Instant
JavaScript

Nigel McFarlane

Wrox Press Ltd.®

Instant JavaScript

First Published   December 1997

Latest Reprint   February 2000

Latest Reprint   March 2000

Published by Wrox Press Ltd,
Arden House, 1102 Warwick Road, Acocks Green, Birmingham B27 6BH, UK.
Printed in Canada
9 TRI 00

ISBN 1-861001-27-4

Trademark Acknowledgements

Wrox has endeavored to provide trademark information about all the companies and products mentioned in this book by the appropriate use of capitals. However, Wrox cannot guarantee the accuracy of this information.

Credits

Author
Nigel McFarlane

Editors
Jeremy Beacock
Dan Maharry

Technical Reviewers
Diana Castillo
Rick Kingslan
Ron Phillips
Tony Pittarese
Richard Stones

Design/Layout/Cover
Andrew Guillaume
Graham Butler

Index
Simon Gilks

Cover image by David Maclean. Digital processing by Andrew Guillaume.

About the Author

Nigel McFarlane is a senior software engineer at TUSC Computer Systems Pty Ltd, based in Melbourne, Australia, where he helps develop telecommunications software. Previously he worked for a major database vendor. He seems to spend most of his professional life trying to work out what it all means, so if you have any ideas please speak up, or alternatively, come to the pub afterwards.

Credit where it's due department

Having your name on a book is wonderful, but I'd be remiss if I didn't point out the contribution of others, some of whom I've relied entirely on, and on whose shoulders I've had the cheek to stand.

Of course it wasn't me; Wrox Press orchestrated the whole thing. Without the leap of faith they took with an unproved person, I'd still be idly wondering: what if? There's a lesson there somewhere about not taking 'no' for an answer. Jeremy Beacock did a particularly good job of alternating between waving the stick and holding the net. Thanks, Jeremy.

It is very difficult to explain in a few words how many gaps and holes the Wrox folk neatly plugged with their expertise, but clearly it's most of the distance between the merely enthusiastic and the reasonably professional so there's that to be grateful for. It's nice wrapping paper too.

Thanks also to my enlightened bosses, Paul Kearney, Bill Jacobs and John Gwyther for making a little space so I could get the thing happening. Also at TUSC, Gerard McDermott was the source of a number of useful JavaScript observations, which opened up areas I might otherwise never have started thinking about. You deserve a medal (made out of a Netscape cookie, of course).

To those people who wonder if they can write a book, the answer is Yes. All that's required is an opportunity, a thimbleful of ability, a bucket of energy and a willingness to commit. If I can do it, anyone can. Don't expect to do anything else for a while, though.

As always, I'm indebted to Phil Muraca, who just keeps on being there. Finally, if this book wasn't such a shared effort with the Wrox staff, and written in computer-ese to boot, I'd dedicate it to my parents, Ron and Jean McFarlane in a second—thank you very much for your endless patience, tolerance and dedication.

JavaScript

Table of Contents

Chapter 7: Disappearing Data 191

Chapter 8: Applets and Java 209

JavaScript

Introduction

JavaScript is a simple programming language that has grown in popularity alongside and as part of the general growth in the World Wide Web and the Internet in the 90's.

The name 'JavaScript' is a bit misleading because JavaScript doesn't have a great deal in common with the similarly named 'Java', another programming language that is often used over the Internet. On the other hand, JavaScript *is* a scripting language (as opposed to an entirely self-contained language), so at least the 'script' part of its name is well deserved. JavaScript is simpler than Java.

The similarity in naming between Java and JavaScript is no accident, however. Programs and pieces of programs written in both languages are used in the World Wide Web to make HTML pages more useful and decorative. Both may be used in the same HTML page, and may even work together. Like Java, JavaScript is spreading its wings beyond simple HTML pages, and is poised to become more generally widespread, thanks both to the hype surrounding its similarly named cousin language, and the fact that it is highly useful in its own right.

Although there are some superficial similarities of syntax between Java and JavaScript, they don't count for much once you consider their different emphases. Software created using the Java language tends to fulfil its aims without much help from other kinds of software. JavaScript, on the other hand, loves to get deeply involved with other software technologies, for example HTML and Web browsers such as Netscape Navigator. Without those other software technologies, JavaScript's utility is limited. So the key to instant success with JavaScript is to use it to get with, and at, other bits of software, particularly (but not only) Web browsers, and that's what this book will help you achieve.

Where JavaScript Exists

Programming languages are used to make programs or bits of programs, and these need to be run, or executed, or triggered, or invoked, or loaded, or whatever term you prefer, by the computer before they have any effect. Many languages require that you carefully prepare your program for execution after you've created its content. That which you type in is generally handed straight to the computer or the computer's operating system where it is executed. JavaScript, however, is an **interpreted** language, and may execute without any preparatory steps on your part. A special, other piece of software (an **interpreter**) must exist to receive and act on your JavaScript program before that can happen.

It follows that in order to do JavaScript things, you need an interpreter and you need a JavaScript program. This diagram shows where these can be found.

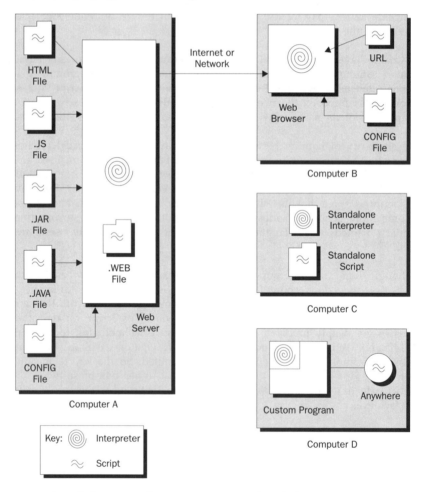

Computer A and Computer B represent a typical Web browser server and client arrangement. The diagram shows that HTML files on the server can contain JavaScript and the browser contains a JavaScript interpreter. This is the most common case, and is called **client-side JavaScript**. When HTML files are fetched from the server into the browser, the JavaScript interpreter in the browser finds and acts on any JavaScript code inside the files, which makes things happen in the browser. It's also the case that the JavaScript code can exist in a non-HTML file of its own, and can be loaded into the browser client separately. This is conventionally stored in a file with a .js extension. More rarely, a `.js` file can be stored in a special format called a `.jar` format that allows various security restrictions to be dropped, but which is otherwise the same. Finally, and obscurely, a `.java` file contains Java code, but it can have JavaScript commands inside the Java code.

Ignoring the other details about Computer A and B for a minute, Computer C is not connected to the Internet at all, and has no browser, but can still do JavaScript. All that's required is a program which does nothing else but interpret the JavaScript language. Then JavaScript scripts stored in files on that computer can be interpreted and run, doing local work only. This is **standalone JavaScript**.

Computer D has a specially written program (made by a specialist programmer) which includes a JavaScript interpreter. Since special programs do special things, it can get JavaScript scripts from anywhere it has access to. This is too specialized a use for this book.

Computer A also has a JavaScript interpreter inside its Web server. An HTML file can have two kinds of JavaScript inside it; one kind interpreted by the browser, the other by the Web server. So the HTML might be affected twice by JavaScript; once as it passes through the Web server, then again when it is displayed by the browser. JavaScript executed by a Web server is called **server-side JavaScript**, which this book only touches on.

A useful technique which can happen on the server side is a partial breaking of the 'JavaScript is always interpreted' rule. At least one Web server allows you to compile your server-side JavaScript scripts so they can be embedded deep in the Web server, yielding performance gains.

Lastly, a user can control a browser via JavaScript. A URL (a World Wide Web address) can contain JavaScript and, in the case of Netscape's browser, can have its configuration controlled from `.js` files.

Of course, the techniques in the diagram could all be mixed together on a single computer, but here the browser is the most useful way to use JavaScript—occasionally one of the other techniques will be discussed.

Origins and Versions

JavaScript was invented by Netscape Communications under the name Livescript 1.0. When Java became fashionable, the name was changed to JavaScript. It first appeared inside Netscape Navigator 2.0. Although invented by Netscape, the language is heavily influenced by other languages, primarily C, but also Java, Perl and other scripting languages. Microsoft Corporation saw the usefulness of JavaScript and released its own variant JScript 1.0, found inside Internet Explorer 3.0 and its Internet Information Server. JScript 1.0 is roughly compatible with Netscape's 1.0 version. Netscape later released version 1.1 of JavaScript inside both Netscape Navigator 3.0 and its LiveWire Web server, but Microsoft only included a few of this later version's features in JScript 1.0. These 3.0 browsers are widely used and partly incompatible, which is a nuisance for JavaScript programmers. Fortunately, Netscape 2.0 is dropping fast in use, reducing one compatibility problem.

Netscape released the language definition for JavaScript to the public, and subsequently agreed with Microsoft and others to create a vendor-neutral standard. ECMA, a standards body in Switzerland produced the standard in July 1997, calling the language ECMAScript. ECMA is an acronym for European Computer Manufacturers Association. This standard is roughly equivalent to JavaScript 1.1, but does not include any HTML features. While this was happening, Netscape released JavaScript 1.2 (with further enhancements) inside Netscape Communicator's Navigator 4.0 component and Microsoft released JScript 2.0 for Internet Explorer 3.0. None of those language versions comply 100% with the ECMAScript standard. Microsoft has also made JScript available as a DLL, which is a programming format that allows the interpreter to be included in non-browser programs.

Both of the major software vendors have said they are moving towards ECMAScript conformance. With Internet Explorer 4.0 containing JScript 3.0, Microsoft claims full ECMAScript compliance. Meanwhile, the number of JavaScript products is increasing. Nombas Inc. has a standalone JavaScript interpreter and a development kit in its ScriptEase product range. Borland International Inc. has a JavaScript-enabled Web server in its Intrabuilder product and Opera Software have announced JavaScript support in their Opera 3.0 browser.

Knowledge That Helps

Basic familiarity with the World Wide Web is assumed in this book. You should understand these terms if you want to learn JavaScript painlessly: Web browser, HTML, URL. You should have a vague idea what MIME types are and what HTTP is, and have created HTML documents. You should have heard of the dreaded CGI, but no experience in that area is required, except for knowing the tags in HTML that support forms.

If you have any experience with third generation languages (3GLs) such as C, Pascal, FORTRAN, BASIC, Java or Visual Basic then you should find JavaScript very easy. Similarly for any form or report building packages such as Oracle's SQL*Forms or Sybase's PowerBuilder. That also goes for any scripting languages such as Unix shell scripts or Perl.

It is particularly useful to have some experience with creating HTML documents that have to look good on at least two different brands of browser—Netscape and Microsoft being the two most popular examples. The compatibility issues surrounding JavaScript are very similar to those surrounding HTML.

Tools You Need

Firstly you need a plain editor for viewing or changing your JavaScript source. The one you use for HTML is good enough. If you use a "WYSIWYG" HTML editor like HotDog to create HTML pages, you'll have to check that the editor supports JavaScript; not all of the brands do. Correct support means the editor doesn't get confused when you start adding JavaScript to your HTML tags. If it does get confused, you'll have to change or go back to a plain text editor like 'vi' or 'Notepad' or 'EDIT'.

For client-side JavaScript you need a Web browser. You need to choose between conservative for cross-browser compatibility and leading-edge for fancy functionality at the expense of some compatibility. The 3.0 releases for Microsoft and Netscape browsers are conservative. The 4.0 releases are leading-edge. If you use restraint, you can still have cross-browser compatibility with the leading-edge versions. Make sure you get the latest minor version of the major version you decide, for example Netscape Navigator 3.04 for Windows 95, not 3.01 for Windows 95.

For client-side JavaScript, it doesn't take long before you want non-trivial forms, or you want to store and recall data for or about the user. You're limited in what you can do here if you don't have a Web server. The server doesn't have to be maintained by you, but it must let you take advantage of its CGI interface—the magic bit of technology required. CGI means "Common Gateway Interface" and lets a HTML page interact with a special program or script that is looked after by the Web server. When writing plain HTML you can avoid needing a Web server by using URLs like **file://C|/temp/test.htm** or **C:/temp/test.htm**, but there's no similar trick for CGI. You need a Web server, and then you need the special CGI programs, or else you're restricted to mostly decorative use of JavaScript. An alternative to CGI is Microsoft's Active Server Pages technology, but the problem is the same regardless of the technology chosen.

There are numerous brands of web servers, some are simple and can run on the same computer you use for your browser, so a connection to the Internet isn't necessary. Some are free to varying degrees. "Very free" ones are Apache for Unix and Fnord for Windows 95/NT. WebSite is an example of a simple-but-flexible commercial PC web server with good reviews.

Getting started with CGI requires some learning. You can give up and get a package that supplies a number of basic services—but this is pointless if you want to create the services yourself. You can also give up if the idea of CGI fills you with fears of having to learn "hard core" programming such as Perl or C – but again, this is not much use if it restricts what you can do with JavaScript in the browser. A better solution is to do CGI in an environment you're already familiar with; JavaScript. ScriptEase from Nombas Inc. is a tool that lets you write CGI programs easily in ECMAScript-compliant JavaScript.

For server-side JavaScript you need a Web server that also has a built-in JavaScript interpreter. Current choices are Netscape's Enterprise Server, Microsoft's Internet Information Server and Borland's IntraBuilder. The most common use of server-side JavaScript is to access a relational database, so if you want to do that you'll have to have one of those that the particular server brand supports. "ODBC-compliant" databases are usually good enough. You have to be fairly organised and understand databases well before this use of server-side JavaScript is more attractive than using CGI as above.

For standalone JavaScript your only choice at this time of writing is Nombas Inc.'s ScriptEase range of products, unless you want to be a Netscape ONE licensee and turn Netscape's JavaScript source code (written in C) into a running product. The ScriptEase:Web Server Edition variant will only work with a Web server (that is, with CGI), so if you want to manage your PC or Web host with standalone JavaScript, you'll have to get the ScriptEase:Desktop version.

These products can all be found on the World Wide Web:

Product	Location
Netscape Navigator 2.02	`ftp://ftp.netscape.com/pub/navigator/2.02`
Netscape Navigator 3.0	`ftp://ftp.netscape.com/pub/navigator/3.04`
Netscape Communicator 4.0	`http://www.netscape.com`
Netscape Enterprise Server	`http://www.netscape.com`
Microsoft Internet Explorer 3.0	`ftp://ftp.germany.eu.net/pub/service/msdownload/ieinstall/ie302/en/`
Microsoft Internet Explorer 3.0 Jscript 2.0	`ftp://ftp.germany.eu.net/pub/service/msdownload/ieinstall/ie302/en/`
Microsoft Internet Explorer 4.0	`http://www.microsoft.com/ie`
Microsoft Internet Information Server	`http://www.microsoft.com/products/prodref/81_ov.htm`
Borland Intrabuilder	`http://www.borland.com`
Opera Web browser	`http://www.operasoftware.com`
Nombas ScriptEase products	`http://www.nombas.com`
Apache Web Server	`http://www.apache.org`
Fnord Web Server	`http://www.wpi.edu/~zik/fnord/`
WebSite Web Server	`http://www.website.com`

HTML Template Files

The easiest way to experiment with JavaScript is via a Web browser. In order to experiment, it is easiest to work with web pages. At the risk of jumping ahead, a simple page such as this gives you a starting point to experiment with. Chapters 1 and 2 explain how to use such a page.

```
<HTML>
<BODY>
My JavaScript test page
<SCRIPT LANGUAGE="JavaScript">
  // JavaScript scripts go here
</SCRIPT>
</BODY>
</HEAD>
```

Typographical Conventions

Several typefaces are used in this book to identify special information.
Here are examples of the styles we use and an explanation of what they mean:

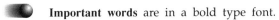 *Advice, hints, or background information comes in this type of font.*

Important words are in a bold type font.

Words that appear on the screen in menus like the <u>F</u>ile or <u>W</u>indow are in a similar font to the one you see on the screen

Keys that you press on the keyboard, like *Ctrl* and *Enter*, are in italics.

Code has several fonts. If it's a word that we're talking about in the text, for example, discussing the **for...next** loop, it's in a bold font. If it's a block of code that you can type in as a program and run, then it's also in a gray box:

```
<STYLE TYPE="text/javascript">
... Some Javascript
</STYLE>
```

Sometimes you'll see code in a mixture of styles, like this:

```
<HTML>
<HEAD>
<TITLE>Javascript Style Sheet Example</TITLE>
<STYLE TYPE="text/javascript">
tags.BODY.color="black"
classes.base.DIV.color="red"
</STYLE>
</HEAD>
```

The code with a white background is code we've already looked at and that we don't wish to examine further.

These formats are designed to make sure that you know what it is you're looking at. I hope they make life easier.

Read On...

The next chapter covers the basic features of the JavaScript language. After that, there is a flood of examples showing various tricks and techniques. Finally, there is a reference section that covers all the language details. All the examples have all been tested with Netscape and Microsoft browsers, or with ScriptEase for CGI and standalone scripts. All the examples that are contained within this book can be found for downloading at our web site—
`http://rapid.wrox.co.uk`. Testing was done on a Microsoft Windows 95 Intel-based PC, and on a Hewlett-Packard HP-UX Unix computer.

Chapter

Language Tour

This chapter describes the basic building blocks of the JavaScript language without becoming bogged down in too much detail. By the end of this chapter, you will be familiar with the basic features that the language has to offer. If a language feature isn't covered here, or the detail seems incomplete, look in the Reference Section at the back of the book. The core features of JavaScript apply to all brands and versions. There is the occasional exception, usually rare, but sometimes applying almost everywhere, especially where the "rule" has only recently been settled.

For the extremely lazy, extremely technical or merely impatient, here is a quick buzzword-laden rundown that briefly summarizes the main JavaScript language features:

- **Third generation language**. JavaScript is cousin to C, Pascal, and Basic.
- **Free-formatted with C-like syntax**. Careful formatting is optional, unlike FORTRAN.
- **Interpreted and loosely-typed**. You don't have to wrestle with a pedantic compiler.
- **Garbage collected with no pointers**. Like Java, someone else cleans up your mess.
- **Floating point numbers and Unicode strings**. Like Perl, basic types are kept simple.
- **Arrays and objects**. Objects are easy and informal, as in Perl, and have properties and methods.
- **Object-based, not object-oriented**. Complex object features are left out, unlike C++ or Java.
- **Null and undefined special values**. Variables and functions can be created anytime, like Perl.
- **Flexible functions**. Bare statements without a **main()** will do. Variable parameters for functions.
- **Highly portable**. Hardware independent, so it can run anywhere, much like Java.

Embeds in other software. Other software provides the input and output facilities and the substance that JavaScript scripts act on, in the form of objects.

ECMAScript terminology

Since ECMAScript is the emerging standard for JavaScript, it's best to learn good habits at the start and use its terminology. The ECMAScript standard only defines the most central features of JavaScript. It broadly categorizes an implementation of the language into three parts, to which is added here a fourth, for clarity. This diagram illustrates how these parts go together to form a JavaScript interpreter.

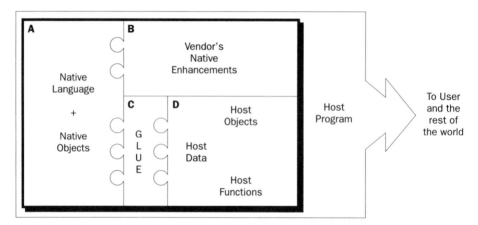

Recall that JavaScript loves to work with other software technologies such as Web browsers. In ECMAScript/JavaScript, a **native** feature means a feature of the language that is solely to do with JavaScript. Such a feature might be the syntax for mathematical expressions, or variable names. Section A in the diagram above represents all the native features which go together to make ECMAScript. Section B shows that each JavaScript vendor might add **native enhancements** to the language to make their product more attractive, but these are still solely to do with JavaScript. Section D shows **host features**, which are features built into some other software that are not directly to do with JavaScript. In a web browser, these might be HTML documents, links, plug-ins, images or form elements. In a standalone interpreter they might be operating system calls or database functions. Finally, section C shows these host features connected to the native language by a little bit of software 'glue'. To summarize, the main software (browser, server or operating system) is said to **host** the JavaScript interpreter; that is all four pieces combined. The ECMAScript standard doesn't find the glue section interesting enough to talk about. Browser vendors like to promote their own proprietary solutions for the glue section using technology brand names like ActiveX and LiveConnect.

A Word on Input and Output

JavaScript relies on host objects for all its input and output needs. It's a bit hard to experiment with the native features without receiving or displaying anything, so here are examples of how to do basic output. These examples print "Hello, World!" on a single line on the screen, and nothing else.

Client-side JavaScript, in an HTML file to be loaded by a browser:

```
<HTML>
<BODY>
<SCRIPT LANGUAGE="JavaScript">
    document.write('Hello, World!\n');
</SCRIPT>
</BODY>
</HEAD>
```

Standalone JavaScript, in a plain text file to be supplied to an interpreter:

```
Clib.puts('Hello, World\n');
```

The functions **document.write()** and **Clib.puts()** are **host functions** (or host methods), not native features of the JavaScript language. All web browsers hosting JavaScript support **document.write()**, but since a standalone interpreter isn't a web browser, it has a different facility. The string **'Hello, World!\n'** on the other hand, is a native JavaScript feature - a string constant. It's very common in JavaScript to see host and native features mixed up closely as in each of these examples. In these examples, the single, **'Hello, World!\n'** line can be replaced with any number of lines of JavaScript.

Variables and Data

You can store information inside pieces of JavaScript code. Here are some examples:

```
var new_value;
var cost = null;
var new_price = 10.95;
address = "23 Short St.";
var result = 'Result unknown';
result = true;
result = 1.08e+23;
result = 0x2Fe3
result = 0377
$name = "Jimmy Zed";
var first = 1, second = 2, last = 10;
```

There are two ways to store data—inside a **variable**, or directly typed in as a **constant**. The example illustrates both with variables on the left of the equals sign on each line, and constant values on the right. Data always has a **type**, so constants each have a type. Variables take on the type of the data they contain, but since variables can contain data of any type, they change types when the data inside them is changed. The variable has no innate type of its own.

Variables are just a piece of space in computer memory referred to by a name that has to follow some basic rules. Normal English words, possibly strung together with underscores ('_') are safest. The first letter must not be a digit. The first time you use a variable name, that variable can spring into existence automatically, but it's best to use the **var** keyword as a hint to the computer to tell it the variable is new, and to keep yourself organized. After you use **var** once, never use it again for that variable. Avoid using variable names that might clash with other uses of the name.

> *Avoid using $ in variable names—neither Internet Explorer 3.02(with JScript 1.0), nor Navigator 2.02 can handle it. Avoid using names that differ only in case like **Fred** and **fred** if you expect to use Internet Explorer 3.02 with JScript 1.0—it can't tell the difference.*

Primitive types

Primitive types are the simple building blocks of all data in JavaScript. The main primitive types are **Boolean, Number** and **String**. They are discussed first. Neither objects nor arrays, which are both important types in their own right, are primitive types.

Boolean, Number and String

The Boolean type has only two values. The constants for these values are **true** and **false** and are only used for truth values. Unlike some languages, **false** isn't exactly the same as **0** (zero), but it will convert to 0 when used where a number is expected, so it's much the same thing.

The Number type is for floating point numbers with zero or more decimal places. There is no separate type for plain whole numbers, integers or bytes. Number constants can be written plainly, in decimal, or in computer exponential or hexadecimal or octal notation. All of these formats are shown in the above example. The Number type can cope with very large (or very small) values and negatives. Very large means up to about 10^{308}, very small means down to about 10^{-308}, if you're mathematically inclined.

The String type is for textual characters. There is no type for representing just one character. A String is a row of zero or more characters as a unit, not an array of single characters. Of course, a String of exactly one character is as good as a single character, so that is the way a single character is represented. There are a few special characters which can be stored in a String, all of which begin with a '\'. The '\n' in '**Hello, World!\n**' above is an example—it adds a newline character to the string. Strings must start and end with single quotes, or with double quotes. You should be careful when putting quotes intentionally inside Strings, and the start and end quotes must match in type.

Special Numbers, Null and Undefined

There are less obvious primitive types and values as well. These are the three special Number values **Infinity**, **-Infinity** and **NaN**. There are also the special types **Null** and **Undefined**.

The three special Number values can't be used as constants, so there is no way to type them in. There are, however, variables called **NaN** and **Infinity** which contain these special values, so those variables can be used where these values are needed. NaN means 'Not a Number' and is the result of a mathematical operation that makes no sense. The Null type has only one value: **null**. **Null** means 'no data'—it's used as a placeholder in a variable to let you know there's nothing useful in there. The Undefined type is trickier. It also has one value: **undefined**, which is often the same as **null**. If a variable's contents are unclear, because nothing (not even **null**) has ever been stored in it, then it's **undefined**, but for convenience, much of the time it acts as if it had a **null** value. Unless you are doing something advanced, **undefined** is usually bad news meaning your script isn't working properly. In the example on page 13, variable **new_value** is undefined because nothing is ever assigned to it. The same is true of the variable **old_value**, because it doesn't appear at all. The safest way to examine these special values is with some special utilities— **isNaN()**, **isFinite()** and **typeof()**—which are described later.

The NaN and Infinity variables may be standard, but they are too new for all but the most recently released browsers. You can, however, create them yourself if you want to stick close to the standard in your scripts. Here's how:

```
var NaN = 0/0;
var Infinity = 1e300 * 1e300;
```

There are two widely available constants that can be used to check infinite values. They are **Number.POSITIVE_INFINITY** and **Number.NEGATIVE_INFINITY**. See the section below on Objects, and the Reference Section.

*Don't rely on the special values printing out the same on all browsers, and don't do mathematics with these values if you're going to create them, as results can be unpredictable. Internet Explorer 3.02 with JScript 1.0 has no idea about **NaN**, it just silently converts to 0 (zero). You can't tell the difference between **undefined** and **null** using Netscape Navigator 2.02, and it doesn't understand **Number.POSITIVE_INFINITY** or **Number.NEGATIVE_INFINITY** either. It is not until browser version 4.0 that NaN is highly bug-free.*

Arrays

Arrays let you store several pieces of data in the same variable. Usually the pieces have a common theme. This can save you creating a heap of variables all with similar names. This is how they work:

```
var month_totals = new Array(12);
month_totals[3] = 1999.95;
month_totals[4] = 'No sales';

var a=4;
document.write(month_totals[a]);
document.write(month_totals.length);
document.write(month_totals);

var days = new Array("Sun","Mon","Tue","Wed","Thu","Fri","Sat");
```

The variables totals and days are made into arrays by the as-yet cryptic code 'new Array(...)'. This does two things. First, the number of items in the array is decided, and stored in a hidden place called '**length**'. In line 1, it's set explicitly to 12. Second, space for some variables (also called array elements) is created, which is equal to the size of the array. Line 2 shows one of those items storing a value. '**[3]**' means the array element with element index 3. Array elements are counted from **0** (zero), not one, so a three element array called **fred** has elements **fred[0]**, **fred[1]** and **fred[2]**. As line 2 and 3 show, array elements can contain different types of data: '**month_totals[3]** = **1999.95**' is an array variable of the Number type, whereas the third line, '**month_totals[4]** = **'No sales'**' is a String type..

Accessing array elements is easy. The first two **document.write()** lines display 'No sales' and '12'. The last line shows a shorthand way of creating an Array and setting all its elements at the same time.

Arrays in JavaScript are closely tied to objects, which are discussed later. In particular, the array indices are not restricted to numbers because of their object-like status. Arrays can also expand in size (in number of elements) just by storing a value in an array element whose index is bigger than any that exists so far. So arrays are quite flexible compared to equivalent concepts in other languages.

> The third document.write() above only needs to report that the variable printed is an object to match ECMAScript. However, Netscape Navigator will print out all the array elements, comma-separated, which is very handy. Navigator 2.02 doesn't know how to do 'new Array', and neither does Internet Explorer 3.02 with JScript 1.0, but it can be simulated with objects— see that section.

One of the things you can store in an array element is another array. An array of arrays can be treated like a multidimensional array, which has a number of uses, particularly in mathematics and graphics. This example creates a two-dimensional array of size two-by-two, and fills it with the values that make up an '**identity matrix**'.

```
var matrix = new Array(2);
matrix[0] = new Array(2);
matrix[1] = new Array(2);

matrix[0][0] = 1;
matrix[1][0] = 0;
matrix[0][1] = 0;
matrix[1][1] = 1;
```

Statements, Blocks and Comments

It's all very well being able to store data, but most of the time it's useful to be able to do something with it. This means writing a JavaScript program or script fragment. A **script fragment** is just a piece of JavaScript that is so small it doesn't deserve to be called a whole program. Most of the examples in this chapter are script fragments. Regardless of what name it has, all JavaScript code consists of a sequence of **statements**. Statements are processed top-to-bottom, one at a time, unless you organize it otherwise. Everything is a statement unless it's a **comment**. Comments are human-friendly annotations which help the reader understand the script's function. Statements can be collected together into a **block**. A block has the advantage that it can act as if it were a single statement, even though it can contain more than one statement. Here's an example program that prints out different text depending upon the value of the variable 'result':

```
var result;
result = 15                            // for this test, set it to 15
result = 5; result = 20;        // then set it again, just for fun

result
= 19;                                  // final value is 19.

if ( result == 15 )
{
    /* this bit won't be printed
   because it's not 15
    */
    Clib.puts('The value is ')
    Clib.puts('still 15')
}
else
{
    /* this bit WILL be printed
       because it's not 15
    */
    Clib.puts('The value has been ');
    Clib.puts('changed to something else');
}
/* end of example */
;
```

Ignore the lines reading '**if..**' and '**else   ..**' for the minute. Notice how some lines end with semi-colon ('**;**') and some don't. In JavaScript semi-colons are the official way of saying a statement has ended. However, JavaScript lets the script writer be care free if, for example, a statement looks like it has finished even though there's no semi-colon, and then the line ends, JavaScript will assume you were lazy and act as though you did put one. It's good practice to *ALWAYS* put a semi-colon as it makes tracking down problems easier. All the examples to date show the simplest kind of statement: just assigning a value to a variable.

Note lines 3 - 6. Line 3 has two statements - '**result = 5;**' and '**result = 20;**'. Also, the single statement, '**result=19;**' is split over lines 5 and 6. JavaScript is a **free-format language**. Provided you always use semi-colons, you can add as many spaces, tabs and blank lines as you like (**whitespace**), provided you stick to the spots where spaces can normally appear. This is similar to HTML. Just like HTML, using a spacing and indentation standard will make the code easier to understand in six months when it is revisited.

There are some comments in this example. The '**//**' characters tell the JavaScript interpreter to ignore everything until the end of the line—this is a single line comment. The '**/***' characters tell the interpreter to ignore everything until the matching '***/**'. This allows comments to span more than one line, although they

17

can still be as small as part of a single line. You can't embed comments inside a String constant. Single line comments will nest, but multi-line ones won't. Additionally, single line comments can appear inside multi-line comments.

There are two blocks in the example above. Blocks are started by left-brace ('**{**') and ended by right-brace('**}**'). In this example each block contains two statements (and a comment, but that's ignored). The line reading 'if..' only operates on a single statement, so a block is used to make two statements behave like one. Notice that blocks break the rules: there is no need for a trailing semi-colon. This is the only exception.

A semi-colon by itself, as in the final line, is the 'do-nothing' statement, so a script reading just ';;;;;' would do nothing 5 times. Finally, since this script uses **Clib.puts()** it's clear this program will only run in a standalone JavaScript interpreter - if it was intended for a browser, **document.write()** would be used.

Expressions and Conditions

With variables and statements, you can store as much data as you like, but eventually you'll want to manipulate it or check it. **Expressions** and **Conditions** are used for these two tasks. Expressions combine values into a new value whereas conditions compare values and return a Boolean truth value (true or false). Conditions are a kind of expression most often concerned with testing logical (truth or boolean) values.

Expressions and conditions combine variables and constant data (and other expressions and conditions) together via **operators**. Except for string manipulation, the operators are mostly identical to those of the "C" and Java languages. An important matter is precedence, which is a set of rules dictating how expressions are interpreted when more then one operator is present. Parentheses, '()' can be used to force a different interpretation to that laid down in the precedence rules. The Reference Section lists all the operators and their precedence.

An operator has to work with something in order to operate. Operators are divided into **unary** operators that operate on one piece of data and **binary** operators that operate on two pieces of data; one on each side of the operator symbol. There is also a single **ternary** operator that uses three pieces of data.

Arithmetic Operators

Arithmetic operators are the familiar mathematical ones and are all binary operators: plus (+), minus (-), divide (/), multiply (*). There is also remainder (%) which gives the leftovers of a division. For example: 9/4 is 2.25, but 4 goes into 9 twice with one left over, so 9 % 4 is 1. This operator is also called 'modulo'. For division of real numbers, not integers, the leftover is a real number, so for example 5.5 % 2.2 = 1.1. Used carelessly, these operators can produce NaN or Infinity: for example, if you accidentally divide by 0.

```
a = 2 + 3;   b = 2 * 3;   c = 2 / 3;   d = 2 - 3;   e = 2 % 3;
```

Microsoft products with JScript version 1.0 truncate floating point numbers to integers before applying %, so 5.5 % 2.2 = 1.

Relational Operators

Relational operators are those used for comparisons and are all binary operators: less than (<), less than or equal to (<=), greater than (>), greater than or equal to (>=), equal (==) and not equal (! =). Discussion of what exactly equals means is deferred for the minute, but it's safe to say if the two things compared are of the same type, then equal means 'the same as' in the common sense way you'd expect.

```
a < b;    a >= b;    a == b;    (a + b) <= (c + d);
```

Logical Operators

Logical operators go hand-in-hand with relational ones. They are **logical and** (**&&**), **logical or** (**||**), **logical not** (**!**). The first two are binary, and the last one unary. These operators let you combine the results of several variable tests into one result. 'Logical and' means both sides must be true, 'logical or' means at least one side must be true. 'Logical not' gives back the reverse of the true/false state of the value tested.

```
a && b;    a || b;    !a;    ( a<=b ) && ( c > d );    !a && b || c;
```

Sometimes logical expressions can get quite complicated. It is best to use parentheses wherever possible, both to aid the reader's understanding and to avoid obscure bugs.

Bit Operators

Bit operators treat Number types as a 32 bit value, which changes bits according to the operator and then converts the value back to Number when done. The operators are bitwise **NOT** (**~**), **AND** (**&**), **OR** (**|**), **XOR** (**^**), **left shift** (**<<**), **right shift** (**>>**), **unsigned right shift** (**>>>**). All are binary, except **NOT** which is unary. The dual right shift operators help keep JavaScript portable between different computers and are derived from Java. These operators aren't yet used much in Web-style applications.

```
a = ~a;    b = b & a;    c = c >> 3;    d = d >>> 1;
```

Miscellaneous Unary Operators

Miscellaneous unary operators: these are **prefix** and **postfix increment** (**++**), **prefix** and **postfix decrement** (**--**), **unary plus** (**+**) and **unary minus** (**-**). Here are examples:

```
a++;    ++a;    a--;    --a;    +a;    b = -a;    b = 2 * a++;    b = 2 * ++a;
```

The unary minus is easiest to understand; it simply makes a negative number positive and vice versa. All the rest are really as valuable for their side effects

19

as much as for their main effect. Unary plus, for example, won't change the sign of a Number (unary minus does that) or its value, so you might think it's useless. Nevertheless, it does force any variable it's used with to undergo type conversion (discussed later), and on rare occasions that can be useful. The pre/post increment/decrement operators just give you a fast way of saying 'a = a + 1' or 'a = a - 1', they increase or decrease the variable they're applied to by one, which is a common operation. Care has to be taken if they are mixed with other operators in an expression, or used in an assignment, as this example shows:

```
a = 5; c = a++ + 2;           // c = 7, not 8;

b = 10; c = ++b + 2;          // c = 13, not 12;

a = 6; b = 11; c = ( ++a == b++ )// not obvious (but c is false as 7 == 11 is
false)
```

When the ++ is placed before the variable it works on, that variable is incremented, and the new value is used in any expression it's part of. However, if the ++ is placed after the variable it works on, the variable's old value (before increment) is used in the expression and then after that's over, the increment is applied as an afterthought. As the last statement in the example shows, it can get confusing if overused.

Assignment Operators

The **assignment operators** are the last general group of operators. Plain assignment (=) is the most obvious one. From one point of view it makes no sense to think of it as calculating any kind of expression, since usually it's just used to copy a value into a variable. But looked at differently, if the value it's copying is the result, and storing that value into a variable is just a side-effect, then it looks like an operator that does nothing to a value except calculate it (and have a side-effect). If this doesn't sound plausible, consider this example:

```
a = 2; b = 2; c = 2;
d = ( a + ( b + ( c + 3 ) ) );        // d becomes 9
d = ( a = ( b = ( c = 3 ) ) );        // d ( and a, b and c) becomes 3
d = a = b = c = 3;                    // d ( and a, b and c) becomes 3
```

Line 2 is fairly straightforward, it's just 'd = a + b + c + 3' with more parentheses than are really needed. In Line 3 we can think like this: c is assigned 3, and passes 3 on, so (c = 3) is 3, then b is assigned that new 3, and so on. Finally, line 4 shows that the parentheses can be dropped, leaving us with a shorthand way of assigning the same value to numerous variables at once.

As for C and other C-like languages, mixing up = and == is a common source of bugs. See the 'Disappearing Data' chapter.

There are other assignment operators: compound ones. All the bit and arithmetic operators can be combined with = in a way which allows simple expressions to be written in a shorthand way similar to ++ and --. Here is an example for plus. See the Reference Section for the rest.

```
a += 3;                        // same as a = a + 3;
```

Other Operators

Three operators don't fit into any category. These are the ternary **conditional operator ?:**, the binary **comma operator ','** and the binary **string concatenation operator +**.

The ternary condition operator is a quick way of assigning one of two values to a variable, depending on some test. It's really just shorthand for a specific kind of **if** statement (**if**s are described in the next section). It works like this:

```
a = 1; b = 2; c = 3; d = 4;
x = ( a > b ) ? c : d;            // x becomes 4
```

If the expression before the **?** (which should be a condition) is **true**, then the expression between the **?** and the **:** is assigned to **x**, otherwise the expression to the right of **:** is assigned to **x**. This can also get quite confusing if care isn't taken.

The comma operator's main use is for passing arguments to functions (described in the next section), but technically it's a binary operator as well. What it does is evaluate its left value, throw the result away, evaluate its right value and pass that on. This might all seem useless until you realize that it allows you to put in your own side effects if you want them. Not advised, but here's an example:

```
a = 2; b = 3; c = 4; d = 5;
x = ( a++, c ) * ( b++, d )        // same as x=c*d; a++; b++; so why bother?
```

The string concatenation operator takes two String values and creates a new String which is the same as the two original strings run together. Some examples:

```
a = 'Red';
b = "Blue";
c = a + b + 'Yellow';             // c becomes "RedBlueYellow".
d = a + 5;                        // d becomes 'Red5'.
```

This is really useful. Since **+** is already used with Numbers as the addition operator however, it can get a bit confusing. In the last line, one value is a String and one is a number, so how does **+** know whether to concatenate or to add them? The section on type conversion explains, but generally you are safe provided the one value that is a string doesn't contain numeric digits. No strings are damaged in the process of concatenation—in fact, a value which is a String type is always constant—unchangeable by any means. If you want to modify a String, you have to replace it wholly with another string. When the + operator is used for string concatenation, it tries hard to perceive its two supplied values as strings.

Finally, there are some operators that don't look much like operators. They are **new**, **delete**, **void**, and **typeof()**. **New** and **delete** allow the creation and removal of objects, a topic covered later.

Delete is not available in Internet Explorer 3.02 or less, or Netscape 2.02. Netscape only officially supports delete in its 4.0 browser, but it won't generate an interpreter complaint if used in the 3.0 Netscape versions. In a language that is already garbage collected, delete has only a little utility.

Void is used for controlling expressions. All expressions calculate a value, which would normally be the result of a comparison or a mathematical calculation. Sometimes it's preferable to just throw the result away, rather than storing it in a variable, particularly if the main aim of the expression is to achieve some side effect, such as changing a host object. **Void** causes the expression to report undefined, rather than what the expression's result would otherwise be.

```
a = 5;
document.write( void (++a) );          // displays 'undefined', not 6.
```

Void is not available in Navigator 2.02 or Internet Explorer 3.02 or less.

Typeof is used for identifying types. Given an expression or variable, it will report a string containing a descriptive word describing the type. See the Reference Section for the exact strings. **Typeof** is one of the rare places where you can refer to a variable that has never been declared with **var** without generating an error. This is especially useful since it allows you to check for the existence of variables with **typeof**.

```
var a = 'anything';
var b;
document.write(typeof(a));          // displays "string"
document.write(typeof(b));          // displays "undefined"
document.write(typeof(c));          // displays "undefined"
```

Typeof() is not available in Navigator 2.02.

Flow Control

Flow control syntax features of JavaScript give the script writer control over which JavaScript statements are executed and when. Without flow control many scripts would be very large, and some would be impossible.

If ... else ...

The 'if ... else ...' statement causes the interpreter to choose between one or two alternative statements and execute at most one set. The syntax is:

```
if ( condition )
    statement or block
```

or

```
if ( condition )
    statement or block
else
    statement or block
```

In the first form, if the condition is met, then the statement or block of statements is done, otherwise it is skipped. In the second form, if the condition is met, then the first statement or block is done, otherwise the second one is. Each possible block is called a **branch**. Since a block has parentheses, but a statement doesn't, it follows that parentheses are optional if there is only one statement in a branch. Some examples:

```
if ( x == 5 )                    // first example
    y = 6;

if ( name == "fred")             // second example
    y = 6;
else
    y = 7;

if ( x == y && a == b )          // third example
{
    x++;
    y++;
}
else
{
    a++;
    b++;
}
```

The statements making up each branch are indented only for ease of reading. Like HTML, it makes no difference to the result if there's extra whitespace included.

While ...

The 'while ...' statement repeats a statement or block based on a condition. Its syntax is:

```
while ( condition )
    statement or block
```

If the condition is met, one repetition occurs. After that, the condition is checked again to see if there should be another repetition, and so on. If the condition is never **true**, then no repetitions at all occur. Care has to be taken that the condition eventually stops the cycle or the loop will go on forever. Some examples:

```
var num = 134 - 1;               // example 1. Find the biggest
factor of 134.
var finished = false;

while ( finished == false )
{
    if ( 134 % num == 0 )
    {
    document.write('The biggest factor of 134 is ' + num);
    finished = true;
```

```
        }
        num--;
    }

    num = 1;                    // example 2. Display all the numbers (never ends).
    while (true)
    {
        document.write(++num + ' ');
    }
```

For ...

The 'for ...' loop statement is similar to the 'while ...' loop but is a bit more complicated. Like the 'while ...' it also allows the same statement or block to be repeated. Usually a count is kept to make sure that the repetition doesn't go on forever. The syntax is:

```
for ( setup; condition; change )
    statement or block
```

The statement or block part is the repeated part. 'setup' is a JavaScript statement that occurs before the first repetition occurs. 'condition' is a JavaScript expression (usually a condition) that is evaluated before the repeated part is started. If it evaluates to true, then another repetition starts. 'change' is a JavaScript statement that occurs just before the condition is re-checked, and which usually effects whether the condition will pass or not. These examples show a very common idiom using the 3 parts within the brackets of the for statement to set, test and update a counter which controls the number of repeats:

```
    var fruit = Array(3);
    fruit[0] = 'apple';
    fruit[1] = 'pear';
    fruit[2] = 'orange';

    for (count=0; count <=2; count++)          // display all fruit.
        document.write(fruit[count]+ ' ');

    var new_line = '<BR>';
    for (loop1=0; loop1 < 5; loop1++)          // display a triangle of T's.
    {
        for (loop2=0; loop2 < loop1; loop2++)
        {
        document.write('T');
        }
        document.write(new_line);
    }

    for (;;)                                   // do nothing forever.
    ;
```

The first loop produces this output:

```
apple pear orange
```

The second loop, which has a further loop inside it, produces this output:

```
T<BR>
TT<BR>
TTT<BR>
TTTT<BR>
TTTTT<BR>
```

The last loop produces nothing and never ends.

Zero or more of the three parts can be left out if they're not needed, but for this command there must always be exactly two semi-colons between the for parentheses, no carefree omissions allowed.

There is a second form of the **for** statement that is specifically for objects. See the objects section for details.

The only other standard flow-control features are the **continue** statement and the **break** statement.

Both should only appear inside a block that is the repeated part of a **for** or **while** statement. These statements give finer control over how a block of statements is repeated. **Break** causes any repetition to stop immediately with no further repetitions. **Continue** causes the current repetition to stop immediately, but the test for another repetition still goes ahead. Some examples:

```
var loop = 0;                    // Example 1. Display all multiples of 7.
while ( ++loop < 200 )
{
   if ( loop % 7 != 0 )
  continue;
      document.write(loop + ' ');
}
```

```
for (loop=1000; loop < 1099; loop++)// Example 2. Find the first number bigger
{                                    // than 1000 that is divisible by 99.
   if (loop % 99 == 0)
  break;
}
document.write(loop);
```

In the 'while' loop, the loop variable will increment through all the values from 0 to 199. The first thing that happens in the loop is the 'if' test, which will pass for all numbers not divisible by seven. Therefore, the branch or body of the 'if' statement will execute. This is the 'continue' statement, which sends control back to the while statement. Therefore, the number will only be written out if the if statement fails, which occurs when the number IS divisible by seven.

In the 'for' loop, the loop variable will increment through all the values from 1000 to 1098 in the ordinary case. However, if the 'if' statement is ever satisfied, the 'break' statement will execute. When, or if, that occurs, control will pass to the statement immediately following the 'for' statement. So in this case, either 1099 or the last value of the loop variable is written out. Of course, the number written out will be 1089 (= 11 times 99).

Functions

Functions allow useful bits of code to be bundled up into a block and given a name so that the bundle can be referred to by its name each time it's required, rather than being re-typed. The syntax for making a function is:

```
function name(arguments)
{
    statements, possibly including 'return'
}
```

and for referring to an existing function:

```
name(argument-values);
```

function is a JavaScript keyword like **var** or **while**. Name is the unique name given to the function, which follows the rules for variable names. **Return** is a keyword similar to **break**, which can only exist inside the function. 'Arguments' is an optional comma-separated list of variables which will be used inside the function, and are similar to the data that the expression operators work with. '**Argument-values**' is a comma-separated list of data items to be used by the function when it's referred to. Three examples:

```
function say_hello()
{
    document.write('Hello. ');
    document.write('Welcome to the say_hello() function. ');
    return;
}

function add_together(first, second)
{
    var result = first + second;
    return result;
}

function add_all()
{
    var loop=0, sum=0;
    for ( loop = arguments.length-1; loop >=0; loop--)
        sum += arguments[loop];
    return sum;
}

// Now make them happen

say_hello();
var answer = add_together(5, 3);
document.write( answer + ' ' + add_together(10, 4) );
document.write( ' ' + add_all(1, 3, 5, 7, 9) );
```

As you can see, most of the effort is in **declaring** the functions, that is, making the JavaScript interpreter aware they exist. This is equivalent to the **var** statement for variables. Only the last four lines make them "go". This script fragment displays this output:

```
Hello. Welcome to the say_hello() function. 8 14 25
```

A bit of terminology can go a long way toward speaking intelligently about functions. When a function is made to happen, it's said to be **called** or **invoked** from the piece of script that refers to it. Data specified between the parentheses when the function is called are known as **arguments** or **parameters** and are said to be **passed** to the function. When a function has a value to hand back to the place it was called from, it is said to **return** that value.

There are several things going on in this example. Firstly, **return** is being used in two ways. If there's an answer to be handed back from a function, **return** hands it back. Otherwise, **return** returns **undefined**. Secondly, sometimes functions have arguments declared, as for **add_together()**. Once the function is running these act just like normal variables, except that they are unavailable outside the function, a bit like how **break** is unusable outside a **for** or **while** loop. Thirdly, even if no arguments are declared, a function can still get at any that are passed to it, as shown in **add_all()**. In this function, no arguments are declared but clearly 5 are passed to it (in the last line). Inside every function is a special Array called **arguments** (it's always present), that can be examined for the number and values of the arguments passed in. This allows a function to handle the less common case where it is passed different numbers of arguments at different times.

Finally, the last two functions have some variable declarations in them—**loop**, **sum** and **result**. These are not accessible outside the function they appear in, but they're not special like the **arguments** Array. They are an example of **scoping**. Scoping means variables are only present in a limited part of the program, to reduce complexity. The rule is that any variable is useable until a close-bracket ('**}**') appears which matches the nearest open bracket ('**{**') BEFORE the spot where the variable first appeared. If that was all, then complexity would indeed be reduced, but the scoping rules also say that its possible to have more than one variable with the same name—if so then the one in the innermost (meaning nearest) scope will be used. An example that shows scoping at work is:

```
var stuff = 'outside';

function do_it()
{
    var stuff = 'inside';
    document.write(stuff);
}

document.write(stuff);          // display 'outside'
do_it();                        // display 'inside'
```

New scopes aren't created inside **if** branches or in **while** or **for** statement blocks. Those kinds of blocks will obey whatever scopes were at work just before they began, however. Only functions produce new scopes.

Earlier, there was some discussion of operators that have side effects in expressions and conditions, such as the pre-increment operator ('++'). The main purpose of expressions and conditions is to return a value that is the result of calculating the expression or condition. Functions can do anything when called, including performing statements that are unrelated to the return value that they pass back. Since functions can participate in expressions and conditions, quite powerful side-effects can occur as this optimistic example shows:

27

```
var tasks_complete = solve_all_world_problems() + keep_everyone_happy();
```

Whatever the statements in these functions are, it's likely they are large and complex ...

JavaScript comes with a few generally useful ECMAScript native functions. See the Reference Section for the gory details. These are **parseInt()**, **parseFloat()**, **escape()**, **unescape()**, **isNaN()**, **isFinite()** and **eval()**. All of these are for String and Number manipulation, except **eval()** which is special.

> *IsNaN() doesn't do much on Internet Explorer 3.02 with JScript 1.0, since NaNs are unknown there.*

The function **eval()** takes a string, examining and running it as though it was a JavaScript scriptlet. This lets the script writer get a string from somewhere else (for example from user input) and run it straight away without starting any new program. This is a very powerful feature, but it also can let the user do all kinds of damage to any variables and functions you have in the JavaScript that lets this happen.

```
var code = 'x + y';
var x = 5, y = 4;
document.write( eval(code) );                           // displays 9
```

Objects

Nothing makes some computer people more miserable than the word object. Fortunately, JavaScript Objects are extremely tame.

What is an object? In general terms, an object is one or more pieces of data and one or more useful functions all collected together into a neat item that can be easily carried around. Usually the data items and the functions are related and work together. Often an object has a particular identity, like 'person', so that it's possible to have many 'person' objects, each one for a different human being. The ability to carry all the stuff about a person or other kind of thing around in one neat item is a very handy and powerful feature of modern computer languages.

Advocates of other programming languages that support objects such as C++, Java, Ada and Eiffel are likely to become enraged by such a simple definition of objects. For those languages, defining and combining objects is a very exact science. However, JavaScript's loosely-typed and interpreted nature is perfectly suited to simple objects, so the definition is a good one, in this case.

Here's an example of JavaScript objects:

```
var thing = new Object;

thing.name  = 'Any old thing';
thing.age   = 59;
thing.hobby = 'moving as little as possible.';
```

```
thing.thing2 = new Object;
thing.thing2.name = "thing's own thing";

delete thing;
```

First, the **new** operator mentioned earlier creates an Object which is put into **thing**. **thing** is still an ordinary variable, it simply contains a new type of value—an Object value. After that's complete, **thing** is neither **undefined** nor **null**. However, Objects initially don't contain much of interest—**properties** have to be added to them, like ingredients combined to make up a meal. Lines 3 to 5 demonstrate the simple syntax used to add properties:

```
object-variable-name.property-name = value
```

Objects can have as many properties as you can find different names for and each property can contain a value of any type, including another object. Lines 7 and 8 show that the **thing** Object has a property that is another Object. Finally, Objects can be got rid of using **delete**. After **delete**, **thing** is **null**.

An object will also automatically disappear if a function ends and that object was created inside the function *and* the function doesn't return the object back to its caller. The Disappearing Data chapter has more to say about mechanisms that make objects go away.

Objects aren't primitive types

There's a very important contrast between an Object and a variable holding an Object. A JavaScript Object is just like a bag of properties in no particular order, and that's a good way of viewing it. However, a JavaScript variable can't contain an arbitrary number of properties, it can hold only one piece of data. So the variable just contains a bit of data that tracks where the bag is (you can't get at this data) and, when there's more than one Object around, which Object bag it is. The actual bag itself is separate from the variable's value.

This is important because up until now, dealing with primitive data has been easy; if a variable contains 2, and another variable gets assigned the value 2, that's fine because 2's are cheap—you can have as many as you like. This is also true for Objects—you can have as many as you like—but it's often the case that one object will be shared between many variables, because it can be too much bother (or even impossible) to copy it. This means **delete** is a bit tricky—it really means "make this variable stop tracking its object". If no variables are tracking an object, then the JavaScript interpreter will throw the object away.

This distinction is particularly important when using functions. Variables can be passed to functions as arguments. Variables can contain primitive types or objects. If you use a primitive type as a function argument, then the argument appearing inside the function is a copy of the one you passed it. This means your original copy can't be damaged from inside the function. However, if you pass an object to a function, a copy *isn't* made, so you are operating on the exact same object inside the function as outside, with consequences to the object that apply even after the function finishes. To summarize—extra care is required passing objects to functions as they are not proof against accidental damage inside the function.

Methods

If you have used another programming language, you might be familiar with concepts such as structures, records, tuples, or forms. An object that only has properties does for you about the same amount as these other common concepts. It's just data. However, objects can also contain **methods**, as this example shows:

```
function ordinary_say_hello() { document.write("Hello."); }

function special_print_name()
{
    document.write("My name is: " + this.name);
}

var thing = new Object;

thing.name = "Fred";
thing.say_hello = ordinary_say_hello;
thing.print_name = special_print_name;

thing.say_hello();
thing.print_name();
```

There are two apparently normal functions here, except that the second one has a mystery variable called **this**. Near the end of the script, two properties of the thing Object apparently have function names stored into them:

```
thing.say_hello = ordinary_say_hello;
thing.print_name = special_print_name;
```

Then right at the bottom, the Object properties begin to look like functions:

```
thing.say_hello();
thing.print_name();
```

A method is just a function that likes to be inside, or be part of, an object. It does this by letting an object's property track it in the same way that properties and variables can track whole Objects. When the method/function is called (as if it were a property of the Object), the special **this** variable becomes available inside the method/function. **this** is a kind of placeholder for whichever Object has called the function, and allows access to all the other properties of the Object the function was called from. It's done like this (no pun intended) so that the function can always get at the properties of the Object it was called from if it needs to, regardless of which Object called it. However, when methods take advantage of the **this** variable, they can't usually be called as a plain function any more.

Therefore, Objects are really bags of properties and methods. In addition, Javascript objects can have a special **prototype** property.

Prototypes and Constructors

Suppose you wrote some JavaScript that stored employee's details in Objects. You might have 20 items of data per employee. If one Object is used for each employee, that's 20 property values per Object, plus maybe 10 handy methods. Every time you add a new employee you have to set 20 properties and 10 methods on the new Object you create. That's a lot of typing. Especially when the methods are all the same for each employee (likely) and half the properties are the same for each employee. And all you'd have for your effort would be an Object, which doesn't sound much like an employee record.

The **prototype** property fixes this, along with another special use of functions—**constructors**. Here's an example of a constructor and a prototype:

```
function display_it()
{
    document.write(this.name);
}

function Employee(name, age)
{
    this.name = name;
    this.age = age;
    this.status = 'Full time';
}

Employee.prototype.address = 'JS Industries, Station St.';
Employee.prototype.contact = '012 345 6789';
Employee.prototype.job = "Appear indispensable";
Employee.prototype.display = display_it;

var person1 = new Employee("Doe, John", 47);
var person2 = new Employee("Doe, Jane", 45);

person1.display() + document.write(" " + person2.contact);
```

The function named **Employee** isn't an ordinary function, because it uses the special **this** variable. It could be used as a method, but not in this example as there isn't any Object property it's being assigned to. Instead it's being used with **new** to create an Object. So this function is put to a third use: neither function nor method, instead it is a **constructor**. The **new** operator assumes its argument is an object constructor and magically 'knows' the constructors name, which is the constructor function's name.

The Object created is a typical one except that the function **Employee** decorates it with extra properties automatically. If you create an object using '**new Object**', you don't get any new properties automatically. So constructor functions add value to the normal object construction process.

The extra properties created by a constructor function can be based on function arguments, since all the usual function rules apply. Therefore, this constructor achieves two ends: firstly it saves typing by letting the script writer reuse the statements in the constructor each time an Object is created; secondly, it's a more meaningful word than just plain Object.

Constructors are only a half solution to the problem of too many properties per Object. If there were 20 properties and 10 methods per Employee object, that would be 30 arguments to the Employee constructor. That is hardly practical. Instead, there is a special property called **prototype**. Properties of the **prototype** property are copied magically into every Object created by the matching constructor. So the two variables **person1** and **person2** both contain the same address, contact, job and display properties, even though the **Employee** constructor didn't explicitly set them. Notice that the word **prototype** is only required once where each **prototype** property is declared. This is a little bit like **var**.

There's one other reason why constructors are useful. In Netscape Navigator 2.02 and Internet Explorer 3.02, you can manipulate existing Arrays, but you can't make one via '**new Array**'. What you can do is make a special constructor that does an equivalent job. Here's how:

```
function MakeArray(size)
{
    var num = 0;
    this.length = size;
    for (var num = 1; num <= size; num++)
        this[num] = 0;
    return this;
}
```

In Navigator 2.02, the 'length' property won't be set either. However, the new versions 4.0x of Navigator and IE will support using 'new Array..' Techniques to overcome this kind of incompatibility are discussed later.

Secret Object Truths

Plain variables and primitive types like Number and String are straightforward. Why bother with Objects? The compelling reason is that if you scratch the surface, Objects rule the world. Here's a many-faceted illustration:

```
var data1 = new Number("5");
var data2 = new String("Anything");
var data3 = data2.substring(1, 4) + data2.charAt(7); // data3 = nythg (!)

var data4 = new Function("a, b", "return (a<b) ? a : b;");  // return lesser
value
data4(3, 5);

var data = new Array(2);
data.0 = "red";                          // same as data[0]
data.1 = "blue";                         // same as data[1]

var data5 = new Object;
data5["shape"] = "square";        // same as data5.shape
data5["old cost"] = 10.95;        // same as data5.old cost (but that's an
error)

var data6 = Math.round(3.45);             // equals 3
var data7 = Date(1997, 7, 27);    // a day of the year
var data8 = new Image();                  // only in browsers
```

Firstly, the familiar primitive types can be treated like Objects:

```
var data1 = new Number("5");
var data2 = new String("Anything");
```

For the Number type, this is nearly useless, but String values have a bit of Jekyll and Hyde about them. On the one hand, a String is just a humble piece of text surrounded by quotes—unchangeable. On the other hand, it's a complex object with a heap of methods that let you search, convert, split and otherwise prod it in a number of useful ways as shown in line 3. JavaScript automatically converts primitive Strings to String objects, so it's all fairly invisible to the script writer. The Reference Section describes all the methods for the String type.

Secondly, Functions are Objects:

```
var data4 = new Function("a, b", "return (a<b) ? a : b;");  // return lesser
value
data4(3, 5);
```

This is only useful for advanced stuff, but if you're desperate to create a function without a name, line 5 shows how.

Thirdly, Arrays are Objects:

```
var data = new Array(2);
data.0 = "red";          // same as data[0]
data.1 = "blue";         // same as data[1]

var data5 = new Object;
data5["shape"] = "square"; // same as data5.shape
data5["old cost"] = 10.95; // same as data5.old cost (but that's an error)
```

The familiar syntax for getting at Array elements is interchangeable with the Object property syntax. Arrays are just Objects with one special difference—the length property of an Array exists and is kept up-to-date automatically by JavaScript. Objects have no automatically updated length property. Similarly, Objects are Arrays. The Array syntax for getting at elements can be used to get at Object properties, except since property names aren't numbers, a string is used inside the square brackets. This is especially handy if the property name contains spaces, or you don't know what the property name is at the time. Objects and Arrays are interchangeable; you can add properties to Arrays and Array elements to Objects, as well as the normal way around. Nevertheless, you only get the length property with an official Array, and it won't count non-element properties.

Fourthly, there are some really useful objects:

```
var data6 = Math.round(3.45);    // equals 3
var data7 = Date(1997, 7, 27);   // a day of the year
var data8 = new Image();         // only in browsers
```

The example illustrates the Math and Date kinds of Objects. These are the only two native JavaScript types not yet discussed. Both contain a host of methods for doing (surprise) mathematical and date-time calculations. Math is also a rare example of a **built-in** JavaScript Object. Built-in objects never need to be created with 'new' before use—one always exists for you to work with.

Fifthly, Objects are the most common way of accessing host features, as the last line of the example shows. Nearly all of the interesting bits of a Web browser look like JavaScript Objects. So Objects it is. Since this nearly brings the discussion of JavaScript native language features to a close, only the word Object appearing with its self-important initial capital letter will stand in future for the plain, native JavaScript type. A type does not describe a piece of data, a type describes a variety of data. The more humble word 'object' will be used to cover any bit of data that operates roughly like an Object; having methods properties, and so on. This is also applies to Arrays/arrays.

Finally, the biggest secret of Objects is that there's always one around you. A given script might look like it just contains plain variables, but these variables are really properties of some object. In ECMAScript, this is the magic global object that you can't see or touch. In browser-hosted JavaScript, each window is an object that contains as properties any variables you care to make up. Every variable is a property of some object—it's just a matter of finding it.

Syntax Support for Objects

For ... in ...

Sometimes an Object's contents are unknown. If it were an Array it would be easy to discover the contents—just look at the length property of the array and start accessing elements starting at 0 (zero). It's not so easy for Objects because the properties of the Object aren't neatly ordered and their names can be arbitrary strings—millions to choose from. There has to be another mechanism.

The **for...** statement discussed earlier has a variant designed for this job. Its syntax is:

```
for ( variable in object-variable )
    statement or block
```

An example:

```
for ( prop in some_object )
{
    if ( typeof( some_object[prop] ) == "string" )
        document.write(" Property: " + prop + " has value: " +
some_object[prop]);
}
```

This example steps through all the properties of the **some_object** variable (presumably containing an object) and displays only those properties containing strings.

Unfortunately, the **for ... in** statement is a trap for beginners. "Ordinary" properties are reported as you would expect, but some special properties never appear. This can be a source of confusion. Typical examples are methods of objects that are supplied by the host, not by the script writer. See the Reference Section.

With ...

The point has been made that every variable is part of an object, which we might call the **current context**, the **current object**, or the **current scope**. Sometimes (usually for typing convenience) we might want to change the current scope. The **with** statement does this. Its syntax is:

```
with ( object )
    Statement or block
```

An example:

```
var unrealistically_long_name = new Object;
unrealistically_long_name.sole_property = new Object;
unrealistically_long_name.sole_property.first = "Ready";
unrealistically_long_name.sole_property.second = "Set";
unrealistically_long_name.sole_property.third = "Go";

with ( unrealistically_long_name.sole_property )
{
    document.write( first + ',' + second + ',' + third '!');   // Ready, Set,
Go!
}
```

To display the three deepest level properties would take long lines of code like lines 3, 4 and 5, were it not for the use of **with** surrounding the line producing the output. Further work could be saved by putting the last three assignments inside the **with** statement as well.

You may be suspicious by now that **document** must be some kind of object in a web browser, and **write()** a method of that object. Absolutely correct.

Type Conversion and Equality

JavaScript is called a loosely typed language because any variable or property can contain any type of data, but this flexibility doesn't come free. Every piece of data still has a type, and there are several situations where decisions need to be made about how to handle those types. To save the script writer the overhead of making those decisions (typical of a strongly typed language), the JavaScript interpreter follows a set of built-in rules. Obscure and hard to find bugs can occur if these rules aren't appreciated by the script writer. Generally speaking, the only time these rules apply is when **type conversion** happens—a piece of data of a given type needs to turn into another type. Some examples of when this might happen are:

```
var u = String(5.35);            // 5.35 or "5.35" ?
var v = "10" + 23;               // "1023" or 33 ?
var w = ( "10.5" == 10.5 );      // true or false ?
var x = new Object;
var y = x + 1;                   // what ?
```

Primitive type conversion

ECMAScript says that a piece of data can be converted to each of the obvious primitive types: Boolean, Number and String. If the piece of data is an Object, then the **valueOf()** method will be used to return a Number, and the toString() method will be used to return a String. If the piece of data isn't an Object, then the JavaScript interpreter does the job itself, internally. These conversions are mostly intuitive—for example, the following values all become **false** when converted to a Boolean value: **undefined**, **null**, **false**, **0**, **NaN**, and **""** (the empty string).

Converting a String to a Number is tricky. Either the String looks like a number or it doesn't. The latter case produces NaN, but the former case isn't simple. Because the Number type has a limit to the number of digits it can store, there is a special piece of agony the interpreter must go through to store the closest possible value to the number represented in the String. This is the business of **rounding**, and applies in the reverse as well; converting a Number to a String. This can be particularly irritating because some JavaScript implementations can cause 6 / 2 to equal 2.99999999 instead of 3—although you usually have to pick more obscure number combinations to see this happening.

The URL **http://developer.netscape.com/library/examples/ JavaScript/rounding.html** contains a JavaScript function that will round a variable that otherwise isn't rounding well. ECMAScript-compliant JavaScript will correctly round. This example reveals at least one problem in most Netscape browser versions; Microsoft browsers generally round better.

```
var x = 0.03;
var y = 0.09+0.01;
var z = 1.23456789012345678;
document.write(x + ' ' + y + ' ' + z);
```

The moral of this example is: don't rely on the built-in support for number rounding if you want to display highly accurate numbers. If you have a JavaScript implementation that isn't rounding well, or if you are doing complex mathematics, then the ultra-safe way to compare Numbers is to use this old trick:

```
var tiny = 1e-10;
if ( Math.abs(value - 1.2345) < tiny) ) // Math.abs() removes the sign of a
Number
{
    document.write("so close it's the same as 1.2345.");
}
else
{
    document.write('some number other than 1.2345.');
}
```

There are a few other subtle conversions that are generally invisible to the script writer—see Reference Sections A and C.

The ability to convert to primitive types freely means that the following examples contain no ambiguities:

```
var u = String(23);          // "23"
var v = Number("44.55");     // 44.55
var w = +("0xFE99");         // 65177
var x = "23.45" - 10;        // 13.45 - minus only accepts Number types
var y = ( "fred" && 23 );    // true
var z = ( "0xFF" & 0xF0 );   // 0xF = 15
```

Easy conversion of mixed types

Given the ability to convert between types at will, the rules describe which conversions will occur when there is a mixture of types present. Step one is to identify what is a legal mixture and what isn't. Here it is according to the ECMAScript standard.

> A mixture of types can only occur for binary operators. If a given binary operator only supports one type, then both pieces of data for that operator must either be of that type, or convertible to that type, otherwise an error results.

This takes care of most cases, such as all the bit operations, multiplication, subtraction and division. All those operators require two numeric (or convertible to numeric) types.

Remove these cases and the **polymorphic** binary operators are left—those that work with more than one type of data. The assignment operators and the comma operator are examples, but they are straightforward. The assignment operators always change the contents of their left-hand data item to match their right-hand item, and the comma operator doesn't combine its two data types in any meaningful way at all.

For all these cases, there's no confusion possible, and no need to do anything except watch for complaints from the JavaScript interpreter.

Hard conversion of mixed types

The problematic operators are the relational operators ('==', '<', '>', '<=', '=>') and the concatenation operator ('+') which is also used for addition. All these operators work with more than one type.

Since some types such as some objects can be converted to either Numbers or Strings, the conversion rules for these hard cases come down to describing which way the two arguments will be converted in which circumstances. All else being equal, arguments that are Objects have a preference as to which of String or Number they will convert to (usually Number, except for the Date type), and that preference can figure in the conversion decision as well.

The easiest case to understand is '+', the addition/concatenation operator. The rule is:

> For + operators, if either argument is a String or converts preferentially to one, then do String concatenation, not addition. Otherwise, neither argument prefers to be a String, so do Number addition.

To apply this test to a specific example ask yourself: would either argument like to be a String? If so, concatenation is in order. The interpreter does the same thing.

For the relational operators, the situation is similar but the case for Strings is 'weaker'.

> For >, >=, <, <= operators, if neither argument can be converted to a Number, then do string comparison, not numeric comparison. Otherwise, at least one argument can be converted to a Number, so do numeric comparison.

To apply this test to a specific example, ask yourself: could either argument be a Number? If so, numeric comparison is in order. The interpreter does the same thing.

Remembering what happens in these two cases can be tricky because it can go either way (Number or String), and it's all a bit obscure. A memory trick that will acts as rough guide is to remember this:

"String plus: either String, String compare: neither Number"

The case of inequality and equality is different again:

> For ==, != operators, first convert any Objects to their preferred primitive types. If the types are still different, convert any Boolean to a Number. If the types are still different, convert the non-Number argument to Number and compare as Numbers. Exception: null == undefined without any conversion required.

To apply this test to a specific example, ask yourself: would both arguments prefer to be Strings? If so, a string equality test is in order, otherwise it's a numeric equality test.

These ECMAScript comparison rules all roughly agree with the pre-ECMAScript versions of JavaScript currently available. There is, however, one particular trap to be wary of.

Netscape JavaScript 1.2 is different

Netscape's JavaScript version 1.2 abandons most of the type conversion rules, incorrectly anticipating the standard. This means "3" != 3, for example.

Fortunately, if you don't explicitly ask for this version of JavaScript when you embed your script in a Web page, it works like the older versions of JavaScript that both the standard and Internet Explorer are closer to. Even more fortunately, in Netscape Navigator 4.0 if you don't explicitly request the 1.2 version, you still have access to all the 1.2 features, except for this specific change.

`===` and `!==` have been proposed for inclusion in the standard to support this variation. Internet Explorer 4.0 supports these operators.

It's also true that bugs in the Microsoft and Netscape implementations make some of the more subtle comparisons unreliable. Early versions get easily confused about comparisons with NaN, null and 0 when type conversions are involved.

Making the hard way easy

The safest way to proceed with comparisons without wasting time tracking obscure bugs and compatibility problems is to use a straightforward approach. First, compare same types only —don't mix Numbers and Strings; second, if mixing is inevitable, force the conversion you want to happen. Finally, avoid comparing things with null; just rely on the fact that conversion to the Boolean type is reliable. This example illustrates these points:

```
var result = ( a+'' == b+'' );            // String comparison forced
    result = ( a-0 == b-0 );               // Number comparison forced
    result = ( !a == !b );                 // Boolean comparison forced

if ( a != null ) { do_something(a); };     // possibly attracts bugs
if ( a ) { do_something(a); };             // more likely to avoid bugs

var message = "total errors: " + num_errors; // always safe
```

Summary

This chapter has described the nuts and bolts of the JavaScript language. The native language contains considerable detail without any reference to other technologies such as Web browsers. With data types, expressions, statements and functions a script could achieve a great deal, if only it wasn't hampered by a lack of facilities for doing input and output. The powerful concept of objects presents an opportunity to collect data and code together in a way that can be quite compact and flexible, especially in the way that object can track other objects via their own properties.

The Reference Section contains more specific information about the language. In the next chapter, we will see how a JavaScript interpreter combined with a Web browser or other host program removes the input/output problem and creates many opportunities for scripts to be usefully executed.

Browsers and other hosts

A JavaScript interpreter can't do much in a vacuum; it needs to work with a host program. The host program supplies all the interesting objects, functions and data that the interpreter operates on. Through these things, scripts can read input from a user, display output to a user, and perform computations in between.

Browsers

JavaScript has its origins in the Internet and the World Wide Web, so it's no surprise that Web browsers are the places JavaScript is most frequently used. In most cases, this is achieved by adding JavaScript scripts to files that normally only contain HTML tags and content.

Adding JavaScript to HTML

An HTML document that contains JavaScript can be looked at from two points of view. Looked at from the outside, there are only a few places in an HTML document where JavaScript scripts can be placed so that they will have any meaningful effect. Looked at from the inside, an HTML document consists of numerous interesting features, which can be manipulated by any scripts that can get at those features. It is the former view that is described here.

Since JavaScript scripts can only be placed in HTML documents in certain spots, opportunities for acting upon the document or the browser displaying the document are limited. What JavaScript in an HTML document is able to achieve is categorized as follows:

- Affect document layout when HTML tags and content are still being loaded by the browser.
- Affect the number of browser windows and window-like objects currently displayed.
- Capture, mimic and modify actions the user of the browser might make.
- Perform basic automation and basic feedback tasks.

Improve on the simple forms that HTML supports.

 Forward user actions onto applets, plug-ins and other foreign bodies embedded in the document.

Terminology: a browser **hosts** a JavaScript interpreter or has a JavaScript interpreter **embedded** in it. Similarly, an HTML document may have JavaScript scripts embedded in it.

<SCRIPT>

The **<SCRIPT>** HTML tag is the main way of connecting JavaScript to HTML. Any amount of JavaScript code can accompany the **<SCRIPT>** tag. It is a paired tag and has a number of variants as this example shows:

```
<HTML>
<HEAD>

<SCRIPT>
  var step=1;
</SCRIPT>                                              // example 1.

<SCRIPT LANGUAGE="JavaScript"> step=2; </SCRIPT>        // example 2.
<SCRIPT LANGUAGE="JavaScript1.1"> step=3; </SCRIPT>     // example 3.
<SCRIPT LANGUAGE="JavaScript1.2"> step=4; </SCRIPT>     // example 4.

<SCRIPT SRC="myfunctions.js"> </SCRIPT>                 // example 5.

<SCRIPT TYPE="text/JavaScript"> step=6; </SCRIPT>       // example 6.
HTML 4.0

</HEAD>
</HTML>
```

Examples from 1 to 4 inclusive show the most common use: **inline** JavaScript. This form is called inline JavaScript because the JavaScript code inside the document is *executed as soon as it is encountered* when the browser is reading the HTML file. In these examples, the JavaScript scripts are very trivial—just assigning a value to a variable—but could easily be quite complex, which would halt reading of the HTML until the script finished.

Each of the first 4 examples illustrates a different point. Example 1 shows that just the plain tag is enough to identify its contents as a script. Example 2 shows that the **<SCRIPT>** tag is designed for all kinds of scripting languages, not just JavaScript (although JavaScript is currently the default for most browsers), and that the language attribute identifies the particular language. The HTML 4.0 standard uses a different attribute, **TYPE**, specifying a MIME type of **'text/JavaScript'** for JavaScript, but only Internet Explorer 4.0 and Navigator 4.0 supports this attribute, so it's less portable. It is illustrated in example 6. If a browser does support scripting generally, but doesn't support the language specified, then the code between the tags is ignored. Examples 3 and 4 show that a particular language version can be specified. If the browser supports that language version, then the code is executed using that language version, otherwise it is ignored. None of 'Jscript', 'ECMAScript' or 'JavaScript1.0' work as language names.

<SCRIPT>

Example 5 shows that a JavaScript script can be retrieved from another file. The value of the **SRC** attribute can be a full URL. This form is particularly handy if you have a large number of JavaScript functions that are used in several HTML documents. Rather than type the functions into every document, store them in a separate file containing pure JavaScript (no HTML) and use **SRC** in every HTML document that needs them. The content of the file will be executed immediately, in the same way as for the earlier cases, but it's not referred to as inline JavaScript because it isn't physically in the same file.

Example 5 should not use the **LANGUAGE** attribute either. This is because the source file is retrieved from somewhere external to the HTML document and therefore the web browser's normal mechanisms for detecting file type should be relied upon. Occasionally there is a problem getting this to work—if so, make sure any web server you use knows that a **.js** file is an '**application/ x-JavaScript**' MIME type with a '**js**' filename extension. You can use URLs in the **SRC** attribute that accesses files on the local disk if you're not using a Web server. No special setup is required in that case.

The two biggest benefits of inline JavaScript are that you can add to the HTML which is being read and rendered in the browser, and you can declare functions for later use.

Inline Scripts

This example illustrates adding to HTML, and using a function. All indenting is just for readability.

```
<HTML>
  <HEAD>
    <SCRIPT>
      function weather_comment()
      {
      if ( !Math.random )                        // doesn't exist in Navigator 2.0
      {
          document.write('<PRE> -- weather called off due to rain --</PRE>');
      }
          else if ( Math.floor((Math.random()*2)) == 0 )
          {
              document.write("<STRONG>It's just awful.</STRONG>\n");
          }
          else
          {
              document.write("<EM>How wonderful it is!</EM>\n");
          }
      }
    </SCRIPT>
  </HEAD>
  <BODY>
    <P>Weather report for today:</P>
    <SCRIPT>
      weather_comment();                         // add special stuff
    </SCRIPT>
    <P>End of report.</P>
  </BODY>
</HTML>
```

In the **<HEAD>** of the example, an inline script is used which does nothing except create a function. This is similar to the other activities that go on in the **<HEAD>**—no document content, but plenty of other setup information. Then in

43

the body, an inline script calls that new function which runs the infamous `document.write()`. The output of the `document.write()` is added to the plain HTML as it is displayed on the screen. This means the body part of the HTML will ultimately contain either this:

```
    <P> Weather report for today:</P>
  <STRONG> It's just awful.</STRONG>
    <P> End of report.</P>
```

or this:

```
    <P> Weather report for today:</P>
  <EM>How wonderful it is!</EM>
    <P> End of report.</P>
```

or for Netscape Navigator 2.02, which has no `Math.random()` method, this:

```
    <P> Weather report for today:</P>
  <PRE> -- weather called off due to rain -- </PRE>
    <P> End of report.</P>
```

and then will be rendered by the browser appropriately.

The important thing to note here is that while the example has managed to affect the HTML delivered to the user, once that HTML is delivered, it's very difficult to change it again.

Where to put <SCRIPT>

An HTML document consists of a **<HEAD>** and **<BODY>** or a **<HEAD>** and a **<FRAMESET>**. There are three reasonable places to put **<SCRIPT>** tags: in the **<HEAD>**, in the **<BODY>**, and after the **<HEAD>** but before the **<BODY>** or **<FRAMESET>**.

In theory, the head contains no document content, only meta-information about the document. In theory, the head is completely read by the browser before any body elements are displayed. This makes the head a good place to put any JavaScript which does invisible setup. This means declaring all functions, native objects and variables in the head, and avoiding `document.write()`. However, both Explorer and Navigator will handle output from the head if you use `document.write()` there anyway.

Another good reason for putting as much script as possible in the head is that the JavaScript interpreter only knows that functions, objects and variables exist after the browser has reached the point where they are created in the HTML document. If functions are declared at the bottom of the document and called from the top, you will get 'function undefined errors' all over the place.

The body is the obvious place to put inline code that can vary the HTML output. If the script in the body starts looking complex, consider putting it in a function declared in the head, and just call it from the body. At the end of the body is a good place to put any JavaScript code that you want to happen when the document is nearly fully displayed on the screen.

Documents containing a frameset instead of a body can't have any JavaScript inside the frameset (except JavaScript URLS, see below). This is a nuisance if you want to vary the frameset details using inline scripts. Instead, you can put a **<SCRIPT>** tag after the **</HEAD>** tag, and use it to write out the whole **<FRAMESET>** content (or the whole **<BODY>** content), avoiding the problem altogether.

Overall, browsers supporting JavaScript are quite liberal about where you can technically put **<SCRIPT>** tags. A script can be responsible for quite a lot of a given document's content as this rather suspect (but browser friendly) HTML example shows:

```
<!DOCTYPE HTML PUBLIC "-//W3C//DTD HTML 3.2//EN">
<SCRIPT>
   with ( document )
   {
      write('<HTML><HEAD>\n');
      write('<TITLE>Nearly all JavaScript!</TITLE>\n');
      write('</HEAD><BODY>\n');
      write('Who needs plain HTML?\n');
      write('<BR><HR></BODY></HTML>');
   }
</SCRIPT>
```

Further variants

These first examples show all the common ways of embedding JavaScript into an HTML file. There are also some additional browser-specific methods. Netscape Navigator 4.0 (and the equivalent Communicator suite) has enhanced security options for JavaScript. The benefits of using these are twofold: your scripts can be protected from prying eyes, and your scripts can do more powerful things. This subject is explained in Chapter 6, including the **ARCHIVE** and **ID** attributes, and **JAR** files.

Four traps

JavaScript code stored in a document by itself is a straightforward matter. Embedding JavaScript into an HTML document, which has another kind of content and format altogether, introduces some problems.

You can't use '**</SCRIPT>**' inside inline JavaScript. When a browser picks through a file's text, it looks for tags indicating where various bits of information begin and end. Once it sees a '**<SCRIPT>**' tag, it goes on the hunt for a matching '**</SCRIPT>**'. So this example is problematic:

```
<HTML><BODY>
<SCRIPT>
var warning = 'do not ever put </SCRIPT> literally in a string';
</SCRIPT>
</BODY></HTML>
```

The whole output of this HTML example is likely to be:

```
literally in a string';
```

when no output was probably intended.

45

The solution is to chop up the tag like this:

```
var hack = '</SCR' + 'IPT>';
var warning = 'do not ever put ' + hack + ' literally in a string';
```

A similar problem occurs with printing any 'special' HTML characters. An example:

```
<HTML><BODY><SCRIPT>
// who's shorter? (He is - she grew up, and he's earlier in the alphabet
anyway).
document.write(('Danny DeVito' < 'Shirley Temple')
?'Danny<Shirley':'Shirley<Danny');
</SCRIPT></BODY></HTML>
```

The HTML produced looks like this, with output only 'Danny':

```
<HTML><BODY>
Danny<Shirley
</BODY></HTML>
```

'**<Shirley**' surely looks like a tag, but is unknown to the browser and therefore ignored. Do this instead:

```
// common knowledge anyway
document.write('Danny&lt;Shirley'); // also use this trick for &gt; and &amp;
```

If the HTML file containing JavaScript script is publicly available on the Internet, there are further problems. There are many browsers that not only don't support a scripting language but haven't even heard of the **<SCRIPT>** tag. When a browser discovers an unknown tag, it is discarded and ignored. In this case, the first example above is likely to produce this ugly output for the reader's consumption:

```
var hack = ''; var warning = 'do not ever put ' + hack + ' literally in a
string;
```

There is a special feature of JavaScript which solves this problem. If the first line of a JavaScript script is the HTML comment start symbol, then the JavaScript interpreter will ignore it, even though it is a JavaScript syntax error. This lets JavaScript code look like HTML comments for browsers with no clue about scripts. This is specific to browsers. An example:

```
<HTML><BODY><SCRIPT>
<!- hide from old, stupid browsers

document.write('JavaScript rules, but not everywhere!');

// end comment -->
</SCRIPT></BODY></HTML>
```

A final problem has more to do with HTML rendering of tags than the tags themselves. Recall the weather example above. In that example, the **document.write()** calls contain strings that are terminated by the newline character '**\n**', meaning "start a new line at this point". In the modified HTML that results, you can see this has happened because the 'End of report' line starts on a line by itself. However, when the HTML is rendered for the user,

new lines don't have any effect on the displayed output, so they are only useful
when someone looks at the HTML source. Another example:

```
document.write('red\n');
document.write('blue\n');
document.write('yellow\n');
```

This does not visibly produce three lines of output. It appears to the user as:

```
red blue yellow
```

To insist on separate lines in the user output, use a **
** HTML tag instead of
a newline.

Taking all these traps into account, the 'Hello World!\n' example of Chapter 1 is
best re-written for browser-hosted JavaScript as follows:

```
<HTML>
 <HEAD>
  <TITLE>First script ever</TITLE>
  <SCRIPT LANGUAGE="JavaScript">
   <!--hide it from old browsers
   // No functions or variables to declare in this case, normally put them
here.
   // finish hiding -->
  </SCRIPT>
 </HEAD>
 <BODY>
  <SCRIPT LANGUAGE="JavaScript">
   <!--hide it from old browsers
   document.write('Hello, World!<BR>');
   // finish hiding -->
  </SCRIPT>
 </BODY>
</HTML>
```

This is a good general pattern to follow, even though it looks complicated for
this simple document.

JavaScript Entities

An HTML **entity reference** is a bit of HTML syntax that lets difficult-to-type
characters be represented. Examples are ** ** and **&Aacute**. JavaScript
entities are an extension to this syntax. An example:

```
<HTML><HEAD>
<SCRIPT>
var pixels_per_unit = 25.4;
var total_units = 8;
</SCRIPT>
</HEAD><BODY>
Bar graph showing number of units:<BR>

<HR ALIGN=LEFT SIZE=10 WIDTH="&{pixels_per_unit * total_units};"><BR>

Bar graph showing units as a percentage of 1000:<BR>

<HR ALIGN=LEFT SIZE=10 WIDTH="&{(pixels_per_unit*total_units/1000) * 100};%">

</BODY></HTML>
```

Unlike HTML entity references, these can only be used in the value part of an HTML tag attribute, as shown, not in normal HTML content. Notice in the second **<HR>** that the result of the JavaScript entity is concatenated with '**%**'. Whatever other characters are in the value part of the tag attribute will concatenate with the JavaScript entity's value. Any JavaScript expression can be used between the braces. JavaScript entities are of limited use. They are supported only in Navigator 3.0+, but the HTML 4.0 standard advises that this syntax be deprecated for this use in a later standard.

JavaScript URLs

A JavaScript URL is a special kind of URL. Mostly, URLs contain some kind of address that leads to a file or an E-mail account or a terminal session when that hypertext link is clicked on. JavaScript URLs are different in that they don't retrieve or send anything, except as a side effect. What they do do is cause the immediate execution of a script instead, without the overhead of any request to a web server.

JavaScript URLs only occupy a single line, so if they contain more than one JavaScript statement, semi-colons should be used. There are three places to put JavaScript URLs.

Interactive

All Netscape browsers, plus Internet Explorer 4.0 support this functionality.

```
javascript:Math.PI * radius * radius
javascript:alert(top.name)
javascript:if ( top.page_number ) { alert(top.page_number.hits); }
```

The web browser user can type JavaScript URLs directly into the browser the same as for any URL. You can use the browser as a simple calculator, as in the first line above. A more common use is as a debugging aid, shown in the other two lines ('**alert()**' is a browser host function—more on that later). Typing JavaScript URLs interactively lets you examine any hidden (or not so hidden) contents of an HTML page; such as variables or properties. The URL has access to all the pages in the current window if frames are present. If the URL is just typed as follows: '**javascript:**' a special interpreter window appears that allows plain JavaScript to be typed in and executed straight away, without the **javascript:** prefix.

As document source

```
<HTML><BODY>
<SCRIPT>
var quiz_results = "Your result for this test was: " + 23 + "%";

function update_results()
{
    quiz_results = "Perfect score!";
}

var tiny = "#define x_width 1\n#define x_height 1\nstatic char x_bits[] =
{0x00};";

</SCRIPT>
```

48

<STYLE>

```
<A HREF="javascript:quiz_results">Click here to see your results</A><BR>
<A HREF="javascript:update_results()">Click here to improve your results</A>
<IMG SRC="javascript:tiny" NAME='Single pixel image'>

</BODY></HTML>
```

You can replace normal URLs in a document with **javascript:** ones. The result of the JavaScript expression will be the contents displayed if that URL is loaded. If the expression result is void, then no action will be taken, except for any side effects. In the first **<A>** tag above, clicking on the link will result in a new page displaying this line:

```
Your result for this test was: 23%
```

If the second **<A>** tag is clicked nothing will appear to happen since function **update_results()** returns **void**. If the first link is clicked afterwards this will be displayed:

```
Perfect score!
```

This also works in client-side image maps, submit buttons, and frames, but not in Internet Explorer 3.0.

The third example shows an image's content coming from a JavaScript expression instead of from a file at a normal URL. This tactic is explained in Chapter 4. Internet Explorer 3.0 cannot do this.

As bookmarks

Netscape Navigator 4.0 will accept interactive JavaScript URLs as bookmarks. To create one just follow these steps. Click from the browser menu bar: Window, Bookmarks, Edit Bookmarks. In the new window select an appropriate folder like 'Personal Toolbar Folder' by clicking on the name, then click File, New Bookmark and enter the JavaScript URL along with the other details.

Care must be taken when creating these kinds of bookmarks. Any document from any source could be currently displayed when a user selects a bookmark. If the bookmark refers to any objects, variables or properties in the current page, extra checks should be included in the bookmark URL. This ensures the bookmark doesn't 'crash' if picked when the user is exploring some unexpected page.

<STYLE>

Styles allow formatting normally specified in HTML tags to be collected together and applied to tags repeatedly as a unit. JavaScript can be used with styles. A syntax is required to identify the contents of a style, with the most common syntax being that of the CSS1 standard, which is what is currently implemented in most browsers.

For JavaScript there are two issues for handling styles: creating them and working with them.

Creating JSSS

Style sheets can be written in several different languages, one of which is JavaScript. JavaScript style sheets conform to the CSS1 style sheet model, so they are equivalent to style sheets written in CSS1 syntax. JavaScript style sheets are known by the acronym JSSS, and are only supported in the Netscape 4.0 browsers. They can be declared in two ways, illustrated here:

```
<HTML><HEAD>
<STYLE TYPE="text/JavaScript">
  tags.P.borderWidth = 100;
  tags.P.borderStyle = 'none';     // or else a very thick border ensues
  tags.B.color = "red";
</STYLE>

<LINK REL=STYLESHEET TYPE="text/JavaScript" HREF="fancystyle" TITLE="Fancy">

</HEAD><BODY>
<P> Spacious paragraph ! </P>
<P><B>Angry spacious paragraph!</B></P>
</BODY></HTML>
```

The use of the `<STYLE>` tag shows that creation of style sheets in JavaScript is just a matter of creating correctly named properties and assigning valid values. Capital '`P`' and '`B`' in the example stand for the `<P>`aragraph and `<B>`old tags respectively. The section describing the browser object model explains what properties exist. The CSS1 concepts of '**classes**' and '**ids**' have a similar syntax.

The `<LINK>` tag in the head of an HTML document is supposed to identify dependencies between this document and other documents in a general manner. One such dependency is a JavaScript style sheet, so this tag provides an alternative to embedding the style sheet data directly in the document.

There are a few special JavaScript functions for JSSS:

```
<HTML><HEAD>
<STYLE TYPE="text/JavaScript">
  tags.H1.color = 'pink';
  tags.H1.margins(1,2,3,4);          // set top, right, bottom, left margins.
                                     // paddings(), borderWidths() exist too.
  tags.H1.rgb(50,50,50);

  contextual(tags.H1, tags.B).fontStyle = "italic";

  function change_it()
  {
    if ( color == 'pink' ) fontStyle = "medium";
  }

  tags.I.apply = change_it();
</STYLE></HEAD></HTML>
```

The first few details of the style details are simple. The **margins()** method is handy shorthand for setting the four margin properties all at once—it just saves typing. The **rgb()** method is similarly handy for specifying colors by value.

The next part of the style takes a bit of getting used to. '**contextual()**' is a method which lets one style depend on another; the equivalent of CSS1 syntax like '**H1 B { font-style: italic }**'. As JavaScript it looks a bit unusual until you realize that **contextual()** is creating an object which has its **fontStyle** property set. **Contextual()** can take any number of arguments, which means you can have any number of levels of tag nesting as a condition for the special style information.

The final part creates a JavaScript function and assigns it to the special property '**apply**' of the current style for the '**<I>**' tag. The **apply** property is an escape hatch for those special cases when it all becomes too hard. When the browser reads a tag and collects together the relevant style information, it first resolves how that tag's details will be displayed. Before displaying the tag details, it checks the apply property. If the apply property is set, then the assigned function is called and, therefore, can then do any last-minute band-aid work required on the tag's ultimate style.

In this example, because **<B>** tags inside **<H1>** tags are shown as italic, some confusion might arise if **<I>** tags are also present inside the **<H1>** tag—they could look the same. The **apply** property is used to avoid this case. The **change_it()** function checks the color the tag details are going to be rendered in and, if the answer is '**pink**', assumes that the **<I>** tag is inside a **<H1>** tag and so changes it to '**medium**' style.

Manipulating Styles

In order for JavaScript to be able to do anything with style sheets apart from specifying them, two things need to be possible: the style details need to be readable, and the style needs to be changeable by JavaScript.

In Internet Explorer 3.0 browsers, it is not possible to read or write style attributes outside the style definition. This means styles are both static (unchanging) and invisible to JavaScript.

In Netscape 4.0 browsers styles can be changed. Additionally, if the style includes a position property of '**absolute**' or '**relative**', then the style appears as a JavaScript Layer object. This Layer object has read/write properties matching all the '**CSS1 positioning**' properties. This lets scripts manipulate the style's location, size, visibility and stacking order in the document. The actual display of the HTML element or layer identified by the style is still static. This means that if a style is changed via JavaScript, any HTML elements already displayed won't automatically change to match the new values. The document that the element is a part of would have to be reloaded first (which might reset the changes anyway). The sole exception is the background color or image for an 'absolutely' or 'relatively' positioned style.

Internet Explorer 4.0 has an innovation called **dynamic styles**. Dynamic styles means that styles are fully exposed as host objects that JavaScript can manipulate after they are created and after the HTML document is displayed in the browser as well. Styles created with the **<STYLE>** tag and styles created with the HTML **STYLE=** attribute are accessible as JavaScript objects. This gives all the functionality of Navigator 4.0 layers, plus the ability to change all the other style properties. A change to one of these properties via JavaScript can result in parts of the document being re-examined and redrawn differently by the browser ('**reflowed**').

See Chapter 9, "Dynamic HTML" for further discussion on manipulating styles from JavaScript.

<META>

This tag in HTML 4.0 provides a way of setting the default scripting language for an HTML document, and the default style definition language. The syntax is:

```
<META http-equiv="Content-Script-Type" content="text/JavaScript">
<META http-equiv="Content-Style-Type" content="text/JavaScript">
```

Since JavaScript is already the default, and Internet Explorer doesn't support JSSS, they're not of much use yet. Netscape 4.0 ignores the tag variants.

Events

HTML events are the main way JavaScript improves its interactivity with the user. An **event** is just a piece of input to the browser, usually from the user. **Event handlers** are bits of JavaScript code that execute in response to events.

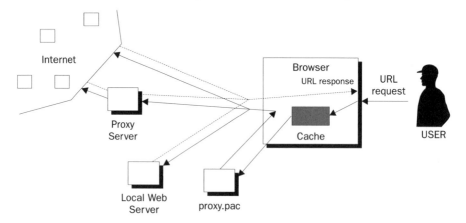

An **event model** describes how events are created and moved around by the software. The HTML 4.0 standard calls events relating to HTML **intrinsic events**. These are the browser events of most interest. The components of the HTML event model are:

- Special conditions causing events to occur.
- Special attributes in HTML tags for each event.
- Scripts to handle each event.
- A JavaScript host object that a given event acts on.
- Control passed temporarily to the JavaScript interpreter when an event occurs.
- Data accompanying the event.

From the script writer's point of view, only the third, fourth and possibly final items require any JavaScript code.

Creating handlers

There are two ways to create JavaScript for HTML events: via HTML tags and via JavaScript host objects.

```
<HTML><HEAD><SCRIPT>
var shouts = 0;
function shout(obj)
{
    alert('What? Just: "' + this.value + '"\n\nLOUDER !!');
    shouts++;
}
</SCRIPT>
<BODY>
Shouting page. Type away, then hit the TAB key.<BR>

<FORM NAME="shouter"> First shout:
<INPUT TYPE="text" NAME="first" ONCHANGE="this.value='LOUDER !!!';return
true;">
<BR> Second shout:
<INPUT TYPE="text">
<BR> Last shout:
<INPUT TYPE="text" NAME="last">
</FORM>

<SCRIPT>
document.shouter[1].onchange=shout;
document.shouter.last.onchange=shout;
</SCRIPT></BODY></HTML>
```

In this example there are three HTML text fields, all with **onChange** event handlers. Since HTML tag attributes are case insensitive, "**ONCHANGE**" could have been written "**onchange**" or "**onChange**". In documentation, the convention is to use **'onChange'**, as will be done from hereon. In JavaScript code, the equivalent property must be lowercase—**'onchange'**, only Netscape 4.0 will allow **'onChange'** as well. Later in this section, and in Chapter 5; where forms are discussed, the implications of this handler are described. For now, run the example and see for yourself, or just note the syntax. The Reference Section has a discussion on the mechanics of events.

Conventions

In the example above, the first text field has the event handler embedded in the HTML tag. Any amount of code can go here, but unless the handler is trivial as in the example, usually a function will be called.

Notice the '**this**' keyword is used. In Chapter 1 it was discussed how '**this**' gives access to the current object or alternatively the object in whose scope the script is running. In the example above, the current object is the specific form element the user changed.

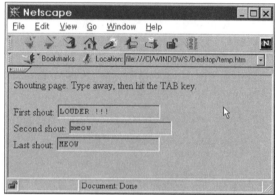

Also notice the 'return' keyword is used. Unlike JavaScript URLs, JavaScript event handlers are supposed to always return true or false although this is: a) not enforced, b) not always necessary, and c) sometimes doesn't even do anything. It is a good habit to get into, though.

The last text field has an **onChange** event handler or **trigger**, but it's not specified in the **<INPUT>** tag. At the bottom of the example is a line with the word '**last**' in it, which is the name for the third text element as specified in the tag. This line allocates the '**shout**' function to the **onChange** event for that element. From JavaScript you can only assign a whole function to an event, not a scrap of code as for the first function. You can assign an anonymous function, if you don't want to declare one, but its harder to read what's going on.

Notice the '**shout()**' function declared in the head also uses the '**this**' keyword, so there is an expectation that it will be used as a method of an object, which is true. The '**shout()**' function also has one argument; '**obj**'. This argument is not used in early JavaScript browsers, and in those cases will always be null. In Navigator 4.0, an Event object associated with the event will be passed to the event handler function, containing interesting bits about the event. Internet Explorer 4.0 looks at a global variable for event details, not a function argument.

Above the line assigning a handler to the last element is a similar line. This does the same thing, but for the middle HTML form element which has no name in the **<INPUT>** tag. This is an example of objects and arrays being (nearly) interchangeable in JavaScript.

Since the '**shout()**' function is declared in the **<HEAD>**, why put the JavaScript event handler assignment script elsewhere in the body? Because the browser works from the top of the HTML document down when displaying it to the user. This means some bits of the document, such as the text elements, appear before others. Before they appear, these elements don't exist, which would make it hard to assign event handlers to them. The assignment has to be done after the elements are created. Assigning handlers inside the element tag is the better method, because this problem is avoided and everything about the tag is in the one place.

onError and event complications

Not all event handlers can be set in HTML tag attributes. The most notable exception is the **onError** event handler of Netscape 3.0 and 4.0. It can be set in the **<IMG>** tag using the **ONERROR** attribute. The event also occurs for windows and frames but there is no tag attribute to use. In those cases it must be set directly from a script. This handler is discussed in Chapter 3.

Secondly, Netscape 4.0 supplies new event management routines in Javascript: **captureEvents()**, **releaseEvents()**, **routeEvent()** and **handleEvent()**. In earlier versions, certain events fired certain event handlers, and that was it. With these new routines, those existing events can move to new places, firing handlers that previously wouldn't have taken part. This is a behavioral change, rather than a new place to put handlers.

Thirdly, Internet Explorer 4.0 allows potential event handlers to be structured in a hierarchical manner. Events move up the hierarchy in a manner called **event bubbling**, starting with the most specific handler possible such as an individual HTML tag, and working up towards more general handlers such as window or document handlers. The event is disposed of when a potential event handler exists to receive the event. The handler is triggered, performs actions, and then may elect to stop the event from bubbling up any further.

Timer events

There are ways of causing a JavaScript script to run other than with a HTML intrinsic event. The JavaScript function **setTimeout()** is an easy alternative:

```
<HTML><HEAD><SCRIPT>
function wake_up()
{
    alert('Fire, Flood, Famine!');        // Try to wake up the user.
    setTimeout('wake_up()', 2000);
}
setTimeout('wake_up()', 2000);            // 2000 milliseconds in the future
</SCRIPT></HEAD></HTML>
```

This page displays an alert box to the user every two seconds. The first time this occurred because the function **wake_up()** was scheduled in the second last line when the document was displayed. It reoccurred because the function reschedules itself just before it ends. The first argument to **setTimeout()** can be any valid JavaScript. If you run this example, you'll see that timers created with **setTimeout()** can be really irritating, but they're good at checking the state of a document or window, performing animation, or regularly reloading a document in case it has changed. This last case is a variant of 'client pull' behavior where the browser regularly updates itself.

Plug-in events

Whenever plug-ins or ActiveX controls are engaged handling **<EMBED>** and **<OBJECT>** tags in HTML, JavaScript can also happen. This is because LiveConnect and ActiveX allow plugins and controls to run specific JavaScript functions or scripts. For Netscape, the **<EMBED>** tag must include the

MAYSCRIPT attribute, or this kind of event won't be allowed. The special file type identified by these tags can actually contain bits of JavaScript script as part of its content. See the Multimedia and Plugins chapter; Chapter 4, for more details.

Java Exception events

A mechanism similar to HTML events is to use Netscape's BeanConnect technology in Netscape 4.0 browsers. This allows JavaScript code to be invoked when a Java exception occurs in an applet, without a lot of extra effort required when the applet is written. Java exceptions are highly flexible things that can happen almost any time.

Other oddities

Watch() and unwatch() object methods are features aimed at easing JavaScript debugging. However, they do provide a general mechanism for calling an otherwise unconnected function when a plain object property has its value changed. This is not strictly an event-oriented mechanism. Chapter 7 illustrates the most common use of this feature.

The server-side JavaScript section describes some further mechanisms which can result in client-side JavaScript running.

Finally, the browser configuration section below describes how dynamic updates to the browser's preferences can occur via JavaScript without any user interaction.

Other Browser JavaScript

HTML documents are not the only way JavaScript scripts can interact with a web browser. There are a number of other places as well. At this time, these are all specific to Netscape browsers.

JavaScript inside Java

```
<HTML><BODY>

<APPLET CODEBASE="local" CODE="start.class" HEIGHT=10 WIDTH=10 MAYSCRIPT>

</BODY></HTML>
```

JavaScript scripts can be embedded in a limited way inside the Java source code that a Java applet is compiled from. Both Java and JavaScript must be enabled in the browser.

The <APPLET> tag, innovated by Netscape is the primary way of embedding Java applets in an HTML document. Although JavaScript scripts always have access to all Java applet internals, Java applets don't always have access to JavaScript objects. The MAYSCRIPT attribute supplied by the HTML author grants permission for that to happen.

JavaScript can be embedded in Java in several different degrees, ranging from mimicry of JavaScript methods directly in Java language syntax through to `eval()`-style execution of any legal JavaScript. This subject is covered in more detail in Chapter 8.

Proxies and proxy.pac

Netscape browsers require access to the Internet or some other network to be useful. One way of managing this access for Netscape 4.0 only is via JavaScript.

A browser on the Internet uses a number of services on the user's behalf. These are the common functions of the browser like web pages, news, file transfer (ftp) and electronic mail. Each of these services demands that the browser connect to a server (such as web servers or news servers) in order to do any useful work.

In the simplest case, the browser connects to servers directly using widely known public address information, but this creates security problems for the computer the browser runs on. Usually there is one or more 'proxy', 'firewall' or 'gateway' interposed between the browser and the actual Internet. Private address information points the browser to the proxy instead of to the world at large, reducing security problems.

For performance or organizational reasons, the browser user might want to pick and choose between proxies (if more than one is available) for each and every URL request made. The proxy configuration file, written in JavaScript, allows the user to set policy stating what kind of URLs go to which servers. Each time a URL request is made, the URL is processed by a JavaScript function in the configuration file that decides how to proceed.

In order to make this easy, the browser supplies some native JavaScript functions for picking apart URLs. These are only available when used in the proxy configuration file. The job of the proxy file is to define the function **FindProxyForURL** and nothing else. Two arguments are always passed: the full URL to be fetched, and the piece of the URL containing the host name only— for convenience of use in the function.

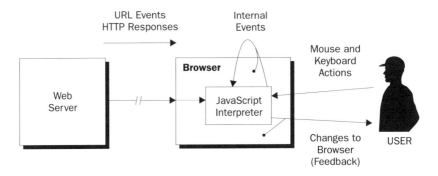

In the following example, imagine a browser is used on a PC in a small corporate Intranet with Internet access via 3 hosts: one for SOCKS (a "secure sockets" protocol) connections, and two for all other 'normal' Internet URLs. There might be two either for redundancy or for performance reasons.

```
// proxy.pac file

function FindProxyForURL(url, host)
{
  if (isPlainHostName(host) || isInNet(host, "192.123.234.0") )
    return "DIRECT";

  else if ( url.substring(0, 6) == "https:" || url.substring(0, 6) == "snews:")
    return "SOCKS sockshost:1081";

  else
  {
    if ( Math.random() < 0.5 )
        return "PROXY proxy1:1080 ; proxy2:1080";
    else
        return "PROXY proxy2:1080 ; proxy1:1080";
  }
}
```

First, note that **String** and **Math** functions are available—this is JavaScript. Second, there are some 'helper' functions used, such as **isPlainHostName()**. These save a lot of complex string operations, and allow conversion between hostnames and IP addresses (the underlying technical name for a computer). Avoid doing conversions, because there is a performance penalty. Finally, the function has to return a string in a specific format; most of the interesting formats are illustrated here. This string advises the browser how to get the URL. See the Reference Section for more details on the individual functions.

In this example, there are three '**if**' branches. The first branch is taken if the user types a URL with a simple hostname (like '**http://localserver/top/index.html**') or a hostname that is in the company network, which is called '**192.123.234.0**' in this example. A direct connection results, using the widely known public addresses for the Web. This is internal to the company, so all the fuss about proxies and security is ignored. The second branch identifies '**https**' and '**snews**' style URLs (which use the magic SOCKS protocol) and reports back to use the special SOCKS proxy. The third branch returns both of the ordinary proxies for everything else. When more than one proxy is returned, the browser tries them in order until it succeeds. To prevent the first one in the list always being used and the other standing idle (even though both work), the **Math.random()** function ensures they are returned in a random order.

This script, usually called **proxy.pac** can be located at any valid URL, so it can be shared by many browser users if desired. To make the browser use such a file, follow these options in the browser menu system:

Navigator 2.0 and 3.0: Choose Options, Network Preferences ..., then choose the Proxies tab in the resulting window. The third radio button "Automatic Proxy Configuration" is the one; click and enter a URL, press Reload to read the new script. Your browser now obeys the new rules. Test by navigating to somewhere well known, such as **http://www.yahoo.com**. On Unix versions of Netscape remember to choose Options, Save Options afterwards.

Navigator/Communicator 4.0: Choose Edit, then Preferences ... In the resulting window, double-click in the left-hand pane on the word Advanced until Proxies appears, then click on the word Proxies. The radio buttons on the right hand side are the same as for the earlier versions of Navigator, so proceed as described above.

If the proxy file's URL is provided by a web server, then that server is contacted 'directly' in order to get the file, so you don't need a proxy file in order to get the proxy file. You can tell that files with a `.pac` extension are special to the browser—just try to load the `proxy.pac` directly into the browser window via its URL and you'll get an unusual error from the browser.

Preferences and prefs.js

In Netscape Navigator 4.0, there is a new method of storing all the preferences that can be set for the browser, such as colors of links, locations of toolbars and sizes of windows. In Netscape 3.0, the browser is restricted to the user preferences accessible from the `options` menu and further changes made possible via the Admin Kit product.

Three scripts

In 4.0, three scripts which are all JavaScript scripts can be used to control the browser. The three scripts are '`prefs.js`', '`netscape.cfg`', and '`config.jsc`'. '`.jsc`' stands for 'JavaScript configuration'. These scripts are consulted by the browser in the order listed when it starts up with later files overriding earlier ones. The first two are stored on the same computer as the browser, and the third one at any valid URL.

The script '`prefs.js`' (or `preferences.js` on Unix) stores all the user preference information. It is read when the browser starts up, and written by the browser when it shuts down, and so can't be changed by hand when the browser is running. If the browser is not running, it can be changed like any text file. If the user manipulates preferences via the Edit menu Preferences... popup, this will change the script when the browser shuts down. The only reason to edit by hand is to add one of a few special preferences that make developing in JavaScript easier—these can't be added from the browser. See the Reference section and Chapter 7. There can be a different `prefs.js` for each user profile created in Netscape 4.0.

The script '`netscape.cfg`' replaces the '`netscape.lck`' file of Netscape 3.0. This script stores user preferences that override the '`prefs.js`' script. It also stores other preferences inaccessible to the user, such as menu options and the 'big-N' animated icon. Lastly, it stores reference information about the '`config.jsc`' script. The `netscape.cfg` script is encrypted so that the browser user can't touch it or read it, giving system administrators a way to permanently set browser features. It can be created by hand, but an easier approach is to use Netscape's Mission Control product. This product contains a Configuration Editor tool that provides a GUI interface for the '`netscape.cfg`' script just like the Edit, Preferences... browser window does for the `prefs.js` file. Mission Control also contains an InstallBuilder tool which can deliver the encrypted '`netscape.cfg`' script to the computer which will run the browser.

The script 'config.jsc', if it exists, in turn overrides the 'netscape.cfg' script. It can have the same range of content as the 'netscape.cfg' script, but is stored as a plain readable file, not an encrypted one. It can be written by the Configuration Editor, or by hand; as for 'netscape.cfg'. It is usually stored apart from the browser user's computer. The script's URL can be used to update a browser's configuration regularly (not merely once at startup time) by including re-read instructions in the local netscape.cfg. This is especially powerful if 'config.jsc' changes between reads—features can be regularly turned off and on like TV channels going off-air. This script's main use is for administrators who need to manage many browser installations at once—all browsers can be configured from one 'config.jsc' URL.

Netscape claims it is possible to alter 200 different items via these scripts. Regrettably, that is too much detail for an 'Instant JavaScript' book.

E-mail and News

Browsers at the 4.0 version level include the ability to send e-mail messages and news posts in HTML format. Where HTML goes, JavaScript can go as well provided the e-mail or newsreader that the message is read with contains a JavaScript interpreter and HTML displayer (as is the case in Netscape Communicator). Then the message in HTML format will run any JavaScript contained within it as would normally happen with an HTML-and-JavaScript web document. This raises a number of interesting possibilities which are reminiscent of Lotus Notes and other workflow style products:

- Including scripts that advise you when your e-mail has been read at the other end;
- providing forms and surveys for readers to fill out;
- demonstrating scripts to others;
- producing multimedia messages, including 'spoken' audio messages.

The techniques to use here are the same as those for scripted HTML documents in general, which are covered in later chapters. If the reader of the message doesn't have a JavaScript/HTML enabled reader, only a plain text document will appear.

Compatibility

Unfortunately, not all JavaScript browsers were created equal. Early versions have only a subset of features of later versions, and some features are buggy in some versions. Netscape and Microsoft have been diverging in their advanced features as fast as possible in order to obtain a loyal customer base. Today's advanced features are tomorrow's backwards-compatibility nightmares.

Handling compatibility requires a two pronged attack: **readership strategies** and **technical tricks**.

Choose readers

If you only intend to use JavaScript to set browser preferences, then readership isn't much of an issue. However, JavaScript is mostly embedded in HTML documents. Who is going to try and read these pages? Answer these questions and avoid masses of work being tripped up by compatibility issues.

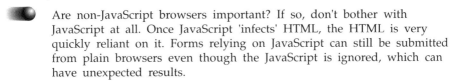

- Are non-JavaScript browsers important? If so, don't bother with JavaScript at all. Once JavaScript 'infects' HTML, the HTML is very quickly reliant on it. Forms relying on JavaScript can still be submitted from plain browsers even though the JavaScript is ignored, which can have unexpected results.

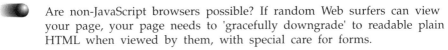

- Are non-JavaScript browsers possible? If random Web surfers can view your page, your page needs to 'gracefully downgrade' to readable plain HTML when viewed by them, with special care for forms.

- Do you control the browser version? In an Intranet application used only within one company, all users may have the same browser. It's then safe to use all features of that version, provided you are willing to upgrade your work if the browser version changes.

If none of the above are the case, then you are left with multiple JavaScript/ browser versions to handle. You can still simplify matters, provided you don't mind losing some readership or having your content look bad in unexpected places:

- Ignore really old browsers. At this time of writing, according to one poll, less than 1% of web surfers use Navigator 2.02.

- Support latest browsers only. This will cut down testing to one browser per vendor, but loses you a significant part of the readership, especially if latest versions are newly minted.

- Advocate one brand only. This cuts compatibility to one (or more) version. If your subject matter appeals mostly to users of one browser, for example Unix or Macintosh, don't bother with the others. Maybe you prefer a particular browser vendor.

Support the most popular browsers. You can still reach 80% of web surfers if you support about 5 to 10 of a given month's most popular browser versions. Web sites like **'www.yahoo.com'** have 'Browser Statistics' sections you can be mystified by.

A safe middle ground at this time of writing is to use the features in Netscape 3.0 JavaScript. Failing all that, you can spend a lot of time making your JavaScript work everywhere and gracefully downgrade everywhere else. Lots and lots of time.

Choose tricks

Here are a variety of tricks for handling different browsers in JavaScript.

Supporting ancient browsers

```
<HTML><BODY><SCRIPT>
<!-- hide from old, stupid browsers
document.write('JavaScript rules, but only here!');
// end comment -->
</SCRIPT></BODY></HTML>
```

Shown earlier, comments hide script source from browsers that don't know
`<SCRIPT>`.

Detecting scripts are ignored

```
<HTML><BODY><SCRIPT>
  alert("Off to the JavaScript page?");
  document.location.href = 'js_top.htm';
</SCRIPT>
<NOSCRIPT>Get a real browser, see it all!</NOSCRIPT>
</BODY></HTML>
```

The `<NOSCRIPT>` tag provides a method of dealing with browsers which refuse
to interpret JavaScript, either because they can't or because the user has turned
JavaScript off. The main use of this tag is to provide some feedback to the user
asking them to go away or else enable JavaScript. It can be used, as in this
example, to show a dummy page which is replaced if JavaScript is enabled.
Although the alert in this case stops the 'real' page from loading automatically,
it can easily be left out.

Detecting versions

```
<HTML><HEAD>
<SCRIPT LANGUAGE="JavaScript">var v = 1.0</SCRIPT>
<SCRIPT LANGUAGE="JavaScript1.1">v = 1.1</SCRIPT>
<SCRIPT LANGUAGE="JavaScript1.2">v = 1.2</SCRIPT>
</HEAD><BODY><SCRIPT>
document.write(v);
</SCRIPT></BODY></HTML>
```

This script shows a simple way of detecting JavaScript versions—at the end, 'v'
contains the highest version supported. If a rough guide is all you need it
should suffice. Unfortunately, all it really tests is the tag attribute. JavaScript for
Internet Explorer 3.0 on the PC and Macintosh are subtly different in features.
JavaScript 1.1 is "supported" in Internet Explorer 3.0 with Jscript 2.0, but doesn't
support all the features in Netscape's 1.1 implementation. Bugs and beta releases
further cloud the water.

There are other ways of gathering information about the browser and JavaScript.

The **navigator.userAgent** property contains a unique string describing the
browser version, brand and platform. Although it doesn't contain the JavaScript
language version, it can sometimes be deduced. For example, Netscape 2.02 has
the string '**Mozilla/2.02   (Win95;I)**' for the Windows 95 32-bit version and
that version is known to support only JavaScript 1.0.

Via Netscape's LiveConnect and Java, the operating system and its version can
be detected, provided Java support is enabled. This script will report '**Windows
95-4.0-Pentium**' for Netscape Navigator 3.03 32-bit for the PC:

```
var str = '';
str += java.lang.System.getProperty('os.name');
str += java.lang.System.getProperty('os.version');
str += java.lang.System.getProperty('os.arch');
document.write(str);
```

This script works for Netscape 3.0 and 4.0 browsers.

For Internet Explorer, the JavaScript version is accessible directly via special native functions. However, this requires at least Jscript 2.0, or else the script will fail with no ability to trap errors. An example:

```
var str = '';
str += ' ' + ScriptEngineMajorVersion();
str += ' ' + ScriptEngineMinorVersion();
str += ' ' + ScriptEngineBuildVersion();
document.write(str);
```

Common output for this example would be '**2   0   1125**'.

As a last resort you can detect the JavaScript version by testing in the script for a specific feature or bug that you know is unique to a given version.

Supporting several versions

Once the JavaScript version is known, there are three main strategies available: **separate pages**, **alternate script blocks**, and **object guarding**. Separate pages means creating separate HTML+JavaScript documents for each language version, and displaying the appropriate one. Alternate script blocks means providing **<SCRIPT>** blocks in the HTML for each version and using an '**if**' test at the start of each so that only the 'right' one does anything. Object guarding is perhaps the most flexible method:

```
<HTML>
... more HTML ...
<SCRIPT>
if ( top.images ) { change_image(); }
</SCRIPT>
```

The **top.images** property is problematic in some browsers, so always calling **change_image()** won't always work. By testing the property against **null**, nothing is done if it doesn't exist. This allows feature-by-feature compatibility without regard to versions, but it also means using a lot of extra **if**s if you use many non-portable features.

Web Servers

Browsers aren't the only place JavaScript is useful. There are several excellent reasons for having a JavaScript interpreter in a Web server:

 to help display HTML documents whose content changes regularly;

 to keep track of a web browser user;

 to handle form data submitted from a browser;

- to permanently store information in files or databases on the server;
- to connect a browser user to other, non-Web systems;
- to get a faster response than other server mechanisms.

Web servers have different characteristics to browsers. The need for compatibility between web servers only extends to the HTTP protocol—nearly invisible to the user and the script writer. Servers aren't necessarily cheap, they usually run in stints of weeks or more, they take some time to set up, and they have administration tasks unrelated to HTML and JavaScript.

Server-side JavaScript varies between web server brands, but it doesn't matter much except to confuse script writers who know client-side JavaScript. A server script writer only needs to know the specifics of one web server to get the job done. At least server-side JavaScript is moving towards ECMAScript compliance—Microsoft's Internet Information Server 4.0 is advertised as 100% compliant.

In this section, the basics of server-side JavaScript are outlined using Netscape's Enterprise Server 2.0 web server and Netscape's LiveWire 1.01 server-side JavaScript compiler as examples. Advancing from client-side to server-side JavaScript moves the script writer into the domain of client-server computing.

Adding server JavaScript

There are three places to put scripts for server-side JavaScript in the example used here.

<SERVER>

Inside an HTML file, a **<SERVER>** tag can be added which appears like a **<SCRIPT>** tag, except that **write()** replaces **document.write()**. This tag is a non-standard tag and it and its contents are ignored, even by browsers that recognize it. It has no tag attributes. An example:

```
<HTML><BODY>
<SERVER>
  // this is JavaScript
  write('Hello, World!<BR>');
</SERVER>
</BODY></HTML>
```

This HTML document is stored at a URL in the web server's web site. If a browser requests it, the document received looks like this:

```
<HTML><BODY>
Hello, World!<BR>
</BODY></HTML>
```

And the browser displays this:

```
Hello, World!
```

64

The **write()** method can produce more interesting output if server objects, properties and variables are used. The script can do other processing invisible to the browser, but that's all.

Source files

Like client-side JavaScript, JavaScript code can be stored in **.js** files, separate from any HTML document. There is no **<SERVER SRC='file.js'>** syntax.

Backquotes

Client-side JavaScript has JavaScript entities, and server-side JavaScript has backquote substitutions. Apart from syntax they are similar:

```
<HTML><BODY><FORM>
<INPUT TYPE="text" VALUE="&{top.name;}">
<INPUT TYPE="text" VALUE=`server.hostname;`>
</FORM></BODY></HTML>
```

'**server.hostname**' is an object property in the web server containing the name of the computer the web server runs on. One other difference is that the client case doesn't supply quotes in the resulting data, but the server case does.

Steps for server-side JavaScript

Making server-side JavaScript work isn't as trivial as client-side JavaScript. A myth exploded: server-side JavaScript is sometimes lumped in with other Web concepts like 'server-side includes' or 'server-parsed HTML'. It is more like 'server compiled JavaScript'. An HTML file containing a **<SERVER>** tag is hardly touched when the user attempts to fetch it via a URL.

Firmly gripping the vendor's manuals for the example server, proceed as follows if you wish to create server-side JavaScript scripts:

Server setup

Ask the local Web Master for access to an existing installation, or hack your way through the install process for Enterprise Server 2.0 and LiveWire 1.01 yourself. With Windows NT, the computer can be both a browser machine and a web server machine. It can do both at the same time, so you can browse your own site. At the end of the install you should have achieved the following:

- Obtained access to the directories for the new web site;
- Installed Enterprise Server 2.0;
- Installed LiveWire 1.01;
- Proved the web site works by browsing it;
- Enabled LiveWire, and restarted the server.

A point of confusion is the Administration Server. This is a second web server at a different URL to the main one but on the same computer, and part of the same installed software. This server can be browsed as well. Its web pages allow you to start, stop and configure the main server. No web pages can be added to it.

A second point of confusion is identifying names. The computer's name, computer user accounts, web server names, and web server user names are all different. Write them down on a bit of paper.

Create an Application

Enterprise Server collects related server-side JavaScript and HTML files into groups called **applications**. **Application Manager** is a special application used to manage the others. All applications have a name which is used in URLs. The manager application's name is '**appmgr**', so its URL is '**http://localhost:80/appmgr**', assuming '**localhost:80**' is the web server's contact address.

Use a browser to run **appmgr**, then use the **appmgr** buttons and forms to make a new application, including a home or index page, and the other details. The method selected for tracking client sessions is particularly important because not all browsers support all methods. Add the directory the new application will live in to the web site's directory structure. Cookies are described later on in the book. Now you are ready to create web site content.

Create HTML files and **.js** files as usual in the new application or look at the samples supplied.

Compile the Application

In order for the web server to run server-side JavaScript fast, it needs to have it in a pre-digested form. If the 'Hello, World!' example above was stored in '**test.htm**', this can be achieved at the DOS prompt:

```
lwcomp -v -o test.web test.htm
```

'**lwcomp**' is the LiveWire JavaScript compiler. A **.web** file contains partially compiled JavaScript, and is used when a browser requests a document in an application that has server-side JavaScript in it. Many **.htm** or **.js** files can be compiled and merged into one **.web** file:

```
lwcomp -v -o test.web test.htm help.htm extras.js
```

The application manager must now be used to stop and restart the application, since the **.web** file has just changed. All preparation is now complete.

Run the Application

An application's pages can be retrieved by an ordinary browser with an ordinary URL such as '**http://localhost:80/myapp/page.htm**' where '**localhost:80**' is the web server, '**myapp**' is the application name, and '**page.htm**' a page in that application. The browser should be able to ignore the **<SERVER>** tags and their content.

The Application Manager presents an alternative method of viewing the application's pages, via Run and Debug buttons. The Run button opens a new window, and loads an application page just like a user entering the URL. The Debug button does the same, but in a special debug mode.

When server-side JavaScript runs, there is normally no way to interact with it, since the web server has no user. This makes debugging hard. The Debug button solves this problem. It loads the application page inside a window split into two frames. The left frame reports debug information about the server-side JavaScript processing, whilst the right frame displays the application page as per normal. Using special **trace()** and **debug()** functions, the script writer can produce extra debug information if desired.

A trap: the application can't be started and stopped while displayed in debug mode. Clear the window first.

Server-side Features

In a Web Server there are no frames, windows or styles, so none of these browser objects exist. Unique to the server JavaScript interpreter are four key objects on one hand, and a group of utility objects on the other.

The four key objects are not in a hierarchy. Instead, they differ in their lifetimes, and in the way different clients (browser users) share them:

- A sole object named '**server**' exists while the web server is up, and is shared by all users of the web server.

- One object named '**project**' for each application exists while the application exists and is shared by all users of that application.

- One object named '**client**' exists for each browser user, from when that user first accesses the server until it is deemed that they have gone away.

- One object named '**request**' exists very temporarily for each URL request made of the server.

The request object contains details of a URL request such as form data or search criteria. The other objects are used to communicate or coordinate between users and requests—often required when one web server is dealing with many different browser users.

The other group of objects; **utility objects**, allows general programming tasks to occur in server-side JavaScript. Native objects such as **String**, **Math** and **Date** are also available. Important examples are:

- The File object can read and write files on the server.

- The Database object can read and write relational databases such as Oracle and Microsoft Access.

67

Catching responses

Sometimes things go wrong when a browser tries to get a URL. If, for example, the URL is not found, a '404 Not Found' message appears in the browser. There is a way of using JavaScript to handle these errors better. It doesn't require server-side JavaScript, but does require fiddling with a web server.

Many web servers such as Apache have redirection options. These allow one URL request to be substituted for another. One such option allows a specific document to load when unusual response codes, like the dreaded 404, occur for a URL. This may be more informative for the user than the plain error message. Since the document is just an HTML document, it can contain client-side JavaScript, which may do any special steps required, such as going to alternative pages, setting cookies or communicating the error with other HTML frames. See Chapter 3; Frames and Windows for how.

An example: the Apache 1.2 web server has a configuration file called 'srm.conf' which maps out how the web server is to manage the local web site. This line added to that configuration file:

```
ErrorDocument 404 /admin/errors/report.html
```

causes 'report.html' to be displayed to the user whenever an unknown (equals 404) URL is requested. Report.html might do some JavaScript in order to inform the web master of the site, display the URL of the failed link, or go to another page.

Consult documentation specific to your Web server for a similar configuration option if you want to use this approach.

Standalone interpreters

A JavaScript interpreter not embedded in some other tool like a browser has few constraints on its behavior. This makes it flexible enough for general scripting and programming tasks. All that is required is that basic system functions be available so the interpreter can do input and output. In one sense, the operating system (Windows or Unix) becomes the interpreter host.

The most visible standalone interpreter for JavaScript is Nombas Inc.'s ScriptEase 4.0 range of products. There are four key offerings: a standalone interpreter, a standalone interpreter specifically for use with a web server, an enhancement which lets scripts send data to each another over the Internet, and a development kit allowing the interpreter to be embedded in a customer's existing application. The company has a range of pre-prepared scripts covering general programming tasks such as databases, networking, distributed computing and Web access. The interpreters have native enhancements to support more traditional data types such as bytes.

Using standalone JavaScript combined with a web server is particularly useful— see the forms and CGI chapter. The Reference Section documents ScriptEase's compatibilities and enhancements.

68

All by itself

Here are two examples of standalone JavaScript scripts, the first from Chapter 1.

```
Clib.puts('Hello, World\n');
```

```
#include "stredit.jsh"

var id    = "Nombas ScriptEase 4.0 JavaScript";
var brand = str_cut_text(brand, "JavaScript");

if ( brand )
    Clib.printf("JavaScript type is: %50.50s\n", brand);
else
    Clib.printf("Not JavaScript? Identity crisis!");
```

Each of these examples would be in a separate file. The ScriptEase interpreter can read a script stored in a file with any extension, so '**.js**' is fine, although '**.jse**' is the preferred extension. '**.jsh**' is the preferred extension for **#include**'d files.

The first example shows the "put string" function **Clib.puts()** which is the equivalent of **document.write()**. The second example uses the "print formatted" function **Clib.printf()**, which does the same thing, but gives fine control over the format of the output. This isn't HTML, so output to the screen or elsewhere appears exactly as you specify it. The '**%50.50s**' characters are an example of a specific format.

The second example also shows a 'hash include' in the first line. This allows another script to be included in the main script, replacing the '**#include**' which is called a **directive**. The HTML equivalent is **<SCRIPT SRC="string.js">**. Any code in the script included is interpreted straight away—in this case it is included so further on the handy function **str_cut_text()** can be used to return a string minus a specified piece, or **null**.

Command line variations

These examples show JavaScript being run from the command line:

```
C:\SE> secon32 example1.jse ready set go

C:\SE> sewin32 "Clib.printf('A piece of pie: %d', Math.PI * 0.2);"

$ se < example3 > output
```

There are different interpreter programs to suit different compatibility issues and different computers. This explains why there are several different commands shown.

The first example shows how to specify a **.jse** file and supply starting information to it ('**ready**', '**set**' and '**go**'). The second example shows directly executing JavaScript without any file, similar to a JavaScript URL in HTML. The last example (using Unix) shows that the interpreter can handle having the source of its script and of its output redirected from/to another file.

Batch files

In addition to the above mechanisms, JavaScript standalone scripts can be embedded in batch files.

On the PC, batch files are .BAT files and are handled as follows:

```
@echo off
SEcon32 %0.bat %1 %2 %3 % 4 %5 %6 %7 %8 %9
GOTO SE_EXIT

// All the script including #include's goes here
Clib.puts("Boo! JavaScript strikes.");

:SE_EXIT
```

When DOS runs this script, only the first three lines and the last are seen by DOS because of the **GOTO**. In the second line, the ScriptEase interpreter is fed the *same* file, and is smart enough to know that a .BAT file means ignore all lines except those between '**GOTO   SE_EXIT**' and '**:SE_EXIT**', which must be the script.

On Unix, batch files have a special start line instead:

```
#!/usr/local/bin/se
    // script and #includes from here on
    Clib.puts('JavaScript back at work\n');
```

This example assumes ScriptEase was installed in the **/usr/local/bin** directory.

CGI programs

CGI is discussed in a later chapter, but for completeness here's a simple example:

```
#include "html.cmm"
CGIOut('<HTML><BODY>');
CGIOut('A CGI test page');
CGIOut('</BODY></HTML>');
```

A CGI program is a program that produces a HTML document. It has a URL, so a browser can request the document. It receives the URL and outputs the document contents directly to the web server which forwards it to the browser.

The CGI program can be written in any language. If the CGI program is a standalone JavaScript ScriptEase 4.0 script, there are two options. The first option is a batch file as described above. The second option is a version of the JavaScript interpreter that has extra support for CGI. In this case, the function **CGIOut()** must be used instead of **puts()** or **printf()** to send the output to the web server.

JavaScript inside JavaScript

Scripts are interpreted and scripts can contain strings of any size and content. So the contents of a string can be a JavaScript script, which might get interpreted at some point. Anywhere a JavaScript string can go, JavaScript script source can be sent.

The native ECMAScript function **eval()** turns a plain string into an interpreted program. The **setTimeout()** and more recently, **setInterval()** functions do a similar thing. In addition, there are ways of 'getting back' script code that has already run. Function objects may report back their code when converted to strings, or have a '**src**' property containing the source. Microsoft browsers grant access to the **<SCRIPT>** tag's contents in a given document.

Scripts in strings plus interpretation allow some quite advanced techniques. ScriptEase exploits **eval()** to do remote debugging of scripts, and to allow scripts to be communicated between remote computers. Functions and objects can copy themselves from window to window in browsers, and rearrange themselves in response to user actions.

Summary

This chapter has described all the cracks and crevices into which JavaScript scripts can be stuffed.

Although HTML pages are the most common place to find JavaScript, there are diverse options. Netscape is increasingly dependent on the language for a variety of tasks. Web servers use JavaScript to turn read-only HTML documents into usefully interactive applications. Fancy web servers do this via server-side JavaScript, simpler ones rely on standalone interpreters and CGI. Standalone JavaScript is a general programming language adaptable to any task. The desperate can put JavaScript inside Java.

For all that, web browsers are still the cheapest, most accessible and easiest way to exploit JavaScript. Compatibility issues are tricky, but once JavaScript is added to HTML, it's hard to go back—you're dependent. Much of this book explores the possibilities of client-side JavaScript.

The next chapter illustrates many simple tricks with browser windows made possible by JavaScript.

Windows and Frames

Without a browser window to display it, there's not much point in creating HTML documents, much less adding JavaScript for special effects. This chapter explains how all the biggest parts of a browser hang together and what JavaScript techniques can be applied successfully to them. The biggest parts of a browser are the browser windows and any frames they might have.

Browser windows and frames live together with HTML documents in an edifice called the **Browser Object Model** or the **Document Object Model**. This edifice is a set of JavaScript host objects. This chapter is mainly concerned with the Window object, which stands for a whole browser window or frame. Nearly as broad in scope is the Document object, which can stand for the whole content of a given browser window. A Window object can often be handled from a JavaScript object called **window**. A Document object can always be handled from a JavaScript object called **document**.

Messing with windows and frames using JavaScript is a game called "who controls the browser?" played between the script writer and the user, with the browser's security features as umpire. The specifics of the security features are covered in Chapter 6; Privacy, Security and Cookies.

The more specific objects in the Browser Object Model are described in later chapters, such as Chapter 4; Multimedia and Plugins and Chapter 5; Forms and CGI.

Window Types

The more you think about it, the more windows there appear to be in a browser. They are controllable to different degrees from JavaScript.

Main browser windows

A browser can display more than one window at once. These windows hold the content the user normally views. Each one is represented by a Window object in JavaScript. They can be opened and closed and their history navigated via JavaScript, with some security limitations. All JavaScript variables and objects in an inline JavaScript script ultimately belong to one Window object. Although windows are mostly used to display HTML documents, non-HTML windows exist as well, such as windows that display a `ftp://` URL.

Windows displaying HTML

HTML documents are the most common contents of browser windows. It is with Window objects that the script writer most often tries to override the user's control of the browser. The Window object's **open()** method or function is particularly important. This function should never be confused with the **open()** method of the Document object, discussed later. Suppose two HTML files exist as follows, plus a third that illustrates the **window.open()** method:

```
<!-- first.htm -->
<HTML><BODY>Boo!!</BODY></HTML>
```

```
<!-- second.htm -->
<HTML><BODY>I'm smaller</BODY></HTML>
```

Here is an example of the **open()** function:

```
<HTML><BODY><SCRIPT>
var win1 = open("first.htm","first",
            "resizable=no,height=200,width=200");

function show_it()
{
  var win2 = window.open("second.htm","second",
            "resizable=no,height=100,width=100");
}
</SCRIPT>
<A HREF="#" ONCLICK="show_it();"> Click me, Alice.</A>
</BODY></HTML>
```

Notice the use of the "#" URL. This is a plain HTML trick that prevents a page from being replaced when a link is followed. However, that won't work on Internet Explorer 3.0. Here is the initial page, shown in Internet Explorer 4.0:

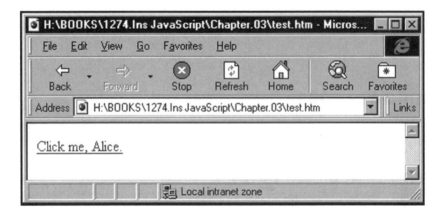

When this page is displayed, a second
window is opened by the inline script:

If the link is clicked in the original window, then a further
window is displayed:

This example shows several important points. The **open()** function provides the
new window with a name (this is separate from its **<TITLE>**) and a set of
window property options. To avoid confusion between window properties and
JavaScript properties, this chapter refers to traditional window properties such
as menus and scrollbars as **decorations**. The options can stop toolbars from
appearing, set the window size in pixels and so on. The **open()** function
returns new Window objects, which the variables win1 and win2 refer to. For
win2, the **open()** function has to be qualified with the object 'window' because
technically, the window isn't the current object for event handlers. For normal
inline scripts, plain **open()** is enough.

The parts of the third argument to **open()** must be comma-separated, not
space separated, and not commas plus spaces. This picky syntax is a trap you
can fall into with monotonous regularity. So a typical **open()** function call
looks as follows:

```
variable-name = open("URL", "window-name", "option=value,option=value...");
```

One design issue in this example is that the 'win2' variable is only local to the
show_it() function. This is usually a bad idea because when the function
ends and the variable goes, you've lost track of the new window. It can be
found again with **open('','second')**, but it's better to keep the variable
somewhere more permanent, like 'win1' in case you want to use it.

Another design issue is that users often don't like unexpected windows popping
up, especially without controls like menus on them, so you need a good reason
to do it. Here are three fair reasons:

75

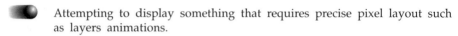 Attempting to display something that requires precise pixel layout such as layers animations.

The window is a temporary popup-style window like help or a user warning.

The features removed are compensated for with buttons, links and images in the new window.

Open() is otherwise quite limited. Security issues prevent you from changing the decorations of an already open window (unless you use a secure script), or a window displaying pages from a different web site. There is no way to prevent the user from closing a window you've specially opened—to detect this you must keep track of a variable

When it's not HTML

Browser windows don't always display HTML documents. Sometimes they display directory information from FTP sites, gopher menus, or just a single image. Windows only have a name if assigned one from JavaScript, otherwise they are anonymous and can't be found. So new windows displaying non-HTML information can't be touched or read by JavaScript. Existing windows which change their contents from HTML to something else will keep their name. If you have a variable referring to such a window, Netscape will set all the existing properties of the object to **'undefined'** (including the **'name'** property—somewhat bizarre). Internet Explorer does a little better, leaving the **'name'** and the **'location'** property intact, but the other properties can't be examined at all for 3.02.

The mail, news and bookmark organizer windows aren't accessible from HTML embedded JavaScript, but configuration preferences, scripted in JavaScript for Netscape 4.0 browsers (discussed in Chapter 2) can affect their appearance and content. These preferences can also control the appearance of the first window that appears when the browser starts up.

Wysiwyg

In Netscape 3.0 only, resizing a HTML window can have an unusual side effect. If the HTML source comes in part from inline JavaScript, the URL displayed in the location bar can change. If the URL is **'http://my.site.com/page.htm'** it changes to **'wysiwyg://56/http://my.site.com/page.htm'**, where **'56'** is some random number.

Such a page is still a normal HTML page, accessible from JavaScript. The new-looking URL just reflects Netscape's attempts to cope with resizing and the page's URL hasn't really changed. Ignore it. An example page that can be resized to show this behavior is:

```
<HTML><BODY><SCRIPT>
document.write('resize for Navigator 3.0 wysiwyg');
</SCRIPT></BODY></HTML>
```

You can't make up a **'wysiwyg:'** URL yourself.

View Source

The page that displays the HTML and JavaScript source for a given document isn't accessible from JavaScript.

In particular, there is no easy way to get the whole contents of the 'View Source' page into JavaScript strings. Internet Explorer 4.0 has an almost equivalent, but separate mechanism for doing this. This mechanism is explained in Chapter 9.

Netscape browsers can be directed to display the View Source window from embedded JavaScript. Do this by opening a window with the URL '**view-source:X**' where 'X' is the fully qualified URL of the document to view. This can be used as a debugging aid.

About, Help and Security Info

In the Netscape browsers, these windows are all just HTML pages, so in theory they are accessible directly from JavaScript. There isn't much reason to do so. If you feel the urge to hack into the browser in order to find out how these windows are named, go ahead. The About page is easiest because it doesn't appear in a new window without a location bar. Microsoft-type windows like Help might be accessible via ActiveX, but why bother—it's just help.

Both Netscape and Microsoft have a software development kit (SDK) that assists in the creation of HTML help pages. Three URLs are good starting points: for Netscape's NetHelp: **http://developer.netscape.com/products/ index.html** for Microsoft's HTML Help: **http://www.microsoft.com/ workshop/author/htmlhelp/**.

Java

The Java interpreter controls two kinds of windows in addition to the space reserved for it with the **<APPLET>** or **<OBJECT>** tags. These are zero or more Java popup 'canvases' and the sole Java console. Both of these kinds of windows can be manipulated from JavaScript via ActiveX or LiveConnect. See Chapter 8; "Applets and Java". New canvases can be created this way, but the console cannot be displayed or hidden from JavaScript. You might want to create a canvas if you want to control a Java applet from JavaScript in an independent window. You might also want to work with the console when debugging your scripts.

Warnings and Dialog Boxes

Depending on your preferences (especially security preferences) there are numerous warnings and dialog boxes that can appear during a web browsing session. Very few of these can be controlled directly from HTML embedded JavaScript. Some can be avoided by the use of secure scripts (described in Chapter 7), or otherwise affected by configuration preferences.

However, three types of popups are custom-made for JavaScript use. They are created with methods of a Window object and are called **alert**, **confirm** and **prompt**:

This is **alert**:

This is **confirm**:

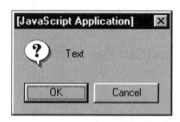

This is **prompt**:

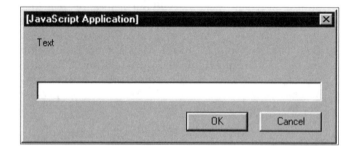

These examples are from Navigator 4.02 for Windows 95. Where 'Text' appears, any JavaScript string can be substituted. Here is a script showing all three:

```
<HTML><BODY><SCRIPT>
var agree = false, notes = '';
agree = confirm('Love pumpkin?');
if ( agree )
    notes = prompt("Its good points?",'Type here');
else
    notes = prompt("Its bad points?",'Type here');
alert(notes + '\nYour mother would be proud.');
</SCRIPT></BODY></HTML>
```

Confirm() returns a Boolean value. **Prompt()** returns a string typed in by the user. **Alert()** returns '**undefined**' which is much the same as not returning anything. The windows are always titled '[JavaScript Application]' or similar words for security reasons so the user can't be fooled into thinking they are something else.

These windows halt the script until the user responds. In Netscape this means halting all JavaScript in the browser. This behavior makes **alert()** and **confirm()** useful as simple debugging aids—use them to step through a script that isn't quite working yet. They are particularly useful for probing an existing page via JavaScript URLs:

```
javascript:alert(document.form1.field1.value)
```

Note the **document** object is used here—this alert displays an HTML field value that is part of an HTML document. These popups aren't HTML-style popups, they just display directly, so end-of-line characters aren't lost. If you want fancy formatting, you have to do it yourself. To duplicate this code:

```
<HTML><BODY>
<STRONG>Snow White accomplices:</STRONG>
<UL><LI>Dopey<LI>Grumpy<LI>Doc</UL>
</BODY></HTML>
```

try this:

```
var message = 'SNOW WHITE ACCOMPLICES:\n'
              + ' o  Dopey\n o  Grumpy\n o  Doc';
alert(message);
```

If you really need fancy formatting, you can simulate these windows with HTML windows, using **window.open()** and display content formatted with HTML tags and form elements, but the window will not be **modal**, that is, the other windows will not be frozen when the new one appears.

Layers, Frames and Scripts

None of these is a window in the user sense. Layers are Layer objects which are either documents, or pieces of documents. Scripts are whole documents taking up part of an existing window, but don't have a Window object of their own. Frames appear as an array of Window objects internally to scripts, but externally they are only a piece of a window. Both layers and frames act like containers for document information, just adding a few properties of their own, such as size and position. They don't have the status of a whole user-visible window—no toolbars or menus.

A Frameset is not a window or an object at all, it is just a convenient tag for grouping and sizing a set of frames. It also provides a place for window event handlers to be specified.

Pop-up Menus

The user can make pop-up menus appear when right-clicking (Unix and Windows 95/NT) on a document. You have to use advanced event handlers in the 4.0 level browsers in order to stop these from appearing.

On Unix only (Netscape 3.0 browsers have two variants of pop-up menus: one for frames and one for non-frames) you can alternate them by turning a non-frame document into a frame – just make a frameset document with a single frame that points to your original document. The reverse can also be done. Then you can disable the 'back' option on these menus as described under 'history' in the next section.

Window Organization

This section describes how windows work with each other. The discussion applies mostly to ordinary HTML document windows, not other windows such as mail readers.

Hierarchy

A browser can have more than one window open. No window is marked as special just because it was first, or because it opened the others—they are all equal. Each of those windows can either contain a HTML document with a **<BODY>**, or with a **<FRAMESET>**.

Each window has a Window object, and each Window object has two important properties **document** and **frames**. The **document** property points to the Document object matching the URL for the window. **Frames** is an array of (possibly zero) frame Window objects. The frames array has a **'length'** attribute which reveals how many frames are *owned* by the main window object.

Consider these HTML documents:

```
<!-- rabbit.htm -->
<HTML><BODY>Rabbit.</BODY></HTML>
```

```
<!-- vsplit.htm -->
<HTML><FRAMESET COLS="*,*">
<FRAME SRC="rabbit.htm" NAME="bunny1">
<FRAME SRC="rabbit.htm" NAME="bunny2">
</FRAMESET></HTML>
```

```
<!-- three.htm -->
<HTML><FRAMESET ROWS="*,*">
<FRAME SRC="rabbit.htm" NAME="bunny3">
<FRAMESET COLS="*,*">
<FRAME SRC="rabbit.htm" NAME="bunny4">
<FRAME SRC="rabbit.htm" NAME="bunny5">
</FRAMESET></FRAMESET></HTML>
```

```
<!-- complex.htm -->
<HTML><FRAMESET ROWS="*,*">
<FRAME SRC="rabbit.htm" NAME="bunny6">
<FRAME SRC="vsplit.htm" NAME="bunny7">
</FRAMESET></HTML>
```

Displayed in small windows, they look like this:

rabbit.htm:

vsplit.htm:

three.htm:

complex.htm:

The value of '**frames.length**' is 0, 2, 3, and 2 respectively. The third example shows that nested framesets don't do anything tricky—each frame is simply added to the **frames** array. The last example shows that if the URL for a frame turns out to be a frameset document, then it *is* tricky—the frames of the second frameset aren't counted in the first frameset, even though it looks the same visually. The structure of these four windows can be illustrated as follows:

81

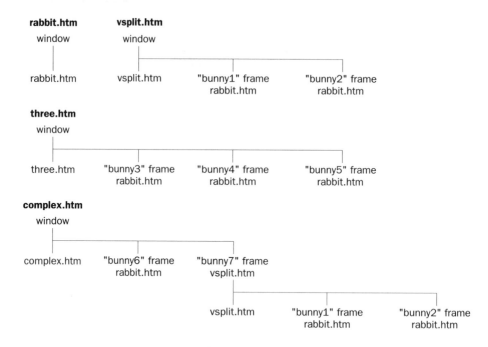

In the fourth example, to reach the lower left document (object) from the original, from the frameset document (called '**top**') in JavaScript requires navigating the object hierarchy like this:

```
top.frames[1].frames[0].document;
```

or

```
top.bunny7.bunny1.document;
```

Frame names are object properties of the Window object as well as 'frames' array members—this is objects and arrays being almost the same again. If frames are deeply nested and documents are complex, referring to distant objects from the top down can be very cumbersome.

Finally, Internet Explorer 3.0 and 4.0, and HTML 4.0 allow floating frames: the **<IFRAME>** tag. Floating frames are specified in the document's **<BODY>** content. Nevertheless, they are added to the 'frames' array of the window containing the document, just as **<FRAMESET>** frames are.

Window references

A well-defined hierarchy of windows, frames and documents brings order to complex HTML documents, but it doesn't make access to those objects particularly easy. Access between windows and within windows is made easier by special object properties.

In HTML, the special URLs **_self**, **_parent**, **_top** and **_blank** are often used to control which window or frame to load a URL into. JavaScript has equivalent variables, called '**self**', '**parent**' and '**top**' which always point at Window objects. These variables are properties of the Window object. '**Blank**' does not exist because it is pointless to refer to a window which hasn't been created. There is also a '**window**' variable which is the same as '**self**'.

Like HTML, the '**top**' variable refers to the Window object representing a whole visible window, regardless of its content. '**self**' refers to the Window object that the script is most directly embedded in. '**parent**' is the same as '**self**' unless '**self**' is a frame, in which case '**parent**' is the window containing self's frameset document.

A script always executes inside the scope of some object. Usually this is the '**self**' window, which means window methods like '**open()**' and '**alert()**' don't require a prefix like '**self.open()**' or '**window.alert()**'. The longer form is required if these methods are used inside an event handler, because the current object there is usually not a window.

Some JavaScript host objects are '**global**'; meaning they are available to use regardless of what object is current. **Math** is an example. '**top**', '**self**', and '**parent**' are like this, so '**top**' in particular is always available to use. They are also updated automatically if windows go away or framesets are replaced with other documents. If all else fails, start from '**top**' and work down.

Decorations

Other elements of a browser window exist as properties of the Window object for that window. Security issues prevent some of these features being changed unless advanced techniques like signed scripts or configuration scripts are used.

- **Status bar**. The message in the status bar can be read and written to, but not the progress indicator. The chapter on Multimedia and Plug-ins has an example.

- **Open()** can create a window without a status bar, by using the 'status=no' option, but there is no way for a plain script or the user to put it back. This is very irritating in Netscape, because, if a window with no status bar is the last one in the browser to shut down, the browser will start up without status bars from then on. The solution is to either edit the browser preferences file by hand, or have JavaScript open a window with a status bar and shutdown the browser again using that window as the last window. In Navigator 4.0, a signed script can expose or remove a status bar.

- **Scrollbars**. Scrollbars can be disabled in new windows via **open()** by using the 'scrollbars=no' option. The user cannot put them back. Frames can also have scrollbars. These can't be exposed or removed once set.

- **Toolbars**. These cannot be read or changed by embedded JavaScript, except for **open()** which can create a window without them, by using the 'toolbar=no' option. The user can put toolbars back at any time if the menubar is accessible.

● **Menubar.** As for toolbars, except once its gone, the user can't get it back.

● **Big N or E icon** (in the top right corner of the browser window). This can only be changed from a configuration script.

● **Window title bar.** The title string is a property of the top-level Document object in the window, not the window itself. The property is called 'title'.

● The title bar and its close and resize icons are added by the computer's operating system, not the browser, and aren't visible inside JavaScript. You're stuck with them, unless you create an ActiveX control that specifically removes them.

Finally, Netscape 3.0 (and 4.0) has a 'kiosk' mode that allows the browser to start up without most of the window decorations. This is done with a command line option; '-k'. In Netscape 4.0 the preferred way of doing this is to use **open()** and a mixture of its options that prevent the user from changing windows. This is called 'canvas mode'. Internet Explorer 4.0 supports this directly with a button on the browser toolbar and calls it 'Full screen mode'. An example of canvas mode which sets the correct options is:

```
<HTML><BODY><SCRIPT>
var details = 'alwaysRaised=yes,titlebar=no,left=0,top=0,width='
    + top.screen.width
    + ',height='
    + top.screen.height;
</SCRIPT>
<A HREF="#" ONCLICK="window.open('about:','test',top.details);">
</A>
</BODY></HTML>
```

The only catch is that the JavaScript must be moved to a signed script or else the 'AlwaysRaised' option (illustrated above) is ignored. The 'AlwaysRaised' option prevents other windows and applications from appearing in front of the canvas mode window.

Concurrency

If several windows and/or frames are downloading web documents at the same time, it's a race that anyone could win. If inline scripts that operate on other windows occur as part of the downloads, chaos can result. Without planning, it's impossible to know whether a variable or object exists yet in a given frame or window used by another window's script.

For Netscape browsers, the situation is not so bad. Using the footrace analogy, as the runners speed down the track next to each other, they juggle a ball between themselves. Only the runner with the ball can interpret a script. This means that for Netscape, you can always be confident that when you set or read a variable it won't change at least until your script ends (when you pass the ball on). However, in Internet Explorer, every runner has a ball, so you can't even be sure about your variables from one statement to the next.

Of course, a variable or object referred to only within its own window is straightforward.

The solutions for the general case are:

- Don't mess with other windows unless absolutely necessary
- Only rely on windows that are known to be fully loaded.
- Use events to wait for windows to finish loading.
- If a critical window closes, close everything related.

Two key window events help achieve this: **onLoad** and **onUnload**. The **onLoad** event fires when a document is fully displayed. The **onUnload** event is a little less trustworthy due to bugs, but fires when a document is removed from visibility. Since these events are document-based, they apply to windows, frames and **<LAYER>** tags. These are the only two window events in HTML 4.0, but Netscape browsers 3.0 and 4.0 have a heap of others. An example of a multi-frame document that alerts the user when everything is loaded:

```
<!-- toplevel.htm -->
<HTML><HEAD>
<SCRIPT>
var total = 0;
var win = new Array();
function ready(w)         // report that this window is ready
{
    win[total++] = w;
    if ( total == 3 ) alert('All rabbits ready.');
}
</SCRIPT></HEAD>
<FRAMESET ROWS="*,*" ONLOAD="top.ready(this)">
<FRAME SRC="newbunny.htm">
<FRAME SRC="newbunny.htm">
</FRAMESET></HTML>
```

```
<!--newbunny.htm -->
<HTML><BODY ONLOAD="top.ready(this);">
Hop.
</BODY></HTML>
```

In this example, the alert only appears when the '**ready()**' function has been called enough times. That is enough by itself to detect everything's loaded. This example also stores the supplied Window objects. In this case there's no real need to do so because the **frames** array already tracks each frame. However, this example can be adapted to the case where separate windows, not just frames, are loaded using **open()**. In that case the '**win**' array is needed to track those separate windows. Finally, you might be tempted to use '**register**' rather than '**ready**' for the function that reports the document is loaded. That is a bad idea, as '**register**' is a reserved word in JavaScript.

History

In the window hierarchy diagram above, each window or frame not only has a document object for its URL, it also has an object called '**history**'. This stores the URLs of all the past documents appearing in this window or frame.

Methods of this object are used to navigate forwards and backwards through the list. The items in the list are just URL strings, not whole documents – you can't probe historical documents with scripts.

The most common uses of history are as follows:

```
<A HREF="#" ONCLICK="window.history.go(-1)">
   Boldly take a step backwards</A>
<A HREF="#" ONCLICK="window.location.reload()">
   Boldly go nowhere</A>
<A HREF="#" ONCLICK="window.location.reload(true)">
   Boldly go nowhere, but making a special effort</A>
<A HREF="#" ONCLICK="window.location.replace(url)">
   Boldly forget the past</A>
```

The first case returns to the previous document, like the user's **Back** button. The second case refreshes the current page. The third does the same, but from its original source (which may have changed). The last refreshes the current page, but also throws out all the history in the process, effectively disabling the user's '**Back**' button.

History features are bug-prone in Internet Explorer 3.0. Even in browsers where they work perfectly, your author isn't keen on them, apart from the occasional '**go(-1)**'.

Window Design

A few design issues crop up when working with windows.

Multiple windows

Simple document display doesn't often involve multiple windows. If you are trying to build an application that makes heavy use of forms, that is another matter. Multiple forms lead quickly to multiple windows.

Because the user can close a window at any time, maintaining a lot of random dependencies between windows just doesn't work well. Not only do you have to check window references before every use, you have to decide what to do when they've gone. Worse still, when a window closes, all the objects and variables inside it vanish forever. Best to choose a simple architecture with fewer tricky possibilities. Two workable options are explored here.

Simple approach

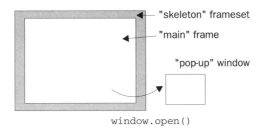

"skeleton" frameset

"main" frame

"pop-up" window

`window.open()`

This example has a maximum of 2 windows. The 'skeleton' window contains one frame only, in which all the action such as form data entry happens. When user issues occur, the second window 'pop-up' appears, but only for temporary matters. While the pop up window is open, the first window can't or shouldn't be modified. To stop the main window from doing anything, always use the same variable to track the popup window opened with **open()**. Then test that variable in all event handlers in the main window to make sure it's correct to go ahead with the event.

The frameset document in this example may appear useless, but it's critical. Control type data can be stored in the main window or its frameset document object. If the sole frame is used to change between pages of the Web application, then the data in that frame is destroyed with each new page. But any data in the frameset window stays intact. If the main window is created without toolbars, the user can't damage the frameset window at all.

Enhancements: it may make sense to allow the user a second popup for Help text, or similar information that doesn't lock the main window. The main menu can also benefit from a second frame in a strip containing buttons or links that allows the user to navigate pages in the other frame.

More complex approach

If you really do need multiple windows at a time, a more complex solution is as follows:

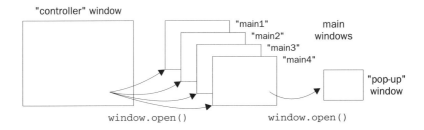

"controller" window

"main1"
"main2"
"main3"
"main4"

main windows

"pop-up" window

`window.open()`   `window.open()`

In this example, the controller window is dedicated to maintaining good order in the application. It does all the opening and tracking of the main windows. If the controller window is shut down by the user, it shuts down all the main windows as well—they can't survive without it. If a main window wants to refer to another main window, it asks the controller window for a window reference via a function supplied in the controller window, like `'top.opener.get_window('form3')'`. Control information is stored in the controller window. Pop-ups and help are managed in each main window as for the simple case, or the controller window can be given responsibility.

A problem with this solution is that the controller window is always visible, and so must contain something sensible to look at—like a toolbar or a control pad. It's ineffective and confusing to users if you try and hide the controller window just by making it very small.

If one of the main windows is guaranteed to always exist, it can take on the role of the controller by being structured as for the simple approach—then no separate controller window is needed. However, there are always cases where the simple approach is limited. One typical such case is where a window displays constantly updating information—you cannot afford to overwrite the window because the user goes elsewhere, so only the complex case will do.

Window event handling tricks

A particularly tricky possibility involving window events is discussed in Chapter 10. It explains how Netscape 4.0 browsers can send event information between windows.

Windows without URLs

A window can avoid the overhead of downloading an HTML URL from some remote place by creating the HTML in the browser. Inline JavaScript can be used to generate the whole HTML document for a window, from another window. There are a few good reasons for doing this:

 the HTML is small and trivial, and Web connections can be slow;

 the HTML depends on some other data currently in the browser;

 the HTML page never ends, or continually refreshes, or other automation.

For greatest portability, the way to do this is to load an empty, dummy page as a place holder when the window is first created and then re-write it straight away:

```
<!-blank.htm -->
<HTML></HTML>
```

```
<!-hello.htm-->
<HTML><HEAD><SCRIPT>
<!--
var txt='<HTML><BODY>Hello, World!<BR></BODY></HTML>'
var win2 = open('blank.htm', 'win2');
win2.document.open();
win2.document.write(txt);
win2.document.close();
// end comment -->
</SCRIPT></HEAD></HTML>
```

This example shows the use of the other common **open()** method—for the Document object. This kind of **open()** destroys the current document, leaving the window ready to receive new document information. document.close() shuts the door on any more data for this document.

Netscape has a few ease of use shortcuts. Its version of **document.write()** is smarter—it will automatically do a document.**open()** if one is required. It is better to get into the habit of doing the **open()** yourself since Microsoft browsers require it. The two files above can be shortened to one and made faster if Netscape-specific enhancements are used:

```
<!-hello.htm-->
<HTML><HEAD><SCRIPT>
<!-- avoid &lt; problems
var txt='<HTML><BODY>Hello, World!<BR></BODY></HTML>'
var win2 = open('about:blank', 'win2');
win2.txt = txt;
win2.location.href = 'javascript:txt';
// end comment -->
</SCRIPT></HEAD></HTML>
```

'**about:blank**' fills a Netscape window with nothing. This is a handy way of giving frames a temporary initial document when you know they are going to be reloaded shortly. This still works in Netscape 4.0, but sometime the window doesn't *look* empty, due to a bug. '**about:blank**' is also available in Internet Explorer 4.0.

Detecting size

Early HTML tried to get away from any need to know sizes of screens or windows, but for more advanced applications the issue rears its ugly head again. There are two things worth knowing: the size of a given window in pixels, and the size of the whole computer screen.

Window size

In browsers version 4.0, window, frame and layer sizes are directly accessible in Window object properties like **innerWidth** and **innerHeight**. See the Reference Section. Prior to those versions, the only way to be sure of window

and frame sizes is to set them explicitly using **window.open()** or tag
attributes, and disable user resizing. For Internet Explorer 3.0 you should be
able to create a special ActiveX control to expose window sizes if you're
desperate.

Screen size

For the size of the user's screen in pixels, version 4.0 browsers have a new
Window property called '**screen**' which is itself an object. It has various
properties describing the screen size—see the Reference Section. In Navigator
3.0, you must resort to LiveConnect and get the data from Java as follows (this
is still JavaScript):

```
if (navigator.javaEnabled())
{
  var obj = java.awt.Toolkit.getDefaultToolkit();
  obj = obj.getScreenSize();
  document.write(obj.width+'x'+obj.height);
}
```

If the user has Java turned off, this won't work, in which case you'll have to
resort to the last possibility: here, and for Internet Explorer 3.0 and Netscape
2.02, you must create a custom Java applet or ActiveX control. Either can detect
the screen size and make it readable from JavaScript. See the chapter on Java
for the Java case. Of course, ActiveX controls will only work on platforms that
Microsoft supports.

Other people's frames

Your carefully organized document can be loaded into a frame in someone else's
document. This creates two problems: any visual effect you've planned can be
spoiled by the content of unexpected sister frames, and the special variable
'**top**' isn't the '**top**' you relied on any more. If the frame wrapping your
document comes from a foreign web site, security limitations can trip you up
as well.

The solution is to reload your document into '**top**', but without touching any
features that might fail due to security. Careful testing by Bob Stewart (see
mailto:webmaster@vmirror.com) yields logic which works with all relatively
modern browsers. Thanks for permission to reproduce, Bob:

```
// First inline code of your document
if (parent.frames[1])
    parent.location.href = self.location.href;
```

The reverse can also be a problem: you are displaying a foreign document in a
frame of your document. Either the foreigner overrides your frames, or their
document isn't accessible any more and won't load. There's nothing you can do
about the former case, except load their document in a separate window
instead—perhaps one without user controls. The latter case is worse, because
they could use the 'HTTP Response' tactics described in Chapter 1. This results
in a valid page being loaded, but not the one you expected. Better to be
philosophical about this happening to start with.

Finally, you might want a page to appear only within a specific frameset document, probably a specific one. This simple test stops it from being loaded alone:

```
// first inline code in your document
if ( top == self )
    self.location.href = "frameset.htm";
```

Keeping windows intact

Some actions a script can take will spoil the appearance of a document. Submitting a form, requesting search results, sending email via HTML or even just clicking a link can stop a document which contains animations or interesting information from staying in good order. The chapter on forms and CGI; Chapter 5, explains the mechanics for forms. The chapter on Multimedia and Plugins; Chapter 4, explains the mechanics for images, animations and links.

Help Windows

You may want to supply help for a window's contents. There are a number of methods to try. Usually you want to help the user with either a small cue, or a more detailed discussion.

Small Cues

A hint is often enough to help the user.

status message

The status message bar at the bottom of a main window is a handy place to cue the user. The biggest catch with it is that if the user can resize the window, you never know how much of your message is exposed to view. The easiest solution is to give up—write and hope. Keep the message short, just in case some idiot has set the system font size to 36 point. It's only a cue after all, not a warning.

There are two properties of the Window object for the status bar: **'status'** and **'defaultStatus'**. The latter sets the status bar permanently, except for when the mouse pointer hovers over an interesting object like a link. Then the 'status' property value is used instead. This means it only really makes sense to set the status property via an **onMouseOver** event. See the discussion in the Multimedia and Plugins; Chapter 4.

You might give up on the status bar because there's not enough space, and create a one line frame across the width of the window at the bottom. Then at least you'd have the full width of the window. You can use the 'Windows without URLs' approach above to fill it whenever you need. Alternatively, you can put a single input text field into that thin frame and write messages into the field. None of these ideas are that much better than just using the status bar.

flyover help

Typically called flyover help, bubble help or tool tips, browsers at the 4.0 level already do this for you, so upgrade if this is critical. Internet Explorer 4.0 has the most support—the **TITLE** attribute of HTML 4.0 is used to show a tool tip over the tag it is part of. Netscape 4.0 will only produce these tiny windows for **ALT** attributes in <**IMG**> tags.

Extraordinarily desperate people will create a small window as a tooltip using window.**open()**, but why bother? It's slow, and it gets very tricky capturing the mouse movements and managing window focus so that the tiny window stays on top while the mouse hovers over the item of interest. Furthermore, browsers limit the minimum size of a window for paranoid security reasons (100x100 pixels in Netscape). To get around this limit you have to use a signed script, or write the tooltip window in ActiveX or Java.

For Netscape 3.0 and Microsoft 3.01 for the Macintosh, it's possible to mimic the Netscape 4.0 behaviour. Use the technique described in the Multimedia and Plugins chapter for swapping images with an onMouseOver event. Make the second image the same as the first one, except that a tooltip appears to be embedded in it. When the images swap, the tooltip appears and disappears.

Detailed information

When nothing but the facts will do, a window with hypertext information in it is just what HTML was designed for. Use **window.open()** and strip the new window of most of its controls, so the user can't Web surf in the help window ... you never can tell how their minds work! There are a number of options for making the window appear on the screen.

Help button

The most pain-free way to proceed is to just use a form button visible to the user. Most browsers don't even require that it be inside a <**FORM**> container. Very straightforward:

```
<INPUT TYPE="BUTTON" VALUE="Help" ONCLICK="show_help()">
```

'**show_help()**' is just your function containing all the **window.open()** **plumbing.**

Context Sensitive Help

A more aggressive approach is to open the help window with information specific to the bit of the window the user is interested in and not the whole window. There are two approaches: the form way, and the hard way.

The form way applies when the document in the window contains a form. Using **onFocus** triggers (described in detail in the chapter on Forms and CGI), keep track of the current field the user is in by updating a separate variable. When a help button as described above is pressed, open the appropriate document for that field. A trivial example:

```
<HTML><HEAD><SCRIPT>
var field = "one";
function help()
{
    window.open("help_"+field+".htm", "help");
}
</SCRIPT></HEAD><BODY><FORM>
<INPUT TYPE="TEXT" NAME="one" ONFOCUS="top.field='one'">
<INPUT TYPE="TEXT" NAME="two" ONFOCUS="top.field='two'">
<INPUT TYPE="BUTTON" VALUE="Help" ONCLICK="window.help()">
</FORM></BODY></HTML>
```

In this example, 'help_one.htm' and 'help_two.htm' are help documents describing an individual field. The example could be varied so that different parts of a single document are displayed instead. This is done by using <A NAME=''> tags in the help file and modifying the function 'help()' above as follows:

```
window.open("all_help.html#" + field, "help");
```

The hard way to do help is to organise matters so that when the user clicks anywhere in the screen, help appears for the item at that spot. In order to do this you must use advanced event features of 4.0 version browsers and lose some portability. The main problems to solve are:

- Convincing the user to click differently with the mouse for help.
- Partitioning the document logically into pieces;
- Identifying the item at the coordinates the user clicked.

For the end users, the normal left click is fine for help if they understand some left-clicks do other things, like following links or setting checkboxes. Otherwise, pick any supported mouse button combination. It's possible to use the mouse to drop a 'help' icon onto the item required, if you want to use all the details of animation available in Dynamic HTML (see that chapter).

Partitioning up the document into pieces is a design approach that lends some structure to the document. Thinking of the document as a jigsaw of rectangular pieces is like making hot spots in an HTML image map. It makes it easier to define what help to show for each X,Y location in the document. Internet Explorer 4.0 does this for you, because all HTML elements are available to capture events. For Netscape Navigator 4.0, you have to use the whole window as one backdrop, and then make sure any areas which are to have help available are displayed via positionable styles, so the events can be captured in a Layer object. This means re-working a plain HTML document into one with positionable styles and layers located over (or containing) every interesting feature of the document.

To identify the item to give help on, use the Event object provided in different ways by the two 4.0 browsers. Then proceed as for the 'form way' above, opening the appropriate help page.

Chapter 9; "Dynamic HTML" and Chapter 10; "Further Topics" explain how to exploit these more advanced concepts. If all else fails, you can always turn to the HTML help software development kits (SDKs) mentioned earlier.

93

Built-in help

In addition to the tactics described, configuration tools like Mission Control can be used to alter the basic menu items and toolbar icons of the browser. Bookmarks can form a simple help index and be locked so that the user can't remove them. Signed scripts in Navigator 4.0 can affect the 'Guide' menu, adding a help item for a specific application. See the chapter on Privacy, Security and Cookies; Chapter 6.

Bad documents and onError

Browsers can be quite tolerant of bad HTML, bad links and bad images. Often the document will finish displaying anyway. Netscape 3.0 and 4.0 have a mechanism to allow it to be equally tolerant of bad JavaScript. This is the Netscape-specific **onError** event handler, present in Navigators 3.0 and 4.0.

Numerous errors can occur due to bad syntax, either when the document is loading, or later on in error handlers, and when **eval()** and **setTimeout()** occur. As a special 'other' case, errors can also occur when loading ('interpreting') an image—examining its URL or its content. When these errors appear the user gets an ugly error box. It is this kind of error that the **onError** handler is designed to manage. An example:

```
<HTML><HEAD><SCRIPT>
var ignore = true;
function catch_error()
{
   if ( ignore ) alert('Ignored ... sort of.');
   return ignore;
}
</SCRIPT></HEAD><BODY><SCRIPT>
onerror = null;
document.write('<BR><A HREF="x" ONCLICK="+++">No error</A>');
onerror = catch_error;
document.write('<BR><A HREF="x" ONCLICK="+++">Warning</A>');
ignore = false;
document.write('<BR><A HREF="x" ONCLICK="+++">Real error</A>');
document.write('<BR>Finished');
</SCRIPT></BODY></HTML>
```

The default behavior is that any error stops the document being read and the error appears. In this example, the **onerror** handler is set three times, and there are three bad pieces of syntax—'+++' is not valid JavaScript.

Firstly, the handler is set to 'null' meaning ignore all errors, so **'No error'** appears, unmolested. Only **<IMG>** tags which have an **OnError** handler in that tag will be treated differently. In that sole case, responsibility for **<IMG>** errors devolves to the specific **<IMG>** tag's handler. That handler has the same choices as the document's **onError** handler.

 Secondly, the handler is set to the **'catch_error()'** function, which returns **'true'** due to the variable **'ignore'**, and pops up an alert (**'ignore'** has no special significance here, it's just a useful trick). When the alert is acknowledged, the **'Warning'** content appears unmolested.

Finally, the handler is called again but returns **false** this time. An error results and the browser gives up loading the document, so **'Finished'** never appears.

Summary

Manipulating Web browsers' windows and frames via JavaScript is mostly restricted to HTML document windows. Using scripts in this area creates tension between the control the script writer and the browser user would like to have over the browser's features.

For basic document-style web pages, especially if they are publicly available on the Internet, keep it simple. Trying to limit the user's behavior is a valid goal, but takes work and should be restricted to special purpose windows. Don't annoy users with extra windows, or useless windows just because you want more control as a script writer—the user can always shut a window down.

For Web based applications, or whole systems delivered with a browser viewer, take a designed approach to limiting the users behavior, so that a minimum of bad things can happen. Most toolbars give the users powers that can unexpectedly change your application setup. Configuration scripts, lockable preferences and signed scripts can enhance the script writers control over the browser beyond the basic features available in HTML-embedded JavaScript. Avoid old browsers for these applications where possible and, where impossible, stick to the simplest effects.

Chapter

4

Multimedia and Plugins

Multimedia activity mostly occurs in a browser. Client-side JavaScript can be used as a control mechanism for fancy items embedded in an HTML document. Some features of the browser itself can be controlled in a dynamic way from scripts. Server-side or standalone JavaScript can play a part feeding the multimedia information to the browser.

This chapter discusses the multimedia possibilities created by combining JavaScript with plain HTML. Further effects are possible by combining JavaScript with Java or Dynamic HTML. Those other possibilities are discussed in Chapters 8 and 9.

A Web browser has a pecking order that dictates how it handles a multimedia item. A file, message or URL making up a multimedia item can be identified either by a DOS-style file extension or a MIME message type. Usually the MIME type will only be available if the item is retrieved from a Web server, rather than from a local filesystem.

The browser uses such an extension and type to identify how to display the item. First, the browser tries to handle the item itself. If that is not possible, the item is handed to a plugin that works with the browser. If there is no suitable plugin available, a helper application (a separate program) is started to deal with it. If there's no suitable helper, the user gets the option of immediately installing a plugin or helper, saving the item to disk, or giving up. For 'plugin', also read 'ActiveX control' for Microsoft browsers. A multimedia item doesn't necessarily have to take up any space on the screen—sound clips, for example, are multimedia items.

HTML Refresher

It pays to look before you leap. Basic multimedia is possible in a browser without using JavaScript. This section is a brief review of what you can get away with using plain HTML.

Color and Visibility

The numerous features of HTML allow colors to be statically chosen for all visible elements of a document, plus the document's background. These features are now mostly deprecated in HTML 4.0 in favor of equivalent style sheet properties, but are still widely available.

Style sheets can further affect the appearance of HTML elements; they may become transparent, occlude other HTML elements, be themselves occluded, be clipped at the edges, or not display at all.

Images

Many single-image formats exist: GIF or PNG for graphics, JPEG for natural images, XBM, and others. GIF, JPEG and PNG have progressive formats so images are viewable as they are loaded. The use of a transparent color in a GIF image makes the image appear to be non-rectangular in shape. Making images look appealing is an art and a science all of its own.

The **<IMG>** tag maps an image of one size into a rectangle in a browser window. The rectangle can be of a different size, scaling the image. The **LOWSRC** Netscape attribute allows a 'quick' image to display while the 'real' one is being retrieved. **<A>** tags can have images in their content, client- or server-side image maps always have images in their content. An image can appear as part of a **<BUTTON>** tag's contents in HTML 4.0. An image can appear due to an **<INPUT TYPE="image">** tag.

The **BACKGROUND** attribute of the **<BODY>** tag lets an image tile the document's background. Style sheet properties with 'background'-type names do the same job.

Client- and server-side image maps and images in hypertext links allow the user to navigate to other URLs, possibly opening new windows in the process.

The 'single pixel image trick' is an old trick involving a tiny image one pixel wide and high. When the sole pixel is transparent, it is a crude method of aligning HTML elements when style sheets are not available. When not transparent, solid color rectangular blocks of any size are displayed. Both effects are achieved using the **HEIGHT** and **WIDTH** attributes of the **IMG** tag.

The 'animated GIF' mechanism inside GIF files allows simple animation by bundling a number of images into the one file. Pauses and endless loops are possible.

For fully animated images, the MPEG, QuickTime (usually MOV) and AVI standards are most common. These mostly require plugins. VRML is used to display 3-dimensional images and animations, possibly with user animation. The **DYNSRC** and **START** attributes of the **<IMG>** tag give crude control over animations in Microsoft browsers.

Images and plugins can be further clipped and overlayed using style sheets).

Sound

Sounds can be included in an HTML document using the **`<EMBED>`** or **`<OBJECT>`** tags. If the sound takes up no visible space in the browser, the proprietary **`<BGSOUND>`** tag of Microsoft, or Netscape's **`HIDDEN`** attribute for **`<EMBED>`** is used. Alternatively, display can be avoided by setting the **`'display'`** style sheet property for the element to **`'none'`**.

Text

HTML text has a few simple effects available. Most of them are achieved with style sheets or pre-style sheet tags, such as **`<FONT>`**. Moving the mouse over a hypertext link updates the status bar with the link's URL. Hyperlinks themselves are visibly different to other text. Microsoft's proprietary **`<MARQUEE>`** tag allows text to roll across the screen in several different ways. Netscape 4.0 allows a different font displayer to be installed into the browser or special additional fonts to be downloaded, if you can be bothered. Flyover help appears for images (Navigator 4.0) or **`TITLE`** attributes (Internet Explorer 4.0).

JavaScript HTML techniques

This section discusses what you can achieve with JavaScript and plain HTML, without stepping into the realm of Dynamic HTML.

Image Events

An image displayed in an HTML document can receive events and, therefore, can have JavaScript event handlers. The reference section summaries which events are available. There are two categories of events:

Real events

Only HTML 4.0 defines any standard events for images. In prior versions, there isn't even an **`onClick`** handler for image maps. Only Internet Explorer 4.0 supports all these events. Netscape 4.0 supports one or two. For portability, restrict yourself to **`onMouseDown`** and **`onMouseUp`** and version 4.0 browsers, or wait for further major upgrades from the vendors.

Netscape supports several proprietary events. These are **`onAbort`**, **`onError`** and **`onLoad`**. These three events are designed to make loading of images a smooth and painless experience for the user, by handling problems as images load. The **`onAbort`** handler occurs when the user cancels the image download. **`onError`** occurs when there is a problem loading the image. **`onLoad`** occurs when an image is fully displayed.

`onError` is useful if your document contains references to many images scattered over a number of web sites—like a compilation page. It cannot be known how many of them will be available when the page loads. Use **`onError`** to turn off complaints, as described in the 'Bad documents' section of the Windows and Frames chapter; Chapter 3.

99

An **onLoad** handler can prevent the user from proceeding before they have fully appreciated your pictures. Advertisements are a case in point. An example:

```
<!-- frameset document -->
<HTML><FRAMESET ROWS="*,*">
<FRAME NAME="rubbish" SRC="advert.htm">
<FRAME NAME="content" SRC="blank.htm">
</FRAMESET></HTML>
```

```
<!-- frame advert.htm-->
<HTML><HEAD><SCRIPT>
function more()
{
    top.content.location.href = "content.htm";
}
</SCRIPT><BODY>
<IMG SRC="buy_it.gif" ONLOAD="more()">
</BODY></HTML>
```

About the only reason for using **onAbort** is to help the user escape from a document that contains a huge, slow image. An example:

```
<HTML><HEAD<SCRIPT>
function run_away()
{
    window.location.href = window.history.go(-1);
}
</SCRIPT><BODY>
Another elephant crowd scene:<BR>
<IMG SRC="peanut_hunt.jpg" ONABORT="run_away()">
</BODY></HTML>
```

Big images should really be viewed in a window of their own, not in HTML, for best possible appearance. One reason for this is that the browser will be better able to exploit the colors that the computer terminal has to offer, which can improve the image's reproduction.

Derived events

If an image is the sole content of another HTML tag, then user events for that tag are probably intended for the image. Several tricks can be achieved by this method.

The main approach with Netscape is to surround the image with an **<A></A>** hyperlink 'container', making **onMouseOver**, **onMouseOut** and **onClick** handlers available. This works in Navigator 3.0 and 4.0, and Internet Explorer 4.0. The alternative is to place the image within a **<LAYER>** tag (a positioned style sheet) which can capture all the HTML 4.0 events. This alternative won't work in Navigator 3.0.

Internet Explorer 4.0's general event model allows mouse actions and keypresses to pass up through the HTML tag hierarchy regardless of tag. This means both Netscape's **<A></A>** alternative and numerous other tag combinations are possible. For Internet Explorer 3.0, the situation is very limited as neither Image objects nor **onMouseOver** triggers are fully functional.

The next section shows how to exploit these tactics.

Using the Image Object

JavaScript lets the scriptwriter create an Image object for an image located at a URL. This is quite special behavior since not many parts of an HTML document can be created separate from the document. You can't create a **<P>** Paragraph object, for example, in any browser. Internet Explorer 3.0 and Navigator 2.02 don't support this Image behavior.

The reference section lists all the properties and methods of this object. The two essential properties are **src** and **complete**:

 src is a read/write property containing the URL of the actual image file represented by the object.

 complete is a read-only property indicating whether the browser has finished attempting to load the image file.

These attributes lead to several consequences. For '**src**', an image file can be replaced with another, whether it is visible in the window display or not. For 'complete', you have to resort to event handlers to find out if the image is fully loaded or not.

When an Image object is assigned a new image URL, it actually represents a scaled-to-fit version of the URL. **HEIGHT** and **WIDTH** attributes in **<IMG>** tags, or constructor function arguments in JavaScript, dictate the size the image file is scaled to fit. If neither are supplied then the image's natural size is used (no scaling). The upshot of this is that any image URL can be assigned to an Image object, and it will always fit exactly the space that object takes up on the browser window.

Replacing an image

Here is the simplest example—replacing one image with another. It's easy to see how the **onClick** handler could be expanded to do more complex work such as retrieving the image URL from a text field the user filled in. Because the Image object underneath is a scaled image, this example will work with any replacement image, regardless of size—try changing the names in the script to any images you have lying around.

```
<HTML><BODY><FORM>
<IMG SRC="http://localhost/tmp/first.gif">
<INPUT TYPE="BUTTON" NAME="Go" ONCLICK="window.images[0].src = 'anything.jpg'">
</FORM></BODY></HTML>
```

Button swaps

The button in the **<INPUT TYPE="button">** tag is rather boring. It's not hard to create two images that look like interesting buttons—one for when the button is selected and one for when it isn't. This is so simple and useful that HTML 4.0 includes a general **<BUTTON>** tag. However, this tag only highlights the edges of any enclosed image when the mouse is pressed. That leaves plenty of scope for very fancy buttons using images. This example makes the mock button change appearance when the mouse hovers over it.

101

```
<HTML><BODY ALINK="black" VLINK="black" LINK="black"><FORM>
<A HREF="javascript:void(0)"
ONMOUSEOVER="window.document.images[0].src='down.gif'"
ONMOUSEOUT="window.document.images[0].src='up.gif'"
ONCLICK="alert('Click!');return false;">
<IMG SRC="up.gif">
</A>
</FORM></BODY></HTML>
```

If the second image looks the same as the first, except for an added small box of text, then this arrangement simulates flyover help (Microsoft tooltips). Since the **onClick** handler fires when the mouse is 'Over' but not yet 'Out' of the image, further changes to the image are possible when the click occurs. For example, an image of a button may generally appear ordinary, change to an image of a highlighted button when the mouse is over it, and change again to an image of a depressed button when the user clicks on it.

This example won't work for Internet Explorer 3.02, so see this page for a free Java applet that does the same thing, and works with both Microsoft and Netscape 3.0 browsers: **http://pw1.netcom.com/~jcheves/mousover.html**.

Making it go faster

Each time the **src** property changes, the browser has to find the image. A lengthy delay can result if the image file isn't cached in the browser and needs to be retrieved over the network. If the image is already loaded, this problem is much reduced. Image objects separate so those in the current document can be used to make image swaps look faster to the user, by preloading the image.

```
<HTML><BODY><SCRIPT>
var poster1 = new Image;
var poster2 = new Image;
var poster3 = new Image;

poster1.src = 'elvis.gif';
poster2.src = 'ghandi.gif';
poster3.src = 'groucho.gif';

setTimeout('top.document.replace("three_wise_men.htm");',10000);
</SCRIPT>
Waiting ...
</BODY></HTML>
```

This example isn't too fancy. It guesses that 10 seconds will be enough for the images to be cached. It could be done better by regularly checking the **complete** property on the three Image objects but, unfortunately, **complete** is buggy in Netscape 4.0 for Image objects created with **new** (although it works in 3.0). The 'complete' property does work for Image objects created with **<IMG>**. Setting **onLoad** handlers via JavaScript is also problematic. The exact timing is not that critical in most cases—other pages can load the same image at the same time anyway. It's often sufficient to get a head start with an Image object at the top of a document in time for it to be displayed furthered down as the page loads.

An alternative to using **setTimeout()** is to have a frameset page instead of a plain HTML document. In this page are two frames; one that is zero pixels in height or width, and the other that fills the screen. The HTML for the zero width or "hidden" frame contains normal **<IMG>** tags for all the needed images. Because none of the frame shows, the user doesn't see those images. The script writer can then check the (non-buggy) 'complete' property in those hidden images for progress.

Controlling animation

Animated GIFs don't give you any control over their animation—they run, and you're stuck with them. Fancy plugins do give control, but often use file formats you can't create without tools. A middle ground, using the Image object, provides crude fully controlled animation. The frames of the animation are a full URL each. When doing this it's important to be confident that all the images are cached by the technique above, or else the animation will start in a very jerky manner (it will improve with time). The following example shows a 'waiting' animation, controlled by the user. In this case the animation images are named 'wait-0.gif' through to 'wait-7.gif' and appear as follows:

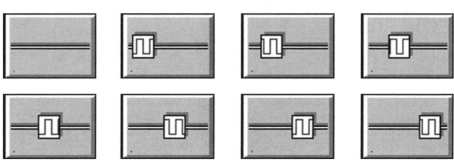

```
<HTML><HEAD><SCRIPT>

// tested with Netscape 4.0 and 3.0

// --- get those images ---
var wait_images = new Array(8);
var wait_loop = 0;

for (wait_loop=0; wait_loop <8; wait_loop++ )
{
    wait_images[wait_loop] = new Image;
    wait_images[wait_loop].src = "wait-"+wait_loop+".gif";
}

// --- start and stop functions ---
var wait_img = 0;     // which image to show
var wait_id = 0;      // remember wait timer.

function wait_start()
{
  wait_img = ++wait_img % 8;
  top.document.images.icon.src = wait_images[wait_img].src;

  wait_id = setTimeout("wait_start();",1000);
}

function wait_stop()
{
  clearTimeout(wait_id);
  top.document.images.icon.src = 'anything.gif';
}
```

```
</SCRIPT></HEAD>
<BODY>
<IMG SRC="anything.gif" NAME="icon">
<FORM>
<INPUT TYPE="BUTTON" VALUE="Wait" ONCLICK="wait_start()">
<INPUT TYPE="BUTTON" VALUE="Done" ONCLICK="wait_stop()">
</FORM></BODY></HTML>
```

In this example, the timing and order of the images are all fully exposed in the **wait_start()** routine, which could be arbitrarily complex. The small box moves from left to right, disappears, and then repeats. However, it could just as easily move right to left, or alternate directions, or jump around randomly. It could start fast and then slow down. Only one function needs changing for each of these effects.

Faking Menus and Popups

The 'button swap' section above shows how to mimic tooltips with images. If you have a large image, then it is possible to mimic other graphical user interface (GUI) elements, like menus. GUI items that require complex user input like dialog boxes are impractical.

The way to do this is to apply a general image replacement technique for this specific problem. The general approach treats the space taken up by the initial image as a canvas (blank area) on which to draw other images. If the 'background' color or texture of the images is the same as the document background, this can appear quite effective, and is sometimes as convenient to do as Dynamic HTML tricks. Consider the following images:

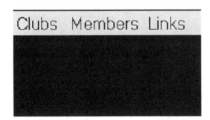 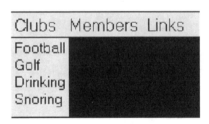

If there are no more than four menu items each in 'Members' and 'Links', the image space can be used to display all the different menus using 4 images. This setup relies on a client side image map as follows (assume the images are 200x100 pixels with each word item being 60x20 pixels):

```
<HTML><BODY><SCRIPT>
var dropped = false;
var menu = 0;
function update(item)
{
   if ( !dropped )    // no submenu yet
   {
      if ( item != 1 && item !=6 && item != 11)
      {
          return;              // user clicked somewhere useless
      }
      if ( item == 1)
      window.document.pic.src = 'fakemenu2.gif';
      // two more if's for other menus ...
   }
```

```
        else
        {
          if ( menu == 1 && item == 1 )
            ; // do the football thing ..
          // 14 more if's for other menu items ...
        }
      }
      </SCRIPT>
      <MAP NAME="menu">
        <AREA COORDS="0,0,60,20" HREF="javascript:window.update(1)">
        <AREA COORDS="0,20,60,40" HREF="javascript:window.update(2)">
      <!-- 5 x 3 = 15 AREA tags total ... -->
      </MAP>
      <IMG NAME="pic" SRC="fakemenu1.gif" USEMAP="#menu">
      </BODY></HTML>
```

The user is first presented with a single menu bar. Clicking anywhere in the image except the menu bar does nothing. Clicking on a menu bar item causes the image to change and a drop-down menu appears. Clicking on an item in the drop-down menu causes some arbitrary JavaScript to run. Clicking in empty space away from the drop down menu still does nothing. A more sophisticated example could clean up the menu bar afterwards or gray-out inappropriate options. The appearance of the drop down menu could be animated via an animated GIF that ran through its images once and then stopped, with the drop down menu fully exposed as the last image of the animation.

Obviously, the example menus are quite plain, but very artistic ones could just as easily be used. Provided that every pixel of the image is covered by an **<AREA>** tag, the user won't notice that some 'hot spots' apparently do nothing when clicked. This is because the mouse point will look the same everywhere on the image. There is no need to lay out the areas in a grid as has been done in this case; it's just convenient for menus. There is no need to stick to menus with this technique either.

Progress meters

Progress meters are tricky to implement with image replacement techniques, because of the many stages progress can be at. It's quite possible to do by creating 100 images for each percentage point of progress, but there's an easier way: use a single pixel image and a frame or layer. This is also easy with positioned style sheets and no images—extend the clipping region of a colored area as progress occurs, to expose more of the area. Here is an example of the image approach.

```
<HTML><FRAMESET ROWS="40,*">
<FRAME NAME="progress" SRC="blank.htm">
<FRAME NAME="test" SRC="bar.htm">
</FRAMESET></HTML>

<!-- blank.htm -->
<HTML></HTML>

<!-- bar.htm -->
<HTML><HEAD><SCRIPT>
function draw(percent)
{
  with (top.progress.document) {
  open();
```

105

```
    write('<HTML><BODY><IMG SRC="onepixel.gif" HEIGHT=10 WIDTH="' + percent*4 +
'"></BODY></HTML>'
     );
   close();
   }
}
var percent = 10;
</SCRIPT>
</HEAD><BODY><FORM>
<INPUT TYPE="BUTTON" VALUE="Progress" ONCLICK="window.draw(percent+=10)">
<INPUT TYPE="BUTTON" VALUE="Backwards!" ONCLICK="window.draw(percent-=10)">
</FORM></BODY></HTML>
```

Although the updates are due to the user here, the **draw()** function could easily be called from anywhere within the code (possible with better error checking on the passed-in value). This example will run more slowly than a style sheet version, but it is extremely portable.

Local processing

Retrieving URLs, for images, animations or otherwise, can be slow. There are a few small tricks that are more efficient than generating a possibly expensive URL request for the Web.

Multimedia without URLs

It may not be necessary to reach across the Internet for animations and images. The simplest thing is to package your multimedia up and deliver it to the disk drive that holds the target web browser, making your pages work that way. If you are installing an information kiosk, or producing a game, that may be enough. A second possibility is to use Netscape's LiveCache feature—see **http://www.netscape.com/comprod/products/navigator/version_3.0/ease/cache/how.html**. This allows web pages normally accessed by a web server to be bundled up into a local file (possibly on a CD) and still be accessible via their full URL. URLs are still used in these cases, but at least they are local to the browser's computer.

Finally, some trivial multimedia can be done directly in the browser.

Inline images

Chapter 2 describes how JavaScript URLs can be used as document content. They can also be used as image content—specifically for an Image object's **src** property. If you can create the contents (not the URL) of an image directly in client-side JavaScript, you can display it without a web server.

Unfortunately, there are two catches. The first is that image content is hard to reproduce from any language. JPEG format is based on mathematical transforms, GIF is compressed (as well as being a proprietary format), PNG is even more complex mathematically, so it's too much trouble. The second is that Netscape has this obscure bug in its JavaScript implementation:

```
'xxx\000yyy' == 'xxx';        // true !
'xxx\000yyy'.length == 3;     // true !
```

An **ASCII NUL** (zero value) character terminates a JavaScript string and, therefore, can't be put inside one. This shuts out most image formats, since they contain binary data and, therefore, randomly contain **ASCII 0**'s.

Even with these issues, the ancient and humble XBM format is still a possibility. This format only allows black and white bitmapped images, but it contains plain text, not binary data, so no ASCII zeros. An XBM file looks like this (this is the file's source):

```
#define trash_width 16
#define trash_height 16
static char trash_bits[] = {
    0x00, 0x01, 0xe0, 0x0f, 0x10, 0x10, 0xf8, 0x3f, 0x10, 0x10, 0x50, 0x15,
    0x50, 0x15, 0x50, 0x15, 0x50, 0x15, 0x50, 0x15, 0x50, 0x15, 0x50, 0x15,
    0x50, 0x15, 0x10, 0x10, 0xe0, 0x0f, 0x00, 0x00};
```

Somewhat ironically, this is a picture of a rubbish bin icon—height 16 pixels, width 16 pixels. Each hexadecimal value represents 8 pixels, each either on or off.

If you put this text in a string, you can assign it to the **src** attribute of an Image object. Chapter 2 under 'JavaScript URLs' shows an example of creating a one pixel GIF this way.

What is this good for? If you refuse to access a Java applet, ActiveX control or plugin from JavaScript, then it's your only way of doing graphics (black and white at that) in a browser with JavaScript. You can create an arbitrary image with patterns, or graphs, or pick up drawing movements made by the user, etc. That is left as an exercise to the reader...

For later sub-versions of Navigator 4.0, such as 4.04, the ASCII NUL bug is fixed, so the other image types are again a possibility—but beware! It is only fixed deep inside JavaScript where images are manipulated—if you try to display a string with an embedded NUL using **window.alert()** or **document.write()**, the bug is back.

Status bar animations

Animating the status bar is a thrill nearly as cheap as XBM images. If you can write a string to it once, you can do so twice...and so on. This Web site lists a number of different scrolling effects in JavaScript with source:
**http://www.geocities.com/SiliconValley/Heights/8583/
js_scroll_category.html**

The debate is still open as to whether scrolling messages annoy the user, but the answer is probably Yes. Here is the least annoying example your author could think of (watch the status bar carefully):

```
<HTML><HEAD><SCRIPT>
var current = 0;
var note = "The scrolling message from hell";
function scroll_it()
{
    current = (current == note.length) ? 0 : current+1;
```

107

```
        defaultStatus = note.substr(0, current)
          + note.charAt(current).toUpperCase()
          + note.substr(current+1, note.length);
        setTimeout("scroll_it()",100);
    }
    scroll_it();
    </SCRIPT></HEAD></HTML>
```

Document re-writing

The progress meters section illustrates how crude animation can be done by re-writing HTML documents. You can rewrite any HTML document, not just an **<IMG>** tag. To make this happen as smoothly as possible follow that same example, but: avoid tables; always use **HEIGHT** and **WIDTH** attributes in **<IMG>** tags; minimize the number of URLs that have to be fetched in order to complete the page; and don't get your hopes up too high.

The URL request trap

In order to stop a browser from making requests of web servers, it's common to install JavaScript event handlers to capture events, or to install **javascript:** URLs to replace 'normal' URLs. However, there is a subtle difference between these two tactics.

When an **onClick** event handler for a link is invoked, it gives the script writer a chance to abort any URL request that would otherwise occur. That link might be in an **<A>** tag or a client-side image map's **<AREA>** tag. If the handler returns **false**, no URL request occurs (this doesn't work in Navigator 3.0, since **onClick** return values are ignored there). However, a **javascript:** URL is still a URL, so substituting it for another in a tag doesn't technically stop the URL request.

This subtle distinction is important, because if the browser detects that a URL is to be loaded, it gives up on the current document. When it gives up, any partially loaded components of the document, such as replacement images, streaming sound files, or animations stop as well. So avoid **javascript:** URLs in favor of event handlers in documents that contain many loading or reloading multimedia objects.

Microsoft 3.0 web browsers don't support **javascript:** URLs in client-side image maps anyway.

Creating pauses and delays

Controlling animation effects often means working with timing issues. One such issue is deliberately creating pauses in processing. Although JavaScript in browsers is good at scheduling events for the future via **setTimeout()** and **setInterval()**, it doesn't contain any **sleep()**, **wait()** or **pause()** style functions like this:

```
do_something();
wait(3);            // three seconds pass impossible
do_something_else();
```

108

Implementing these is a bit tricky. There are two solutions:

- brute force
- stop thinking about it

The brute force solution looks like this:

```
function wait()
{
    var loop;
    for ( loop=0; loop < 10000; loop++)
        123.45 * loop * 67.890;
}
```

This function grabs the browser and doesn't let go until it has finished. The mathematics in the body of the **for** loop is just to give the computer something to do other than examining and incrementing the **loop** counter. This is heavy work for the browser's computer, but it works. The only problem is that it runs at different speeds for different browsers, and may not stop all browser windows if the browser is 'threaded' so that each window runs independently (e.g. Internet Explorer).

You can write a calibration function that detects the speed of the browser's computer and modifies the loop total accordingly, but it will only turn a guess into a rough estimate.

"Stop thinking about it" saves you from trying to breed a flying pig. Browsers think in terms of scheduling incoming events—items that need doing, either immediately, or at some time in the future. In order to do this they need to keep referring to their list of outstanding events to see what's due to be done. This approach doesn't fit well with the idea of "just stop for a second". You can usually re-express your goal as a series of events to be scheduled and use **setTimeout()** instead.

JavaScript and Plugins

Plugins allow clever multimedia effects such as coordinated sound and picture, and specialized graphics. Depending on the individual plugin, JavaScript can control these effects to varying degrees.

To refresh on terminology: when a browser retrieves a URL resource from the web, the resource arrives in a message with some identifying information. One part of this information is the MIME type—which uniquely describes the type of content the message contains. An ActiveX control is not a plugin—Microsoft Internet Explorer supports both ActiveX controls (general access to the browser computer) and Netscape-style plugins (intended to have little access to the browser computer).

As a script writer, before you can control a multimedia effect created by a plugin, you need to know four things. They are that the MIME type for the multimedia URL is known by the browser; that a plugin is installed for that

MIME type; that an **<EMBED>** or **<OBJECT>** tag exists for the multimedia effect, and that the effect has loaded into the browser. Only when all those things have occurred does JavaScript have any chance of affecting the plugin.

Often it is sufficient to warn users of a Web page that a particular plugin is required by putting a note in that page, or by letting the browser warn the user itself. You can usually be confident that common plugins are present, such as those supplied with the browser at installation. Alternatively, you can focus on the users interested in your page (who are likely to be correctly installed) and let the rest cope as they may. However, on the Internet there is no controlling user's browser installation so, technically, you should check (via a script) before making assumptions about how plugins can be controlled.

Plugin Object Model

The following diagram illustrates the essential parts of the browser object model for plugins. This is for Netscape Browsers 3.0 and 4.0. The 'embeds' array also exists in Microsoft browsers, but none of the other stuff.

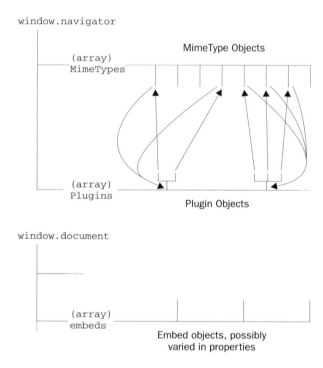

There are two parts to the model, one part relating to installation, and the other relating to specific HTML documents.

Installation Plugin Objects

Details of what plugins and MIME types have been installed in the browser are exposed to client-side JavaScript. There are two important object types: MimeType and Plugin. The reference section documents their details. They are collected into arrays called **mimeTypes** and **plugins**. These arrays are accessible from the **window.navigator** object. Netscape recently documented the **window.components** object—this object has properties with the same names that refer to those arrays as well.

Every MIME type either has a plugin, or it doesn't. Each MimeType object in the **mimeTypes** array has a property **enabledPlugin** which is either **null** or refers to a Plugin object in the **plugins** array. If it is **null**, it means that MIME type must be handled by some other means. Only one plugin can handle a given MIME type.

One the other hand, every Plugin object in the **plugins** array looks like an array of MIME types. A Plugin object has a few descriptive properties but mostly its properties point to MimeType objects in the **mimeTypes** array. Each plugin can handle more than one MIME type, but no plugins can share MIME types.

If you type in the URL **about:plugins**, you will see a report based on these browser objects for the currently installed plugins and their MIME types. You can see from the source of this page that it merely uses these objects.

There is no reason to modify these objects from JavaScript. There is only one reason for examining them:

Detecting correct installation

It's no use trying to control a multimedia object in the browser if it's handled by an unexpected plugin. Fortunately, the MIME type of the multimedia URL and the plugin preferred is usually known in advance by the scriptwriter. This gives enough information to write a script that will detect the situation when it arrives at a user's browser. This kind of testing is required:

```
var known = true;

if ( ! navigator.plugins["QuickTime Plug-In"].enabledPlugin )
    known = false;         // the expected plugin is missing

else if ( ! navigator.plugins["QuickTime Plug-In"]["video/quicktime"])
    known = false;         // its not configured for our type
```

Once a missing plugin is detected, there are two choices: let the URL load, but script around it without touching it, or exclude the tags with the URL from the source HTML. Using the **known** flag from the above example:

```
function rewind_it()
{
    // ... rewind a quicktime movie back to frame 1.
}
if ( known )
{
```

```
document.write('<EMBED SRC="film.mov" HEIGHT=260 WIDTH=320'
           + 'CONTROLLER=true LOOP=false AUTOPLAY=TRUE>');
   document.write('<INPUT TYPE="BUTTON" VALUE="Play" ONCLICK="rewind_it()">');
}
else
{
   // only use standard HTML parameters
   document.write('<EMBED SRC="film.mov" HEIGHT=260 WIDTH=320');
}
```

Similarly for avoiding the whole problem:

```
if ( known )
{
   document.write('<EMBED SRC="film.mov" HEIGHT=260 WIDTH=320'
              + 'CONTROLLER=true LOOP=false AUTOPLAY=TRUE>');
   document.write('<INPUT TYPE="BUTTON" VALUE="Play" ONCLICK="rewind_it()">');
}
else
{
   document.write('<IMG SRC="get_quicktime.gif" HEIGHT=260 WIDTH=320>');
}
```

Document Plugin Objects

Detecting that a browser is configured with the plugin you want to use is only half the battle. To interact with the multimedia URL it must be loaded into the browser. Just like the rest of an HTML document, this means a JavaScript host object will be created when that part of the document is reached. Just because the object is created doesn't mean that the whole related URL has been loaded—this is similar to the Image object. This object is called a plugin instance.

The 'embeds' property is an array which contains one Embed object for each **<EMBED>** or **<OBJECT>** tag in the document. Internet Explorer 3.0 differs on this property—it is **window.document.embeds** in Netscape browsers and **window.embeds** in Explorer 3.0 only. A simple hack fixes this:

```
var myembeds = ( typeof(window.embeds) == "undefined" )
? window.document.embeds
: window.embeds;                    // use 'myembeds' from now on
```

The elements of the array appear in the order that they appear in the HTML source. The ugly part of the embeds array is that every Embed object has different properties and methods, depending on the plugin used to handle the URL. In Netscape these properties are only accessible to JavaScript if the **MAYSCRIPT** attribute is included in each **<EMBED>** tag. Otherwise, the embedded object is only controllable by plugin-specific attributes in the **<EMBED>** case, or **<PARAM>** tags in the **<OBJECT>** case. The plugin-specific parameters are only available from JavaScript if the plugin supplies them as Embed object properties (or by retrieving the whole tag as a string—as in Internet Explorer 4.0).

To find out the properties and methods a given plugin supplies, you have to lookup information supplied by the plugin vendor (usually accessible on their web site). This is also the case for tag attributes specific to the plugin.

To find out if all the Embed objects have been created for a document, just use a synchronization tactic such as document **onLoad** handlers—see the chapter on Windows and Frames under 'Concurrency'. Alternatively, you can repeatedly check the **embeds.length** property until it is as large as the number of embedded objects in the page.

Controlling Plugins Objects

There are two degrees of control over plugins from JavaScript. Whether they are available depends on the individual plugin. They are:

 Embed object properties and methods

Embed object properties and methods + callback functions

Apart from an Embed object, a plugin instance can cause a specially named JavaScript function to run. If the function exists, the plugin will run it at appropriate times. Since the function is written by the script writer, not the plugin vendor, this gives an escape hatch for the script writer to do special actions on behalf of the plugin.

Simple Object Properties—Live Audio

LiveAudio is a Netscape plugin installed by default with Navigator 4.0 designed for sound files. It supports several sound formats. When a LiveAudio plugin instance is created, perhaps in response to a tag like **<EMBED SRC="tidal.wav">**, an Embed object is created in the 'embeds' property of the browser. **http://home.netscape.com/comprod/products/navigator/ version_3.0/multimedia/audio/how.html** describes the properties and methods of this object. Particularly noteworthy is the **IsReady()** method, which is just like the 'complete' property of the Image object. This mechanism can be used to tell if the sound file is fully downloaded yet. The RealAudio plugin does not support any callback functions, so control of the plugin instance is one way—from the script writer to the plugin instance.

To illustrate a whole plugin, here are the properties and methods quoted from that document. These methods are very typical of plugins. In this list **int** (integer) is just a convention meaning a whole number is expected, rather than a string or fractional number:

Controlling functions (all Boolean):

```
play('TRUE/FALSE or int','URL of sound')
stop()
pause()
start_time(int seconds)
end_time(int seconds)
setvol(int percent)
fade_to(int to_percent)
fade_from_to(int from_percent, int to_percent)
start_at_beginning() = Override a start_time()
stop_at_end() = Override an end_time()
```

113

State indicators (all Boolean, except the last, which is an integer):

IsReady() = Returns TRUE if the plug-in instance has completed loading
IsPlaying() = Returns TRUE if the sound is currently playing
IsPaused() = Returns TRUE if the sound is currently paused
GetVolume() = Returns the current volume as a percentage

Callback functions – Shockwave Flash

ShockWave Flash is a plugin from Macromedia **http://www.macromedia.com**. The plugin displays sound and animation combined with a scripting language of its own, all bundled up into a multimedia file downloaded via a URL. When an **<EMBED>** tag specifies a ShockWave Flash file the tag's **NAME** attribute must be set.

When the plugin instance is created, the Embed object contains specific methods and properties as for the LiveAudio plugin. Because it is a different plugin, however, the properties and methods are different. If the **NAME** attribute is set to **demo**, the plugin instance will look for the JavaScript function **demo_DoFSCommand()**. If the function exists, then it may be called from within the plugin instance at different times in the display of the loaded file.

This JavaScript function is invoked, runs and then ends in response to a call made by the plugin. Inside the function might be a number of calls to methods of the Embed object that matches the plugin instance. This function could also draw new HTML buttons in a separate frame to be used to control the plugin, or display a prompt for the user in a **confirm()** dialog box. The plugin passes several arguments to the function that can be used to control what tasks the function performs each time it is called. These arguments come from information inside the downloaded file.

If another ShockWave Flash file is embedded in the HTML page, but with a different NAME attribute, it has a separate custom function, which would be called independent of the other embedded object.

This plugin does not create a special property to indicate when the file has completed its download. Instead, the callback function can be called when the file is fully loaded. If unique arguments are supplied to the function, the function can use them as a cue to detect that the download has finished.

See **http://www.macromedia.com/support/flash/ts/documents/ tn4160.html**.

Summary

Where an HTML page contains images, but no animation, JavaScript can add simple animation. Where an HTML page contains fancy media used by browser plugins, JavaScript can often control the fancy media in ways beyond the control of the user. In either case, event handling for images and the like are very limited in most browsers, since HTML 4.0 support is not widespread yet.

Performance is an issue with multimedia. Some simple animations are possible inside the browser without retrieving anything over a network. The Image object can be used to cache and preload images so they can be presented speedily for the user.

Using plugins carries its own risks. Unless the scriptwriter is in control of the user's browser, anything can be configured in the browser when a multimedia document is downloaded. To robustly handle this situation the scriptwriter must go to extra lengths to detect plugin support if the user is to be spared warning messages.

Chapter

5

Forms and CGI

With JavaScript, a browser's form elements take on some of the attributes of '4GL' form-building packages and spreadsheets. Without JavaScript, HTML form elements aren't that flexible—all plain HTML form elements can do is send any user data directly to a Web server. Some HTML tags like `<INPUT TYPE="button">` are entirely useless without JavaScript.

CGI (and similar mechanisms, like server-side JavaScript) allows data submitted by a form to be usefully directed or processed. If an HTML form has its data submitted to a Web server that doesn't have CGI in place, the submitted data is thrown away at the server, or causes an error to be returned to the browser.

There are many ways to skin a cat when it comes to submitted form data. In addition to those methods already mentioned, other Web server architectures like ASP, ISAPI and NSAPI can be exploited. This chapter focuses on CGI, since it is the simplest and most accessible.

Forms

JavaScript can interact with HTML forms directly in a number of ways. It can:

- write out form element tags with inline JavaScript, as for other HTML
- act as form element event handlers, via tag attributes or host object properties
- read and modify form element values
- construct form elements in a limited way

It is beyond these basic tasks that JavaScript adds real value to forms and HTML. The higher level tasks that JavaScript can achieve are:

- validating and correcting user data
- performing calculations on user data
- storing and forwarding user data
- controlling user navigation through the form

All these tasks add up to smoother form operation, since these activities can be done within the browser on the local computer. Without JavaScript, every check or change requires that the form's details be passed to a Web server, which can slow processing considerably.

Form objects

HTML forms are part of HTML documents, so it's no surprise that form-style tags are reflected in JavaScript as objects that are properties of the Document object.

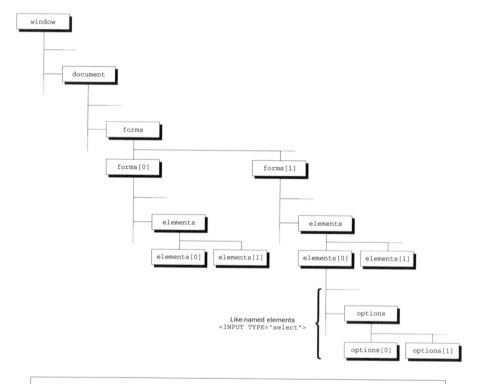

The diagram above shows the basic structure of the forms part of the document object model. The specific methods and properties are listed in the Reference Section. Key details are described here.

Form Objects explained

An HTML document can contain more than one form, so the '**forms**' property near the top of the hierarchy is an array with an array member for each form. These objects have as properties all the important attributes of the **<FORM>** tag. HTML documents can have text fields and buttons without any **<FORM>** tag. If this is the case, then a single form object is created in **forms[0]**. If form controls exist both within and outside a **<FORM>** tag, then the ones outside the tag are ignored.

Each form object has an '**elements**' property that is an array. Each array element is one of the form controls in the form. The form controls populate the array in the same order they appear in the HTML document (not as they appear on the screen). **<INPUT>**, **<BUTTON>**, **<TEXTAREA>**, and **<SELECT>** tags are represented as a 'forms' array element, one for each instance in the document. This includes **<INPUT TYPE="HIDDEN">**. Effectively, a 'form control' and a 'form element' are equivalent—the former emphasizes what the user visibly sees, the latter emphasizes an object the script writer sees.

It's best to think of the individual element objects as being a generic 'input' type of object, rather than being specifically a checkbox or textarea object. These objects have in common '**type**', '**value**', '**name**', and '**form**' properties. The '**type**' property allows you to distinguish from within JavaScript what type of tag was used to create the element. The '**value**' property is the current value of the control, the '**name**' property reflects the **NAME** attribute of the tag and the '**form**' property refers back to the '**forms**' array element that this form control is a part of. In addition to these basic properties, there are properties which only apply to some types of control, and properties for event handlers (described further on). See the comparison tables in the Reference Section.

Generally, none of the form or form element objects visible in JavaScript can be created or deleted. Some of their properties can be usefully set, like the element 'value' property, but the structure of a given form can't be altered, except by re-writing the HTML using inline JavaScript or Internet Explorer 4.0's dynamic access to the source.

For most form element types, this two-level hierarchy of forms and form elements covers it all. The **<SELECT>** form control is the exception. Within the element object for each **<SELECT>** tag is a property '**options**'. This is an array of objects, one for each **<OPTION>** tag within the **<SELECT>** tag. The type of these **<OPTION>** tag objects, is Option. The Option object is a rare example of an HTML-related object that can be created independent of any HTML document. This makes it similar to the Image object (see Chapter 4). Option objects can replace existing objects in the '**options**' array of a **<SELECT>** element, allowing changeable menus. This is not possible with Internet Explorer 3.0

Access to form elements and their properties is demonstrated with this form:

```
<HTML><BODY><FORM NAME="patient">
Insanity checklist. Enter number of weeks: <INPUT NAME="weeks" TYPE="text">
Hearing voices? <INPUT NAME="symptom" TYPE="checkbox">
Seeing things? <INPUT NAME="symptom" TYPE="checkbox">
Clothing preferences:
<SELECT NAME="diet">
<OPTION VALUE="napolean"> Napolean Bonaparte
<OPTION VALUE="strangelove"> Dr. Strangelove
</SELECT>
<INPUT TYPE="submit">
</FORM></BODY></HTML>
```

These properties are all valid for the document:

```
with ( top.document )
{
  forms[0].name;                    // = 'patient'
  forms[0].method;                  // = 'GET' (the default)
  forms[0].elements.length;         // = 5
  forms[0].elements[0].value;       // = '', the user can change it.
  forms[0].elements[0].onchange;//  null, no handler.
  forms[0].elements[1].name;        // = 'symptom'
  forms[0].elements[2].checked;     // = 'false', the user can change it.
  forms[0].elements[3].options.length; // = 2
  forms[0].elements[3].options[1].value; // 'dates'
}
```

Note that the 'value' property of the 'text' element is always a string, even though the user is prompted for a number in this example.

The form element objects have a further useful feature that isn't covered by any property. In Chapter 2, there was some discussion on conversion of JavaScript types. To refresh, JavaScript objects are converted to strings where strings are expected, via the toString() method of the object. For form element objects, the conversion conveniently re-creates the HTML that the object reflects. Therefore, this example produces a form with two identical input fields:

```
<HTML><BODY><FORM>
<INPUT TYPE="text" NAME="twin" VALUE="me too"><BR>
<SCRIPT>
document.write(document.form[0].element[0]+'<BR>');
</SCRIPT>
</FORM></BODY></HTML>
```

Naming form elements

With more than one form, or with many form elements, using array indices quickly becomes confusing, as the above example shows. Fortunately, form and element tags are accessible via their names as well, since objects and arrays are nearly the same thing in JavaScript. The **NAME** parameter of the appropriate tag is used as the property name. Here are the same properties using the property names instead of array indices:

```
with ( top.document )
{
patient.name;                      // pointless
patient.method;
patient.elements.length;    // pointless if all names are known
patient.weeks.value;
patient.weeks.onchange;
patient.symptom[0].name;    // this line and the next - special handling
patient.symptom[1].checked;
patient.diet.options.length;
patient.diet.options[1].value;
}
```

The 'named' notation is a lot clearer and almost identical structurally. There is one catch. In the source HTML document, the **NAME** attribute for both checkboxes is 'symptom'. This might be by design, or possibly even required (as for mutually exclusive radio buttons). If the checkboxes are referred to by array indices, there is no problem. However, properties present a difficulty: an object can't have two properties with the same name, whether it is a form element or not.

The solution to this problem is that the property name no longer refers to just one of the elements. Instead, it refers to a new, intermediate object. In Navigator, this object's type is '**InputArray**', and it is a JavaScript array. Each similarly named element is then a member of the '**InputArray**' array. This array often cryptically appears when buggy scripts are run with Netscape browsers. It helps to remember that each form element is just a type of input item, and therefore an '**InputArray**' is just an array of such items.

Using names can make life a lot easier, especially if they are short. For the unimaginative, and the pathological haters of array syntax, use names such as '**form1**'. A big trap with naming elements is forgetting to avoid the numerous reserved words and other property names. The 'Disappearing Data' chapter, Chapter 7, covers this possibility in more detail. A simple example for now is:

```
<HTML><BODY><FORM>
Flagpole juggling survey. Enter pole length: <INPUT TYPE="text" NAME="length">
</FORM></BODY></HTML>
```

Clearly the '**document.forms**' JavaScript object already has a '**length**' property, since it is an array.

Form events

HTML intrinsic events are the main way the script writer catches and processes form input. If the user turns JavaScript support off in the browser, any form elements will have their default behavior. The reference section describes the full gory details of which events are supported where. Chapter 2 describes features common to all events. Events commonly used in form processing are described here.

Here is an example that shows how event handling makes HTML more interactive and useful:

```
<HTML><HEAD><SCRIPT>
function applause()
{
  var answer = "Man is correct!\n" +
        "Man crawls when young, walks when adult and uses a cane in old age\n"
+ "\nShould you meet a riddling Egyptian Sphinx, you'll be perfectly safe";
  alert(answer);
}
</SCRIPT></HEAD>
<BODY><FORM>
<H1>Riddle Page</H1>
What goes on four legs in the morning, two during the day and three in the
evening?
<BR> <INPUT TYPE="radio" ONCLICK="alert('You seem confused too')"> A confused
table
<BR> <INPUT TYPE="radio" ONCLICK="alert('Perhaps you've had too much Sun?')">
The Sun
<BR> <INPUT TYPE="radio" ONCLICK="applause()"> Man
</FORM></BODY></HTML>
```

In this simple example, the event handlers give the user additional information not otherwise displayed with the document.

The **onReset** and **onSubmit** events are the only ones that apply to a whole form. These events match the default actions of the **<INPUT   TYPE="submit">** and **<INPUT   TYPE="reset">** tags, and can be applied to the **<FORM>** tag as well as to the submit/reset **<INPUT>** types. Use of these events is of debatable value, because the **<INPUT   TYPE="button">** tag can be used to do the same job in a safer way with an **onClick** handler. If the form must still be submittable for non-JavaScript browser users, then any checks that might have been done in these handlers will be ignored anyway.

The '**onClick**' event handler is probably the most common handler used. The main uses are for detecting checkbox and radio button changes and for carrying out arbitrary actions, such as opening new windows. The '**button**' type of the **<INPUT>** tag relies almost entirely on the **onClick** handler in order to do anything useful.

Alongside **onClick** is the **onChange** event. This event occurs when the user moves the cursor away from a form element whose value has been changed. Typically, this is a '**text**', '**textarea**', or '**select**' element. Except for Internet Explorer 4.0, usually only one of **onClick** and **onSubmit** is available in a given element.

The **onBlur** and **onFocus** event handlers occur when the user moves between fields in a form, and between frames or windows. Their main use is to control the way the user navigates between fields. In current browsers, they can be tricky to use portably and aren't advised for doing simple checks on fields.

Apart from these events, many other events are defined in HTML 4.0 for form elements. These events such as **onMouseMove** and **onKeyPress** are rarely available or used for HTML forms.

The main problem with events is trying to anticipate exactly how they will occur. Just knowing all the event handlers possible is not enough information. A simple example is clicking on a text input field when another text input field currently holds the cursor. A number of events may result from this one action—**onBlur** and **onChange** in the original field, **onClick** and **onFocus** in the new field. The order in which these events occur is not standardized or consistent between browsers. If the handlers for these events further mimic user actions by calling form element object methods like **click()**, **blur()** or **focus()**, then matters become quite complex. Too much reliance on the exact order of events will produce non-portable, fragile code that isn't even backwardly compatible.

Microsoft 3.0 handler trap

Internet Explorer 3.0 provides us with a good example of the complexities of event handling. In that browser, **onChange**, **onBlur** and **onFocus** handlers can behave very inconveniently. When one of these event fires, the browser reacts to the event with some internal actions, then calls an event handler, then does some further internal actions to finish up.

122

Unfortunately, the further internal actions can undo just the thing you've been trying to achieve in the handler. An example:

```
<INPUT TYPE="radio" ONCLICK="this.checked=false">
```

This line attempts to keep the radio button unset, even if the user clicks it. However, the browser applies the results of the user's click after the event handler finishes, so it's set anyway.

To avoid these effects, defer processing until all the event handling rubbish is finished. This approach, which is compatible with other browsers, applies your handler as you expect. Try clicking the second radio button in this example:

```
<HTML><BODY><SCRIPT>
function real_handler()
{
   document.forms[0].r[0].checked=true;
}
</SCRIPT><FORM>
<INPUT NAME="r" TYPE="radio">
<INPUT NAME="r" TYPE="radio" ONCLICK="setTimeout('real_handler()',1)">
</FORM></BODY></HTML>
```

Current field problems

Another example of event handling differences stems from the concept of a '**current field**'. When an **onBlur** trigger fires, what should the current field be, where should the insertion point be, what field if any should gain focus? Microsoft and Netscape browsers answer differently at the 3.0 level. An example:

```
<INPUT TYPE="text" ONFOCUS="this.blur()">
```

The handler attempts to make the field read-only, by automatically blurring it as soon as it gains focus. This won't work in Internet Explorer 3.0 for two reasons: firstly, because of the trap described above; secondly because that browser requires that one field always be in focus. In that browser, you can only put focus somewhere else, not take it away from a field. This also won't work in Navigator 3.0. In that browser, you can have no fields focused, and a time-out delay isn't required to do it. However, there is a bug that leaves the insertion point in the current field if it is blurred from its own handler. The upshot is that this code will work for both browsers:

```
<HTML><BODY><SCRIPT>
function defocus()
{
   window.document.forms[0].two.focus();
}
</SCRIPT><FORM>
<INPUT NAME="one" TYPE="text" ONFOCUS="setTimeout('defocus()',1)">
<INPUT NAME="two" TYPE="text">
<SCRIPT>document.forms[0].two.focus();</SCRIPT>        <!-- starting field -->
</FORM></BODY></HTML>
```

Types of form

Form elements can be collected together for a number of purposes. It pays to notice the general class of task the form is intended for, because once identified, techniques to follow become obvious. This section describes some general classes of forms, and the attendant issues.

Controls and Calculators

The simplest use of a form is a single button marked 'Just do it'. Such a form is typically used to control the browser or the user's navigation in the browser. The form elements used don't contain any data, or else the data they do contain is ignored. The point of the form is to make something else happen.

For such a form, there is usually little need to go beyond **onClick** event handlers. No data is required from the user; so many events are meaningless. No '**submit**' or '**reset**' form elements exist. Form elements may be unrelated. The form acts much like a collection of HTML hyperlinks. The appearance of buttons and checkboxes adds visual variety to a page whose only other features might be links, text and images. A simple example, that allows the user to navigate between several pages via buttons, is often called a '**button bar**':

```
<!--frameset.htm-->
<HTML><FRAMESET ROWS="50,*">
<FRAME SRC="control.htm">
<FRAME NAME="main" SRC="home.htm">
</FRAMESET></HTML>


<!--control.htm-->
<HTML><BODY><FORM>
<TABLE BORDER=0><TR>
<TD><INPUT TYPE="button" VALUE="My Home"
ONCLICK="top.main.location.href='home.htm'">
<TD><INPUT TYPE="button" VALUE="Games"
ONCLICK="top.main.location.href='game.htm'">
<TD><INPUT TYPE="button" VALUE="Links"
ONCLICK="top.main.location.href='link.htm'">
<TD><INPUT TYPE="button" VALUE="Help"
ONCLICK="top.main.location.href='link.htm'">
</TR></TABLE>
</FORM></BODY></HTML>
```

A similar but less simplistic use of forms puts the JavaScript interpreter under the user's control. The JavaScript interpreter supports basic mathematics and logic, which can perform calculations on the user's behalf. In this case, the calculation is done in the following stages: user input, processing & user feedback. Note that the entire process occurs without accessing any other URL. Just like the button bar example above, no form data is forwarded anywhere. Unlike the button bar, the user might enter values into the form which are processed locally. There is still no need for a 'submit' button, or a button performing a submit action, but a 'reset' button might be used to clear the form. Because the user can enter data, the script writer might need to validate that data in case rubbish has been entered, or control the user's navigation through the elements of the form. If the window containing the form closes, the form data is gone.

The classic example of this kind of processing is a calculator. A calculator just takes input from one place and produces output in another. A trivial example (which could do with some better error checking—more on that later):

```
<HTML><BODY><FORM>
<H4>Centimeters to Inches and back again converter</H4>
<INPUT TYPE="text" NAME="cm" ONCHANGE="this.form.inches.value = this.value *
2.54">
<INPUT TYPE="text" NAME="inches" ONCHANGE="this.form.cm.value = this.value /
2.54">
</FORM></BODY></HTML>
```

Type any number into either field, and see the other field update.

A very simple example of a desk-style calculator can be found at `http://www.people.cornell.edu/pages/avr1/calculator.html`. This alternate page points to a number of similar examples, some of them even useful, but not all of them are pure JavaScript, so view the HTML source of each to confirm: `http://www.yahoo.com/Computers_and_Internet/ Hardware/Calculators/Online_Calculators/JavaScript/`

Fire and Forget

The most common kind of form on the Internet is used to collect data from the browser user and is then submitted once to a remote system. The user rarely, or never, sees the data again in the form that it was entered. The two most common styles of these 'fire and forget' forms are **search requests**, and **registration or feedback forms**. These forms are the kinds that HTML was designed to support when **<FORM>** tags were first added to the HTML 2.0 standard. The form data is submitted to a Web server where it is processed by a specially developed system.

These kinds of forms have some features which combine to make them 'one use only' forms. The form is contained in a single HTML document. The fields in the form are usually very simple: the user starts at the first one, works down, and then submits. Once such a form is submitted there is often no need to retain the form information in the browser—the document containing the form is replaced with something else. The user rarely has a reason to return to the form document, unless it is to start again. The data that the user enters is rarely rejected—at worst it might produce no useful results. The information in the form doesn't have any complex relationships with other data, and doesn't need to be maintained in the browser after the user has submitted it.

These forms are simple to construct because they rely heavily on the principle of '**harmless data**'. No matter what the user enters, the system to which the data is submitted will cope. There is no need to coordinate the form data with other information in the browser or maintain it in some special state. JavaScript in the browser might do some validation on the data, but that's about all. Often these forms can be constructed in plain HTML without any JavaScript at all.

An example of a simple 'fire and forget' style form is this page from Wrox:

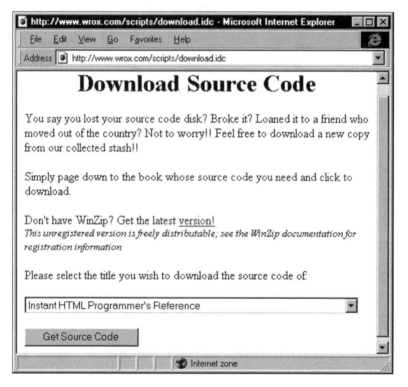

Other examples can be seen at **http://www.yahoo.com**, and **http://www.hotbot.com**

Shopping Carts

When forms need to span more than one HTML document, a '**shopping cart**' or '**shopping trolley**' is a design approach that overcomes some limiting factors of HTML.

A common use of forms is to allow users to place orders for goods. Shopping cart forms meet this need. The name derives from the user's typical behavior—they browse through the web site looking at goods, collecting desired items the same way that shoppers operate in a supermarket, and then buying them at the end. The equivalent of a physical shopping cart or trolley in a web form is a temporary storage place for form data.

Simple 'fire and forget' style forms would be enough for the job if it weren't for three issues.

The first issue is the matter of document size and presentation. Web sites selling goods act as ordering systems, but they also have an advertising and sales function. If the site has many items for sale, a simple form solution would result in a huge HTML page that can be scrolled at length, takes a long time to load, and has possibly hundreds of form fields. Web sites selling goods are better off mimicking the large printed catalogues that used to be delivered in the days before television (or now in the electronics industry). The user can turn to specific sections of interest, and choose items from each. This allows smaller HTML pages and better advertising focus on the user.

The second issue is that there is nowhere in plain HTML to temporarily store form data. For browsers without JavaScript support, there is no choice but to maintain the shopping cart with the Web server and ask the user to submit each item so it can be stored in the cart. Then a final extra submit tells the server the cart contents should be purchased.

The third issue is that HTML forms can't span several HTML documents. This makes the design goal of splitting any form into separate documents difficult.

With a modern browser, JavaScript comes to the rescue for all these issues. The tasks involved are as follows:

- create a permanent place for the shopping cart
- create forms in each page of the catalogue
- organize for each form's data to be captured in the cart
- submit shopping cart data if the user decides to buy

A full example follows. First, the creation of a shopping cart—the 'simple approach' to multiple windows described in the 'Windows and Frames' chapter is used here. The shopping cart will be stored in a frameset document, one frame used to control the catalogue paging and another to display the actual pages.

```
<!--catalog.htm -->
<HTML><HEAD><SCRIPT>
var cart = new Object;        // The whole cart

function Item(name, price, quantity)        // cart item constructor
{
this.name = name;
this.price = price;
this.quantity = quantity;
}
</SCRIPT></HEAD>
<FRAMESET ROWS="50,*">
<FRAME NAME="buttonbar" SRC="buttons.htm">
<FRAME NAME="page" SRC="welcome.htm">
</FRAMESET>
</HTML>
```

Each property of the 'cart' object will be an ordered item. Each ordered item will have its own product code, making it unique. The control frame is ordinary; it doesn't even use a form:

```
<!--buttons.htm -->
<HTML><BODY><TABLE BORDERS=0><TR>
<TD><A HREF="big.htm" TARGET="page">Big stuff</A>
<TD><A HREF="medium.htm" TARGET="page">Medium stuff</A>
<TD><A HREF="small.htm" TARGET="page">Small stuff</A>
<TD><A HREF="order.htm" TARGET="page">Place order</A>
</TR></TABLE></BODY></HTML>
```

The front page is just an introduction for the user:

```
<!--welcome.htm-->
<HTML><BODY>
Welcome to the Obscure Emporium! If no one wants it, we've got it!
</BODY></HTML>
```

Here is an image of the first page the user sees:

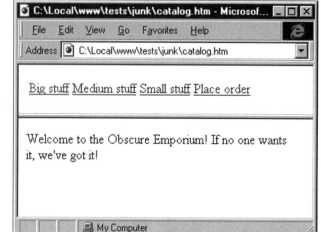

The catalogue pages all follow the same pattern. The first one is shown here:

```
<!--big.htm-->
<HTML><HEAD>
<SCRIPT>
function recall_selection()
{
if (top.cart["CH"])
    {
document.frm.c1.checked = true;
document.frm.v1.value = top.cart["CH"].quantity;
    }
if (top.cart["LV"])
    {
document.frm.c2.checked = true;
document.frm.v2.value = top.cart["LV"].quantity;
    }
if (top.cart["AO"])
    {
document.frm.c3.checked = true;
document.frm.v3.value = top.cart["AO"].quantity;
    }
}
</SCRIPT>
<BODY ONLOAD="recall_selection()">
<SCRIPT>
if ( top == self )            // make sure this is a frame.
self.location.href = "welcome.htm";
</SCRIPT>
<FORM name="frm">
Big stuff for sale today.<BR>
Check the items required and enter a quantity for each<BR><BR>
<BR>
<INPUT TYPE="checkbox" NAME='c1' ONCLICK="document.frm.v1.value='0'">
<INPUT TYPE="text" NAME='v1' MAXLENGTH=2 SIZE=2
ONCHANGE="top.cart['CH']=new top.Item('Combine Harvester',145000,this.value)">
```

128

```
Combine Harvester - $145,000.00
<BR>
<INPUT TYPE="checkbox" NAME='c2' ONCLICK="document.frm.v2.value='0'">
<INPUT TYPE="text" NAME='v2' MAXLENGTH=2 SIZE=2
ONCHANGE="top.cart['LV']=new top.Item('Lunar Vehicle',6000000,this.value)">
Lunar Re-entry Vehicle - $6,000,000.00
<BR>
<INPUT TYPE="checkbox" NAME='c3' ONCLICK="document.frm.v3.value='0'">
<INPUT TYPE="text" NAME='v3' MAXLENGTH=2 SIZE=2
ONCHANGE="top.cart['AO']=new top.Item('Arctic Ocean',123,this.value)">
Arctic Ocean - $123.00
</FORM></BODY></HTML>
```

If the user navigates to this page, it appears as follows:

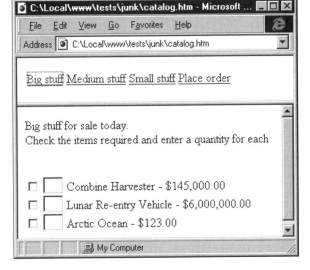

In this example, two letter codes ('**CH**', '**LV**', '**AO**') are used for each product line. Anything could be used. The example isn't formatted very well, nor does it do good validation—if the user ignores the instructions, problems can occur. Its main point is to show how items are put into the shopping cart using an **onChange** trigger. The '**recall_selection()**' function demonstrates how the form is loaded with any existing selections the user has made. This allows the page to be abandoned and revisited without any information being lost.

The last page is the ordering page that submits the data in the shopping cart to a Web server. Here it is:

```
<HTML><BODY>
Your order currently consists of:<BR>
<SCRIPT>
var i;
var linetotal = 0, subtotal = 0;

for ( i in top.cart)
{
document.write(' Item: '+top.cart[i].name);
document.write(', '+top.cart[i].quantity+' at '+top.cart[i].price);
linetotal = top.cart[i].quantity * top.cart[i].price;
document.write(' each is: '+ linetotal + '<BR>');
subtotal += linetotal;
}
```

```
document.write('<BR>Total due is: '+subtotal+'<BR>');
</SCRIPT>
<FORM METHOD="POST">
<SCRIPT>
var item;
for (i in top.cart)
{
item = '<INPUT TYPE="hidden" NAME="'+i+'" VALUE="'+top.cart[i].quantity+'">';
document.write(item);
}
</SCRIPT>
<BR>
Credit Card details (you won't feel a thing)
<INPUT TYPE="text" NAME="card_number">
<INPUT TYPE="submit" VALUE="Buy Now">
</FORM>
</BODY></HTML>
```

Typical output from this page might be:

The shopping cart details are extracted twice, once for the user to review, and once to create hidden fields (they could be visible if desired) in the form that is submitted. The data submitted consists of field name-value pairs; in this case, the name is the two-letter product code and the value is the number of items bought.

Notice that these forms (and all other submitted forms) make assumptions about the program at the Web server site that will receive the submission. In this case, the script writer assumes that such a program knows prices for all the items on sale, knows what the two-letter codes mean, and knows that the number supplied is a quantity, not a price. The form document and that program are a deliberate match.

This coordination between the server side and the browser side can require a lot of work if they are maintained separately. A more sophisticated strategy is to have the server side create the HTML and JavaScript in the client side automatically, so that updates need only be done on the server side. This can be done with either server-side JavaScript or CGI programs. The section on CGI below has examples.

Data management forms

Beyond forms that submit data only once are forms that are used to manage existing data. Typically, this data is in a database accessible via a Web server. Databases tend to support four important operations: **insert**, **update**, **delete** and **fetch**. Forms that are submitted only once are equivalent to just one database-style operation, typically insert (e.g. registration forms) or select requests (e.g. search engine queries). To fully support database-style operations requires a more sophisticated approach.

Browsers versus 4GL tools

Because browsers and Web servers have a client-server relationship, and because JavaScript provides a generally flexible programming language for controlling the browser, it may seem that a web browser is a good tool to use as a database client development tool. However, it is only a primitive tool for such uses, compared with more specialized "4GL" database tools. On the other hand, 4GL database tools are primitive tools for developing Internet document retrieval systems, so that makes it even.

Traditional 4GL database clients provide a great deal of programmer support, being custom built for databases. Some of the features they support with little effort are:

- automatic validation of simple types
- 'pick lists' or 'select lists' recalled dynamically from the server
- logic for insert, delete, update and fetch operations
- automatic coordination of master-detail records
- support for multi-record forms
- fully synchronized operation
- log-in and security features

Few of these things are built into a web browser. To mimic a complex data management-style form in a web browser can be a lot of work and can generate a lot of JavaScript. Even then, it is possible the form document can't be crafted by hand, because it may require an up-to-the-second view of the database. In this case, the form document must be partially generated by a CGI program or by server-side JavaScript each time it is displayed.

There are no total obstacles to achieving the features that 4GL tools support. If your goal is to explore the possibilities, feel free. If you have limited time, there are efficient ways to proceed.

Strategies that ease implementation

The simplest strategies are to avoid the technology or avoid the problems.

The technology can be avoided in a number of ways. Custom tools instead of browsers or Java applets instead of JavaScript can be more productive for complicated forms, if the user base allows it. JDBC is a well-defined Java standard for accessing databases, and the number of commercial Java applets supporting form-style interfaces to databases is increasing. Of course, Java applets are embeddable in HTML documents.

Avoiding the problems means keeping it simple. Two very time-consuming processes when developing data management forms are supporting in-place editing and supporting master-detail record coordination. The next two sections look at reducing the effort needed for each. A third consumer of time is validation of user data, discussed in detail later. If the form is complex, this can take up considerable time. However, as described in the chapter on 'Security, Privacy and Cookies', in a public arena like the Internet, validating the data in the browser is no guarantee of anything when the submitted data arrives at the server end. If that is your case, it might not be worth adding any user validation at all.

A further easy trap to fall into when working with databases is to reflect the database structure directly in the fields of a document's forms. This is not so bad for a simple document based on just one database record, but if there are 3 types of records in the database with 14, 15 and 16 fields each, a complex document might end up with all 45 fields displayed. Lots and lots of JavaScript can easily result from trying to keep them organized. In this case, a better approach is to focus on the task the user is trying to achieve with a given form, and supply only the fields necessary, regardless of the underlying database structure. When the data is submitted to the Web server back-end, that back-end is responsible for sorting through the data, away from the user's view. This is '**transaction processing**', a standard technique in the world of databases: the type of task is identified, just the needed data is supplied, and then some dedicated program grinds through the logic required to make it all happen.

In-place editing

In-place editing occurs when the one form is used for both retrieving and modifying data. The advice of this section is **don't do it** use the alternative, which is to break up the functionality into many simple forms.

In-place editing looks good to the user. The user sees a single form, typically with a number of button options, one for each form function. Typical button options are 'add', 'display', 'delete' and 'modify'. When the user presses a button, the form is submitted as usual. When the submission returns with a new HTML document, it is exactly the same form. Usually only the data in the form has changed, so there is little that is new for the user to absorb. Here is a simple example—the source HTML is not important, it is the general look of the screen that is the point here:

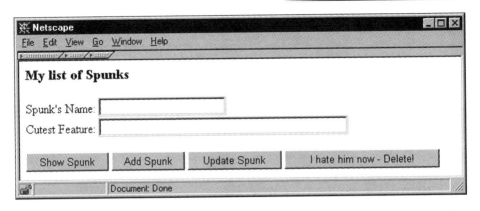

The row of buttons perform different functions, but the user only ever sees this one screen. This kind of setup is hard work for the script writer (especially a non-spunk script writer!). Nearly all such screens are not going to have forms as small as this one, either. A typical sequence of user actions in such a screen illustrates why it is difficult:

- The user partially fills in an empty form with search or fetch criteria, and submits.

- The form is replaced with an identical form containing the fetched data.

- The user modifies the fetched data and submits, causing an insert, update or further search.

- The form is replaced with an identical form containing the changed data.

There are many such sequences of steps. This requires a complex form that records many states because it is not always clear what action the user intends when changing the fields. Is it new search criteria for a fetch, or new data being inserted? What action did the user do last? Two deletes in a row may not make sense. These states are usually stored in JavaScript variables, and may include duplicating some or all of the form's data. These states have to be preserved somewhere in case the form document reloads or is submitted, and might have to contribute to the submission process as well. Argghhh!

A simpler approach is to separate out each operation into its own document. The key to this approach is to retain 'seed data', also called the 'current key'. These values are enough information to identify the current data and to communicate between documents.

Here is an example based on scheduling waiter's shifts in a restaurant. If the waiters are all frustrated actors, chances are the staff will need to be regularly reorganized. A 'duty' in this example is a match of a shift (a time period) and a particular person. In order to avoid dedicating the rest of this book to script extracts for this one scenario, only the essential features are included:

```
<!--main.htm - the top level document -->
<HTML><SCRIPT>
var shift_id = null;                // current key values
var staff_id = null;
</SCRIPT><FRAMESET ROWS="50,*">
<FRAME SRC="actions.htm">
<FRAME NAME="page" SRC="blank.htm">
</FRAMESET></HTML>
```

```
<!--actions.htm - controls for the user -->
<HTML><BODY>
<A HREF="fetch.htm" TARGET="page">Show duties</A>
<A HREF="insert.htm" TARGET="page">Add duty</A>
<A HREF="delete.htm" TARGET="page">Delete duty</A>
<A HREF="update.htm" TARGET="page">Update duty</A>
</BODY></HTML>
```

These documents are similar to the shopping cart example.

```
<!--fetch.htm - search form to get current duties -->
<HTML><FORM>
Enter shift name: <INPUT TYPE="text"><BR>
Enter staff name: <INPUT TYPE="text"><BR>
<INPUT TYPE="submit" VALUE="Get Duties">
</FORM></HTML>
```

This form doesn't use the seed data, because the user is doing a new search. If the search succeeds, the page generated by the system behind the Web server might look like this:

```
<!--results.htm - data resulting from the search -->
<HTML><BODY><FORM>
   Shift Name - Waiter Name - Rate - Tips <BR>
<INPUT TYPE="radio" ONCLICK="top.shift_id='3'; top.staff_id='13';">
Evening - Manuel - $10/hr - No Tips<BR>
<INPUT TYPE="radio" ONCLICK="top.shift_id='3'; top.staff_id='22';">
Evening - Elmer - $2/hr - Tips allowed<BR>
<INPUT TYPE="radio" ONCLICK="top.shift_id='3'; top.staff_id='9';">
Evening - Woody - $12/hr - Tips allowed<BR>
</FORM></BODY></HTML>
```

Output from this HTML looks like this:

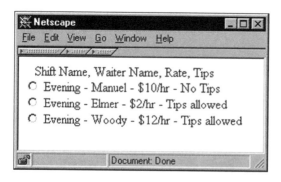 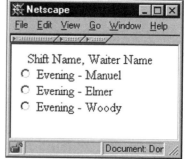

When the user selects one of the three displayed duties, the seed values for that duty is saved. The other three documents use these values. The update case, **update.htm**, might look like this:

```
<HTML><FORM>
<INPUT TYPE="hidden" NAME="shift_id" VALUE="&{top.shift_id}">
<INPUT TYPE="hidden" NAME="staff_id" VALUE="&{top.staff_id}">
<SCRIPT>
document.write('Current shift period: '+top.shift_id+'<BR>');
document.write('Current staff member: '+top.staff_id+'<BR>');
</SCRIPT>
<BR>Hourly Rate:
<INPUT TYPE="text" NAME="rate">
<BR>Tip policy:
<SELECT NAME="tips">
<OPTION VALUE="Y"> Tips allowed
<OPTION VALUE="N"> No tips allowed
<OPTION VALUE="R"> Customers tipped for staying
</SELECT>
<BR><INPUT TYPE="submit" VALUE="Update">
</FORM></HTML>
```

The only problem with this example is that the user is left wondering what a
'**staff_id**' and a '**shift_id**' is. However, if this URL was returned by a CGI
program rather than being hand-written, and the two id's were passed to that
program, the real name for the shift and the staff member could be inserted
into the document instead. The section on CGI discusses the mechanics of
parameter passing. When this form is submitted, the replacement document
might be merely:

```
<HTML><BODY>Update succeeded.</BODY></HTML>
```

The delete and insert cases follow in a similar manner. The insert case wouldn't
need to use the seed values, as new user data would be the issue. It might
check the new data doesn't clash with the current seed values.

Master-detail coordination

Master-detail coordination means coordinating two forms so that they always
match. Some 4GL products do this for you automatically, but that automatic
process can create a dozen event handlers. In a web browser, you might have
to script that many JavaScript event handlers manually in order to achieve the
same effect.

The classic example of master detail coordination is an order-entry system. In
such a system, one purchase order from a customer consists of a number of
individual items required (entries) plus general information such as the
customers name, order number and the date (the order). The details are entered
into a computer to track the order. All kinds of rules apply: an order must
have at least one entry; if an order is deleted, all the entries are deleted; when
an order is added, entries must be added; when the user displays an order, all
the matching entries should be displayed.

There are several problems here for the Web developer:

- how to display and manage multiple records at once
- how to coordinate two forms
- how to ensure that when submitted, both forms succeed or fail together

135

The section on display techniques describes methods of displaying multi-record sets. Coordinating forms is discussed here. Ensuring two submissions stand or fall together is discussed in the 'Complex Problems' section.

Finding an easy solution to coordination problems means using a similar pattern to that in the previous section. Functionality supplied to the user should be broken up into numerous, simple forms. In that previous section, the concept of seed or key data was used to target each simple form at specific data. A similar approach can be used here, but in a repeated way. Using the order-entry example, an important observation is that entries can't exist without an order. This means that the order details 'drive' the entry details—the order details must be specified before the entry details can be known. This allows the forms to drive the user's responses in a step by step manner. Here is a stripped down example showing insertion of an entry into an existing form:

```
<!--main.htm - the top level document -->
<HTML><SCRIPT>
var order_id = null;              // current order key
</SCRIPT><FRAMESET ROWS="50,*">
<FRAME SRC="order_actions.htm">
<FRAME NAME="order_page" SRC="blank.htm">
</FRAMESET></HTML>
```

```
<!-- order_actions.htm - controls for the user -->
<HTML><BODY>
<A HREF="fetch.htm" TARGET="order_page">Show order</A>
<A HREF="insert.htm" TARGET="order_page">Add order</A>
<A HREF="delete.htm" TARGET="order_page">Delete order</A>
<A HREF="update.htm" TARGET="order_page">Update order</A>
</BODY></HTML>
```

These two documents are almost identical to the last example. The '**fetch.htm**' document would be similar as well. Since this example is about inserting an entry into an order, not displaying an order, assume the user has displayed an order, which set the seed '**order_id**' value to 55, and then clicks the 'Update order' button. In the previous example, this would be a single document. In this example, the document is a frameset with the same structure as the top level frameset, but focussed on an entry, not an order. When this new frameset is displayed, the user sees three frames: a top row, a left column, and the remainder.

```
<!--update.htm - let the user change an order or its details -->
<HTML><SCRIPT>
var entry_id = null;              // current entry key
</SCRIPT><FRAMESET COLS="100,*">
<FRAME SRC="entry_actions.htm">
<FRAME NAME="entry_page" SRC="order_update.htm">
</FRAMESET></HTML>
```

The **order_update.htm** document just contains a normal form, with a submit button and a hidden field containing the **order_id** stolen from 'top.order_id'. When the user changes the form details (the order details) and presses submit, the order is changed, but no entries for the order are changed, so that document isn't illustrated. Here is the suspiciously familiar 'entry_actions.htm' page:

136

```
<!-- entry_actions.htm - controls for the user -->
<HTML><BODY>
Choose entry action:<BR>
<A HREF="fetch.htm" TARGET="entry_page">Show entries</A><BR>
<A HREF="insert.htm" TARGET="entry_page">Add entries</A><BR>
<A HREF="delete.htm" TARGET="entry_page">Delete entries</A><BR>
<A HREF="update.htm" TARGET="entry_page">Update entries</A><BR>
<BR>
<A HREF="order_update.htm" TARGET="entry_page">Back to Order Update</A><BR>
</BODY></HTML>
```

The '**
' tags are present only because this menu appears vertically on the left—a layout choice. The only frame remaining is the one in the bottom right-hand corner of the window that fills most of the space. The 'entry_actions.htm**' document gives the user the choice of four forms; just like the '**order_actions.htm**' document does, but focused on entries. The difference is that for the 'order' screens (the master record), the seed value is just '**top.order_id**', but for the 'entry' screens (each a detail record), the seed value is the combination of '**top.order_id**' and '**top.order_page.entry_id**'. This fully specifies which entry is being operated on. For displaying current data, displaying orders requires no **order_id**, unless the user searches for it specifically. Similarly, for displaying an order's entries, no **entry_id** is required, but the **order_id** is.

Using this approach, the user has to jump around a little more than for a single integrated screen, but the script writer is spared a lot of coordination work, and the user can only make one simple and safe change at a time. If this seems a little confusing, try fully implementing the example in the previous section on 'in-place editing', then convert it to a fully working ordering system that has no entry records (and therefore no master-detail coordination), and finally add support for entries as described here.

Stripped of validation and other features that make these forms robust, there is only a very small and manageable amount of client-side JavaScript required. You are still required to create server-side JavaScript or CGI programs in order to service the submitted data.

Finally, master-detail coordination is an example of working with one-to-many relationships. One order has (possibly) many entries. These relationships can occur in "**chains**", for example: one order has many entries; one entry has many parts; one part has many suppliers. The approach described here can be applied to such chains which have more than one "**link**" (to burden an overused word with further meaning)—just keep nesting the framesets and adding seed values at each level. Only one record is ever operated on at a time, but the set of current seed values puts that record into a context.

Complex problems

Some database style problems are worth keeping well away from.

Database Integrity

You can never be sure that the data submitted by the user in good faith will be accepted by the database. It may be conflict with other data and be rejected, or the database may become corrupt and fail entirely. This means error handling is required, as described under the CGI section. That in itself is no great chore, but trying to anticipate or detect integrity problems before submitting is a great deal of effort for little benefit, or else is a hobby. Best to submit, wait and see what happens, and then act on the outcome.

Multiple submits

Each submit is a single action (an HTTP request) that is independent of all other requests. Submitting several times, say for several different forms on the same page, is several different actions. It is again a great deal of effort to impose some kind of coordination system (usually called a transaction model) on such sets of submit operations so that they succeed or fail together. The difficulties of backing out from partially complete sets of submit operations are immense, not to mention the user's ability to interfere by shutting down the browser at an instant. A better approach for the desperate is to use inline JavaScript to create an additional form, containing a duplicate of every field of every form to be submitted, then copy all the values across and submit that new form as a single item. A specialized server-side program then handles the complexity of the combined data.

Form Display Techniques

There are several display techniques using JavaScript that build on the basic **<FORM>** tags of HTML.

Read-only fields and boilerplate

Sometimes form data in a document shouldn't be changeable by the user. Boilerplate text and read-only form fields can achieve this.

Boilerplate text is just all the content of a document that doesn't change. If a document is dynamically produced, like the results of a search query, then plain HTML text can be displayed. The catch with displaying form data this way is that JavaScript cannot change it, unless Dynamic HTML techniques are exploited. If form content displays a mixture of form controls and boilerplate text, and that form can be submitted, then there should be a hidden field duplicating each boilerplate data item, or else those items won't be submitted with the rest of the data.

To make existing form controls read-only, there are two alternatives: don't let the user get near the control or change the control's state back as soon as the user changes it. The first possibility is covered under 'Form events' and is perhaps a better approach for **text**, **password** and **textarea** fields. Alternatively, to change a field back to what it was before the user touched it, try these various tricks:

```
<HTML><BODY><FORM>

<!-- This case works for "text", "textarea" and "password" types -->
<INPUT TYPE="text" NAME="first" VALUE="Important"
ONCHANGE="this.value=this.real">
<SCRIPT>
document.forms[0].first.real = document.forms[0].first.value;
</SCRIPT>
```

```
<!-- This case works for all checkboxes and for radio button groups of one -->
<INPUT TYPE="checkbox" NAME="second" ONCLICK="this.checked=!this.checked;">

<!-- This case works for radio button groups of more than one button -->
<INPUT TYPE="radio" NAME="third" CHECKED>
<INPUT TYPE="radio" NAME="third" ONCLICK="this.form.third[0].click()">
<INPUT TYPE="radio" NAME="third" ONCLICK="this.form.third[0].click()">

<!-- This case is solely for SELECT -->
<SELECT NAME="fourth" ONCHANGE="this.selectedIndex=this.realIndex">
<OPTION SELECTED VALUE="A"> Apples
<OPTION VALUE="B"> Banana
</SELECT>
<SCRIPT>
document.forms[0].fourth.realIndex = document.forms[0].fourth.selectedIndex;
</SCRIPT>

</FORM></BODY></HTML>
```

"**Submit**", "**reset**", "**button**", "**hidden**" and "**image**" input types can't have their values set directly by the user at all, so they are ignored. Their normal action can be disabled with an **onClick** handler if desired.

Bugs: Internet Explorer 3.02 ignores the handler in the "**password**" case. Navigator 3.0 may crash if asked to display a radio button group of only one button. For radio buttons and select lists, Internet Explorer 3.02 has a trap in the use of its event handler—see the heading titled 'Explorer 3.0 handler trap'. The "**file**" input type is problematic for event handlers—it appears to be buggy in all Netscape versions and you can't even be sure it is present at all with Explorer 3.0, since it's added to the browser's computer via a patch.

There are other solutions. HTML 4.0 has a **READONLY** attribute for form elements which is the ultimate solution, but it is only supported in Internet Explorer 4.0. A Java applet that displays a single piece of text can be exploited from JavaScript—see Chapter 8. A normal **<INPUT>** form control of type "**button**", "**reset**" or "**submit**" can have its displayed value changed via JavaScript—although the user can still push the button, they can't change the displayed value. Finally, a Netscape **<LAYER>** can be used to write out a scrap of text in a specific position over a document. The Layer solution has the advantage that it can be made wider if the new text is longer than the old.

Menus

The **<SELECT>** and **<OPTION>** tags with their single and multiple pick variants are the main mechanisms for displaying menus, but there are a few alternatives and subtleties.

The alternatives for drop-down menus are to use image map swaps as described in the 'Multimedia and Plug-ins' chapter, Chapter 4, or to take advantage of positionable styles with Dynamic HTML. For plain, static menus that don't scroll or drop down, any set of clickable items such as a button bar can suffice.

However, the **<SELECT>** and **<OPTION>** tags have a trick or two of their own. As noted in 'Form objects' you can create your own **Option** objects, and change menus on the fly. There are some restrictions, however. It won't work in Internet Explorer 3.0, for one.

139

Replace a menu item

This is straightforward. The Option constructor function takes two arguments: the contents of the **<OPTION>** tag, and the **VALUE** attribute.

```
<HTML><BODY><FORM NAME="cafe">
<SCRIPT>
function to_morning()
{
document.cafe.food.options[2] = new Option('M1', 'Garlic Muesli');
}
function to_evening()
{
document.cafe.food.options[2] = new Option('M2', 'Garlic Quiche');
}
</SCRIPT>
<INPUT TYPE="button" VALUE="Halitosis Cafe Morning Menu"
ONCLICK="to_morning()">
<INPUT TYPE="button" VALUE="Halitosis Cafe Evening Menu"
ONCLICK="to_evening()">
<SELECT NAME="food">
<OPTION VALUE="B1">Garlic Bread
<OPTION VALUE="S1">Garlic Soup
<OPTION VALUE="M1">Garlic Muesli
</SELECT>
</FORM></BODY><HTML>
```

Remove or Gray Out a menu item

Removing items from a menu is easy. To remove the last item in the example above:

```
document.cafe.food.options.length--;
```

To remove an intermediate item, all the items can be moved up to fill the gap, or the item can be blanked out. From within JavaScript:

```
document.cafe.food.options[1] = new Options('XX', '         ');
```

To initialize an item with blanks from HTML is trickier. The browser will collapse sequences of spaces into a single space. This is fine if other menu items have non-space strings. However, if all the menu items are formed from spaces, the menu will be only one character wide. An alternative is to fill the menu item with non-breaking spaces, which aren't collapsed when HTML is read. An example in HTML:

```
<OPTION>     </OPTION>   <!—4 spaces -->
```

In JavaScript, four non-breaking spaces isn't the same as four ordinary spaces. Plain space has character code 32. Non-breaking space has character code 160, or in hexadecimal notation 'A0'. Therefore, in JavaScript, four such characters are written as '\xA0\xA0\xA0\xA0'. If a menu control is part of a submitted form, and the item picked contains non-breaking spaces, then these different values will be sent with the submission as well. Any receiving CGI program or server-side JavaScript will then have to cope.

Because the text in the select menu items isn't HTML, only limited formatting options are available. This is much the same as **alert()** boxes. There is no way to fade a menu item, indicating it is unavailable. The best you can do is remove it entirely, or give the user some simple cue like surrounding the item's text in parentheses, and use an **onChange** event handler to complain if they pick it anyway.

Add wide menu items

If you attempt to add menu items that have text wider than the widest current item, the new item will appear truncated. There are two ways around this.

First alternative: plan ahead. Allocate enough space for all possible items. This option allocates 5 spaces:

```
<OPTION VALUE="X"> Hi    </OPTION>
```

or, if the menu is built from JavaScript originally:

```
var spaces5 = new Option('Hi\xA0\xA0\xA0', 'X');// \xA0 is the   character
```

Second alternative: re-write the whole **<SELECT>** contents, changing the HTML.

Changing the number of items

You can add menu items quite simply, but the browser doesn't cope perfectly. An example:

```
with (document.cafe.food)
options[options.length] = new Option('D1', 'Garlic Ice Cream');
```

Under Windows 95, a drop down menu still appears, but that menu now has a scrollbar to accommodate extra items, rather than simply expanding in size. At least the non-drop down version looks normal. To have the menu drop down to a new length, you have to re-write the whole **<SELECT>** tag.

Multi-Record Forms

There are several approaches to displaying more than one record at once in a document. The simplest is to have a **<FORM>** container for each record, which is straightforward. However, if all the records are to be part of a single form, some other approach is necessary.

Repeating controls

A form can have multiple elements with the same name, so a simple solution is to use the same form elements repeatedly. Ten records with a street and suburb field each means ten text fields named '**street**' and ten named '**suburb**'. This may only require plain HTML. The main disadvantage is that many form elements lined up in a document can be hard on the eyes. This approach makes adding records difficult, unless extra, spare fields are supplied. When the data is submitted, a large amount of data is sent, which can exceed the limits of some CGI systems and which can take some effort to extract in the receiving program.

List Viewers

A flexible approach is to store records in a set away from the user's view and only display the 'current' record. An example:

```
<HTML><HEAD><SCRIPT>
function Horse(kind)          // constructor - add other parameters as required
{
   this.kind = kind;
}

var list = new Array(0);   // the list of records, each an object.
var current = 0;
list[current++] = new Horse("Arab");
list[current++] = new Horse("Quarterhorse");
list[current++] = new Horse("Palamino");
list[current++] = new Horse("Gelding");
list[current++] = new Horse("Shetland Pony");
list[current++] = new Horse("Hack");
list[current++] = new Horse("Mule");

function next(form)
{
   if ( current + 1 < list.length )
     form.kind.value = list[++current].kind;
   else
     form.kind.value = '';
}
function previous(form)
{
   if ( current > 0 )
     form.kind.value = list[--current].kind;
}
</SCRIPT></HEAD><BODY><FORM>
<INPUT TYPE="text" NAME="kind">
<INPUT TYPE="button" VALUE="Next" ONCLICK="next(this.form);">
<INPUT TYPE="button" VALUE="Previous" ONCLICK="previous(this.form);">
</FORM>
<SCRIPT>
current=0; document.forms[0].kind.value=list[0].kind;
</SCRIPT></BODY></HTML>
```

It is easy to see how insert, delete, and update operations could work on the JavaScript '`list`' Array via user-buttons. The one visible record acts as a "letterbox slot" into the list. More than one row at a time could be displayed using this approach. In order to submit anything, arrangements similar to the shopping cart example would have to be made.

Selectable HTML

HTML form controls don't provide very flexible layout options. If visual display is an issue, it may be better to render the records in boilerplate HTML, with only minimal form controls. This example reuses the data of the previous example:

```
// ... 'list' initialisation ..
</SCRIPT></HEAD><BODY><FORM><TABLE BORDER=1>
<SCRIPT>
var i;
for (i=0; i < list.length; i++)
{
document.write('<TR><TD><INPUT TYPE="radio" NAME="horse" VALUE="'+i+'">');
document.write('<TD>'+list[i].kind+'<TD>Other horsing around ...<TR>\n');
```

```
}
</SCRIPT></TABLE></FORM></BODY></HTML>
```

This example looks better but lacks any editable fields. Any record can be selected by checking its radio button. The value of the radio button contains enough information to identify the record—seed data again. In this case, the seed is the index of the '`list`' array. If that array didn't exist, perhaps because the page was the output of some search query, the seed data is sufficient to use as a query used to display the record in an editable form.

<Textarea>

Textarea tags provide a form control for multi-line input, which sounds perfect for multiple records. Their only obvious restriction is that their content must be plain text only, which is rather primitive.

For display only of multi-record data, you may find textareas of basic use. There are two traps. The first is that Windows and Unix differ over the end-of-line character, one requiring '\r\n', the other just '\n'. Fortunately the '\r\n' combination works in both places, so use that. A portable example displaying 3 lines:

```
<TEXTAREA ONCHANGE="this.value='ten\r\ngreen\r\nbottles';">
No bottles yet
</TEXTAREA>
```

Unfortunately, the Macintosh requires just '\r'. If you want portability on all three platforms, you will have to avoid literal characters altogether. Instead, test the operating system using one of the compatibility techniques in Chapter 2, set a variable to the correct characters, and use that variable instead.

The second trap is the autowrap feature of the textarea. If a line extends past the physical width of the textarea, and the **COLS** attribute is set to a value, then the line will be broken unpredictably into two, spoiling the display.

If the user can change the textarea's contents, the situation is much worse. Textareas were designed for plain text, not formatted information. Their word-wrapping behavior formats plain text nicely, but makes data entry of line-oriented information very difficult. You can't stop the user adding additional lines beyond the value of the **ROWS** attribute, and if the **COLS** attribute is set you can't stop the user from entering a long line that gets word wrapped, and that is then indistinguishable from two separate, smaller lines.

With careful processing of the textarea's value, you can reformat user input, but really this is so limited, it is not recommended. Desperate tactics: use a 4.0 browser and capture each keystroke the user makes over the textarea control and insert it into the textarea's value yourself from the scripting side.

Validation

Using JavaScript to check user-entered data in a browser gives the user better feedback. It also makes the program (CGI or otherwise) that has to consume the submitted data easier to write if it can assume the data is legal values.

Validation models

When to check the data the user enters is a design issue for validation. The options are form level validation, field level validation and key level validation.

Form level validation is the easiest. When the user attempts to submit the data, use an **onSubmit** or **onClick** event handler, check the user's work and reject the submission with an **alert()** pop-up if there are problems. If two fields depend on each other and the user picks a bad combination, a form level check can be too delayed for the user.

Field level validation isn't any harder, except more handlers are required. When the user leaves a field, or changes its state, the handler fires and an alert occurs if there is a problem. Unless the handlers are carefully organized to prevent the user from moving on when an error has occurred, a form-level re-check is required as well. This careful organization is very time consuming if portability and backwards-compatibility are issues because of the complexities of event models, discussed earlier.

Key level validation is an attempt to stop users from typing forbidden things at all. Trying to guarantee only uppercase alphabetic letters in a text field is an example. An event captures each keystroke and allows it or ignores it. This degree of control has little to recommend it for forms, unless you are trying to implement your own keyboard shortcuts. It has its uses in Dynamic HTML, discussed elsewhere. This book advocates form-level validation, with additional field level checks whenever special cases arise. A simple example showing a mixture of the two is as follows:

```
<HTML><HEAD><SCRIPT>
function validate()
{
  with ( window.document.forms[0] )
  {
    if (    country.value.length != 2
    || !parseInt(postal.value,10)
    || parseInt(postal.value,10) < 0
    )
      {
        alert("Evidently you're lost.");
        return false;
      }
  }
  return true;
}
</SCRIPT></HEAD>
<BODY><FORM ONSUBMIT="validate()">
<H3> Where are you? </H3>
<BR>Enter your two letter country code:
<INPUT TYPE="text" NAME="country"
ONCHANGE="this.value=this.value.toLowerCase()">
<BR>Enter your postal code:
<INPUT TYPE="text" NAME="postal">
<BR><INPUT TYPE="submit">
</FORM></BODY></HTML>
```

This example does most validation in the **<FORM>** event handler. A minor correction is applied in the first **<INPUT>** tag to provide the user with some quick and harmless feedback for that particular tag.

Regular Expressions

Netscape 4.0 browsers and Internet Explorer 4.0 support regular expressions. These make some validation tasks extremely simple, and are worth using if you can always rely on these browsers.

A regular expression is like a JavaScript string that must follow a specific format. Regular expressions use this format to describe another string format. When a normal string is examined with a regular expression, a conclusion is drawn about whether, or how, that normal string matches the format of the regular expression. So regular expressions are an analysis tool for strings—very handy for user input.

Regular expressions can appear in two places: new **String** object methods, and the **RegExp** object. See the Reference Section for all the method names. The critical detail for validation is that the **match(regexp)** method of a **String** object returns **true** if the string is in the format dictated by the **regexp** regular expression, otherwise **false**.

These regular expressions are delimited by **/** characters instead of ' or " quotes in JavaScript source. The **RegExp** object is only used if a regular expression is stored in a string rather then embedded literally in the script source. In that case, the **RegExp** object acts like a little engine that converts and manages the string-embedded regular expression. This second case is an uncommon use of regular expressions.

A typical example:

```
var str = "Eany Meany Miny Mo";
var bool = null;
bool = str.match(/Meany/);      // true-contains 'Meany'
bool = str.match(/^E/);         // true-starts with 'E'
bool = str.match(/[Nn][^yY]/);  // false-all n's and N's have a trailing y or Y
```

Regular expressions can be quite complex. Their syntax is copied exactly from the same feature in the Perl language. The Reference Section describes the JavaScript functions that support regular expressions.

For the really gory details on regular expressions, visit this Perl URL: **ftp://ftp.netinfo.com.au/pub/perl/CPAN/doc/manual/html/pod/ perlre.html**. Perl documentation on the Web may automatically relocate you to an identical document at a closer site, so don't be too surprised if you end up somewhere else.

Numbers

Text, textarea and password form controls accept strings, not numbers. If the form demands a number from the user, it needs to be converted. Here is the worst thing to do:

```
Seats: <INPUT TYPE=TEXT ONCHANGE="if (!(this.value-0)) alert('Number
required');">
```

This example relies on automatic type conversion from a **String** to a **Number** to check the user's response. Apart from the fact that it will fail if the user types 0 (zero), the interpreter will fail entirely if the user types 'se#$a%jjz' or any other rubbish—of course, users are all geniuses and never do things like this.

A better solution is to use two built-in JavaScript functions: **parseInt()** and **parseFloat()**. Both take **Strings** and attempt to read **Numbers** from them, either an integer, or a floating point number. This can be somewhat successful, especially **parseInt()** which can read numbers in bases other than 10 if needed. These functions are unusual in that they are not part of any obvious JavaScript object. Examples:

```
var num1 = parseInt('23', 10);      // decimal
var num2 = parseInt('1AB2', 16);    // hexadecimal
var num3 = parseFloat('garbage');   // returns NaN
var num4 = parseFloat('123.45');
```

Unfortunately, these functions have two failings. First, they return **NaN** if the conversion fails, which is fine except that old browsers like Navigator 2.02 and Explorer 3.02 with JScript 1.0 can't cope with **NaN** or return **0** instead, leaving you to wonder what really happened. Secondly, both functions stop trying to read the string as soon as a number is successfully read. This example doesn't fail:

```
var num5 = parseFloat('3.1415926junk');      // num5 = Math.PI (roughly).
```

More irritatingly, neither does this:

```
var num6 = parseFloat('11.22.33');                    // num6 = 11.22
```

There are two alternatives: accept the first thing typed and discard the rest, or examine the user data thoroughly. The latter case means writing your own versions of **parseInt()** and **parseFloat()** that return **NaN** even if there is training garbage—for **parseFloat()** that is about 70 lines of JavaScript if thorough checking is done. Accepting the first thing typed works like this:

```
<SCRIPT>
function check_num(obj)
{
if (!parseInt(obj.value)) alert("Number required");
else                      obj.value = '' + parseInt(obj.value);
}
</SCRIPT>
<INPUT TYPE="text" ONCHANGE="check_num(this)">
```

With **parseInt()**, the second argument is critical. It says what mathematical base to interpret the number in. Humans use base 10, the digits zero to nine. Without it, the interpreter will 'do its best' with the first argument and might conclude it is any of octal, decimal or hexadecimal. If dumb users add leading zeros, '033' will be read as 27, because it looks like an octal number. Always specify the base.

These Netscape 4.0 regular expressions will pass or fail a string as an integer and as a floating point number, including leading and trailing spaces, but won't tell you if they are effectively Infinity or not:

```
str.match(/^[ ]*[+-]?\d+[ ]*$/);                          //integer
str.match(/^[ ]*[+-]?\d*\.?\d*([eE][+-]?\d+)?[ ]*$/);//floating point
```

Validation Masks

Masks are similar to regular expressions, but less complex and easier to support across all browsers. The idea is that a format dictates allowable values for a field. Users of report creation tools and spreadsheets will be familiar with format masks—validation masks are a similar thing, but for input, not for output.

The simplest example is entering a monetary amount. This could be handled as a number, but dumb users might add '$', ',', '.' or even 'Y' symbols (damn, where's that pound sign on my keyboard). A mask can solve this by only accepting specific characters.

```
<SCRIPT>
function check_mask(value,mask)
{
int i;
if ( value.length != mask.length ) return false;
for (i=0; i<mask.length; i++)
    {
if ( mask.charAt(i) == '#' )                      // digit required
    {
if ( !parseInt(value.charAt(i)) ) return false;
    }
else                                              // exact match required
    {
if ( mask.charAt(i) != value.charAt(i) ) return false;
    }
    }
return true;
}
</SCRIPT>
<INPUT TYPE="text" ONCHANGE="check_mask('$##.##',this.value)||alert('Bad
value');">
<INPUT TYPE="text" ONCHANGE="check_mask('$####.##',this.value)||alert('Bad
value');">
```

In this example, the **check_mask()** function has a simple matching criteria: strings to check fail unless they exactly match the mask, except for certain character positions that may be any digit. The first input field can accept values from '$00.00' to '$99.99', the second from '$0000.00' to '$9999.99'.

Regular expressions to do the same job would be:

```
str.match(/^\$\d{2}\.\d{2}$/);     // $##.##
str.match(/^\$\d{4}\.\d{2}$/);     // $####.##
```

Domains, Lookups and Picklists

Another way to constrain a field's value is with a **domain**. A domain is just a set of allowable values for a variable or field. Some such sets can't be fully listed, such as every instant in the day. Others can, like the set of months of the year.

Where the set can be listed, a lookup is a function that checks a value against that set. A picklist displays the members of a domain as a guide for the user to choose from.

```
<SCRIPT LANGUAGE="JavaScript1.1">
// times of the day
function is_time_domain(value)
{
var num = parseFloat(value);
return ( !isNaN(num) && !isInfinity(num) && num >=0 && num <2400 );
}

// months of the year;
var months = new Array('Jan','Feb','Mar','Apr','May','Jun',
'Jul','Aug','Sep','Oct','Nov','Dec');
function check_domain(domain, value)
{
if ( domain == 'TIME' )    return is_time_domain(value);
if ( domain == 'MONTHS' )  return months.[value] && true;
}
</SCRIPT>
<INPUT TYPE="text" ONCHANGE="check_domain("TIME",this.value) || alert('Re-
do');">
<INPUT TYPE="text" ONCHANGE="check_domain("MONTHS",this.value) || alert('Re-
do');">
```

The most common form of a picklist is a simple menu using a **<SELECT>** tag. If the set of valid values in the domain are highly dynamic, e.g. available taxis in a taxi fleet, then the picklist is only as up-to-date as the time when the document was last loaded. If this isn't recent enough, a picklist can be created using **window.open()** to create a small scrollable window of values. This window is then the picklist. When a value is chosen, the window updates the field in the original document via a handler. Such a small window can load a fresh URL every time it is opened, and therefore is always up to date.

Server Checks

If all else fails, the data in a form can be submitted to the Web server for validation by server side JavaScript or a CGI program. The only costs are in development time and performance, and of course, you must have development access to the Web server environment.

Avoiding CGI development

If you don't want to write CGI programs or server-side JavaScript, or you can't because you don't have development access to the Web server where your pages are stored, there are a few alternatives.

Using e-mail

A form can send its data to an e-mail address via a '**mailto:**' URL instead of a 'http:' URL. To do this, just use **<FORM ACTION=mailto:fred@obscure.com ENCTYPE="text/plain">**. This feature isn't supported in Internet Explorer 3.0 or in the version of Netscape Navigator 4.0 that is separate to the Communicator suite. There is no way to send e-mail without the user being warned, except for these possibilities: use of a signed script, or if the user has turned off email warnings in the browser preferences. Of course, the Web browser must have access to an e-mail service to start with.

Using cookies

A form's contents, or any data, can be packed into a cookie (see Chapter 6 for how) and stored with the user's browser. Each time the user visits the web page containing JavaScript, that JavaScript can examine the cookie and be reminded of what the user entered. This is limited in some respects—if the user uses a different browser, or removes the file containing their cookies, the data is lost. Cookies stay with the browser that received them, so they are not generally portable once saved.

Using custom packages

There are numerous commercial and free packages available on the Internet which are pre-build CGI programs. Web Site administrators are more likely to allow installation of well-known packages than your one-off custom program. A simple example is a clock image that displays the time. Here is a bit of HTML that uses such a tool and the image that results:

```
<img src="/cgi-bin/clock.exe?format=secs">
```

 In order to get this clock to update, image swapping techniques explained in Chapter 4— 'Multimedia and Plug-ins' need to be employed.

This particular example comes from the free utility available at `http://www.geocities.com/SiliconValley/6742/`

CGI

Whole books can (and have) been written about CGI programs and their interaction with forms. There isn't room in this book for a detailed examination of CGI issues, but CGI is so closely related to HTML forms, that the mechanics need some explanation

What has CGI to do with JavaScript? To understand how to script inline JavaScript in a browser, first understand what a browser is—obvious. To understand how client-side JavaScript acts when forms are submitted, understand how CGI submissions affect documents. To understand how to script standalone JavaScript programs that benefit a website, understand what CGI itself is.

For a detailed discussion of the CGI standard, see `http://hoohoo.ncsa.uiuc.edu/cgi/`

What is it?

CGI is a specification that applies to Web server software. CGI stands for **Common Gateway Interface**. Its goal is to provide a mechanism for URL requests that can't be handled internally by the server itself. There is no requirement that a Web server implements the CGI specification, but it is so useful, few Web servers do without it.

A Web server responds to a request from a browser user by using the user-supplied URL to locate some data. This data is then sent back to the browser. In the ordinary case this is done by finding and opening a file, reading its contents and sending that content. An HTML file is a typical example. CGI provides an alternative. Instead of finding and opening a file, the Web server finds and runs a program. The output of the program is the content that is send back to the user. The program that was executed then ends.

The CGI specification describes what information is transferred between the Web server and the CGI program, and how this should be done. Because operating systems like Windows 95 and Unix vary, the approach used to implement CGI can be slightly different, but the three main types of transferred information remain the same:

 administrative data about the URL request passed to the CGI program

 form (and cookie) data from the browser passed to the CGI program

 new (usually HTML) document passed from the CGI program back to the Web server

Because CGI programs are separate programs they can be written in any language. The content that makes up such a program is never revealed to the browser user. It is only such a program's output that ultimately reaches the user. Chapter 2 shows a very simple CGI program written in JavaScript, in the 'standalone JavaScript' section.

GET versus POST for form data

There are two methods of submitting form data to a Web server: **GET** and **POST**. The **GET** method attaches the form data to the end of the URL in the submit request, separated by a '**?**' character from the rest of the URL. The **POST** request sends the form data as a separate, but attached message in the submit request. Both methods use a special code for the data so that it isn't confused with other parts of the submit request.

The two methods have different strengths.

Since **GET** attaches the form data to the URL, the request can be 'remembered' as a bookmark. The browser user can view it. However, URLs have a maximum length, so **GET** is no good for forms with lots of data. **GET** is intended to be used where the form submission doesn't change the web site it's sent to at all. Search engine requests are a classic example.

POST form data is attached separate to the URL and can be any size, so it is reliable for all forms. The user can't see the **POST**ed data, which might be a blessing. However, **POST** requests don't have unique URLs like **GET**. Very, very, big **POST** requests can create problems for little Web servers with only simple CGI support. **POST** requests are meant to be used where the form submission changes or stores something on the web site. Registration forms are a classic example.

In the administrative data passed to a CGI program is a variable called **REQUEST_METHOD**. The CGI program can use this variable to tell which way form data was posted. For many CGI programming tools, this is detected automatically so there's no need for the CGI programmer to do much. No restriction prevents a CGI programmer from ignoring the general intent of the **GET** and **POST** methods.

JavaScript, Forms and CGI combined

When a browser displays a document containing a form, the ultimate behavior desired is that the user can carry out these steps:

- fill in the form
- submit the form
- have the submitted data handled automatically and invisibly
- be returned to the form, or see some feedback saying the submit worked

A number of concepts have to be drawn together to achieve this:

- The **<FORM>** tag specifies a URL to submit the form data to (the **ACTION** attribute)
- The **<FORM>** tag specifies a window to display the 'submit' response in (the **TARGET** attribute)
- An HTML form can originate from a CGI program's URL rather than from a plain URL

Suppose a currently displayed HTML form generated from a CGI URL submits to that same URL (the default action) and displays the results of the submission in the current window (the default target). Then with one CGI program and its URL all the above behavior is achieved. When the HTML form is first called up, it is generated from the CGI URL. When it is submitted, the submit data goes back to the CGI URL, which generates and returns the HTML form again. Presumably the CGI program also does something with the data submitted.

The important point is that the CGI program is called two ways: once just as a document generator, and once as both a form submission handler and as a document generator.

This is the standard way CGI is used with web browsers. As the next few sections show, there are several ways of varying the submission process.

Managing submits

The generated HTML form might contain inline JavaScript. If the regenerated document replaces the existing one after a submit, then all the JavaScript variables and objects in the document are lost. If this data is precious, actions and targets must be organized so that it isn't wiped out. The 'shopping cart' and 'secret server checks' examples earlier in this chapter organize matters carefully for this reason.

Netscape browsers preserve the data in an HTML form after a submit occurs, in case the replacement form is the same one. If so, the data is put back again. This does not happen for JavaScript variables. Internet Explorer 3.0 doesn't have this behavior—you always lose your form data when the form is replaced after a submit. This can be worked around. Suppose this document is generated from a CGI program:

```
<HTML><BODY><FORM>
<INPUT NAME="lonely" TYPE="text" VALUE="I'm here!">
</FORM></BODY></HTML>
```

The 'lonely' field will always be filled. A CGI program could read the old value of the field on submit, and put it back in the generated document. Here is such a CGI program, written in ScriptEase 4.0 standalone JavaScript:

```
var lonely_field = CGIGetVar("lonely");

if ( ! lonely_field ) lonely_field = '';  // program called without submit data

CGIOut('<HTML><BODY><FORM>\n');                    // regenerate the HTML
CGIOut('<INPUT NAME="lonely" TYPE="text" VALUE="');
CGIOut(lonely_field);                              // field is reset here
CGIOut('">\n"');
CGIOut('</FORM></BODY></HTML>\n');
}
```

Each time the CGI program is run, the VALUE attribute of the text field changes to any value submitted.

Otherwise, the simplest way to avoid wiping out data is to choose a target window away from the submission window, if the user requires no feedback. The next simplest is to avoid submitting from the form in question entirely, as described next.

Hand-made submits

Both **GET** and **POST** style requests can be made from an HTML document that has no form, using JavaScript.

For **POST** requests, the only way to achieve this is to create or use an HTML form in another document. The 'shopping cart' example above does this. Whatever data is required is copied into that form. Typically, that form is in a frame of zero height or width so that it doesn't show. This also allows the user to continue interacting with the main document while the submission is underway.

152

For **GET** requests, the URL containing the form data can be constructed by hand without any HTML, but it still requires a (possibly hidden) window to be loaded into. Use **window.location.href** or **document.replace()** to apply the new URL. The format of the URL is:

```
http://host/path?name1=value1&name2=value2&name3=value3...
```

Where **name1**, **name2**, **name3** are HTML 'name' attribute values for fields, and **value1**, **value2**, **value3** are the field values. If two form elements have the same name, there should be two **name=value** pairs.

That alone, however is not enough. URL syntax demands that the URL follow encoding rules so that no special or dangerous characters appear. JavaScript provides the life-saving **escape()** function to do just this, and **unescape()** to change back, if necessary:

```
var my_url = 'http://search.yahoo.com/bin/search?p=help me please!';
var fixed_url=escape(my_url);
```

The 'fixed' version looks like this:
http://search.yahoo.com/bin/search?p=help+me+please%21

Reporting CGI errors

CGI programs might not always be successful. If the program fails for any reason (data corruption, lack of resources or a bug, typically), the browser will report a fatal error to the user. In this case all you can do is fix the originating problem. A less serious case is where the CGI program detects something has gone wrong, and can't complete normal processing. An example is the case when submitted data can't be stored in a database due to clashing data.

When the error is not a fatal one, you can either display a special error page, or redisplay the current page with an error message. The next two examples show both methods. The example checks the entered name to see if it is boring, and if so, reports an error.

Separate page for error:

```
function show_html()
{
  CGIOut('<HTML><BODY><FORM>\n');
  CGIOut('Enter surname ...');
  CGIOut('<INPUT TYPE="text" NAME="surname">');
  CGIOut('<INPUT TYPE="submit">');
  CGIOut('</FORM></BODY></HTML>');
}

var surname = CGIGetVar("surname");
if ( ! surname )                          // called without 'submit'
  show_html()
else
{
  if (    surname.toUpperCase() == 'SMITH'
       || surname.toUpperCase() == 'WONG'
       || surname.toUpperCase() == 'SINGH'
       || surname.toUpperCase() == 'TRAN'
     )
```

```
            CGIOut('<HTML><BODY>Warning! Boring name alert!</BODY></HTML>');
      else
        show_html();
}
```

Same page always displayed, plus optional error:

```
function show_html(err_text)
{
  CGIOut('<HTML><HEAD><SCRIPT>');

  if ( err_text )
    CGIOut('var error_string = "'+err_text+'";\n');
  else
    CGIOut('var error_string = null;\n');

  CGIOut('if (error_string) alert(error_string);\n');

  CGIOut('</SCRIPT></HEAD><BODY><FORM>\n');
  CGIOut('Enter surname ...');
  CGIOut('<INPUT TYPE="text" NAME="surname">');
  CGIOut('<INPUT TYPE="submit">');
  CGIOut('</FORM></BODY></HTML>');
}

var surname = CGIGetVar("surname");

if ( !surname )
  show_html();                  // called separate to 'submit'
else
{
  if (   surname.toUpperCase() == 'SMITH'
      || surname.toUpperCase() == 'WONG'
      || surname.toUpperCase() == 'SINGH'
      || surname.toUpperCase() == 'TRAN'
  )
     show_html('Warning! Boring Name.');
  else
     show_html();
}
```

The variable '**error_string**' only appears in the browser. The variable '**err_text**' only appears in the CGI program. The browser always checks the variable '**error_string**' via inline JavaScript when loading the HTML, to see if anything went wrong.

Special CGI behaviour

The 'submit' mechanism of HTML forms is just a part of the HTTP protocol that underlies all the communication between browsers and Web servers. If you are creating a CGI program, the opportunity exists to fiddle with this communication in a number of ways. You might consider *Wrox's Beginning Linux Programming* for more detail on these CGI techniques:

 No-Parsed-Headers. The HTML output of the CGI program can be sent smoothly and directly to the browser without interference by the Web server if this feature is used. It allows a CGI program to output all the response to a URL request, not just the content of the response.

Server-push. A CGI program can send a document repeatedly to the browser, like a film that flicks forward frame-by-frame very slowly. Each document can be different. This technique is quite limited since proxy servers between the user and the CGI program don't generally support this feature.

No Content. A CGI program can specify that there is no new content to display. This will preserve the document in the browser that sent the submit request, instead of overwriting it with a new document.

Cache control. A CGI program can specify if the document sent should be cached by the browser, and if so, for how long. If 'do not ever cache' is chosen, then the script writer can be confident that the CGI program will always be invoked to regenerate the HTML document, instead of missing out because the browser's cache is at work.

There is no way to do a **POST** or **GET** submit-style operation from a CGI program to the browser. To do something like that, see the cookies section in Chapter 6.

Summary

HTML forms are quite primitive in some respects, merely passing the user's data to some third party with no other processing. Client-side JavaScript can enhance HTML forms so that many features present in specialized form-handling software packages are available in the browser. Validation of user data is a primary example. Because the browser environment isn't optimized for complex data management tasks, attempting these tasks with JavaScript is most successful if the design is kept simple.

HTML forms must send their data somewhere, and CGI programs are a common destination. Although only touched on in this book, server-side JavaScript provides an alternative to CGI. The mechanisms are slightly different, but the patterns of interaction between browser and Web server are the same.

CGI programs can be written in standalone JavaScript, or a variety of other computer languages. Using the same language in the browser and in CGI reduces confusion a great deal. The interaction between browsers, Web servers and CGI programs can be non-trivial, and these elements need to be integrated properly before the desired effect is achieved. Once integrated, processing tasks are shared between the browser (in client-side JavaScript) and the CGI program.

Privacy, Security and Cookies

JavaScript scripts used on the Internet expose a number of risks. Allowing any arbitrary script, written by a possibly anonymous scriptwriter, to do something unknown to a trusting person's computer is a risk for that trusting person. On the other hand, to allow an anonymous person to obtain a script that is someone else's property presents a risk to the script writer.. There are numerous mechanisms available that can address these safety issues.

What your script does to your property is your own concern. It's when your property and scripts are mingled with other people's property and scripts that risks arise and people are likely to become annoyed, upset or even litigious. Privacy matters set the boundaries of what shouldn't or can't be shared. Security matters set the boundaries of good behavior when there is a need to share. **Security hobbles** prevent scripts from crossing either kind of boundary without appropriate permission.

Privacy

One person's treasured privacy is another person's jail cell. Security hobbles that grant privacy to one participant in a shared system take functionality away from someone else. The three main players in such shared systems are browser users, script writers and webmasters.

If a security system is in place, then browser security hobbles are not generally enforced. So privacy issues only really apply in an unsecured environment, such as ordinary use of the World Wide Web.

Privacy for Browser Users

For users of JavaScript enabled browsers, requesting a URL represents a risk if it contains JavaScript. Without security hobbles, JavaScript could seize control of the browser, or possibly the browser's computer. The simplest form of privacy for the user is to turn JavaScript support off in the browser via the browser preferences. This can't be done from within a JavaScript script, except via the **navigator.preference** property in Netscape Navigator 4.0, and even then the browser must be shut down and re-started for it to take effect.

A number of JavaScript bugs that create security risks have been identified in version 3.0 and 4.0 browsers. To avoid as many of these as possible, make sure you have the latest version of the browser available. For example, at this time of writing Netscape Navigator 4.04 is the latest, not 4.02 or 4.01. This Web page: `http://www-genome.wi.mit.edu/WWW/faqs/wwwsf?/html` is a good starting point for JavaScript security bug information.

There are several kinds of security hobbles that protect the browser user's privacy.

I/O restrictions

It is nearly always true that client-side JavaScript is restrained from doing any input or output without the user's permission. Generally, the user can be confident that no changes are occurring to the local computer outside of the browser, but there are exceptions. Writing to files, to network connections and to the display are the main sources of risk. Of these, display-related restrictions are discussed further on. The file and network cases are generally impossible, except for the following possibilities.

Local scripts

If a browser loads a script directly from the local computer without using a web server, then that script can do anything the language and host objects allow. The user may get a warning and an option to back out, depending on how the browser's security preferences are set up. Internet Explorer 3.0 with JScript 2.0 (and later versions) allows script writers to read, write and create any file on the browser's computer using JavaScript facilities directly. This is achieved with the JavaScript **FileSystemObject** and **TextStream objects**.

JScript 3.0 adds the **File** and **Folder** objects which allow local files to be removed or renamed, as well as created or changed. This is only possible for Internet Explorer 4.0, however, and browser security options must be lowered by the user as well.

Netscape JavaScript can also write to local files, but there is no direct support in the language. Instead, Java objects supply this functionality—objects which must be accessed via LiveConnect. Here is an example of writing a user-supplied string to a user-supplied filename. See Chapter 8 for further information about the mechanics at work here:

```
<HTML><BODY><SCRIPT>
function save_it(filename, filedata);
{
    netscape.security.PrivilegeManager.enablePrivilege("UniversalFileWrite");
    var jo_file   = new java.io.FileOutputStream(filename);
    var jo_stream = new java.io.DataOutputStream(jo_file);
    jo_stream.writeChars(filedata);
    jo_stream.close();
    netscape.security.PrivilegeManager.disablePrivilege("UniversalFileWrite");
}
</SCRIPT>
<FORM>
File Name: <INPUT TYPE="text" NAME="file"><BR>
File Data: <INPUT TYPE="text" NAME="data"
                  ONCHANGE="save_it(this.form.file.value, this.value)">
</FORM></BODY></HTML>
```

This example also requires some agreement from the user before it can go ahead. See the Security section.

Java connections

A browser that supports Java applets can make network connections. With ActiveX or LiveConnect, JavaScript scripts can control these applet connections. Chapter 8 describes how.

However, without a security agreement, the connections are limited. Java applets are downloaded via a URL in an **<APPLET>** or **<OBJECT>** HTML tag. Only the computer supplying the page for that URL can be connected to. If the tag includes a **CODEBASE** URL, then the computer at that codebase URL is the only possibility for connections.

A more subtle possibility stems from the fact that one Java applet may converse directly with another. However, the part of the Java system that loads applets also ensures that applets from different sites can't communicate. This prevents one applet from exploiting the network connections available to another.

Cookies

Cookies are described in a later section of this chapter. The cookie data available to web servers doesn't include any very private information such as the user's name, so risk from cookies is minimal. Long-lived cookies are stored in a file on the browser's computer. However, this file is a plain data file with a maximum size of approximately 1200 Kilobytes for Netscape. Other than taking up space, this file doesn't do anything outside the browser environment. A cookie file will normally be only one or two Kilobytes.

Netscape Mission Control

The **netscape.cfg** file of Netscape 4.0 browsers can be configured to give away control of the user's preferences. A JavaScript script stored elsewhere under someone else's control assumes the task. In a company environment, this usually poses no privacy risks.

Window limitations

The main form of output from client-side JavaScript is not to files and network connections, but to the browser itself. JavaScript can affect windows in a browser in three ways:

- Write new content to browser windows.
- Change window decorations such as toolbars and menus.
- Modify JavaScript host objects and variables within windows.

The user can have more than one browser window open at a time. The user can also have more than one URL per window if frames are present, and those URLs can come from different web sites.

If it were not for a number of security hobbles, JavaScript could use its control over windows to:

 Forge or manipulate content displayed from other web sites, therefore, misrepresenting it.

 Make the browser uncontrollable by the user.

 Wreck the JavaScript data and objects stored in windows displaying other web sites.

Two concepts are central to the window security features that prevent these things from happening.

Every Window is an Island

To understand window security restrictions, first take a step back and reflect on the ECMAScript standard.

In ECMAScript terminology, an 'execution environment' is a stage on which scripts can perform (execute), whether they are standalone or client-side scripts. When an execution environment is created, such as in a browser, a good question is: what is the current object? The standard states that all built-in objects and built-in functions in a script are part of a special 'global' object; the current scope when that script starts executing. Even functions like **parseInt()** can, therefore, be viewed as a method of an object.

However, there is not just one 'global' object in a JavaScript-capable web browser. Instead, the browser has a 'global' object for each browser window currently open. These global objects each have a property **'window'** which refers back to that global object. These window properties provide a named hook so that the script writer can get access to that global object.

Each global object is like a bucket in which all the data specific to the window can be stored, making it easy to access. Therefore, the **'window'** property sits at the top of a hierarchy (or a pool) of data that includes all the JavaScript variables, objects and host objects in that window. If the window is closed, everything owned directly or indirectly by the global object is tracked down and cleaned up.

This makes each window fully self-contained and independent. It makes it easy to keep scripts from interfering with other windows, since they can only ultimately belong to one global object. Viewed from the JavaScript perspective, the browser is not a single hierarchy or pool of properties and objects, it is a number of them.

Unfortunately, life is rarely that simple. In reality, one window will often contain JavaScript variables that refer to objects or properties in other windows. A simple example is the **window.open()** method—the return value can be stored in a variable in the containing window but refers to the global object in the newly created window. Similarly, the newly created window's global object has an **'opener'** property referring back to the old window.

At the time of writing this, the ECMAScript standard doesn't specify how the communicating-between-globals system works. The answer for browsers is LiveConnect or ActiveX glue software. This glue is effectively invisible except when window ownership issues are important. The owner of a window is the host address of the window's main URL, for example **'www.this.com:80'**. Attempts to work with properties or methods in a different window first have to pass checks based on the owners of the two windows. This script can be used to show the dynamic behavior involved:

```
<HTML><BODY><SCRIPT>
var win2 = null;

function open_local() { top.win2=window.open(window.location.href,'test'); }

function open_remote() { top.win2=window.open('http://www.wrox.com','test'); }

function show_it()
{
   window.document.forms[0].one.value = top.win2;
   window.document.forms[0].two.value = top.win2.name;
   window.document.forms[0].three.value = top.win2.location.href;
}
</SCRIPT><FORM>
<INPUT TYPE="button" VALUE="Open local window" ONCLICK="open_local()">
<INPUT TYPE="button" VALUE="Open remote window" ONCLICK="open_remote()">
<INPUT TYPE="button" VALUE="Show window details" ONCLICK="show_it()">
<INPUT TYPE="button" VALUE="Go backwards" ONCLICK="window.history.go(-1)">
<BR>
Type of win2: <INPUT NAME="one" TYPE="text"><BR>
Name of win2: <INPUT NAME="two" TYPE="text"><BR>
URL  of win2: <INPUT NAME="three" TYPE="text"><BR>
</FORM></BODY></HTML>
```

When displayed, the document looks like this:

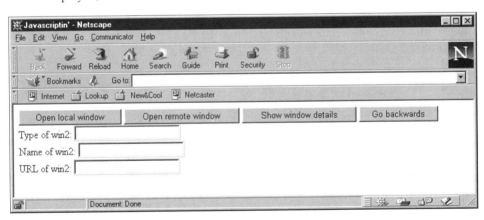

This HTML page has three purposes:

- Create a second window with a URL that is either at the same web site as the main window, or at a different one.

- Display some state information about the second window.

- Provide content for the second window when the URL for that window is at the same web site.

161

The 'Show window details' button is used to report the current state of the auto-created window.

The following discussion pertains to Netscape behavior. Before pressing either of the open buttons, reporting the current state produces an error because the second window is not open and therefore **'win2'** is not yet an object. If a local window is opened, the name and URL will display correctly. If a remote window is opened, then an error results trying to get its URL (assuming you don't own the Wrox Web site). If you navigate with that new window back to a local web page, either via the 'Open local window' button or directly using the window toolbars, the URL is accessible again.

When the window is off-limits, Netscape's error is:

"Access disallowed from scripts at **http://mysite/tests/remote_test.htm** to documents in another domain".

This message assumes that the **mysite** site is where you are doing the testing.

If the second window is closed, a number of obscure errors can occur, depending on the version and whether Java is enabled or not. It is better not to examine a closed window object, except to test if the window IS closed by looking at the boolean value **window.closed**.

If this script is run with Internet Explorer 3.0 and JScript 1.0, none of the second window's properties are accessible, including **window.closed**. This shows that JavaScript inter-window access is not a requirement for all browser tasks.

Every Window is Free

Without security arrangements granting the script writer special privileges, some browser features can't be removed from the user's control. These are:

- Existing windows can't have toolbars or other window decorations removed or added.

- Documents from other sites loaded into frames can't have their events stolen by the frameset.

- Windows can't be created so small that the user can't read the contents.

- Windows can't permanently obscure other windows, or grab the user's input focus and keep it.

The Reference Section describes which methods require special privileges before they can be used. In particular, 'canvas' or 'kiosk' mode, in which a single window takes over the whole screen and requires special privileges for Netscape 4.0 browsers. For these browsers, the user can drop the above restrictions on scripts by changing their browser preferences—as described in the 'Privacy For Scriptwriters' section.

Resource limiting features

Browsers are designed to limit the user to a fraction of the resources of the browser's computer:

- Disk space. Pages loaded from a given web server can't consume more than 80 Kilobytes of space in a Netscape browser's cookie file—more than that can be consumed with Internet Explorer. Creating new JavaScript Image objects, or writing new HTML pages, is still subject to the caching restrictions that the browser user puts in place when setting the browser's preferences. If the user has all caching turned off, Images or pages won't be cached if they aren't part of a currently displayed window.

- Memory. Internet Explorer 4.0 allows the user to place an upper limit on the amount of memory that a newly downloaded ActiveX control can consume. Otherwise, browsers can still consume large amounts of memory. The video memory used for graphics and windows is easy for most browsers to consume, especially if there are many windows, frames and images displayed.

Such memory protection systems aren't foolproof. Even for normal memory and non-ActiveX controls, this script fragment will bring most browsers quickly to their knees (don't try this unless you're willing to re-boot):

```
<HTML><BODY><SCRIPT>
var big_string = "double me up!";

while (true)
{
    big_string = big_string + big_string;//20 iterations equals all your memory
}
</SCRIPT></BODY></HTML>
```

Memory limitations also apply to Java applets in Netscape Navigator. Sometimes these applets are 'cleaned up' to save memory, which can also impact JavaScript. See Chapter 8 for further details.

- Network Connections. JavaScript scripts might open many windows, but the maximum number of connections set by the user via preferences will still be observed. Any additional windows will have to wait for a free connection.

- CPU. Netscape browsers and Internet Explorer 4.0 will abort any JavaScript script that executes more than one million "instructions" (a vague term used by the vendors, probably meaning one JavaScript statement) before finishing. This is designed to prevent scripts from locking the user out of the browser permanently, not to prevent the browser from consuming large amounts of CPU time. This feature can be annoying if you are trying to do long, complex calculations with the interpreter. The user still has access to window menus and toolbars. There is also a workaround: break the task into steps and only run one step at a time. Here is a before and after example:

```
<HTML><BODY><SCRIPT>
var total = 234;
var new_items = 2555666;
function dumb_add()            // addition for people with only one finger
{
  while (new_items)            // won't complete: 2,555,666 iterations > 1,000,000
  {
    new_items--;
    total++;
  }
}
dumb_add();
alert('New total is: '+total);
</SCRIPT></BODY></HTML>
```

In the workaround case below, the browser will still be busy 99% of the time, but because the executing script breaks off regularly for a millisecond, the browser is satisfied that the user still has a chance to do things. The browser will, therefore, be able to respond to user input, but only slowly; especially if that input means other scripts need to run. At the same time, the long-running script will be able to eventually complete all its processing.

```
<HTML><BODY><SCRIPT>
var total = 234;
var new_items = 2555666;

function dumb_add()            // Do addition for people with only one finger
{
    var steps = 10000;        // don't run for too long
    while (new_items && steps)
    {
  steps--;
  new_items--;
  total++;
    }
    if ( new_items )
  setTimeout('dumb_add()',1);
    else
       alert('New total is: '+total);
}
dumb_add();
</SCRIPT></BODY></HTML>
```

Other risks

There are other risks for the user when using a browser on the Internet, but few of them involve JavaScript. The following, however, do:

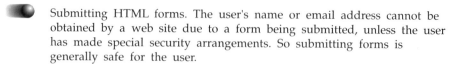 Submitting HTML forms. The user's name or email address cannot be obtained by a web site due to a form being submitted, unless the user has made special security arrangements. So submitting forms is generally safe for the user.

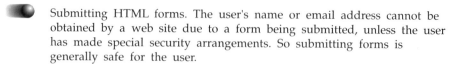 JavaScript cannot silently e-mail a user when the user browses to a web page. The user always gets the opportunity to confirm or cancel the submission.

164

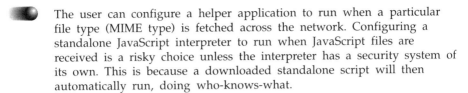

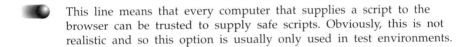

The user can configure a helper application to run when a particular file type (MIME type) is fetched across the network. Configuring a standalone JavaScript interpreter to run when JavaScript files are received is a risky choice unless the interpreter has a security system of its own. This is because a downloaded standalone script will then automatically run, doing who-knows-what.

In modern browsers the user can release all of the restrictions in the browser that require a security agreement. To do this in Internet Explorer 4.0 go to the Options dialog box and under security set the minimum security level to None. In Netscape 4.0 browsers, shutdown all of the Netscape windows and modify by hand the **prefs.js** file. That file is stored in the Netscape installation area, there is one for each browser user. Add this line and restart the browser:

```
user_pref("signed.applets.codebase_principal_support", true);
```

This line means that every computer that supplies a script to the browser can be trusted to supply safe scripts. Obviously, this is not realistic and so this option is usually only used in test environments.

Privacy for Script Writers

For script writers, the two main privacy issues are preventing scripts from being stolen, and preventing scripts from being wrecked. The task is harder for JavaScript than it is for Java or other kinds of program because the script source and the executable program are one and the same.

For standalone scripts, neither issue is a problem, unless someone else has access to your computer or your account. If those scripts are used as CGI programs behind a web server, then there is also no problem, unless the web server itself has a security problem. See the 'Privacy for Web Masters' section for an exception.

For server-side JavaScript, the scripts are stored and executed with the web server, so provided that server is secure, no web user can access them. HTML files sent to the user are stripped of any server-side JavaScript in the web server before delivery.

For client-side JavaScript, the situation is much worse. There is no way to systematically protect JavaScript code except by entering into a security arrangement with the user. There are a few partial solutions.

Hiding source code

Client-side JavaScript has virtually no protection on the Web. You might as well give up, and accept that the work you do is there to be stolen and modified as any web user sees fit. It is non-trivial (except for experts) to break-in to a web site and damage your original HTML and **.js** files, so at least that which your web server delivers to users remains in good order, even if they do something with it afterwards. If such a break-in concerns you, use a tried-and tested Unix host such as Linux for your web site and test its security with the SATAN tool:
`http://www.fish.com/satan/`.

165

Once the JavaScript is in the Web browser, there are only a few things that can be done to protect it. In particular, this code does not protect anything:

```
<HTML><HEAD>
<SCRIPT SRC="secret.js"></SCRIPT>
</HEAD></HTML>
```

The JavaScript in the file **'secret.js'** may not appear when the user chooses to 'View Source' for this document, but its URL is obvious. The user only needs to type the full URL for the file into the browser, retrieve the file, and then do 'View Source' again. Internet Explorer 4.0 scripts are the same, because they have a URL as well.

For a user on the Web who views publicly available HTML, there are few foolproof tactics for protecting or hiding client-side JavaScript. The nearest thing is to embed your JavaScript in a Java applet, using the Netscape LiveConnect features of Java. That is a lot of work for non-trivial JavaScript. See Chapter 8 for details of how to do this.

An easier but less effective tactic is to protect your scripts by making the job of copying them less palatable, rather than impossible.

Making it too much effort

For those inclined to steal your source, there are some simple barriers that will make the job harder, and encourage the culprit to give up. The most common tricks that make scripts difficult to read are:

- Put the whole HTML or JavaScript file contents on one line. Many CGI programs that produce HTML don't put line breaks into the generated HTML file. This helps keep the file as small as possible, improving download performance. You can do the same with your JavaScript **<SCRIPT>** sections. The script stealer has to create a formatting program to fix this, or do it by hand. If your JavaScript code is CGI generated, it is easy to apply a filter to the output which turns all return characters into spaces.

- Use obfuscation (confusion) techniques. It's possible, or even common, to write really unclear code that no one can understand. Since JavaScript has a syntax related to C, you might gain some inspiration by looking at the yearly "C obfuscation contest" winners: **http://reality.sgi.com/ioccc/**.

- Use a **code-shrouding** program. Such a program takes your readable JavaScript source and translates it to equivalent source, but with formatting removed and all symbolic names replaced with randomly generated names. You keep the original source, in case you need to make further changes—which are re-shrouded as needed. An example showing a function before and after shrouding:

```
// before
function calculate_interest(principal, percent_rate, yearly_calculations, term)
{
    var factor = 1 + percent_rate/yearly_calculations/100;//one lot of interest
    return principal * Math.pow(factor, yearly_calculations * term);
}
```

```
// after
function a01(a02,a03,a04,a05){var a06=1+a03/a04;return
a02*Math.pow(a06,a04*a05);}
```

The new function works the same but its meaning is now a near mystery. JMyth is one such tool for JavaScript—**http://www.geocities.com/ SiliconValley/Vista/5233/jmyth.htm**.

Unfortunately, such tools have severe limitations. Firstly, as the example shows, built-in objects, methods and properties can't be renamed. These are often a large part of the code, and can give away the code's intent. Secondly, the translation is almost guaranteed to produce non-working code if **eval()**, **setTimeout()** or **setInterval()** are used, since their string arguments are actually code in disguise. Translators are usually too dumb to detect these more complex cases, so the arguments refer to original names, not translated ones. There are other similar problems which translators can't easily detect as well. Finally, if the document is a frame, referring to functions or variables in another frame, the translator has the further job of coordinating all the changes across documents.

Leaving aside these limitations, you may still find such a tool useful.

Making it impolite

If you put a copyright statement in comments at the top of your code and ask that it should not be used by others, or at least, if it is, then it is attributed back to you, people might just do it. If the information is "published" (exposed on the Web is an example) then you automatically have some copyright rights in countries that respect the Berne convention (most countries), provided you identify yourself as the author.

In the end, worrying about theft is probably not productive. The main problem is identifying when your script has been taken and used elsewhere, and by whom. This is almost impossible to enforce or police on the Web. Most client-side JavaScript code is small and uninspired, and uses well-known techniques that aren't new in any case.

Discouraging onlookers

When a user requests a URL from a web server, the downloaded file may pass through many systems that make up the network before reaching the user. All those systems have the opportunity to read the data as it goes past. Browsers include support for a network protocol called the Secure Sockets Layer (SSL). If support for this is turned on, then all data sent between the browser and any web servers with the same support will be hidden from intermediate systems.

167

However, once the user has the data, such as a **.js** file, they may do anything with it without using secure means, such as forwarding it using e-mail.

Privacy for Webmasters

For Webmasters, there are a few JavaScript issues that create problems on the web site's computer.

CGI-BIN trap on Windows NT

Standalone JavaScript scripts require an interpreter. If that standalone script is used as a CGI program, the interpreter is typically stored with the web server. By convention, a directory called cgi-bin is used. However, on Window NT, this exposes the interpreter to the web user's control—they can submit URLs that have attached script commands, which are then executed by the interpreter. Such commands could read or delete files, or cause other similar problems. Put the interpreter elsewhere for Windows NT web sites.

Chapter 2 has an example of how a ScriptEase 4.0 JavaScript interpreter can be controlled via command line arguments.

HTML form submissions

An issue affecting both server-side JavaScript and standalone JavaScript in CGI programs relates to form submissions. Forms are submitted from web browsers, and without security agreements, the data in a web browser is insecure. An HTML form which submits to a web server can be pulled apart by a hostile user (maybe it's a tax form), mimicked or rewritten in another page and submitted from that page. If the form is normally subject to complex JavaScript validation, all that validation can be ripped out by the hostile user and data submitted that would otherwise be stopped by validation. Alternatively, the user could write a different form that submits to the same CGI program.

Therefore, the receiving JavaScript can't assume the form data is in good order just because some users have proper client-side JavaScript validation in place. Making this assumption when it's not true can result in the CGI program failing.

If the submitting user is not trustworthy, as on the public Internet, then all the submitted form data should be thoroughly checked in the server-side JavaScript or CGI program to avoid surprises. Relying on client-side JavaScript only works in a secure environment such as a corporate Intranet.

This trivial example illustrates why any kind of assumption about public form data is bad. This is the original:

```
<HTML><BODY><FORM ACTION="update.cgi">
Enter account balance:
<INPUT TYPE="text" ONCHANGE="if (!parseInt(this.value))   this.value='NO-
BALANCE';">
<INPUT TYPE="submit">
</FORM></BODY></HTML>
```

This is a copy hacked by a hostile user:

```
<HTML><BODY><FORM ACTION="update.cgi">
Enter account balance:
<INPUT TYPE="text">
<INPUT TYPE="submit">
</FORM></BODY></HTML>
```

In the first case, the form will always submit a valid, numeric balance, or else the special string "**NO-BALANCE**". It might, therefore, seem reasonable for the '**update.cgi**' program to expect only these values. However, the hacked copy submits to exactly the same CGI program and can accept any string, including negative numbers and random garbage. Therefore, the CGI program cannot afford to trust the client-side JavaScript in an insecure public arena.

eval()

Because of the trap with form submissions, data supplied by the user is highly suspect and should be checked thoroughly. Use of **eval()** in web server JavaScript should be examined very carefully if the argument passed to this method comes from the user, or else unexpected statements might be run. Standalone JavaScript that supports functions like **system()** or **popen()** calls are equally cause for concern, because the user data used as arguments to these functions might cause unexpected programs to run..

Security

JavaScript security issues are mostly confined to the World Wide Web. Security issues for non-CGI standalone JavaScript scripts are the same as for standalone scripts in any language.

For the Web, the basic security model supplied by web browsers keeps JavaScript scripts harmless and restricted, and browser users anonymous. As a script writer, you may want to overcome one or both of these restrictions. In order to do so, you must come to a security arrangement with the user.

Script-based security

Privacy restrictions in a browser are at the user's discretion. If you want the restrictions lowered for your script, you have to convince the user and provide systematic support so that it happens smoothly. Technically, this is achieved by **signing** the script, and by embedding the script in a compatible web page to be viewed by a compatible browser. Netscape and Microsoft browsers have different systems for handling signed programs, but both are based on the same concepts. Netscape calls it **object signing**, Microsoft **Authenticode**. These systems are more commonly used for signing other downloadable and executable items such as plugins, ActiveX controls and Java applets, but it is client-side JavaScript that is of interest here.

Microsoft's signing system cannot be used to directly sign JavaScript scripts. Only Netscape 4.0 supports a full signing system for JavaScript. Internet Explorer 4.0 Scriptlet functionality can control how scripts are used to a degree, but it is not a complete or robust security solution.

169

Signing of scripts has to be done in a manner that prevents tampering, or else there is no value in it. This means using some kind of secret code. Computer encryption and cryptography provide such codes. These subjects are very complex, so the details are only touched on here. For a thorough discussion, see this site **http://www.rsa.com/rsalabs/newfaq/home.html**.

In summary, the steps for signed JavaScript are:

- Prepare the HTML page correctly.
- Create special functionality in the in-line JavaScript correctly.
- Sign the script.
- Ask the user to grant access to the script when it is loaded.

Using HTML tags to support security

Chapter 2 covers basic use of the **<SCRIPT>** tag with **LANGUAGE** and **SRC** attributes and the **<OBJECT>** tag. That is enough for plain in-line JavaScript, but not for signed scripts. There are three problems from the HTML perspective:

- How to tell the difference between signed scripts and plain scripts.
- How to prevent unsafe plain scripts and signed scripts from interacting.
- How to stop users and hackers altering inline JavaScript to exploit signed features.

The Netscape approach is to provide a general mechanism that works with all client-side JavaScript. Solutions for the three problems above are explained in turn.

Telling signed and unsigned scripts apart

Netscape signed and unsigned scripts are distinguished with a new type of file. This type could be specific to JavaScript, but instead a general format that works with all files is used. This is called a JAR archive, invented by Sun Microsystems. One such archive can contain many files. The **<SCRIPT>** tag has an **ARCHIVE** attribute which specifies the archive name. The **SRC** attribute is still required to identify the specific JavaScript file. An example:

```
<SCRIPT ARCHIVE="stock_updates.jar" SRC="ticker.js"></SCRIPT>
```

This way, the signing information is attached to the archive and the actual JavaScript source is the same as always. Assembling a JAR archive is part of the signing process and is discussed later.

For inline JavaScript that is embedded in an HTML file, signed **<SCRIPT>** tags can be identified by the use of an **ID** attribute, plus an **ARCHIVE** attribute— either in that tag or in an earlier tag:

```
<SCRIPT ARCHIVE="misc.jar" ID=1> var first = 1; </SCRIPT>
<SCRIPT ID=2> var second = 2; </SCRIPT>
```

Keeping signed and unsigned scripts from interacting

Keeping signed and unsigned scripts separate is simple. Normally inline JavaScript and event handlers share all the JavaScript data in the page. Nothing stops one piece of script from using any of the data, such as form elements or other JavaScript functions, even if it comes from a signed script. So the rule is: "all signed or none signed". This way the page is entirely secure or entirely insecure. If you miss adding one ID to piece of script in a page, then the security is blown for all the pieces of script.

You can make it more complex than these simple rules if you wish: see `http://developer.netscape.com/library/documentation/ communicator/jssec/index.htm`.

Preventing signed scripts from being changed

The problem of preventing changes to scripts is complex. Suppose an HTML page has three secure inline blocks of JavaScript specified via three `<SCRIPT>` tags. What stops someone saving the document to disk, modifying it and then presenting it to others as a "safe" script? Inline scripts are open to abuse since they are delivered exposed to the user with the rest of the HTML. The solution is extra, separate checking of the document.

This extra checking uses the HTML `ID` attribute. This attribute is a way of identifying a particular occurrence of an HTML tag. So an `ID` can be used to identify every inline script and every tag with event handlers in a page. There is a Netscape rule that says: every signed HTML page containing inline scripts must have at least one JAR archive, even if there is no `SRC` attribute. This creates a place to put data for the extra, separate checks. Every script piece, including handlers, must have a separate `ID` value, except for `<SCRIPT>` tags with `SRC`, since that `SRC` file is in the JAR archive anyway.

The extra checks take the form of a checksum or hash value for each piece of script. When the HTML page loads, the script pieces are picked out and hashed, and the new hash value compared with the one in the JAR archive matching the ID of that script piece. A match means all is well. A non-match means the page has been interfered with—a security breach. This arrangement means the HTML document can be loaded via a normal URL whether it's signed or not. If a security breach is detected then the document will be treated as an unsigned script.

The upshot of all this is that the HTML document must be separately processed once by its author so the JAR archive can be filled with the hash values. This is called **page signing**. JavaScript URLs and JavaScript entities can't be signed and, therefore, can't be used in the normal way in HTML. They can still be written out via a **document.write()** inside a `<SCRIPT>` tag.

```
<HTML><BODY>
<SCRIPT ARCHIVE="special.jar" ID="1">
   document.write('first script piece');
</SCRIPT>
<SCRIPT ID="2">
   document.write('second script piece');
   document.write('<A HREF="JavaScript:alert(\'still piece two\')">Click me</
A>');
```

```
</SCRIPT>
<FORM>
<INPUT TYPE="button" VALUE="Click me" ID="3" ONCLICK="alert('piece three');">
</FORM></BODY></HTML>
```

Why would Netscape encourage an approach that requires extra administrative tag attributes when writing HTML pages? One reason might be that this system allows several different web sites to contribute to the one HTML page in a mutually trustworthy way. That means several different companies can have their Web services connected together into one integrated package. That, in turn, might be the beginning of integrated and public inter-company software applications.

Writing Secure Scripts

Marking inline JavaScript with special HTML attributes is only half the content of signed scripts. The script logic itself must be created as well. Special features beyond plain JavaScript's capabilities must be required in the script or else there's no point signing anything

There are two sources of special features: JavaScript itself, and Java.

Within JavaScript the available features are identified in the Reference Section. Outside of signed scripts, these features do nothing. Example features are:

- simple parameters such as the **alwaysRaised** option of the **window.open()** function
- whole functions such as **enableExternalCapture()**
- access to otherwise private data such as writing into windows that display other web sites.

Via ActiveX or LiveConnect, Java is the main mechanism that signed JavaScript uses for special features. Chapter 8 on Java and Applets describes how JavaScript can generally exploit Java. Plain Java is restricted to a harmless subset of the Java functionality, just as plain JavaScript is restricted to harmless control of the browser. Signed scripts (or signed applets) can gain access to the rest of the Java functionality. Writing to local files and connecting to an arbitrary computer over the Internet are two possibilities.

Chapter 8 on Applets and Java describes the Java security model, which signed JavaScript scripts must subscribe to. From the immediately practical perspective, the key points for 4.0 browsers are:

- The Java Security Manager controls all the signed (secure) access in the browser. This means that JavaScript scripts have to appeal to it before any special abilities are granted.
- Appeals by JavaScript may require user confirmation, even though the script is signed, because that is what the Java security model demands. A signed script might be denied permission by the user, and never gain those permissions, so some error checking is required.

By convention, a signed script only requests specific special abilities for short sections of script, and then lets go of them. This is to minimize the time that permissions for special abilities hang around. It's not strictly required that this convention be followed, and it's not followed at all for Internet Explorer 4.0.

Here is a simple example of a signed script, for Netscape 4.0 browsers. This example turns the user's toolbars on and off every second. That'll teach them to think again before accepting signed scripts...

```
<HTML><BODY>
<SCRIPT ARCHIVE="sample.jar" ID="1">
function handler()
{
  alert('Very cautious of you - commendable');
  return true;
}

window.onerror = handler;                    // called if user denies access

function flash_toolbars()
{
  netscape.security.PrivilegeManager.enablePrivilege("UniversalBrowserWrite");
  window.personalbar.visible = ! window.personalbar.visible;
  window.toolbar.visible     = ! window.toolbar.visible;
  netscape.security.PrivilegeManager.disablePrivilege("UniversalBrowserWrite");
  setTimeout('flash_toolbars()',500);
}
flash_toolbars();
</SCRIPT></BODY></HTML>
```

Signing Scripts

Once the client-side JavaScript content is created, that content must be signed. Signing the content lets the user confirm the origin of the script. They can then make a decision about whether to accept it or not. Signing scripts is different for Netscape and Microsoft 4.0 browsers.

Signing In Theory

The big three sources of confusion over signing are human roles, terminology and how it all hangs together.

Human roles means who is providing the secure information, and what the intended audience is. For signed scripts, the script writer is providing the information and the intended audience is any web user who will accept the script. This might seem obvious, but there are other kinds of signing that can happen on the Internet. Apart from similarly signed objects like plugins and applets, whole web sites can be signed, or a single e-mail note can be signed. For these other applications the roles can be different. Here scripts are the focus.

Some terminology. The central concept is a **digital certificate**, or **digital ID**. This is the thing that is exposed to users and is just a piece of data like everything else in computing. **Certificate authorities** (or CAs) are organizations that issue certificates. Certificates contain **digital signatures** which identify specific

173

individuals. Developers have to manage digital signatures. Digital signatures are formed using techniques called **message digests** and **hashes**. Tools used by developers and users that aid the signing process implement these techniques. At the bottom of the pile is a theory called **public key encryption**, which makes the whole system go. If the developer loses his personal keys that are part of the public key encryption method, it's all over and necessary to start again at the top with a new certificate.

Why all these concepts? Because it matches the way people work. Suppose you were a bank and a customer asked you for a line of credit, like a credit card or a home loan. You wouldn't just supply the money without checking the person out—you would ask for proof of identity. If the person just pointed to themselves and said "This is me", you wouldn't be satisfied. You would require them to do two things: provide proof, and provide a signature. Proof just means getting other people you trust to point to that person and say "Yes, he is who he says he is". Those other trustworthy bodies tend to be large, conservative organizations, like other banks, social security, medical benefits or driving registration authorities. Once proof is produced, each time the customer asks to withdraw money their signature is provided, and you contact your trusted friends to see if there have been any problems with that signature since its last use. In the real world this last check might be relaxed, but not in the Internet.

In the case of the Web, the user is the bank and the script writer is the customer seeking access to the browser's features. The web browser holds certificates for a number of trustworthy bodies—certificate authorities. The script writer has a code-signing certificate issued by a certificate authority, who has scrutinized the script writer first. The script writer signs scripts with a pen (a signing tool) and ink (the keys supplied with the certificate), and includes a photocopy (certificate) of the signature of the trustworthy body (the certificate authority) to confirm his identity. When the user loads the signed script, the script writer's signature is examined. If it is unknown then the certificate authority's signature is examined. If it is a known certificate authority the script writer's signature passes, the script is accepted and the script writer can get at the browser's secure features. The user can be warned via special browser dialog popups when this is happening. These dialogs serve to explain to the user who wants to do what to their browser.

So much for theory.

Signing In Practice

In practice, there are three different approaches:

 Doing without the hassle

 Netscape 4.0 object signing

 Netscape 4.0 page signing

For these processes, the script writer needs to be properly setup. The requirements are a computer that has installed the browser that is the target browser for your end-user of the web page containing the signed script. Ideally this should be your development computer as well. If not, you will need FTP access to that development computer. Your browser computer needs Web access. You need an email account that you can read, but it doesn't have to be on your computer (i.e. RocketMail remote email accounts are sufficient).

You must also have a certificate in order to do the signing.

Doing without the hassle

As a developer, the signing process can get in the way of your development—slowing you down. To get going quickly you have two choices: disable security or develop using local files only. Afterwards, you can re-instate security or move the files to a web server. To disable security, read the section above entitled 'Other Risks'. Developing locally means using a **file:** URL for the topmost document and keeping all references relative so that the files can be easily moved later.

Obtaining a Certificate

All of the signing methods require that you obtain a personal certificate. There are four classes of certificate, ranging from 1 to 4. Class 1 one means minimal identity checks on you. Class 4 means even your hair follicles have been inspected. For testing, Class 1 is sufficient, but only Class 2 and onwards carry sufficient credibility to count for anything in the real world. Class 2 and onwards are not free. Most of the popular CA organizations don't bother supplying Class 1 certificates.

Certificates require numerous personal details and a method of payment. You'll also have to wait several days. There are different kinds of certificates, so get the right one: a developer, code or object signing certificate (all the same thing).

The certificates used for testing in this book came from Thawte Certification, **http://www.thawte.com**. Their service is international and doesn't currently suffer from U.S.-specific restrictions. It also allows you to deal with a more local representative who can comply with your country's specific privacy laws. This is very handy if you don't like accumulating charges for international phone calls.

Actually acquiring the certificate starts with applying via the Certificate Authority's web site, using your browser to fill in a form. Next you do the paperwork and payment. Finally, when the certificate is ready you retrieve it from the CA's web site, again using your browser. This last step appears to happen by magic, but just follow the instructions and use a simple nickname for the certificate, avoiding a password if possible. As for the discussion on cookies further on in this chapter, your browser is responsible for maintaining the certificate. Your browser is actually a certificate database; storing all the certificates you ever acquire in browser configuration files. Once the certificate is stored, you can view its details via the browser's security options.

There is one other piece of data that is stored. This is your encryption key for the certificate. It is stored in a separate file, often with a .p12 extension. Lose this file, and you've lost control of your certificate. If you accidentally delete the certificate, you can get it back if you have this file. Otherwise, this file doesn't come into play.

Object signing

Object signing signs things stored outside an HTML document only. Applets, plugins and .**js** files are examples, but this method doesn't sign anything between **<SCRIPT>** and **</SCRIPT>** tags. This is the simplest way to sign Netscape scripts. If you can limit your client-side JavaScript to external .**js** files only—do it this way. This means event handlers must be assigned from scripts, not specified in HTML tags. This is a lot of bother from the script writer's perspective, but the actual signing is easier. A simple example which illustrates signing and use of signed features by toggling the location bar:

```
// greeting.js

netscape.security.PrivilegeManager.enablePrivilege("UniversalBrowserWrite");
top.locationbar.visible = ! top.locationbar.visible;
netscape.security.PrivilegeManager.disablePrivilege("UniversalBrowserWrite");

if ( Math.random() > 0.5 )
  document.write('Happy Birthday!<BR>');
else
  document.write('Merry Christmas!<BR>');
```

```
<!-- object.htm -->
<HTML><BODY>
Welcome to the random acts of kindness page. Just for you:<BR>
<SCRIPT ARCHIVE="greet.jar" SRC="greeting.js"></SCRIPT>
</BODY></HTML>
```

You can't sign a plain .**js** file. The file must be put inside a JAR archive. A JAR archive has two parts: a JAR format, and a JAR file. The JAR format is a group of files set up in a particular arrangement. A JAR file is a single file that collects together all the files in the group. The JAR format is quite detailed and tricky. You can read about it here if you wish:
http://developer.netscape.com/library/documentation/signedobj/ jarfile/index.html.

It's hard work and error prone assembling a JAR file by hand, so it's better to use a tool. Netscape has two tools. One of these is the JAR Packager; an applet that provides a simple, handy GUI that does the job. Because the applet is stored on your local computer, rather than downloaded from a remote URL, it can create the JAR file locally as well. For some reason, this tool has virtually disappeared from Netscape's Web site—you may have to buy Mission Control 4.0 (not a cheap utility) in order to get it.

The alternative is a command-line tool called **Zigbert**, which is free. Zigbert suffers from slow development—probably because it currently has no competitor. At this time of writing, version 0.6 is the latest. Do not use version 0.5—buggy. It is available for Sun Solaris, Microsoft Windows 95/NT and Silicon Graphics IRIX computers. Look here for documentation and a download location:
http://developer.netscape.com/software/signedobj/. With Zigbert, you can look forward to several manual steps, and in the case of a PC, the DOS prompt. Presumably version 1.0 will improve this situation, but you can get by with 0.6.

What you can do with Zigbert 0.6:

- Create the JAR format around your **.js** files.
- Inspect your browser's certificates from the command line.
- Sign your **.js** files stored in the JAR format with a certificate.
- Confirm all is well with the signing and the certificates.

What you can't do with Zigbert 0.6:

- Locate your certificate data
- combine your JAR formatted files into a JAR archive

The Zigbert download provides **zip** and **unzip** tools to cover the latter omission, the former requires hand-copying files. The Zigbert manual explains the gory details, but in summary, get the certificate from the Certificate Authority first and then follow these steps:

- Download the Zigbert tool and install it in a new, empty directory.
- Copy the **key3.db** and **cert7.db** Netscape certificate files to the same directory.
- Make a sub-directory, e.g. **test**, in the current directory. Put your **.js** files in there, e.g. **greeting.js** from the example above.
- Sign using the certificate nickname: **zigbert -d"." -k"my thawte cert" test**
- Move to the test directory: **cd test**
- Make the JAR file using the supplied zip program: **zip -r greet.jar ***
- Move the JAR file to the same directory as **object.htm**.

Your author had problems with Zigbert for his particular PC setup, which this fairly radical command fixed:

```
copy C:\windows\system\msvcrt40.dll C:\windows\system\msvcrtd.dll
```

Only do this if you know what it means, or if you're stuck and don't have an **msvcrtd.dll** already.

Your signed JavaScript should now run in the browser without any user warnings and without any security hobbles.

Page signing

The Netscape object signing case above is all very well, but it doesn't allow signing of event handlers and inline JavaScript code, only **.js** files. An extra level of complexity is required to cover this more extensive requirement.

177

Consider this example, similar to the last:

```
<!-- page.htm -->
<HTML><BODY>
<SCRIPT ARCHIVE="greet2.jar" SRC="greeting2.js"></SCRIPT>
<FORM>
<SCRIPT ID=1>

netscape.security.PrivilegeManager.enablePrivilege("UniversalBrowserWrite");
top.locationbar.visible = ! top.locationbar.visible;
netscape.security.PrivilegeManager.disablePrivilege("UniversalBrowserWrite");

document.write('Random act of kindness button: ');
</SCRIPT>
<INPUT TYPE="button" VALUE="Go Ahead" ONCLICK="greet()" ID=2>
</FORM></BODY></HTML>
```

and the **greeting2.js** file:

```
// greeting2.js
function greet()
{
  if ( Math.random() > 0.5 )
    alert('Happy Birthday!');
  else
    alert('Merry Christmas!');
}
```

As for the last section, the Zigbert tool is required. Again, the 0.6 release is lacking in functionality. For page signing the situation is more serious: there is almost no functionality in Zigbert to support page signing. However, the Zigbert download file includes a workaround. The file **signpages.pl** is supplied to do the job. This tool takes the certificates (you copy them into place again) and the HTML file containing the JavaScript, and produces a JAR file using **zigbert**, **zip** and an ounce of intelligence.

There is one major catch. **signpages.pl** is written in the Perl language! Fortunately, Perl is a free tool. The web site **http://www.perl.com** is a good starting point for information about Perl. A hitch with Perl is that it is ultimately available in C code which must be compiled up before you can use it. For this task, Perl is just a means to an end, so the Perl executable is all you need to find. Not too hard if you're working on Unix, but problematic on the PC. Look here for a copy of Perl for Windows 95/NT **ftp://ftp.netinfo.com.au/pub/perl/CPAN//ports/win95/Standard/x86**. Files with a '**tar.gz**' extension can be unpacked under Windows by renaming them with a '**.tgz**' extension and then using an unpacking tool such as 'WinZip'.

Perhaps you might have Perl installed in **C:\local\perl**. Make sure the **PATH** variable includes the directory containing **zigbert** and **zip**, and then use the magic command::

```
\local\perl\bin\perl signpages.pl -d"." -k"my thawte cert" page.htm
```

The signpages.pl script will warn you if any **<SCRIPT>** blocks are missing **ID** attributes, so you can't get a bad JAR file.

178

You now have a JAR file ready to use without any security warnings or hobbles in place. If you want to check that the page signing process does secure the HTML file against tampering, try removing one of the **ID** attributes and reload the page. The browser will now report that the page is unsigned when the page is reloaded.

User-based security

User-based security means forcing the user to login to a web server before any of its documents, scripts or server-side programs can be used. Once the user supplies the correct information, they are trusted to download the web pages. The computer protocol underneath the Web (HTTP) doesn't provide comprehensive support for user logins, so you have to make do with the basics available.

There are three main approaches, none of which require much JavaScript. They are:

 use the HTTP authentication system, which requires special web server configuration

 use an HTML form that supplies a username and password to a CGI program (or server-side JavaScript) when submitted, and which returns a cookie that can be used to track the user afterwards. If your server-side JavaScript connects to a database, this is the preferred method. Any passwords sent to the server in this manner are exposed to the view of anyone intercepting the message on the way, so it is not a perfect solution.

 Server certificates.

These kind of high jinks with the browser are beyond a JavaScript book, so only a few pointers are supplied.

The first two options are described in **http://www.webthing.com/ tutorials/login.html**. If you decide to use the latter technique, you will need a method of encrypting the supplied password in your CGI program and possibly in the browser as well. If the CGI program is written in JavaScript, this URL contains an industrial strength example of password encryption, although there are many simpler (and possibly less secure) ways to validate passwords: **http://www.mlab.dnj.ynu.ac.jp/~uchiyama/md5java.html**.

The third approach uses the same technology as signed scripts, but otherwise isn't covered here. You require a server certificate instead of an object signing certificate to proceed.

Cookies

Cookies are a form of data passed both ways between web browsers and servers. Cookies sent to a user's browser have some very light implications for privacy. Cookies can be managed from JavaScript.

Cookie theory

It might sound like an obscure branch of theoretical physics, and might possibly have some similar-looking enthusiasts, but the mysteries of cookies are quick to penetrate.

Cookies enhance Web requests

The communication between web browser and web server is defined by the HTTP network protocol. That protocol says that each URL request and its response is a pair of messages independent of the past and the future. Without something fancy like JavaScript and frames, there is no method for maintaining information between requests, and no mechanism to let the web server receive or send any such information. Cookies are an enhancement to HTTP that let this happen. Originally proposed for standards consideration by Netscape Communications (their proposal is at **http://www.netscape.com/newsref/ std/cookie_spec.html**), the most official specification is easily readable here: **http://www.cis.ohio-state.edu/htbin/rfc/rfc2109.html**. Most of the basic points of the specification are covered in the following sections.

Each URL or HTTP request made by a browser user is turned into lines of text called headers for sending to the web server. When the web server issues a response, the same happens. Cookies are just extra header lines containing cookie-style information. This is all invisible to the user. So user requests and web server responses may occur with or without invisible cookies riding piggyback.

A key point is that the piggybacked cookies in the web server response get stored in the browser once received. Although a browser also reports its current cookies to the server when it makes requests, the server generally doesn't save them. This is almost the reverse of HTML form submissions: the browser has the long-term responsibility for the data not the server; the server says what to change, not the browser. However, the browser can use JavaScript to set its own cookies as well.

Anatomy of a Cookie

A cookie is much like a JavaScript variable, with a name and a value. However, unlike a variable, the existence of a cookie depends on several other attributes as well. This is because cookies can arrive at a browser from any web site in the world and need to be kept separate.

A cookie has the following attributes:

name

A cookie name is a string of characters. The rules are different to JavaScript variable names, but commonsense applies: use alphanumerics and underscores. Avoid using '$'. Cookie names are NOT case-sensitive. To really understand the naming rules, read the HTTP 1.1 standard. 'fred', 'my_big_cookie' and 'user66' are all valid cookie names. There are no reserved words or variable name limits.

value

The value part of a cookie is a string of any characters. That string must follow the rules for URLs which means the **escape()** and **unescape()** functions should be applied if one is set by JavaScript. The name and string together should be less than 4095 bytes. There are no **'undefined'** or **'null'** values for cookies, but zero length strings are possible.

domain

If two different web sites are viewed in a browser, they shouldn't be able to affect each other's cookies. Cookies have a domain property that restricts their visibility to one or more web sites.

Consider an example URL **http://www.altavista.yellowpages.com.au/
index.html**. Any cookies with domain
'www.altavista.yellowpages.com.au' are readable from this page. Domains are also hierarchical—cookies with these domains: **'.altavista.yellowpages.com.au'**, **'.yellowpages.com.au'** and **'.com.au'** could all be picked up by that URL in the browser. The leading full stop is required for partial addresses. To prevent bored University students making a cookie visible to every web page in the world, at least two domain portions must be specified.

In practice, the domain attribute isn't used much, because it defaults to the domain of the document it piggybacked into the browser on (very sensible), and because it's unlikely that you would want to share a cookie with another web site anyway.

path

In a similar manner to domains, the path attribute of a cookie restricts a cookie's visibility to a particular part of a web-server's directory tree. A web page such as **http://www.microsoft.com/jscript** might have a cookie with path **'/jscript'**, which is only relevant to the JScript pages of that site. If a second cookie with the same name and domain also exists, but with the path " **(equivalent to '/')**, then the web page would only see the first cookie, because its path is a closer match to the URL's path.

Paths represent directories, not individual files, so **'/usr/local/tmp'** is correct, but **'/usr/local/tmp/myfile.htm'** isn't. Forward slashes ('/' not '\') should be used. Trailing slashes as in **'/usr/local/tmp/'** should be avoided. That is why the top-level path is " **(a zero-length string)**, not '/'.

The name, domain and path combine to fully identify an individual cookie.

expiry time

The expiry time provides one of two cleanup mechanisms for cookies (see the next section for the other). Without such mechanisms, cookies might just build up in the browser forever, until the user's computer fills up.

The expiry time is optional. It is a moment in time. Without one, a cookie will survive only while the browser is running. With one, a cookie will survive even if the browser shuts down, but it will be discarded at the time dictated. If the time passes when the browser is down, the cookie is discarded when it next starts up. If the time dictated is zero or in the past, the cookie will be discarded immediately.

secure flag

This is a true/false attribute, which hints whether the cookie is too private for plain URL requests. The browser should only make secure (SSL) URL requests when sending this cookie. This attribute is less commonly used.

Browser Cookie restrictions

Browsers place restrictions on the number of cookies that can be held at any one time. The restrictions are:

- 20 cookies maximum per domain.
- 4096 bytes per cookie description.
- 300 cookies overall maximum.

RFC 2109 says at least these maximums. Netscape's specification and browsers say at most these maximums, in an attempt to guarantee that all your disk space won't be consumed.

If you rely heavily on cookies, you will soon exceed the Netscape limit of 20. In that case, that browser will throw out one of the 20 when the 21st arrives. This is a source of obscure bugs. It is better to use only one cookie and pack multi-variable data into it via JavaScript utility routines—4096 bytes is quite a lot of space. Internet Explorer doesn't have the 20 cookies per domain limit.

The Netscape file that the cookie data resides in when the browser is shut down is called **cookies.txt** on Windows and Unix, and resides in the Netscape installation area (under each user for Netscape Communicator). It is a plain text file, automatically generated by the browser on shutdown, similar to the **prefs.js** file. The user can always delete this file if the browser is shutdown, which removes all cookies from their system. An example file:

```
# Netscape HTTP Cookie File
# http://www.netscape.com/newsref/std/cookiespec.html
# This is a generated file!  Do not edit.
www.geocities.com FALSE / FALSE 937972424   GeoId    2035695874900187870
.linkexchange.com TRUE  / FALSE 942191819   SAFE_COOKIE      3425efc81808cebe
www.macromedia.comFALSE / FALSE 877627211   plugs    yes
```

The large number in the middle is expiry time in seconds from 1 January 1970. From this example, you can see that most web sites set one cookie only, and then it only contains a unique ID. Web sites often use this ID to look up their own records on the visitor holding the ID.

The equivalent files for Internet Explorer are stored by default in the **C:\WINDOWS\COOKIES** directory in .TXT files with the user's name. These are *almost* readable. Ironically, if you copy the files to a Unix computer, they are easily readable.

JavaScript and cookies

Using JavaScript, cookies can be accessed from the browser, from a CGI program and from server side JavaScript. The first two methods are examined here.

In the Browser

Cookies in the browser revolve around the JavaScript **window.document.cookie** property that first appeared in Netscape Navigator 2.0. This property is unlike other JavaScript object properties for a number of reasons:

- It isn't really related to its parent object, in this case the document object.
- Although it's singular in name, it holds all the visible cookies—but it's not an array.
- If you set the cookie property, its new value won't always match what you set it to.

The property's contents (it's a string) doesn't even look complete—what's going on? An example value:

```
bookmark1=face.htm; my_id=541263; quote=Et%20tu,%20Brutus
```

The 'cookie' property is really just a service point for managing the browser's cookies. It doesn't directly represent the current cookie data. This is different to the other properties in JavaScript, such as the forms array which exactly matches each **<FORM>** tag. When you set the **'cookie'** property, your data is handed to the browser's cookie management software. When you read the **'cookie'** property, you get a report in a single string of the cookies that are currently visible and unexpired for the current window's domain and path. Only name and value attributes are supplied in this report.

This means that when looking for a specific cookie, you must pick the **'cookie'** property's string apart. You can't know when a cookie expires or will be visible without explicitly re-setting it. When setting a cookie, you must use a string in a specific format. That format is:

```
[name]=[value]; expires=[date]; path=[directory]; domain=[domain-name]; secure
```

The items in brackets are supplied by you—leave the brackets themselves out. Each semi-colon separated item is optional, except the first. The '**[value]**' part must be run through the **escape()** function first. The date for **'expires'** requires the exact format that the **toGMTString()** method of the Date object produces:

```
// example date: 'Mon, 13 Oct 1997 12:40:34 GMT'
```

Managing cookie strings can be maddening because of the way they work with **document.cookie**. Fortunately Bill Dortch solved much of the problem for everyone. This URL **http://www.hidaho.com/cookies/cookie.txt** contains **SetCookie()**, **DeleteCookie()** and **GetCookie()** routines that do most of the hard work. The URL can easily be converted into a **.js** file.

In CGI Programs

Sometimes CGI programs are responsible for a URL's content. A CGI program is called at the end of a URL request, so it can read the cookies that the browser reports. A CGI program also produces the URL response, so it can set cookies that the browser will remember.

This example is standalone JavaScript written in ScriptEase 4.0. It is launched from a **.BAT DOS** file, is intended as a CGI program and shows cookie reading and writing:

```
@echo OFF
C:\local\install\ScriptEase\win32\secon32 %0.bat > %OUTPUT_FILE%
GOTO SE_EXIT

// JavaScript script starts here

var this_moment = new Date;

var all_cookies = Clib.getenv('HTTP_COOKIE');     // Received from browser

// Output HTTP/URL Response Headers
// puts() is like document.write()

Clib.puts("Set-cookie: test_name=test_data;\n"); // Sent to browser in header
Clib.puts("Date: " + this_moment.toGMTString() + "\n");
Clib.puts("Content-type: text/html\n\n");

// Output HTML

Clib.puts("<HTML><BODY>\n");
Clib.puts("Cookie report from browser:<BR>");
Clib.puts(all_cookies);
Clib.puts("</BODY></HTML>\n");

// JavaScript script ends here

:SE_EXIT
```

This example does not use the customized-for-CGI ScriptEase JavaScript interpreter, because it is easier here to see the 'raw' response headers that include the cookie data. The line containing **'Set-cookie'** shows a new cookie being sent to the browser; **'test_name'**. The format for this line is usually the same as that written to the **'document.cookie'** property (see above). The line containing **'getenv'** shows the CGI program reading the cookie information sent by the browser. The web server puts it in an environment variable, usually in the same format as is read from the **'document.cookie'** JavaScript property

Notice the **'Date:'** header line. If cookie headers are added with an expiry date, the **'Date:'** header tells the browser what the time was in the CGI program when the expiry was set. This helps the browser avoid becoming confused about when the cookie should expire.

Because of differences between Web servers, the CGI headers in this example may need subtle changes for a specific server even though the style shown here is quite standard.

Using Cookies

Cookies can be put to a number of simple uses. When cookie problems occur, this JavaScript URL is very useful for debugging. It produces a readable report if many cookies are present:

```
JavaScript:alert(document.cookie.split(';').join('\n'))
```

Logging in users

Cookies can be used to force browser users to supply usernames and passwords before viewing Web pages. Web servers already have a mechanism for doing this called 'HTTP Authentication', but if you don't like that system, you can use cookies instead. The steps are:

- Create an ordinary HTML form to accept username and password.
- Submit that form to a 'login' CGI program that validates the form details.

The user name and password might be validated against entries in a private file on the web server, like /etc/passwd on Unix.

- Have the login CGI program return a failure page if the details are wrong.
- Have the login CGI program return the first real page if the details are right.
- Return a special cookie to the browser if the details are right.

This cookie is used to track the user when browsing through pages of the web site.

- Each page on the site should be accessible through a second CGI program. This second program checks the cookie before delivering the requested page.

This is because a user might try and get around the login screen by going directly to the URL of another page. The cookie created cannot be as simple as **'login=true;'**, because an expert user might see this cookie and just create it with a JavaScript: URL next time he enters the web site thus avoiding the login again. The cookie value should be different each time the user logs in (perhaps containing an encrypted time) so that subsequent checks can confirm that the value supplied is recent.

In general, this is not a highly secure login mechanism, but it does prevent unknown users from easily entering your web site. It is less efficient than 'HTTP Authentication'.

If you don't have the opportunity to use CGI programs, you might think that the password can be checked in client-side JavaScript, and then proceed directly to the next page. Yes it can, but it's not secure, because the browser user can always view the JavaScript source and therefore workaround the password-checking code.

Cookies as Bookmarks

There is no way to automate the creation of bookmarks from JavaScript. There is no way to automatically navigate to a specific bookmark. Cookies can be used to workaround these restrictions.

A cookie with an expiry date set way into the future will exist effectively forever. A cookie whose value is a URL can always be used as a bookmark. A simple example:

```
<!-- redirect.htm -->
<HTML><HEAD>
<SCRIPT SRC="cookie_functions.js"></SCRIPT>
</HEAD><BODY>
<SCRIPT>
function go_there()
{
  if ( GetCookie('favorite') )
  {
    window.location.href = GetCookie('favorite');
  }
}

setTimeout("go_there()",10000);              // 10 seconds delay
</SCRIPT>
Returning you to your favorite location on our website ...
</BODY></HTML>
```

Provided the **'favorite'** cookie has been set at some time in the past, the user can be returned there automatically. This cookie could be set by client-side JavaScript, either automatically or in response to some user input, or it could be set in the browser in the response from a CGI program.

More than one bookmark is possible—use more than one cookie, or if the Netscape 20 cookie limit is close, concatenate all the bookmarks together into one cookie's value and unpack them when needed.

User Preferences

Along with bookmarks, cookies can be used to store a limited range of user preferences. The range is limited because of security hobbles. As for the last section these can be set in a number of ways.

186

Common preference choices might be:

- background color
- choice of frames or no-frames display
- choice of in-line images or text only display
- choice of navigation menu style
- font size

As the page is downloaded, inline JavaScript can check for special preference cookies and switch to the appropriate page, or adapt the page layout as required.

User Profiling

A web site can use a cookie to track a user's movements around the site. Web servers already have facilities for tracking the number of times each web page gets loaded, but cookies allow extra information to be supplied. Without the user's agreement, nothing can be stored in the cookie that exposes the real identity of the user, but the cookie can be used to show that the anonymous user is the same anonymous user as last time. Also see 'cookie traps' later.

Visit Counter

Possibly the simplest use of a cookie is to store a number in it and increment it each time the user loads a page that lies in the cookies domain and path. This gives the HTML author a simple way of establishing familiarity with the user. An example:

```
<HTML><BODY><SCRIPT SRC="cookie_functions.js"></SCRIPT>
<SCRIPT>
var visits = GetCookie("counter");
if ( visits && parseInt(visits) )
{
    SetCookie("counter", ++parseInt(visits) + "");
    document.write("Hello old friend on your "+visits+" visit<BR>");
    self.location.href = "top.html";
}
else
{
    var expires = new Date();
    expires.setTime(expires.getTime() + 3E11);    // about 10 years = "forever"
    SetCookie("counter", "1", expires, "");
    document.write("Welcome, Stranger.<BR>");
}

</SCRIPT>
<A HREF="top.html">Enter here</A>
</BODY></HTML>
```

Shopping Carts

Recall from Chapter 5 that shopping carts work around the limitation that HTML forms are restricted to one document. If you don't want to use a hidden frame and JavaScript variables to store the cart's contents, you can use cookies. There isn't much difference. The main benefit is that cookies are easier to

187

submit to a web server—you don't have to recreate an HTML form, they are submitted directly with every URL request. The main disadvantage is that you have to pack your cart items into and out of the cookie, which can be annoying.

Cookie traps

Chapter 7; Disappearing Data, points out some common traps with cookies.

From the point of view of security the web site **http://www.doubleclick.com** is worth considering. As briefly discussed in user privacy, cookies can't expose a user's true identity. However, they can be used to identify that an anonymous user is the same anonymous user as last time. This site has an advertising network that collects profiles of browser users by using cookies. The first time the user views an advertisement from this network the cookie is set. Subsequently, when the user views a page anywhere in the network, the cookie is discovered, and the user's presence is reported back to the network's data-collection service. Like tracking a wild animal, cookie footprints reveal the users habits which advertisers can then take advantage of. The next time the user views a page in the network, an advertisement appears tailored to the user's current habits. If you like tea, everywhere you go will eventually advertise tea leaves.

Summary

Privacy and security concerns serve to make client-side JavaScript a complex matter.

By default, the browser user is safe, and the client-side JavaScript script writer is not. The script writer's activity is restricted by security hobbles and the scripts are exposed to the user's whim. For JavaScript outside the browser such as server-side JavaScript and standalone JavaScript in CGI programs, the script writer has the same protections as any general programming language.

Half-hearted attempts at security such as code shrouding may keep the ignorant and lazy at bay, but ultimately provide no security at all. In order to be properly secure, a complete solution involving digital certificates is required. This is not usually free and requires extra organization and tools. Users may need to be educated as well.

Cookies are a mechanism that resides in the gray area between secure and insecure. Useful for maintaining data in the browser client and for tracking browser users, they have some light implications on security. Their behavior in browsers is unusual compared with other browser features, and can only be controlled from the browser via JavaScript.

Chapter

7

Disappearing Data

Reading a JavaScript book is one thing; debugging an uncooperative script is another. Because JavaScript is interpreted, the feedback you receive about your script's health is mostly limited to warnings about syntax problems. Once syntax problems are overcome, the few run-time diagnostics available generally translate into "I tried to do it, but something didn't exist".

JavaScript is intended to be a quick-and-easy interpreted and interactive language, often requiring only a few statements. There is no compiler rigorously checking your scripts before allowing them to be used. Consequently, it is very easy to become sloppy in your programming habits. Many problems are due merely to this.

Apart from the poor human creating the scripts, there are some genuine traps. This chapter outlines these traps and serves as a memory jogger for problematic issues highlighted elsewhere in the book. Know Thy Enemy—or Enemies as the case may be.

Finally, there is a brief treatment of debugging techniques.

Problems with language basics

If you are new to programming or to JavaScript, you are going to make all these mistakes. Old hands will nod sagely and say "Oh yes, the single-equals problem". Don't be fooled, they do it too. Even now. Think of these mistakes as a rite of passage and a fact of life.

A 'Dangling ELSE' leaves you dangling

Sometimes it is not clear which `'if'` a given `'else'` belongs to. The indenting designed to make it clear can just make it worse. This case has both bad formatting and a logic error:

```
if ( result != "win" )
   if ( result == "lose" )
      do_lose();
else
   do_win();
```

In this example, you never win. The `'else'` branch belongs to the inner, second `'if'`. No amount of formatting will make the interpreter think otherwise. The way to avoid this is always, always use curly brackets (braces)— then the trap cannot be fallen into. You can win in this re-cast example:

```
if ( result != "win" )
{
  if ( result == "lose" )
  {
    do_lose();
  }
}
else
{
  do_win();
}
```

This book is itself guilty of avoiding the braces at times. The excuse of limited space is merely a plea for clemency rather than a defense ...

= isn't always equal to the task

This is a very common typo:

```
var x = 1; if ( x = 0 ) alert ("made it");
```

Probably this was meant:

```
var x = 1; if ( x == 0 ) alert ("made it");
```

Chapter 1 describes how the equality operator can be viewed as an expression. Expressions can appear in `'if'` statements. The mistaken example above is therefore not a syntax error; in the `'if'` part the variable **x** quietly gets reassigned the value **0**, is then evaluated for truth or falsehood, passes, and the alert incorrectly appears.

Netscape browsers are helpful enough to produce this alert if such a situation is detected. JavaScript processing is not suspended just because the window appears. This is different to the behavior of the **window.alert()** method, and to that of normal syntax error messages.

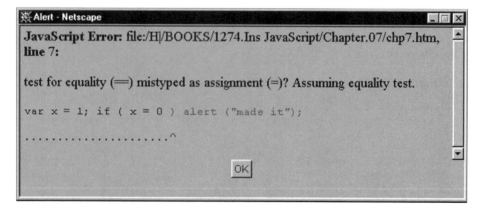

An idiom is a form of expression. This is a common idiom used in JavaScript and other C-like languages:

```
var result = false;
if ( result=calculate_it() )
  use_it(result);
```

You might want to use this idiom without the interference of the Netscape popup. If desperate, avoid the popup as follows or assign outside the **'if'** altogether:

```
var result = false;
if ( result=calculate_it(), result)
  use_it(result);
```

FOR ... IN ... has it in for you

As briefly described in Chapter 1, the **for** ... **in** ... syntax is used to find the names of all the properties of a JavaScript object. The problem is that it does not always work as you expect—some properties don't appear and some objects don't seem to have any properties at all. You can do little about this because it is a product decision made by the developers of the JavaScript interpreter. Usually this problem only occurs when you are hacking into the browser "off the beaten track" for your own devious ends.

Your only strategies are:

 know the property names in advance

 appreciate why they are hidden from inspection and accept it

To know an object's properties in advance, resort to documentation such as this book's Reference Section. The only other tactic possible is to probe the object in question one property at a time using array syntax. This takes a very long time, and is only for the desperate. An example for 4.0 browsers which finds all the lower-case single-character properties of the Document object:

```
function probe(obj)
{
  var i;
  var code = 'a'.charCodeAt(0);

  for (i=0; i < 26; i++)
  {
    if ( obj[(code+i).toString()] )
      alert ('found property: '+ (code+i).toString());
  }
}

probe(top.document);
```

A larger and more complex version could find all the properties of an object, but just finding all properties with six letters or less is 300 million tests—hardly worth it unless you enjoy running scripts overnight.

According to the ECMAScript standard, a given property of an object has a few **attributes** describing that property, such as property name and value. One such attribute is the **DontEnum** attribute. If this attribute is present, then the property won't be revealed by a **for...in...** loop. This is how object properties are excluded in such loops.

There are several reasons why some host object properties have this attribute. The simplest one is that some properties aren't interesting. Every method of an object is also a property of that object. It is pointless trying to interact with a method property if the object is a host object. An example for Navigator 4.0:

```
<HTML><BODY><SCRIPT>
alert(document.open);
document.open = "Fruit Salad";
alert(document.open);
</SCRIPT></BODY></HTML>
```

This script displays the following alerts, and messes up the document object in the process. The **open()** method is not accessible afterwards for creating new browser windows.

A second reason for non-enumerable properties is that some host objects don't follow the same rules as JavaScript. Java is an example. The JavaScript property **'java.lang'** isn't really an object, but a package of object type (**class**) libraries—**'java.lang.io'** is a subpackage of that package, but also isn't an object. A package is merely a group of related objects collected together. The classes are stored on disk and it isn't easy, efficient or even that useful to sift through them looking for **'java.lang'** members that might be objects. Therefore this item and the others relating to Java can't be enumerated at all.

Falling foul of types

It is so easy to do quick-and-dirty client-side JavaScript. A loosely typed language really saves a lot of mucking around otherwise spent organizing the right kind of data for the right kind of variables. Once finished, specially gifted people called users come along and expose gaping holes in your scripts, because JavaScript may well have untyped variables, but all the data itself is fully typed.

Chapter 1 describes how type conversion works in JavaScript. The most common trap is to develop all your scripts with Netscape 4.0 browsers and then discover that it doesn't work on any other browsers because you rely on the special behavior of Netscape's JavaScript 1.2 **!=** and **==** operators. Don't use **<SCRIPT LANGUAGE="JavaScript1.2">** when developing, unless portability is not required. It's probably safest to leave the **LANGUAGE** attribute out altogether, since JavaScript is the default browser scripting language anyway. If you must specify it, use **LANGUAGE="JavaScript"**.

Chapter 5 described validation and the numerous evils of converting user input into numbers. If your CGI program is crashing, your email is not arriving properly, or JavaScript is popping up errors on some obscure browser, first go back and check that all numeric values entered by the user are carefully validated.

Finally, older browsers have limited JavaScript support for types, also described in Chapter 1. If you want to support those browsers, don't be fancy with **nulls, NaNs, typeof()**s or **Array** objects.

Missing <SCRIPT> portions

If syntax errors are occurring in client-side JavaScript, but the script looks perfect, review the discussion in Chapter 2 on embedding JavaScript in HTML. Certain combinations of characters confuse the browser and it can give up believing that a script is present.

A related problem is restricted to 16-bit versions of the Netscape browsers developed for Microsoft's Windows 3.1 platform. If a single piece of HTML-embedded JavaScript exceeds about 32 Kilobytes, the remainder will be silently discarded due to memory limitations. Syntax errors, or 'XX not found' errors will result. There is a simple workaround—break up **<SCRIPT>,</SCRIPT>** tag pairs that contain a lot of JavaScript into several smaller ones.

Problems with variables

Variables are ultimately properties of objects and object models, but their use is so common that a few specific remarks are warranted.

Variables belong to somebody

In client-side JavaScript, the current object is usually the **window** object. This is easy to forget by the time you write '**var   x=0;**' for the 100th time. If you want to access a variable from an HTML event handler or another window, you should identify it by its owning object:

```
<INPUT TYPE="text" ONCHANGE="window.user_input = this.value; return true;">
```

```
top.opener.frames[0].my_time = "11:53";
```

If you don't, you may just set a property on the current object, rather than on the current window (usually a form input control like a text field) where it will usually remain, ignored.

String truncation

Beware of string constants that are over 80 characters. Some earlier browsers can't handle them. Just break them up into smaller chunks—it is easier to read anyway. This example has only short strings but it illustrates the principle:

195

```
var big_string  = "first chunk "
              + "second chunk "
              + "third chunk ";
```

Beware of the null character problem in Netscape browsers:
"xxx\000yyy".length is only 3 except for recent Netscape 4.0 releases; the **'y'**
characters are lost to view. For all browsers, attempting to display such a string
with **alert()** or **document.write()** is generally buggy.

Finally, **document.write()** can be used to output a string as a piece of
HTML. However, any repeated spaces in the string will be collapsed together,
and end of line characters are ignored. Instead, use the HTML non-breaking-
space character like this:

```
var try1 = "Left        Right\n\n\nBelow";
var try2 = "Left     Right<BR><BR><BR>Below";

document.write(try1);                // wrong
document.write(try2);                // right
```

Naming problems

Choosing names for variables is more error-prone in JavaScript than in other
languages.

There are a few specific traps:

- Variables are case sensitive, but not strictly everywhere—JScript 1.0
  generally and Netscape JavaScript 1.2 event handlers are exceptions.

- Cookie variable names are not JavaScript variables, so different rules
  apply there—see the 'Problems with Cookies' section.

- Limitations on variable name size aren't well advertised and vary
  between interpreters, so use shorter names.

The more general problem, which applies mostly to client-side JavaScript and
complex standalone scripts, is that numerous names are off-limits. A very
harmless looking example:

```
var int = 23;        // reserved word
var name = "Fred";   // changes an existing property
var open = true;     // dumps an existing method
```

The variable **int** is a problem because **'int'** is a reserved word. This is easily
detected by the interpreter. The **name** variable is more obscure. In client-side
JavaScript the current object is usually the **window** object. That window object
already has a property called **'name'**. After this script fragment is run, the
window's name has changed—mostly harmless, unless another window relies on
the old name for this one, in which case there will be problems. The open
variable has problems as discussed earlier—the **window** object has now had a
method replaced with a simple data value, and it can't be reversed.

● The 'events and forms' section illustrates further examples of these problems.

● Chapter 10 describes how scope chain concepts also contribute to this problem.

● The reference section describes all the reserved words and other names that are already taken. The best advice is to avoid the lot.

A further naming issue derives from the advent of style sheets and Dynamic HTML. Because of these innovations, HTML tag names now appear as objects and properties within client-side JavaScript. Although they are always capitalized and generally contained within the style parts of the document object model, these names should be avoided as well, or else confusion can ensue. Some HTML tags are common: variable names like **I**, **SUB**, **MAP**, **HEAD**, **CODE**, **A**, **DIR** and **BASE**. Avoid. Particularly avoid using all-uppercase variable names for constants; a practice common in many programming languages.

Just around the corner is the XMP standard. This is a complementary markup language to HTML that allows a document to define its own, unique tag names. This makes it even more important to stay out of the habit of using uppercase names, as these arbitrary names will probably be reflected as JavaScript objects as well.

Problems with events and forms

Beyond trivial uses, events and forms are the most difficult aspect of client-side JavaScript to script in a robust and portable manner. Variations between browsers make designing complex forms to suit everyone akin to tightrope walking.

Events

Numerous event issues are covered in Chapter 5. If your event handlers aren't doing anything, the most common reasons are listed here. The Reference Section contains further information on event handlers.

● You are forgetting to return **true** or **false**, and you need to.

All event handlers should in theory return **true** or **false**. A common problem occurs when a handy function normally meant for non-event scripts is used in an event handler. It is easy to forget that **return** has to be explicitly stated in the event handler. In this example, the hyperlink is always followed, no matter what conclusion the **isValid()** function reaches:

```
<HTML><BODY><SCRIPT>
function isValid(str)               // test if strings start with 'A'.
{
   return (str.substr(0,1) == 'A');
}
</SCRIPT>

<FORM NAME="test">
<INPUT TYPE="text" NAME="stuff">
```

197

```
<BR>
<A HREF="javascript:alert('Valid')"
    ONCLICK="isValid(top.document.test.stuff.value)">
test it
</A>
</FORM></BODY></HTML>
```

The **onClick** handler should read:

```
ONCLICK="return isValid(top.document.test.stuff.value)"
```

In this particular case, a Netscape 3.0 browser design flaw that causes a return value of **false** to be ignored specifically for the **<A> onClick** handler further complicates the matter.

You are incorrectly using the **this** property.

This script runs fine, but (probably unintentionally) creates a property on the Text input type object called **'total_clicks'**. It is this property that is incremented, not the property of the same name that belongs to the **'window'** object—mostly useless behavior:

```
<HTML><BODY><SCRIPT>
var total_clicks = 0;
</SCRIPT>
<FORM>
<INPUT TYPE="button" VALUE="Click Me" ONCLICK="this.total_clicks++">
<INPUT TYPE="button" VALUE="Show Total" ONCLICK="alert(window.total_clicks)">
</FORM></BODY></HTML>
```

You are testing with a Unix version of Netscape Navigator 3.0.

onBlur and **onFocus** event handlers don't work at all with this browser.

You are using a Netscape **onUnload** event handler.

This handler is buggy for all Netscape browsers and can be very unreliable. Avoid.

You forgot that event models differ between browser brands

Chapter 5 describes how subtle differences in event handling behavior make controlling the input cursor and navigation in a form problematic.

Errors and Undefined data

If your event handler is causing JavaScript complaints, first check if the tag for the event handler is **<INPUT TYPE="text">**. If so, you should check that validation is not causing type conversion problems, as described earlier.

If not, then you may be falling prey to problems illustrated in this example:

198

```
<HTML><BODY><FORM NAME="location">
Address:
<INPUT TYPE="text" NAME="address">
Delivery Method:
<INPUT TYPE="text" NAME="method"
ONCHANGE="alert(top.document.location.method.value)">
</FORM></BODY></HTML>
```

There are two problems with this document. The first is that the **onChange**
handler always reports "**undefined**". This is because the form control's name
("**method**") clashes with the property of the Form object also called **method**. Do
not use Form object property or method names as **<INPUT>** item names. The
second problem is similar. The form's name is **'location'**, but forms are
properties of the document object and Microsoft browsers already have a
location property of the document object. Therefore, while this will work for
Netscape, it may confuse Microsoft browsers.

Discussion on scope chains in Chapter 10 discusses some further complexities of
this problem.

Otherwise, there is a further scenario that causes confusion. The script writer
starts with a document, usually much more complex than this:

```
<HTML><BODY><FORM>
Want one? <INPUT TYPE="checkbox" NAME="box1" VALUE="yes" ONCLICK="alert('Why
not!')">
</FORM></BODY></HTML>
```

and decides to enhance it. Rather than wreck the existing tags, text is copied
and experimented with:

```
<HTML><BODY><FORM>

<SCRIPT>var state = false;</SCRIPT>
<INPUT TYPE="checkbox" NAME="box1" VALUE="yes"
       ONCLICK="alert(top.document.forms[0].box1.checked)">

Want one? <INPUT TYPE="checkbox" NAME="box1" VALUE="yes" ONCLICK="alert('Why
not!')">
</FORM></BODY></HTML>
```

In this case, the first checkbox always reports **'undefined'** even though a
Checkbox object has a **checked** property that reflects the state of the box. The
problem is that there are now *two* input elements named **'box1'**, so the
JavaScript object **top.document.forms[0].box1** is an **InputArray** object
(so-named by Netscape), not a **Checkbox** object and has no **checked** method.
The **onClick** handler should read:

```
ONCLICK="alert(top.document.forms[0].box1[0].checked)">
```

The Forms and CGI chapter, Chapter 5, discusses this feature further.

Problems at load time

When an HTML document is loaded into a browser, the HTML elements are exposed to JavaScript sequentially and any embedded objects such as images, applets and plugins load at their own pace. It is no use trying to access a JavaScript object that doesn't exist yet.

Store as much JavaScript as possible in the **<HEAD>** section of the document as described in Chapter 1. Avoid other problems by following the advice of Chapter 3 and use the **onLoad** event handler. Chapter 4 describes how to ensure that images and plugins have fully loaded.

Obscure Netscape problems

Firstly, avoid the **onUnload** handlers as noted earlier.

Secondly, there is a complication with **<A>** hypertext links. The browser assumes that if a link is clicked and any **onClick** handler returns true, then the current document is to be replaced. Normally this is a fair assumption, but not when the **HREF** attribute's URL is a **javascript:** URL. This URL might return void, meaning no action is to be taken. Nevertheless, the browser ceases to load any embedded items that are still loading, assuming they are to be overwritten anyway. To avoid this problem, use a URL of **javascript://** (i.e. nothing but a JavaScript comment) and perform other actions required in the **onClick** handler. This will only work for Netscape 3.0 and higher.

Finally, there is a plain bug with Netscape 4.0 browsers that are version 4.03 or less: an **onLoad** handler for an image loaded via an Image object does not do anything. An **onLoad** handler for an image loaded via an **<IMG>** tag does work.

Problems with the browser object model

In addition to variable, event and form reasons, there are other traps within the JavaScript browser objects that can make data appear to vanish.

Omitting 'document'

One of the most common problems is to forget the **document** property. A script writer might make all the right moves: name every tag, window and frame with the **NAME** attribute, avoid reserved words and use window references to ensure the correct object is being referred to—but still can't get it right. This is a long, but typical example:

```
var temp = top.user_window.body_frame.user_form.comment_field.value;
```

This is the fixed version:

```
var temp = top.user_window.body_frame.document.user_form.comment_field.value;
```

A less common issue which can cause confusion is this script:

```
alert(top.document);
```

This will cause an error with Internet Explorer 3.0, 4.0 and 4.01), but for Netscape, the alert which does appear contains nothing. When a JavaScript expression type-converts a Document object to a String, the result is just a zero-length string. This is probably for security reasons.

It's not the expected browser

For Netscape and Microsoft products, the browser models are not the same. Your non-trivial JavaScript-enabled HTML document is almost certain to fail if you test it on only one browser and then expect it to run on another. You have to use the compatibility tricks described in Chapter 2 to work around areas where they differ.

Image and Option objects are a common example. Internet Explorer 3.0 does not generally support them. No Microsoft browser supports the Plugin, MimeType or Layer object. No Netscape browser supports the **scripts** array property or the **event** Window property of Microsoft browsers.

The 4.0 level browsers differ considerably in the objects that reflect style sheet properties in an HTML document. The Dynamic HTML chapter, Chapter 9, has some discussion of compatibility issues.

Worst of all, advanced features of the event handling models in the 4.0 browser brands are sufficiently different to almost guarantee non-compatibility. If you aren't willing to do some serious thinking to ensure that your event handling logic works in both places, then don't expect it to be portable.

General naming problems

The 'Problems with variables' section describes the pitfalls of poorly named variables. This is really the case for objects of all descriptions. The general rules are:

- If an object reflects an HTML tag, don't let the **NAME** attribute's value clash with any property or method of its parent object.

- Don't use reserved words from any of the reserved words lists.

- Don't use all-uppercase letters lest they be confused with HTML tag names.

Problems with cookies

Cookies are already designed to appear and disappear according to the path and domain of the currently viewed HTML document, and due to their own expiry time, so creating a flock (a jar?) of them is asking for trouble. Cookies can make life extremely complex and are slow to debug and fix if problems occur.

For trouble-free client-side cookies: keep the number used to one, set the path to ` ' ` (the most general path), and either set no expiry time or an expiry time that is way, way in the future.

For trouble-free server-side cookies: cookies arrive separately to form parameters; you can have both a parameter and a cookie with the same name, so keep them separate. When writing **Set-cookie** headers to send to the client, make sure they are written *before* the **Content-Type:** header, and don't forget a **Date: header** if the connection is likely to be slow.

Most cookie problems occur in the browser:

Disappearing cookies

There are many valid reasons why a cookie might not appear:

- The expiry time for the cookie has been reached, and it has disappeared normally.

- Your document stored at some URL like **http://www.test.com/ public/file.htm** is trying to use a cookie with a path like **/public/part1/section1**. The URL is too general for the highly specific cookie.

- The user reloaded a window or frame's URL and the newly loaded document contained instructions to re-set the cookie with an expiry time in the past, so it goes away immediately.

- The user reloaded a window or frame with a different URL, and since the domain or path of the new URL no longer matches, the cookie isn't visible.

- You are using too many cookies—you've hit the Netscape 20 cookie limit and a cookie has been discarded (usually the oldest, least used cookie).

- You created the cookie without an expiry date, and then shutdown the browser. The cookie is not written to the cookie file, and is gone.

A cookie might disappear if there are two windows running that have similar URLs. The first window may rely on a given cookie, but the second window may just as easily delete that same one.

Finally, cookies aren't very permanent. The user can always delete the cookie file when the browser is shutdown, or use **javascript:** URLs to delete a cookie directly in the browser.

Cookie value won't change

You set and set and set a particular cookie, but no matter what you do, you just can't get that new value back from the **document.cookie** property. One of several things is happening:

- Your cookie handling routines aren't quite right. Try the standard ones advocated in Chapter 6.

202

- You are trying to set a cookie that isn't accessible from the current document's URL. Check the path and domain attributes you are supplying.

- You have two cookies with the same name, because the path attribute isn't correct somewhere. When you read the cookie, you get the other one that you didn't touch. Test this with the debug URL in the Privacy and Security chapter, Chapter 6.

- Your expectations of the **document.cookie** property are too high. Re-read the section on this property—not all the cookie information is available.

Cookie values change for no reason

One of the most attractive reasons for using cookies is as a repository for global data—data that is not attached to any window or document, and is accessible everywhere. However, this comes with a catch.

The catch is coordination. Unless specific security measures are taken, the user can open as many browser windows as desired, and interact with them in any order. This makes it easy for one window or frame to interfere with a cookie set by another window. If the two windows view the same URL, interference is more likely than not. It is nearly impossible to guarantee that a window can update a cookie to a specific value and be confident at a later point that the cookie is unchanged.

To see this, just imagine a form which sets a cookie when a button is pressed. Later when the user submits the form, the expectation is that the cookie will be sent with the submission. However, if two windows A and B both show the form, the user can do this: click the button in A; click the button in B; submit in A. The cookie is sent with the wrong value.

Debugging techniques

There are a number of effective debugging techniques available for JavaScript programs, ranging from the trivial to the complete.

Browser JavaScript

For HTML-embedded JavaScript, the crudest debugging tool is **document.write()**. Even if it messes up your HTML document, at least you get some feedback while you are testing. Coupled with a **window.open()** command, you can send the output to another window if you desire.

JavaScript used for proxies or preferences in Netscape browsers is not amenable to debugging—you have to try it, and if it doesn't work, try it differently. At least the preferences are also exposed to HTML-embedded JavaScript if secure scripts are used.

Alerts

Using **window.alert()** functions embedded in inline JavaScript scripts is the simplest way of stopping the JavaScript interpreter at a given point or points when a document is loading. The message in the alert box can reveal the value of any interesting data as well. This is the simplest way to debug complex logic that involves lots of **if** statements and function calls—just add an alert to the suspect branch or function and you'll know whether it's being executed or not. Alerts are particularly effective with **javascript** URLs as well.

javascript: URLs

Once an HTML document is fully loaded, **document.write()** isn't of much use. Inline alerts won't help if the script has finished running. **javascript** URLs allow you to probe the browser and document and see what the current state is. This example shows a window's URL:

```
javascript:alert(top.location.href);
```

However, **javascript** URLs can be used more generally. Provided you are patient and careful, any amount of JavaScript can be included. This example displays all the element numbers of the first form that have value properties:

```
javascript:var i; for (i=0;i< document.forms[0].elements.length;i){ alert(i); }
```

Finally, any function or method in the browser that is otherwise available to JavaScript can be called. This means you can force a form **submit()** directly, perform a **click()** on a button, or call any of your own functions. This example deletes a cookie using the popular routines, which are assumed to be included in the document somewhere:

```
javascript:DeleteCookie("biscuit3");
```

Java console logging

If you don't want to disturb a document when it is loading, but you want a record of what happened, you can log information to the Java console. You can watch the console as the document loads or examine it after the fact. The approach is very similar to **document.write()**, just embed statements as follows at strategic points in your script:

```
java.lang.System.out.println("Window name is: "+top.name);
```

This version does not write an end-of-line character to the console:

```
java.lang.System.out.print('more..');
```

This works for Netscape 3.0 and 4.0.

File logging

If logging output to the console is not permanent or spacious enough, the client-side JavaScript can write to files on the test computer's local disk (assuming it has one). All that is required is that security hobbles in the

browser that prevent this type of behavior are turned off. The Privacy and
Security chapter, Chapter 6, describes how.

Watch points

Netscape 4.0 introduces watch points. Watch points allow code to execute when
a property is changed. Only debugging tools normally take advantage of these,
but they are equally useable directly by scriptwriters. Here is an example
derived from remarks by Netscape's Brendan Eich, the JavaScript inventor.

```
<HTML><BODY><SCRIPT>
function display_it(id,oldval,newval)
{
   document.write('test.' + id + ' was: ' + oldval + ' - now is: ' + newval
+'<BR>');
   return newval;
}

var test = new Object;

test.watch("prop", display_it);      // start watching property "prop"
test.prop = "first";
delete test.prop;                     // still watch even with the property gone
test.prop = "second";
test.unwatch('prop');                 // stop watching property "prop"
test.prop = "third";

</SCRIPT></BODY></HTML>
```

The key is the special **watch()** and **unwatch()** methods which exist for every
object, like **valueOf()** and **toString()**. You register interest in a specific
property and nominate a function to call when it changes. The function can do
anything, including making the change different by not returning the new value
passed to it as an argument. The output of this example is:

```
test.prop was: undefined - now is: first
test.prop was: first - now is: second
```

Debuggers

Both Microsoft and Netscape have browser JavaScript debuggers that are nearing
final release as this is written. If you prefer an Integrated Development
Environment ('IDE') style of development, where the one tool is used for
development, testing and debugging, these tools may appeal. Third-party
companies such as Acadia (**www.acadians.com**) also have JavaScript
development tools.

Server-side JavaScript

Although only briefly covered in this book, server-side JavaScript also supports
techniques for debugging.

Firstly, all the techniques for client-side JavaScript are relevant to a degree as
the server-side scripts ultimately produce client-side HTML and possibly client-
side JavaScript as well. However, these cannot be used to halt server-side
JavaScript as it runs, or confirm that a piece of JavaScript is executing on the
server.

205

Secondly, since server-side JavaScript is securely 'behind' or 'within' a web server, the web server's file system can be used to create log files. The **File** object of Netscape's Enterprise Server is an example of a mechanism that allows this. Since a web server is involved, the server's own logs can be exploited to see URL requests, form parameters and cookie data travelling to the server and back. Server-side code often interacts with relational databases, and such products have logging system of their own.

Finally, Chapter 2 briefly notes integrated features in server-side systems such as Netscape Enterprise Server, which allow the script writer to see an execution trace of the server side code as it occurs.

Standalone JavaScript

Since standalone JavaScript has much the same flexibility as any third-generation programming language, the options for debugging are numerous.

As for client-side JavaScript, the quickest and dirtiest method of debugging is to write out debug information, for example:

```
Clib.puts("Current PATH is: " + Clib.getenv("PATH") + "\n");
```

The example of a client-side **alert()** in standalone JavaScript is a little harder to duplicate. Standalone JavaScript is not embedded in a complex browser-like application that supplies lots of support for graphical objects like alert boxes.

Nevertheless, it is not many lines of script to produce an alert box. Standalone JavaScript versions like ScriptEase 4.0 for Windows 95 have a library of functions that give access to the Windows 95 graphical user interface. If you are new to programming, that is a large and time-consuming can of worms to open. However, if you have a desire to program graphical user interfaces, feel free.

File logging

The **Clib.puts()** example above just writes data to the display window that the script was run from. It is just as easy to log to a file. Only a few lines are required:

```
var fp = Clib.fopen("logfile","w");          // open log file for writing

Clib.fprintf(fp,"%s", "My logged message\n"); // write out a formatted line
Clib.fputs(fp, "My other logged message\n");  // write out just a string

Clib.fclose(fp);                              // close the log file neatly
```

The **fputs()** and **fprintf()** lines appear as often as logged messages are necessary.

206

CGI emulation

When a CGI program goes wrong, it's often not easy to see why, since a web server, not a human, controls it. However, a CGI program can be run without a web server, provided it receives input matching the input a web server would supply. If the program is written in a flexible scripting language like JavaScript, this is not hard to setup, but it is beyond the scope of this book.

Debuggers

As for the browsers, a debugging tool for ScriptEase 4.0 standalone JavaScript is nearing release at this time of writing.

Summary

The interpreted and loosely-typed nature of JavaScript means that errors are often reported without detailed explanations of what went wrong. The ability to add names to the object hierarchy of a browser can result in obscure errors when new names clash with existing ones.

Elements of a browser that can appear and disappear cause the same thing to happen to the data they make available to JavaScript. Windows, cookies and separately loaded items such as images are all examples.

However, there are plenty of ways to probe a given script's behavior, ranging from simple interactive inquiries to full-blown visual debugging environments. Simple techniques are often sufficient to pick up the commonest problem cases. For the rest, you must accept that convenience of an interpreted language gives flexibility with one hand, but with the other puts the onus on the script writer to use a degree of care.

Chapter

8

Applets and Java

Just as plugins and images can be controlled by client-side JavaScript when embedded in an HTML document, so too can Java applets. However, the interaction between JavaScript and Java is more complex and flexible than between JavaScript and plugins due to the fact that Java is a whole programming language of its own. This is especially the case for Netscape browsers.

Using JavaScript, you can knit together Java applets embedded in a Web page with other elements of the page and each other. Java plus HTML plus JavaScript lets you create applications, not just applets.

This book assumes you have no prior knowledge of Java. Nevertheless, there are some things you might want to achieve with JavaScript that just can't be done without a little Java. This chapter explains how to do those tasks, the technical basis behind them, and the noteworthy Java concepts that are needed to make sense of it all.

Standalone JavaScript doesn't yet have any reason for interacting with Java. This chapter only discusses client-side JavaScript interacting with client-side Java.

Java basics for JavaScript scriptwriters

For a detailed tutorial on Java, try **http://java.sun.com** or one of the many Java books available. There is only a superficial treatment here.

Sanity check

There are only a few reasons to delve into Java from the JavaScript script writer's perspective:

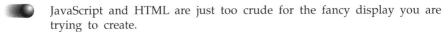 JavaScript and HTML are just too crude for the fancy display you are trying to create.

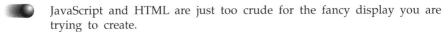 You want to use signed JavaScript scripts.

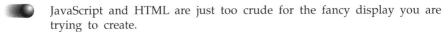 You want to communicate with a program on a web server from the browser.

You want to tie applets and HTML together into a cohesive application.

There are features missing in JavaScript, available only in Java.

You want to use it "because it's there".

Java and JavaScript compared

As for JavaScript scripts, Java programs come in standalone and host-embedded varieties. In Java terminology, these are 'applications' and 'applets' respectively. Similarly, there are client-side and server-side applets, although server-side applets are called 'servlets'. Only client-side applets are discussed in this book.

From the point of view of a person using someone else's Java applets, applets look much like plugin data or ActiveX controls. A Java applet is loaded over the Web from a file of indecipherable binary data using a special HTML tag such as <OBJECT> or <APPLET> in an HTML document. Applet activity is often restricted to a specific rectangle on the screen, allocated to it by the tag, or to special windows that the applet opens itself.

However, internally JavaScript and Java aren't that far apart. Both have syntaxes that borrow common elements from the C language. Both have object concepts. Both can be loaded into browsers via URLs. JavaScript scripts rely on an interpreter in the browser; Java applets also rely on a browser interpreter except that second interpreter has a fancy name: the JVM—the Java Virtual Machine. In both cases, the interpreter makes the program or script portable across different types of computer.

From the point of view of development there are three crucial differences between the two languages:

Firstly, Java source code requires an extra preparation step before it is useable. This step, called **compilation**, takes the readable Java source in a **.java** file and puts an indecipherable stream of binary **bytecode** data into a **.class** file. This serves to check that the developer's readable code is syntactically correct and secure. It is also this bytecode format that is loaded across the Web and interpreted by the JVM. Because the format is indecipherable, it can't easily be embedded in HTML files as JavaScript can. Since the applet source never appears in the browser, there is no 'View Source' option for Java applets.

Secondly, types and objects have a much larger hand in Java than JavaScript. Java is strongly typed, not loosely-typed, so the developer must use String variables for String-typed values and nothing else. The Java language syntax doesn't hide the developer from objects, as is sometimes the case in JavaScript. Java requires object concepts from the very beginning. Quick program or script fragments like JavaScript event handlers aren't possible—only whole objects can be created in Java. This all requires a more careful approach on the developer's behalf. The developer spends a lot of time getting **classes** right—classes define the type of an object in a way that is much more specific than the simple constructor functions of JavaScript.

Thirdly, Java does not come with ready and immediate access to the browser's features. It does have its own useful libraries of objects, but these are aimed more at creating whole applications with Java, rather than accessing the parts of the browser that the Java interpreter is embedded in. It is extra effort to get at browser features such as HTML form elements in documents. This difficulty stems from the Java designers' initial desire to keep Java separate and isolated from other software systems. Amongst their goals were simplicity and security.

Because of these three things, the development model for Java is a little different to JavaScript. With JavaScript, you create your HTML page, decorate it with script bits that act on that page's objects, and load it into a browser to see if it works. With Java, you first create whole objects yourself and compile them to see if they have problems. If not, the resulting bytecode files are loaded via a special tag in an HTML document, and you see if they work within the restricted area of the screen allocated to them.

Finally, scratch the surface and the terminology used in each of the two languages can vary considerably. This is perhaps the main obstacle for the script writer.

Java's special browser status

From the outside, Java applets can appear like any form of multimedia, such as images or plugin data. Thinking there is no difference at all is an assumption trap for the script writer. There are a number of special behaviors that set applets apart.

An applet of objects

Images, sounds, animation and other items embedded in an HTML document are loaded across the web from one file each (JavaScript image animation, described in Chapter 4, is an exception). An AVI movie, for example, isn't usually split across a number of files.

Java is not like that. A single applet usually consists of many objects stemming from a variety of classes. In the simplest case, each class type has a separate file. Each class needs separate fetching across the network (it's not hard to be more efficient that this). The JVM part of the browser consolidates them to form the complete applet.

The implications for the script writer are:

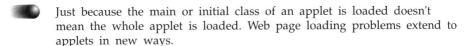 Just because the main or initial class of an applet is loaded doesn't mean the whole applet is loaded. Web page loading problems extend to applets in new ways.

Some or all of the classes can be (and are) permanently stored on the browser's local computer disk, because they are commonly used and there are big performance gains. A browser should have compatible versions of these classes for your Web application's applets.

Because classes can be stored on the local computer. Sometimes they can be used by the script writer *without* any applet being present in the browser. Because these local classes exist, JavaScript can rely on them for some operations like file writing. This is convenient and also saves duplicating functionality across two languages.

In a more complex (but still typical) case, these separate files are often grouped together for performance reasons into single `.zip` or `.jar` files, both at Web sites and in the browser's local install area. However, the idea of separate files for separate classes is still a cornerstone of Java's architecture.

Applets die unwillingly

Suppose an HTML document containing an image and some JavaScript is loaded into a browser window. If the user then browses to a different URL, you would expect that the first document, its image and its script variables would be gone, whatever 'gone' means. This example illustrates:

```
<HTML><BODY>
<SCRIPT>

if ( typeof(saved) == "undefined" )
    var saved = 10;
else
    saved *= 2;

alert(saved);
</SCRIPT>
<IMG SRC="anyimage.gif">
<FORM><INPUT TYPE="text"></FORM>
</BODY></HTML>
```

To run this example, view it and then go back one and forward one, via the browser buttons. This test shows that the alert always shows 10 so the variable **saved** is not saved. You would expect browser caching of the two files (the document and **anyimage.gif**) to work for you, but the document's state from the last time the document was viewed is gone. Otherwise the alert would show 20 on the second viewing, and double each time you repeated the test.

However, life is not always that simple. If you use a Netscape browser, or Internet Explorer 4.0, and type something into the sole field before the above test—the sole field's value *is* remembered. So, there are exceptions to the rule that nothing is remembered.

Java is a big exception. When you leave a URL that contains an applet, that applet is not necessarily wiped away. When you return to the URL, not only does the applet remain loaded, but also the applet's state (all of its variables and objects) is fully preserved as well. This is not an absolute—there are a number of reasons why you can't rely entirely on it—but it is the common case and a fair guide. It's even possible that the applet continued to work after the URL was left.

The implication for the script writer is knowing when applets are loaded or 'fresh' (i.e. have yet to run for the first time) is a non-trivial affair.

See 'Handling Java from JavaScript' for the gory details.

Applet Gossip

Because Java applets have the power of a programming language behind them, they have the potential to communicate with each other. Images don't normally do this—otherwise there might be some unusually entertaining Web sites to visit! The mechanism for such communication might reside purely within Java; be assisted by HTML-supplied tag information; be enabled by glue technologies like ActiveX or LiveConnect; or occur via intermediate JavaScript scripts.

The implications for the script writer are:

- JavaScript can interact with a single applet.
- JavaScript is a useful intermediary for tying together applets.

The Authority of Java

Because Java is held in high regard on the Internet, some of the responsibilities otherwise held by the non-Java parts of Web browsers have been given to it. In particular, Java has taken on the role of security manager for many aspects of the 4.0 browsers. This is especially the case for Netscape. See the section 'The Java Security Model' for the details. Plugins and ActiveX controls rarely provide fundamental services to the browser in a like manner.

The implication for the script writer is that JavaScript scripts must appeal to the Java security manager if they want to perform insecure operations. The section on the Java security model explains.

Creating Java Applets

It is likely that a JavaScript script writer will take advantage of an existing applet, rather than do any Java development, but if you're pushed to it, here are the steps required:

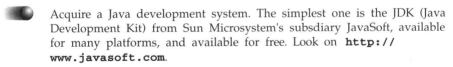

- Acquire a Java development system. The simplest one is the JDK (Java Development Kit) from Sun Microsystem's subsdiary JavaSoft, available for many platforms, and available for free. Look on **http:// www.javasoft.com**.

- Understand the tools. The JDK comes with a **javac** program that is the compiler, and an **appletviewer** program that lets you test your applets without a browser. The javac compiler does NOT combine your various custom Java classes together into a .jar file. You need a JAR packager program to do that, also available from Sun.

- Set up your environment. When a Java class is compiled, at least three things have to be right, apart from the program content. First, the magic **CLASSPATH** environment variable must be set to an appropriate directory. Second, that directory must contain all the library classes needed for the compilation. This means going to the browser installation, looking for .jar or .zip class file libraries and copying and unzipping them in the **CLASSPATH** directory. Thirdly, the class to be compiled must have a filename that **matches** the class name, except for the addition of a **.class** extension.

- Compile the Java source. This is as simple as **'javac MyClass.class'**. The compiler will warn you of most problems. A **.java** file results, which is the bytecode file.

- Move the bytecode file to the Web site and embed its URL in some HTML page.

Crossing the language boundary

The actual lines of code required to go from one language to the other are very simple. The concepts behind the code need a little more appreciation. In order to communicate between the two languages, both must be turned on in the preferences or options windows of the browser.

How Java and JavaScript interact

To reduce the confusion, keep in mind that JavaScript and Java are two separate interpreter environments. In JavaScript, only JavaScript types, objects and syntax are allowed. In Java, only Java types, objects and syntax are allowed. These rules can never be broken.

If two human beings speak different languages, then an intermediary who knows both is required. So it is with Java and JavaScript, and the intermediary is LiveConnect for Netscape or ActiveX for Microsoft. The intermediary's job is to **convert** from one language to the other. There are four things to convert:

- Primitive data types.
- Objects.
- Method and function calls.
- Events.

These things have roughly the same meaning in both Java and JavaScript languages, which makes the intermediary's conversion job relatively easy and efficient.

Direct conversion occurs for primitive data types, method calls and events. Direct conversion means a basic element of one language is duplicated as a similar basic feature of the other language. So a JavaScript Number type is represented by a Java Float type when it is passed to Java.

Wrapping occurs for objects where the conversion is not so easy. Representing objects can be very messy if they contain other objects or have inheritance/ prototype features. Instead of making a complete copy of the original, a placeholder is supplied in the second language. This placeholder "stands in" for

214

the real object. Working with the placeholder in the second language causes the intermediary to coordinate updates with the original object still stored in the first language.

This table describes the conversions that occur. Java is unlike JavaScript in that there are both primitive types, and classes representing the primitive types. Literal values always have a primitive type (e.g. **float**) but variables objects may be of the equivalent class type (e.g. **Float**).

Starting from JavaScript	Result in Java	Starting from Java	Result in JavaScript
Primitive Types			
Undefined	Cannot be converted	**null**	**Null**
Null	*String* or **Object**	**boolean byte char short int long float double**	Cannot be converted
Boolean	**Boolean**	**Boolean**	**Boolean**
Number	**Float**	**Float**	**Number**
String	*String*	*String*	*String*
Objects			
host object	**JSObject** wrapper	**JSObject** wrapper	real JavaScript object
real JavaScript object	**JSObject** wrapper	any real Java object	wrapped Java object
wrapped Java object	real Java object	array of objects	wrapped Java object that allows array indices.
Method calls			
Wrapped Java object method call	method call on real Java object	**JSObject.call()**	named method of real JavaScript object called
Wrapped Java object's property is used	property of real Java object is used	JSObject.get_member() JSObject.set_member()	property of real JavaScript object is used
		JSObject.get_slot() JSObject.set_slot()	array element of real JavaScript object is used
Events and Exceptions			
		Java exception thrown	JavaScript **onError** event

Handling Java from JavaScript

Recall that JavaScript is a loosely-typed language. Within JavaScript, values are converted between types automatically as appropriate. This policy applies to interacting with Java as well—all the conversion is done for you automatically, making the process particularly easy.

Java connection points

Java objects appear in the JavaScript browser object model as though they were host objects. Access to Java is achieved through the properties and methods of these objects. There are two kinds: applet objects and local class library objects.

window.document.applets

Just as **window.document.embeds** is an array of Plugin objects embedded in an HTML document, **window.document.applets** is an array of the applets in that document. If the HTML tag describing the applet has a **NAME** attribute, this can be used to identify the particular applet:

```
window.document.myapplet;
```

Each of the JavaScript array members is an object. Every Java applet has a main object that is the center point of the applet. The objects that are JavaScript array elements are placeholders for the main objects of applets. The properties of those objects match certain properties of the applets' main objects.

How do you know what properties apply to what applet? There are three options:

- Make the applet yourself.
- Look at the applet source code.
- Find documentation on the applet.

"Hello, World" the applet way

This is the Java source file **Hello.java**:

```java
import java.applet.Applet;
import java.awt.Graphics;

public class Hello extends Applet
{
  public String greeting = "Hello, World";

  public void greet()
  {
    repaint();
  }

  public void paint(Graphics g)
  {
    g.drawString(greeting, 5, 15);
  }
}
```

You might notice some superficial similarities with JavaScript immediately. To understand all the implications of this applet is beyond this book; but there are two crucial points:

 Public and private features. In JavaScript, properties and methods of objects are always exposed to the script writer (except for the technicality of the `'internal'` property attribute, described in the ECMAScript standard). In Java, each property and method of a class *may* be exposed. The **public** keywords in this example expose a property **greeting** and two methods **greet()** and **paint()**. This may remind you of Internet Explorer 4.0 Scriptlets—so it should; they are designed to mimic this Java behavior.

This class is the main class of the applet. You can tell because the magic `'extends Applet'` keywords are present. In this case, the applet has no other classes beyond certain standard ones, although that is only obvious to a Java programmer.

This applet might be displayed in an HTML document such as this:

```
<HTML><BODY>
Applet:<BR>
<APPLET CODE="Hello.class" WIDTH=200 HEIGHT=100></APPLET>
</BODY> </HTML>
```

The page looks like this:

In fact, this applet does very little (just displays 'Hello, World') and stops. It doesn't even use the property **greeting** or method **greet()**. That is because those things are designed to be used from JavaScript.

Controlling the applet from JavaScript

This alternative HTML might be used with the applet from the last example:

```
<HTML><HEAD><SCRIPT>
function change_it()
{
  if ( document.my_message.greeting == "Hello, World" )
  {
    document.my_message.greeting = "Don't Panic";
    document.my_message.greet();
  }
```

217

```
      else
      {
        document.my_message.greeting = "Hello, World";
        document.my_message.greet();
      }
   }
   </SCRIPT></HEAD><BODY>
   Applet:<BR>
   <APPLET NAME="my_message" CODE="Hello.class" WIDTH=200 HEIGHT=100></APPLET>
   <FORM>
   <INPUT TYPE="button" VALUE="Try it" ONCLICK="change_it()">
   </FORM></BODY> </HTML>
```

In this example, the HTML form button and JavaScript script instruct the Java applet how to act. That's all there is to it. The applet's greeting property is set directly from JavaScript, and then the **greet()** method is called to display it. This two-step process can be reduced to one step by calling **greet()** with arguments. Here is a modified (and shorter) version of the **applet** source that allows exactly that:

```
import java.applet.Applet;
import java.awt.Graphics;

public class Hello2 extends Applet
{
  String greeting = "Hello, World";
  public void greet(String new_greeting)
  {
    greeting = new_greeting;
    repaint();
  }

  public void paint(Graphics g)
  {
    g.drawString(greeting, 5, 15);
  }
}
```

Here is the modified HTML file that exploits the modified applet from JavaScript:

```
<HTML> <BODY>
Applet:<BR>
<APPLET NAME="my_message" CODE="Hello2.class" WIDTH=200 HEIGHT=100></APPLET>
<FORM>
<INPUT TYPE="text" ONCHANGE="window.document.my_message.greet(this.value)">
</FORM></BODY> </HTML>
```

In this example, whatever the user types in appears in the applet. This is shorter, but since the Java property **greeting** no longer has the **public** keyword, it can't be examined, should you want to check it. That is easily solved if it becomes a problem.

It's not hard to see how even a simple applet like this is useful—it can provide read-only fields that update dynamically in a Web page, for example. That is something that otherwise requires HTML 4.0 support.

Finally, notice how both the HTML file and the Java source needed to be changed when an enhancement was made. This shows how closely the two languages become tied to each other once you start them interacting with each other.

Java methods aren't that flexible

What if the number or type of the arguments varies in the **greet()** call from JavaScript? Display the page above and try:

```
javascript:void(document.my_message.greet(0x12))
```

or

```
javascript:void(document.my_message.greet('xx','yy'))
```

In the first case, JavaScript converts the type successfully. In the second case you should see a message like this:

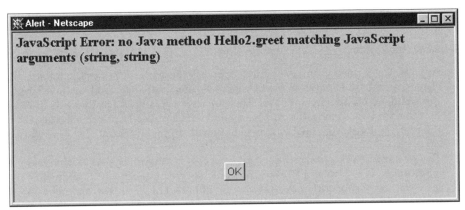

Java methods are not generally as flexible as JavaScript methods. Each method usually has an exact number of arguments with exact types. The moral to the story is: don't rely on type conversion; be organized enough to always supply the right number of values of the right types.

Java methods can return values

The Hello2 applet can easily be enhanced to return the number of successful "hello's". A modified version of the previous example:

```java
import java.applet.Applet;
import java.awt.Graphics;

public class Hello2 extends Applet
{
  String greeting = "Hello, World";
  int     count    = 0;
  public int greet(String new_greeting)
  {
    greeting = new_greeting;
    repaint();
    return ++count;
  }

  public void paint(Graphics g)
  {
    g.drawString(greeting, 5, 15);
  }
}
```

219

The **greet()** method of this modified applet would be called as follows:

```
var js_total = document.my_message.greet("What?");
```

js_total is just an ordinary JavaScript variable which would contain a value of type Number after the Java method returns.

Arguments and return values can be objects.

The **greet()** function can be enhanced to return a Java object rather than a primitive type, or accept such an object as an argument. That is how objects in the applet other than the main applet object can be handled from JavaScript. The next section has more to say on that subject. The function could also be enhanced to accept a JavaScript object as an argument or return value. That is covered in the 'Handling JavaScript from Java' section.

window.Packages

Applets are formed from class files. Some of these class files are standard classes. Just as the browser object model is the meat and drink of JavaScript, so the standard classes are for Java. These classes are stored locally with the browser, and for Navigator 3.0, Navigator 4.0, Internet Explorer 4.0 but not Internet Explorer 3.0, can be accessed directly from JavaScript.

The **window.Packages** property gives access to these classes. Inconveniently, 'packages' is a JavaScript reserved word, so the uppercase P is required. These Java classes are formed into a hierarchy, but it's not an object hierarchy (a hierarchy of object instances), it's a class hierarchy (a hierarchy of object types), with each class appearing at most once. The hierarchy is multilevel so these are all valid classes:

```
window.Packages.java.lang.io.System;
window.Packages.netscape.application.Plugin;
window.Packages.sun.tools.debug.StackFrame;
window.Packages.somethingsoft.stuff.Special;          // imaginary case
```

Apart from the **Packages.java** case, the first word after **Packages** is by convention the name of a company that invented that part of the class hierarchy, hence **'sun'**, **'netscape'** and the new hopeful **'somethingsoft'**. Technically, such a name should be preceded by **'org'** or **'com'**, in a similar way to domain names, but in reverse. Because the **'java'**, **'netscape'** and **'sun'** cases are so commonly used, these three cases *only* are also accessible *without* the **Packages** keyword:

```
window.java.lang.io.System;
window.netscape.application.Plugin;
window.sun.tools.debug.StackFrame;
```

The online documentation for developers at **http://java.sun.com** describes the whole hierarchy of classes.

Using local classes from JavaScript

Several example of using these classes have been illustrated already. From the Disappearing Data chapter, Chapter 7, a simple example:

```
java.lang.System.out.println("Window name is: "+top.name);
```

This example writes the supplied data out to the Java console, and looks straightforward. However, there is a complexity: the hierarchy referred to is a hierarchy of classes, not objects. So when the **println()** method is called, what object does it belong to? In this second example from Chapter 2, where is the return data extracted from?

```
str = java.lang.System.getProperty('os.name');
```

The answer is that methods of a Java object can optionally be **static**. Normally a method is associated with an object, so there is one per object of a given class. Static methods are associated with the class, not a particular object (class instance), so there is one *total*, independent of, and shared by, all objects of the class. This imaginary applet illustrates:

```
import java.applet.Applet;
import java.awt.Graphics;

public class Example extends Applet
{
    static public String data = 'test'; // always available, shared by objects

    public void first()              // available when an object is present
    {
    }
    static public void second()      // available without an object
    {
    }
}
```

The **second()** method is **static** and therefore can be used like the **println()** method, without any object being needed. The **first()** method is not; it cannot be used that way. The **data** variable (a class **attribute**) is also static, so it is accessible—there will always be exactly one copy of the variable. For JavaScript script writers, the moral to this story is that static Java methods and attributes are the easiest to use.

For non-static members, a different approach is required. From the Privacy and Security chapter, Chapter 6, this Netscape-only JavaScript function exploits local classes:

```
function save_it(filename, filedata);
{
    netscape.security.PrivilegeManager.enablePrivilege("UniversalFileWrite");
    var jo_file   = new java.io.FileOutputStream(filename);
    var jo_stream = new java.io.DataOutputStream(jo_file);
    jo_stream.writeChars(filedata);
    jo_stream.close();
    netscape.security.PrivilegeManager.disablePrivilege("UniversalFileWrite");
}
```

221

The lines starting **'netscape**...' exploit static methods as above. To use other Java methods, first a Java object must be created, and then the method can be invoked from this object. In this example, two JavaScript objects that wrap one Java object each are created: **jo_file** and **jo_stream**. The calls to the security manager request permission to write to the local filesystem via these objects, which otherwise wouldn't be allowed. If this were Internet Explorer, capability signing would be used instead for the same result. See Chapter 6.

This example is effectively 'arms-length' Java programming—the whole example is written in JavaScript. No Java object or method is ever directly touched—only Java object wrappers and Java method wrappers. Each time a Java method wrapper is called, processing 'descends' into the Java language, does the work and then returns to JavaScript. The second 'new' operation shows how a wrapped Java object can be handed to a wrapped Java method as an argument. When it is passed to Java it all unwraps properly and the real Java method is called with the real Java object.

In order to fully exploit this feature you need to be conversant with the Java standard class hierarchies. If you are, you can achieve quite a lot using JavaScript that would otherwise require an applet. The only catch is that this approach is slower than directly using an applet, because of all the wrapping and unwrapping that goes on.

Understanding the applet lifecycle

As remarked earlier, applets can have some odd behavior when loading or running. If the applet you are trying to manage from JavaScript disappears, spits errors, won't start or is generally difficult, review these details.

When applets are loaded

Inside Java there is a bit of functionality called a **class loader** that is responsible for retrieving applet class files from across the Internet. It is a lazy soul. It only retrieves applet files when they are absolutely needed. This means an applet can spend a long time in a partially loaded state if it has sufficient classes at hand to do useful work.

For a currently running applet, you can be confident that the main class of the applet has loaded—otherwise the applet couldn't have started. If you call a method of an applet from JavaScript, and that method requires additional classes to be loaded, then execution will halt while the class loader fetches whatever is needed. However, there are two traps. Firstly, this can result in very jerky behavior if the applet irregularly stalls to augment itself with further classes. Secondly, browsers have a security hobble that prevents JavaScript from making network connections. For Netscape browsers less than version 4.0, this hobble extends to the network connections used to retrieve applet class files. In those cases, if JavaScript calls an applet method that needs classes loaded, an error will occur.

To avoid both of these problems, the applet creator should enhance the applet so that when it starts, all the classes are retrieved straightaway. Such a task is outside the scope of this book.

What applets are doing

Applets lead complex lives. An image is either loading or loaded, but applets can be in any one of six states. Three of these start the applet up and three shut it down.

Ready ... Set... Go

The official names for the three startup states are **Loaded**, **Initialized** and **Started**. When a new document with an applet is displayed in the browser, the applet quickly passes through each of these states, ending with Started.

Loaded means the main class of the applet has been retrieved by the class loader.

Initialized means the special `init()` method of the applet has been called. This gives the applet designer a chance to do some preparation work before the applet is officially started.

Started means the applet is running, or expecting user input.

Stop... Relax ... Forget it

The official names for the three shutdown states are **Stopped**, **Destroyed** and **Disposed**. When an applet is due to be removed, or the browser is shutdown, the applet quickly passes through each of these states, ending with Disposed.

Stopped. The applet is not running but all its state (data and objects) is intact.

Destroyed. The special `destroy()` method of the applet has been called. This gives the applet designer a change to do the some cleanup before the applet finally goes away.

Disposed. All the applet's content is discarded—it is gone.

Browser interference

For Microsoft browsers, the use of these states is straightforward. When a URL with an applet is displayed in a window, the three startup states are run through. If the URL is replaced with another one, the shutdown states are run through. Netscape browsers are not so easy.

Netscape browsers attempt to give applets more flexibility. They do this by allowing applets to survive as long as the document they are a part of is retained somewhere in the browser's history. If a URL containing an applet is moved to history because the user displays a different URL, the applet is merely stopped, not destroyed. If the original URL is returned to, the applet is started again.

The consequences are that without planning ahead, the script writer can't tell if the applet is running for the first time, or continuing from where it last left off. The way to defeat this is to get the Java applet to set a JavaScript variable in

223

its **init()** method. When the document loads, if the JavaScript variable exists, the applet is running for the first time. If it doesn't, the Java applet is picking up where it left off. See 'Handling JavaScript from Java' for how to do this.

There is a further complication with this system. If the user creates a very long history of pages, all with applets, a great deal of the computer's resources will be spent holding on to Stopped applets that aren't visible. The Netscape browsers handle this by setting an arbitrary maximum of 10 applets held in this way. If more than 10 occur, some will be moved to Destroyed and then Disposed. If the page is returned to, those applets will be restarted from the beginning. This is not easy for the script writer to handle—better to accept that the applet was aborted in an untimely way and start again. However, the limit of 10 can be lifted higher for Netscape 4.0 with this JavaScript statement:

```
netscape.applet.Control.setAppletPruningThreshold(99); // 99 applets? - plenty.
```

Netscape remarks that the Macintosh version of Navigator has a limit of 1, not 10, but that hasn't been verified in the production of this book.

Finally, there is a second complication. Java is a general programming language and there are ways of avoiding the strict interpretation of these six states. The best the browser can do is *label* the applet as being in one of the states, and hope that its functionality follows suit in the expected way. An applet need only re-write the **stop()** method of the Applet class to achieve this. In a perfect world this would be documented with the applet ...

How to start again

If you are confused about the state of a given applet you can force a complete reload from the remote location the applet came from as follows:

 simultaneously, Shift and the Reload button on Netscape browsers

 simultaneously, Ctrl and the Refresh button on Microsoft browsers

How to detect the Java version

This URL will report the version of the JVM running inside your browser. Applets should be developed to support this version.

```
javascript:alert(java.lang.System.getProperty('java.version'));
```

Handling JavaScript from Java

The Java language doesn't automatically give easy access to the browser's HTML features, such as form elements. By communicating from Java to JavaScript, JavaScript's access to those features can be exploited by Java. This requires knowledge of Java, which this book doesn't pretend to cover, but the important features of this interaction are briefly discussed.

The **MAYSCRIPT** attribute of the **<APPLET>** tag, and the Java **JSObject** and **JSException** classes provide the mechanism with communicating with JavaScript. These features are Netscape innovations applying to Navigator 3.0 and 4.0, Internet Explorer 4.0, but not Internet Explorer 3.0.

MAYSCRIPT

If the **MAYSCRIPT** attribute is not present, no communication from Java to JavaScript is possible. You can always go from JavaScript to Java. The reason behind this is that an HTML document author or a JavaScript script writer might want to use a third party applet, but might not trust the applet enough to be willing to expose their own work to that applet. Without **MAYSCRIPT**, the applet is trapped in Java-land. Chapter 2 has an example of **MAYSCRIPT**.

If there is more than one applet embedded in a given page, some may have the **MAYSCRIPT** attribute and others not. This is a more flexible arrangement than page signing, discussed in Chapter 6, where all the JavaScript is signed, or none of it is. However, flexibility creates a complication. Because Java applets can interact with each other directly, a non-**MAYSCRIPT**ed applet might try to get access to JavaScript by communicating with a **MAYSCRIPT**ed applet that does have access. That could be bad.

Such a security hole is prevented by the class loader that applets rely on to get into the browser in the first place. Two applets share a classloader only if the **CODEBASE**, **ARCHIVE** and **MAYSCRIPT** attributes for both applets' tag match *and* if the applets are embedded in the same document. Otherwise, they have a separate classloader each. So, on a typical single page of applets, there might be two classloaders used: one for **MAYSCRIPT**ed applets, and one for the rest. This has the additional limitation of preventing applets in different frames (for example) talking directly to each other under all circumstances. For those applets, **MAYSCRIPT** and JavaScript must be used, or else Netscape 4.0's BeanConnect enhancements to LiveConnect investigated.

'Errors and events' below illustrates what happens when there are mixups with **MAYSCRIPT**.

JSObject

Just as JavaScript relies on the **document.applets** and **Packages** JavaScript objects to get access to Java, Java relies on objects of the **netscape.javascript.JSObject** Java class. This class is used for all possible types of JavaScript objects, no matter what **typeof()** might report for the object.

JSObject.getWindow()

It's fine to use **JSObject** to represent all JavaScript objects within Java, but how do you get the first such object? **JSObject** has a static method called **getWindow()** which returns a Java object that wraps the JavaScript object that **window** tracks. This example applet illustrates:

```
import java.applet.Applet;
import netscape.javascript.*;      // required for JavaScript access

public class Test extends Applet
{
    JSObject window;            // to match the JavaScript one of the same name
```

```
    public void init()
    {
       window = JSObject.getWindow(this);
       // .. more stuff ..
    }

    // .. more stuff ..
    }
```

Since the **init()** method is responsible for organizing the applet before it really gets going, it's a logical place to grab the JavaScript **window** object. Stored in a property of the class, it's available from then on. See the Errors and Events section for why you might grab the window object outside **init()** instead.

Finding a JavaScript object

Once you have the window object, it's just a matter of stepping through the JavaScript object hierarchy until you reach the bit you want. This **Java** code snippet locates the **window.document.location** object using the **getMember()** method of the **JSObject** wrapper object to return a second wrapper object for the specified sub-object:

```
// ... more ...
JSObject win = JSObject.getWindow(this);
JSObject doc = (JSObject) win.getMember("document");
JSObject loc = (JSObject) doc.getMember("location"); // found it
// ... more ...
```

Using JavaScript properties and methods

The **getMember()** method is one of four methods that can be used to work with the JavaScript properties of a JavaScript object wrapped up in a **JSObject**. There is no **getProperty()** method; instead **'member'** is used to mean those properties which are named, and **'slot'** is used to mean those properties referred to by array indices. This **Java** code fragment changes the current URL for the window.

```
// assume 'loc' exists from the last example
String href    = (String) loc.getMember("href");      // get the old URL
String new_url = "about:blank";
loc.setMember("href", new_url);                        / replace it
```

For array indices, the pattern is similar. Imagine the **location** object was actually an array and the **href** property was instead the third array element (**location[2]**). A Java code fragment again:

```
// assume 'loc' exists from the last example
Number i      = 2;
String href   = (String) loc.getSlot(i);   // get the old URL
String new_url = "about:blank";
loc.setSlot(i, new_url);                    // replace it
```

With both of these cases, note that literal Java values like "**about:blank**" and 2 weren't used as method arguments. The arguments must always be objects (Java-speak: inherited from **java.lang.Object**), so the only choices really are the Java types Boolean, Float, String and **JSObject**.

For JavaScript methods, such as **location.reload()**, the situation is similar, except the **call()** method is used. Since JavaScript supports variable numbers of arguments, but Java doesn't, a little extra effort is required:

```
// ... more ...
JSObject window = JSObject.getWindow(this);

Object args[2];
args[0] = new String("Sales this month");
args[1] = new Number(23);

window.call("show_summary",args);   // = window.show_summary('Sales this
month',23);
// ... more ...
```

Executing any JavaScript code

It's also possible to run an arbitrary piece of JavaScript from within Java. This includes declaring new JavaScript functions, or attaching new properties to existing JavaScript objects. If you specifically prefer the floating point mathematics in JavaScript (there's no real reason to) you can do this:

```
// find the area of a circle, radius 2, using JavaScript
JSObject window = JSObject.getWindow(this);
Number area = (Number) window.eval("Math.PI * "+2+" * "+2);
```

Notice how the addition sign can be used for string concatenation in Java the same as JavaScript. This functionality is the easiest way to interact with JavaScript browser objects as these examples show.

Populate an HTML text field with a Java value:

```
JSObject.getWindow(this).eval("window.document.form1.field1.value = " +
java_string);
```

Make an alert appear with a Java string as the message:

```
JSObject.getWindow(this).eval("alert('message from Java')");
```

In both these cases, the wrapped copy of the JavaScript window object is only temporarily created—long enough for the **eval()** method to pass the statements to JavaScript and return.

Since the class file is compiled into an unreadable binary format, the bits of JavaScript in the class file are very difficult for the browser user to look at. This may be the best way for script writers to protect their code from being stolen, but it is a great deal of effort to go to, and is *still* not as secure as digital signing, because of the possibility of a hacker decompiling the applet. If the JavaScript is stored as Java strings, possibly with a simple encryption like the 'rot13' encryption used on the Internet in the days before encrypted email, then it is a great deal of effort for even a hacker to get the script. But it's still possible: all a suitable maniac requires is a reverse Java-compiler (a decompiler) and time better spent on something else.

Doing without JSObject

You may not have the luxury of **MAYSCRIPT** for some imponderable reason. Internet Explorer 3.0 and Netscape 2.02 don't have a **JSObject** Java class at all. Either makes it hard to communicate from Java back to JavaScript, but not impossible. JavaScript to Java can still be done, so that it allows Java methods to return values back to JavaScript when called. JavaScript can also read and set any public properties of Java objects. The hard part is to give a running applet the ability to affect JavaScript when *it* wants to. There are two approaches.

The simpler of the two is just to call a Java applet method that executes for most of the time. If that applet method only returns when there is information for JavaScript, then Java nearly controls JavaScript. Here is an example which searches for prime numbers greater than 10000. This is Java:

```
import java.applet.Applet;
import java.awt.Graphics;
import netscape.javascript.*;

public class prime extends Applet
{
  static int maybe_prime = 10000;

  public int calculate()              // find the next largest prime number.
  {
    int divisor = 0;
    while (true)
    {
      maybe_prime++;
      for (divisor=3; divisor<maybe_prime; divisor++)
        if ( (maybe_prime % divisor) == 0 )
          return maybe_prime;
    }
  }
}
```

This is the HTML document:

```
<HTML><HEAD><SCRIPT>
function show_it()
{
  for(;;)
  {
    alert (document.prime.calculate());
  }
}
</SCRIPT></HEAD><BODY ONLOAD="show_it()">
  <APPLET CODE="prime.class" NAME="prime" WIDTH=150 HEIGHT=25></APPLET>
</BODY></HTML>
```

This is all rather ugly since it consumes a lot of the computer's resources and nearly locks up the browser, but it may be enough for crude jobs. A more complex example might wait in Java for applet input from the user, and return a string instruction that the JavaScript script can examine and act on, before passing control back to the applet again.

A better approach is to imagine JavaScript and Java are communicating over a network. It's easy to create a public Java string in a Java class that is readable and writeable by both Java and JavaScript. This string (or any data) can be used as the network—it is a shared buffer. Both Java and JavaScript support polling (repeating) timer concepts (**setTimeout()** and **SetInterval()** in JavaScript, timer threads in Java). That is all the equipment required for communications. Setting up Java timers is beyond this book but the JavaScript side is easy to see:

```
<HTML><HEAD><SCRIPT>
function read_buffer()
{
  if ( window.sender.buffer == "empty" || window.sender.buffer == "complete" )
    return;
  alert(window.sender.buffer);              // process the data
  window.sender.data = "complete";
}
</SCRIPT></HEAD><BODY ONLOAD="setInterval('window.read_buffer()',100)">
<APPLET CODE="sender.class" NAME="sender" WIDTH=150 HEIGHT=25></APPLET>
</BODY></HTML>
```

This is how such a system proceeds. Activity starts inside Java, since it is Java trying to communicate with JavaScript:

- The Java applet writes the string "**empty**" to the **buffer** Java variable on startup.

- When there is something to send, the **buffer** variable is changed by the applet to whatever is required.

- The applet waits with a polling timer until the variable changes to "**complete**" (in communications terms, this is called an 'acknowledged protocol', meaning every data transfer is confirmed back to the sender).

Meanwhile, on the JavaScript side:

- The JavaScript script has been waiting for the word "**empty**" to disappear, and reads the new data when it arrives.

- It then changes the buffer to "**complete**".

- When that happens, Java sets the variable back to "**empty**" until the next bit of data is to be sent.

Not to be relied upon for blinding speed, but the browser and the user are free to do other things, and the two systems are now able to communicate.

Errors and Exceptions

The Java compiler and interpreter are very fussy about data types and so on, so numerous errors that are hard to track down in JavaScript yield a message almost immediately in Java. However, problems can still happen. In Java, bad things usually result in "an exception being thrown". An **exception** is just a particular type of Java object. The fact that it is **thrown** means that some piece of code that could have been well-behaved encountered an unusual condition and issued a complaint instead. The complaint takes the form of an exception object which is catered for by special Java syntax distantly related to **'if'** statements.

There are different classes of Java exceptions. The
`netscape.javascript.JSException` class is just for JavaScript-related
exceptions. Java code that calls JavaScript can be written to either specially
handle this exception type, or leave it up to someone else. Unlike the
`JSObject` class, the `JSException` class doesn't reflect any object in the
browser hierarchy.

Because this class is really for Java programmers, its details aren't of much
interest to a script writer. However, script writers need to understand that
`JSException` exceptions (and Java exceptions generally) can cause JavaScript
`onError` event handlers to execute. This only occurs if an exception is thrown
and it is not **caught** (captured and handled) inside the Java applet. This applet
shows the case where a **JSException** is handled without using the JavaScript
`onError` handler:

```
import java.applet.Applet;
import netscape.javascript.*;

public class Test extends Applet
{
  public void test_it()
  {
    JSObject win = JSObject.getWindow(this);
    try {
      throw new JSException();        // by any means, a JSException is created
    }
    catch (JSException e) {
      JSObject.getWindow(this).eval("alert('Exception detected)"); // caught it
    }
  }
}
```

In this applet, the **catch** statement ensures that the Exception never reaches
JavaScript. The content of the catch block does choose to show a **JavaScript**
alert, but it could just as easily be silent.

This second applet raises an exception which does result in the **onError**
handler firing, if there is one:

```
import java.applet.Applet;
import netscape.javascript.*;

public class Test extends Applet
{
  public void throw_it() throws JSException
  {
    throw new JSException("Test Exception");
  }
}
```

The JavaScript code to handle the exception looks like this:

```
<HTML><HEAD><SCRIPT>
function error_alert(message)
{
  alert(message);
  return true;
}
onerror = error_alert;
```

```
function throw_it()
{
  document.x.throw_it();
}
</SCRIPT></HEAD><BODY ONLOAD="throw_it()">
<APPLET MAYSCRIPT CODE="Test.class" NAME="x" WIDTH=150 HEIGHT=25></APPLET>
</BODY> </HTML>
```

and the alert produced by the **onError** handler looks like this:

Notice that in this case, the Java method **throw_it()** specifically states that a **JSException** exception can result from that method being called. This is a Java language requirement. When the document is fully loaded, the **onLoad** event handler causes JavaScript to call the Java **throw_it()** function. That function aborts with an exception (deliberately), ending the Java phase, and throwing control back to JavaScript. That is when the **onError** event handler fires.

There is one further possibility that can occur if a Java applet attempts to exploit JavaScript features when the **MAYSCRIPT** attribute is missing. An exception will result as for the other cases but not if the attempt is made inside the applet's **init()** method. The applet has yet to start when the **init()** method is called, so the normal exception system isn't supported. Instead, the user will be warned on the status line of the browser window that a **MAYSCRIPT** attribute is missing.

The Java Security Model

Apart from the general security provided by a browser, Java has its own security system. Both Netscape and Microsoft browsers take advantage of that security system in order to control access to dangerous features such as the writing of files on the browser's local computer. Each vendor does it differently. The model is used for the whole browser, not just for the JVM part of it.

For Microsoft Internet Explorer 4.0, the Authenticode code signing system allows the Java security information to be included as data with the code being signed, whether Java or JavaScript. Apart from organizing the signing process, described in Chapter 6, there are no implications for JavaScript scripts. A correctly signed script will be able to exploit secure Java features via ActiveX the same as non-secured features.

For Netscape Communicator 4.0, the security information must be included as part of the content of JavaScript scripts and Java applets. The script can be signed or not signed. If not signed, the user will be warned when particular

231

secure features are requested. It is a scriptwriting task to setup the security access properly, and the details contributed by Java are discussed here.

Java security theory

Security normally applies to people—login accounts, locks on doors or identity checks. Those people who are considered 'safe' have passwords, keys, and ID which give them access to computers, rooms and expensive nightclubs. People aren't the issue for the Java security model. Foreign code loaded into a browser is—whether it is Java or JavaScript code.

Java 1.1 security

The security model adopted for the 4.0 browsers is based on the security model innovated for the 1.1 release of Java.

For this model, the precious resources that need to be kept safe are called **targets**. A target is a general name—it could be anything deemed important. For Java, it means classes that do possibly insecure things, like network connections or file writing. For JavaScript it means all those Java classes plus various features of the browser only available to signed scripts, like the **'alwaysRaised'** option of the **window.open()** method in JavaScript 1.2.

The access mechanism for these targets is called a **privilege**. Once a suitable privilege is **granted**, the target's precious features may be exploited. Before they actually are exploited, a switch must be thrown to put the target in unsafe mode—this is called **enabling** the privilege. The privilege ought to be **disabled** when it is finished with.

The protagonist that requests privileges be granted is called a **principal**. That is also a general name—anything could be a principal. In the case of Java, the principals are **codebases**. A codebase means a place that program code originates from. A place that program code originates from means a URL, and a URL means a file like a Java **.class** file, a JavaScript **.js** file, a Java-embedded HTML file or any other suitable format for code or scripts such as **.jar** files.

So a principal (a script or program) requests privileges be granted for particular targets such as Java classes or browser features, and once they are, enables those privileges, performs the functionality of interest, and disables them until that functionality is needed again. The questions remaining are: who grants the privileges, and what privileges? The browser grants, either automatically by verifying an attached digital certificate, or by prompting the user for permission. The Java standard plus the browser maker defines the privileges, so you have to refer to documentation. See the Reference Section for Netscape's list. This diagram summarizes the interactions:

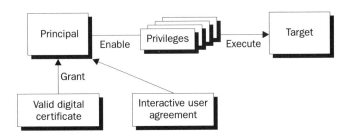

Manageable Privileges

The security system is supposed to be 'fine grained'. This means that the features that are targets are primitive and numerous in nature, and can be granted individually. This is beneficial for programmers who want close-up control of the system, but can be an administration headache. Simple operations like creating and copying a file might require privileges for several targets to be granted. More complex scripts might ask for dozens of privileges. Whether it's the user that has to grant the privileges interactively, or the developer who has to organize the signed scripts, this is not so practical.

A macro target is a target which is a collection of other targets. By requesting privileges on a macro target, all the privilege requests for the collection are made. Macro targets usually group a small number of like-minded targets, like all file targets, or all networking targets. This serves to reduce the administration problem somewhat. Macro targets are used in exactly the same way as other targets.

Microsoft's Internet Explorer 4.0 goes one step further, introducing security zones. A security zone is a just a collection of targets, macro or otherwise that specifies a whole security profile for a given principal (script or file). This way, all the required targets are bundled into a single named item. The browser can then be loaded with a number of security zones, and scripts and applets indicate which zone they require privileges for. The zone description can be "dumbed down" sufficiently that the user can make an informed decision about whether to grant access or not.

Netscape use of features

You may well be sick of the sight of this JavaScript function, since this is its third appearance:

```
function save_it(filename, filedata);
{
    netscape.security.PrivilegeManager.enablePrivilege("UniversalFileWrite");
    var jo_file   = new java.io.FileOutputStream(filename);
    var jo_stream = new java.io.DataOutputStream(jo_file);
    jo_stream.writeChars(filedata);
    jo_stream.close();
    netscape.security.PrivilegeManager.disablePrivilege("UniversalFileWrite");
}
```

All the pieces should fall together for this example now. The **privilege manager** is the part of Java and of the browser that allows privileges to be enabled and disabled. It is stored in local class files with the browser so it is directly accessible from JavaScript whether an applet exists in the HTML document or not. To review: this chapter discusses calling Java methods from JavaScript and the Java security model; Chapter 6 discusses the general mechanics of signed scripts.

The only thing not shown is the granting of privileges. There is no JavaScript required for this—the browser takes care of it when the URL containing the script is loaded.

Summary

The features that Java and Java applets make available in browsers create new horizons for JavaScript scriptwriters. Via glue technologies like ActiveX and LiveConnect nearly all the features of Java can be exploited from JavaScript. However, this doesn't come for free: performance is not quite as good as for a pure Java applet and the necessity of learning many Java concepts can be burdensome. In the end, to fully exploit the two languages together, learn both.

Two important issues when dealing with Java are applet lifetimes and security. The former can easily confuse the situation when the script writer is testing JavaScript web applications. The latter is indispensable if the script writer wishes to exceed the ordinary bounds of the browser's functionality.

Chapter

Dynamic HTML

Web pages vary greatly in their appearance. Some HTML web documents are merely informative, being no more than heading-laden text. Some Web documents are both informative and interactive, such as HTML documents containing forms and a liberal dose of JavaScript. Magazine-style documents, strewn with images, applets and plugins, and sporting fancy styles, headings, colors and typefaces can be quite impressive visually, especially if backed-up by a good graphic artist. Via a few JavaScript multimedia tricks such as those outlined in Chapter 4, images can add a degree of animation. However, for truly impressive Web pages, nothing beats the possibility of independently animating every single tag in a document and its contents, either in response to user actions, or without the user needing to do anything at all. This possibility is offered by **Dynamic HTML**.

Client-side JavaScript, with its timing mechanisms and access to host objects that reflect a document's content is absolutely crucial for Dynamic HTML. Viewed from the JavaScript perspective, it is the script writer that creates dynamic behavior in a document that is otherwise just an inactive load of HTML.

As is the case for the Java language, Dynamic HTML is a subject rich in information that really requires a book of its own. Only the most important features are touched on here.

What is Dynamic HTML?

The term Dynamic HTML is somewhat vague. In a general, hand-waving sense, it means any HTML document in a browser that exploits one or more specific technical features in order to create one or more specific visual effects. From a practical point of view, that is hardly a useful description.

Defined as a technology

Dynamic HTML can be viewed as an evolutionary improvement in browsers, rather than an entirely new, alien technology.

JavaScript commands like **window.alert('Frivolous Text')** provide a very simple mechanism for changing that which a browser displays. Such features are provided by a host object (the **window** object in this case) and have been available since the earliest days of JavaScript. As browser versions increased, more host objects became available, and the extent of JavaScript's control over the browser environment grew. With the 4.0 browsers, the host objects available have reached a kind of critical mass, sufficient to allow very detailed control over the elements of a document, especially in the Internet Explorer 4.0 case. Taking advantage of this detailed control—ordinary JavaScript applied to newly exposed document features—is all Dynamic HTML really is. An important aspect of this control is that it happens *after* the document is fully loaded and rendered into the browser.

Put another way, four technologies contribute to Dynamic HTML:

- JavaScript
- Styles
- HTML
- the DOM—the Document Object Model

By the time all the latest enhancements for these technologies are rolled together, compatibility levels between Netscape and Microsoft 4.0 browsers are lower than you might otherwise hope for.

JavaScript

JavaScript itself does not contribute much that is new towards Dynamic HTML, other than providing a programming mechanism for the host objects innovated by the other technologies. It is the authority that orders those objects' behavior. One exception in the 4.0 browsers is the method **setInterval()**, which is a very handy alternative to **setTimeout()**. Some Dynamic HTML techniques are repetitious—**setInterval()** allows a piece of script to run periodically.

Styles

The properties that make up styles are the meat and drink of Dynamic HTML. By altering these style properties, the script writer can change the appearance of an HTML document even after it is fully rendered on the screen. Styles may be expressed in a number of ways, but the most common approaches, which are the ones that contribute to Dynamic HTML, are based on these standards:

- CSS1: Cascading Style Sheets level 1
- CSS-P: Cascading Style Sheets - Positioning (currently draft)

In addition, there is a CSS2 draft standard now, but it is not implemented in either of the major 4.0 browsers. These standards can be viewed at **http://www.w3c.org**.

Internet Explorer 4.0 has an enhancement to style sheets called **filters**. Filters may be used for a number of additional effects beyond style sheets' normal capabilities.

HTML

With the advent of HTML 4.0, the **STYLE**, **CLASS** and **ID** tag attributes proliferate widely over most tags. These attributes allow style information to be attached to tags, all accessible from JavaScript. The **<DIV>** and **<SPAN>** tags have new importance because of their ability to associate arbitrary chunks of HTML with a style.

Particular to Netscape 4.0 browsers are the **<LAYER>** and **<ILAYER>** tags. Although these tags have no official future and are made somewhat redundant by the CSS-P draft standard, they do provide a useful host object. Only use **<LAYER>** if you are happy to commit to Navigator 4.0.

DOM - the Document Object Model

The Browser Object Model defines all of the JavaScript host objects in the browser. The Document Object Model describes only those parts of the browser model that depend on the currently displayed HTML document. Because of the widespread adoption and therefore importance of HTML, the object model for HTML is undergoing standardization. DOM is that standard, with level 1 (part 1) released in draft and implemented in Internet Explorer 4.0 only.

The exposure of the DOM to JavaScript gives access to all the pieces of an HTML document. Apart from allowing style manipulation and so on, this exposure also gives access to the original HTML source text from within JavaScript. Previously, you could only 'View Source' the HTML source interactively.

As a consequence, the DOM allows the **content** of an HTML document to be changed after the document is loaded. Although the DOM isn't mandatory for Dynamic HTML, the content changing behavior that it enables is the most dynamic aspect possible.

This standard can be viewed at **http://www.w3c.org**.

Defined as an art form

Dynamic HTML can be viewed as a mode of expression for communicating with people, like other visual art forms such as painting, dance, or the iconized, mouse-driven graphics of a computer's desktop.

Like plain HTML, Dynamic HTML appears in a web browser window. Unlike plain HTML, the possibility of images, icons and text moving and reacting to each other creates a new mode of communication that the user must learn to interact with. This kind of interaction is particularly important when browsers are run in full screen mode, such as at information kiosks or via Netscape's Netcaster. In those cases, the user's normal mode of interaction for navigation tasks (via browser toolbars and menus) is not available, and Dynamic HTML features must substitute. The user must learn that key elements of a Dynamic HTML page mean that certain effects will follow.

The ability to position HTML elements at exact locations on a page allows elements to overlap. HTML is normally strictly two-dimensional, but overlapping elements require some organization in the third dimension. However, browsers are not capable of full three-dimensional effects, and in any event all that is really required is a **stacking order** for overlapping elements. A stacking order merely says which item is on top or which other item. So a browser window that is 800 pixels by 600 pixels, with perhaps 6 or less items in its content laying on top of each other, is called two-and-a-half dimensional, or 2.5-D, since the third dimension is much smaller in size than the other two. Rather than overlapping items with a whole third coordinate, the stacked items are said to have a **z-order**. A z-order is a convention that orders overlapping items based on an arbitrary number that is assigned to each item by the script writer.

Dynamic HTML draws inspiration from several other well-established media. It is strong on animated presentation graphics and slide shows. It is also similar to video digital editing, in that it allows effects like panning, wipes, zooms and insets. Dynamic HTML also draws from the world of animation, as it allows crude but flexible animation features. Because HTML documents can be textual, Dynamic HTML also allows some unique tricks of its own—menu expansion is a simple example.

For good examples of the potential of Dynamic HTML, see the following Web pages:

- **Presentation**. Use Navigator 4.0 to view this hype from Netscape:
  `http://developer.netscape.com/devcon/jun97/key_1/directs.html`

- **Video editing**. Use Internet Explorer 4.0 to view this simple page:
  `http://www.microsoft.com/sitebuilder/columnists/samples/Scale2.htm`

- **Animation**. Use Navigator 4.0 to interact with this winner of the Netscape 1997 Dynamic HTML contest:
  `http://developer.netscape.com/devcon/jun97/contest/freefall/index.html`

- **Menu expansion**. Use Internet Explorer 4.0 to navigate through this Microsoft documentation:
  `http://www.microsoft.com/workshop/prog/ie4`.

Dynamic HTML has its limitations as well. It may be a visual art form that can produce useful interrelationships between textual and iconic elements on a page, but because of these effects it is a poor vehicle for communication with disabled users. It is difficult to do drag-and-drop style operations, for example, if you are blind. It also isn't widely accessible outside the two major browsers. Therefore it is a less conservative approach than plain HTML.

What's possible without JavaScript

You should already be familiar with most of the features of HTML and CSS1 style sheets. They are briefly reviewed, as they are the building blocks for the more animated features of Dynamic HTML.

Font control

Styles provide all the text control features normally found in word processors; font size, weight, family and decorative features such as underlining.

Text spacing

Styles provide margin, padding and border spacing features which are **block formatting** information equivalent to 'paragraph formats' in word processors.

Positioning

Styles allow the element to which they apply to be located away from the normal position it would adopt when rendered by the browser. Absolute positioning allows the element to appear anywhere.

Superimposition

With absolute positioning a possibility, elements can overlap. The style mechanism defines the z-order that resolves which elements appear on top.

Visibility and display

Elements can take up visual space in a document, or they cannot be allocated any at all, much like hidden form fields. If they do take up space, then they can be visibly present (the normal case) or just withhold that space from other uses, like the Netscape proprietary **<SPACER>** tag.

Clipping

The content of a styled element takes up a set area, known as a bounding box. If the element's content exceeds the capacity of the bounding box, it may be clipped. Clipping means the overflowing parts of the content do not appear.

Filters

Internet Explorer 4.0 supports a filter enhancement to styles that allows additional effects to be laid on top of other style information.

<DIV> and <SPAN>

Styles normally apply to a specific instance of an HTML tag. Sometimes the piece of content to be styled doesn't easily fit into one of the predefined tags. The **<DIV>** or **<SPAN>** tags can be used to mark out an arbitrary section of content. **<DIV>** provides a line break before and after the content.

241

<LAYER>

The **<LAYER>** tag is an alternate syntax for absolutely positioned styles. It applies to Netscape 4.0 browsers only, and is considered a failed experiment in the sense that Netscape now advocates use of the **'position'** style property instead. That property is part of a standard, whereas layers aren't.

Embedded animation

Chapter 4 briefly describes the options for embedding already-animated objects into web pages, such as progressive GIFs.

JavaScript DOM host objects

Provided that an HTML document is correctly composed so that the HTML markup in it is well-ordered, the HTML tags fit together in a hierarchy. Consider this example:

```
<HTML>
<HEAD>
<TITLE> Pink Page </TITLE>
</HEAD>
<BODY>
<H1>Think Pink!</H1>
<BLOCKQUOTE>
All marshmellows, azaleas, but <STRONG> not </STRONG> panthers welcome.
</BLOCKQUOTE>
</BODY>
</HTML>
```

Re-stated as a diagram it appears as follows:

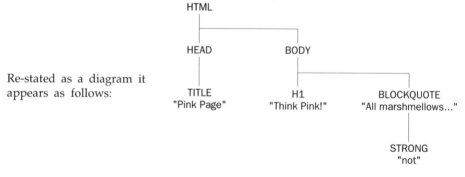

In the Document Object Model (henceforth DOM), each tag in a given document is supposed to have its own object. From this simple example it is easy to see how this could create quite large hierarchies. Imagine if these objects were named after their tags. To access a given tag's object from JavaScript would require quite long object references, possibly as follows:

```
top.document.html.body.blockquote.strong.contents; // doesn't quite work like
this
```

This example is not too bad, but a complex document could be far worse, especially since most documents have more than one paragraph and you need to know which one you are talking about. An HTML table alone adds three levels of objects to the hierarchy. This example doesn't include any style information either. There has to be a better way, and there is.

Hierarchies versus Collections

Users of databases will be familiar with the idea of extracting important data out of a large database by use of a query. Users of event-driven systems would be familiar with extracting important data out of a large flood of events using a filter. In both cases, a reduction method is available to expose only the interesting data. For HTML host objects in JavaScript, collections are the equivalent approach. A collection is just a group of related objects, which in JavaScript translates into an array of objects.

Therefore the DOM offers two ways of accessing host objects: by navigating the object hierarchy directly which might be quite a lengthy process, and by extracting a collection of interesting items from the hierarchy and then looking at them directly.

Often the script writer will know exactly which object is wanted, and will extract a collection from the hierarchy that reduces to the single object desired. At other times, a collection might be extracted that contains a group of matching items. Occasionally the scriptwriter might see fit to go poking through the hierarchy in detail if some complex analysis is required of the document. So both approaches have their place.

If a collection object is changed, the hierarchy is updated as well, and vice versa. The objects are the same in both cases, so the system is fully coordinated.

Object hierarchy

The DOM standard describes the important objects that are used to represent an HTML document inside a program such as a browser. Unfortunately, it does not yet (at this time of writing) describe the gory details of how this is to work in client-side JavaScript, nor is the standard complete or even ratified. So it is a bit early to be labeling browsers as compliant or non-compliant to the DOM.

What is easy to say is that Internet Explorer 4.0 is the first available browser to include support for the central, important features of the DOM. At this time of writing it is the only such browser. Since the DOM standard is yet to be completed, it is hard to claim that Internet Explorer 4.0's implementation is compliant to that standard.

The DOM has two key things to say: all the tags in an HTML document must be accessible as objects and it must be possible to retrieve the HTML source that those tags objects originate from. Only Internet Explorer 4.0 provides extensive functionality for both.

Meanwhile, the more obvious objects available to JavaScript in earlier versions of browsers still exist, such as forms and images. However, these are now considered separate to the 'main event'—the DOM. Of course, they still represent a convenient and compatible way of achieving a range of tasks within the browser.

243

Navigating the hierarchy

For Internet Explorer 4.0, locating an arbitrary tag's object revolves around the **document.all** property, which is itself an object. **'All'** means all the tags in the document, but there's a catch: a few tags are missing. These are the **<HTML>** and **<HEAD>** tags, and all the tags used inside the head. So **'all'** really means "all the parts of the body of the HTML document". Any **<SCRIPT>** tags in the head can be retrieved another way via the **scripts** collection.

This example appeared earlier, but here its **<HEAD>** is missing, and each body tag has an **ID** attribute:

```
<HTML>
<BODY ID="page">
<H1 ID="intro">Think Pink!</H1>
<BLOCKQUOTE ID="quote">
All marshmellows, azaleas, but <STRONG ID="extra"> not </STRONG> panthers
welcome.
</BLOCKQUOTE>
</BODY>
</HTML>
```

This JavaScript illustrates a number of points about tag object access:

```
var tag_object;

tag_object = document.all.page;              // The <BODY> tag
tag_object = document.all["page"];           // The <BODY> tag
tag_object = document.all[0];                // The <BODY> tag

tag_object = document.all.extra;             // The <STRONG> tag

tag_object = document.all.quote;             // The <BLOCKQUOTE> tag
tag_object = tag_object.children.extra;      // ... the ID="extra" sub-tag
tag_object = tag_object.parentElement;       // ... back to <BLOCKQUOTE>
```

The three lines at the top show that the **all** object is an array-style object, similar to the **document.forms** or **window.frames** objects in the browser. It has two crucial differences. Firstly, its properties are named after the **ID** attribute of their respective tags, not the **NAME** attribute. Secondly, all the document's tags appear in the array, not just the top-level tags, as the middle line of the example shows. This is because the **all** property is a collection.

The last three lines illustrate how to move around the object hierarchy. Every tag object has these properties that hold the object hierarchy together and make navigation through it possible:

- **children**—an array of the tags immediately contained within this tag
- **parentElement**—a simple property pointing back to this tag object's parent tag object
- **all**—an array of all the tags contained directly or indirectly within this tag

The first two properties, plus the **children.length** property (recall it is an array) are enough to step through all the tag objects in the hierarchy. The hierarchy is a 'tree' structure, and since the tags are added to the hierarchy in the order they are discovered in the HTML source document, you can find all the tags by stepping through all the children arrays, and the children's children, and so on. In computer science terms this is a **'pre-order traversal'** of the hierarchy.

Working with tags via HTML source

There's not much point navigating the object hierarchy if there is nothing worth having in there. Therefore each tag object has four further properties: `innerText`, `outerText`, `innerHTML` and `outerHTML`. Each of these properties contains a different variant on the tag's contents. This table explains which to choose:

	Content only	Content and HTML tags
Include markup used by tags	`outerText`	`outerHTML`
Exclude markup used by tags	`innerText`	`innerHTML`

'Content only' means the script writer only wants to see that which is marked up by HTML tags and not the tags as well. 'Include space used by tags' applies mostly to *replacing* the HTML source—it means that the piece of document to be replaced should include the tags that mark the beginning and the end of the piece (such as **`<DIV>`** and **`</DIV>`**). You replace HTML source by assigning a string to one of these properties.

The alert boxes for this example are shown below:

```
<HTML><BODY>
<H1 ID="test" STYLE="color:blue">My    <EM>Important</EM>    test</H1>
<SCRIPT>
alert(document.all.test.outerText);
alert(document.all.test.innerText);
alert(document.all.test.outerHTML);
alert(document.all.test.innerHTML);
</SCRIPT>
</BODY></HTML>
```

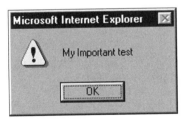

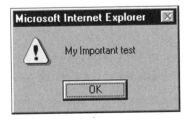

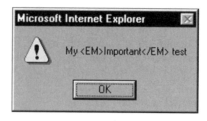

It is not until you try to change the document using the `outerText`/
`innerText` properties that a difference appears between those two properties.
The `outerText` case removes the delimiting tags as well as their content.

There is a further subtle effect at work in this example. Notice that the last two
alerts do not retrieve the HTML source exactly as it appears above—there are
spaces missing, and the quotes around `'test'` are gone. The HTML source is
actually **reconstructed** from the browser's understanding of the document. This is
slightly different to the 'View Source' window that shows the original HTML
document verbatim. Usually no meaningful information is lost. Note that
retrieving the source of a JavaScript script or a JavaScript function does not
suffer from this problem.

If you set `innerText` or `outerText` properties, the text you supply will
appear literally in the browser. If you set `innerHTML` or `outerHTML`, any tags
in the new text will be interpreted before display.

Working with tags via properties

Reading and setting the source for an HTML tag object is not very convenient if
you are only interested in a single feature of that tag, such as an event handler
or a tag attribute. There is a better way—each tag object has properties for all
the valid tag attributes. This is consistent with the older-generation objects such
as form text field objects, and works in exactly the same way.

A tag may have an attribute that isn't in any standard—recall that HTML is
only an advisory markup language—or may have an attribute value that doesn't
make sense. Such detail might be meaningful to some specific Web server or
HTML editor, even if browsers pass over it. It's hard to anticipate unknown
attributes, so properties on the tag object aren't created for them. Tag objects
support three special method properties that give access to these unknowns:

- `getAttribute()`—extract any attribute's literal value.
- `setAttribute()`—set any attribute to any value.
- `removeAttribute()`—throw an attribute for a given tag away.

Finally, the `style` property of a tag object is itself an object. Its own properties
match any CSS1 or CSS-P attribute for that tag. Stylesheet names translate to
JavaScript property names directly, except that hyphens are dropped in favor of
a capital letter. So `color` becomes `color`, but `background-color` becomes
`backgroundColor`. These properties of the `style` property aren't as all
encompassing as you might think, but Internet Explorer 4.0's features are
sufficient to make them very powerful when used. The features mean that:

246

- All style properties can be written, which is the commonest case.

- Only style properties originating from a **STYLE** attribute in the tag can be read.

- Style information defined in **<STYLE>** tags is available elsewhere, not in the tag object.

Object collections

Sometimes the script writer isn't interested in a whole HTML document's structure; just a slice of it. A typical example is user input via HTML forms. Usually you don't care how many nested **<OL>** tags surround the form—you just want to get at it. In JavaScript, a collection means an array object, and the like-minded objects are stored one per array element.

If it wasn't for object collections, the Navigator 4.0 browser would have very little dynamic HTML capability. Even Internet Explorer 4.0 would lose some important flexibility.

Using a collection is the easy part: access the correct array element, or a conveniently named property of the collection object, and you have the same object that you would have found if you had gone poking through the object hierarchy for it. For tag objects, this means access to the **style**, **innerHTML**, **getAttribute()** properties and so on, as described above, but beware! most of these properties are specific to Internet Explorer 4.0.

The trick is to find or make the collection in the first place. There are several sources of collections.

Pre-created collections

Some objects are so useful that they are always available from JavaScript. It's tempting to call them 'built-in' collections, but that term already means 'native JavaScript features' in ECMAScript language, so it is best not to overuse it.

An obvious example of a readily-available collection is the **document.forms** object. Clearly this is a collection of **<FORM>** tags in the current document. Similarly, the **document.images** array is a collection of **<IMG>** tags, and the **document.form[0].elements** array is a collection of **<INPUT>**, **<SELECT>** and **<TEXTAREA>** tags (assuming there is at least one form present in the document). Viewed from the DOM perspective, you can say that all JavaScript-enabled browsers provide some DOM collections, but only one (Internet Explorer 4.0) supports the DOM hierarchy directly. For the rest, the DOM hierarchy is 'invisible'.

For Internet Explorer 4.0, a further example is the **document.styleSheets** object which is an array/collection of objects, one per **<STYLE>** or **<LINK>** tag present in the document. Each of the collection elements has a property **rules**, which is an array/collection of the individual CSS rules. Internet Explorer also has a **scripts** collection for all the **<SCRIPT>** sections in the document. Of course, **document.all** is the most useful pre-created collection for that browser.

For Netscape Navigator 4.0, there are three collections that contain style information: **ids**, **tags**, and **layers**. It is the third of these, **layers**, which provides much of the Dynamic HTML functionality for that browser. The **layers** collection contains an object for every tag that has an *absolute* or *relatively*-positioned style. It also contains every instance of the **<LAYER>** tag. Each object in the **layers** collection contains properties matching all the CSS-P style attributes. The other two collections are mostly used for (statically) specifying JavaScript style sheets (JSSS).

With all these pre-created collections, you might wonder if there is a 'CSS Object Model', 'Script Object Model', or worse still a 'Collections Object Model' that describes a hierarchy of pre-created collections. There are some remarks in the DOM draft standard about support for the collections present in the 3.0 browsers, but beyond that you are mercifully spared another standard.

In-hierarchy collections

A few collections are bundled up inside the DOM object hierarchy itself. Since only Internet Explorer 4.0 has the DOM hierarchy, they are specific to that browser:

 children—for each tag object, all the tags directly contained in this one.

 filters—for each tag object, any style filters applying to this tag.

You might prefer to see the **style** property of each tag as a collection, but technically it's not an array object, since there's no **length** property.

User extracted collections

The most useful form of collection for complex HTML documents is the one you make yourself. Internet Explorer's DOM features provide two ways of extracting a collection:

```
var id_collection  = document.all.item("id23");
var tag_collection = document.all.tags("P");
```

The first case draws out the tag objects for all of the tags in the document that have **ID="id23"** as an attribute. The second case draws out all the tag objects from the document that are **<P>** tags.

Each tag object is referenced as an ordinary array member. There is also a shorthand notation for the **item()** method which allows a single tag object to be extracted. This script fragment illustrates both cases:

```
var all_headings = document.all.tags("H2");
all_headings[0].styles.color = "blue";               // 1st H2 now looks blue

var third_checkbox = document.all.item("boxlist1", 2);  // get the 3rd checkbox
```

Waking up HTML with JavaScript

The main thrust of Dynamic HTML is to make elements of a displayed HTML document change appearance and/or move around. The elements of the HTML document can be woken up from their normally static and unchanging state in a number of increasingly dramatic ways:

- no change at all
- change special embedded items only
- change appearance by modifying style sheets
- move existing elements within the page
- modify the document's fundamental content and structure

The first possibility is just plain HTML and style sheets, and doesn't require JavaScript or in fact any special effort. The second is covered elsewhere in this book where forms, multimedia, windows and Java are discussed. The remaining three possibilities are discussed here.

Simple appearance changes

You have built an HTML document, and you like it the way it is. You don't want to mess around with its layout or content, but somehow you would like it to be a bit more responsive to the user's input, or just a bit more flashy. Otherwise, you'd like the document to stay put. A classic example is highlighting a particular detail when an **onMouseOver** event occurs.

The way to achieve this kind of effect is to change style sheet properties. This is straightforward for Internet Explorer 4.0. Netscape 4.0 browsers require a more complicated approach, unless you abandon style sheets and go back to image swaps, as discussed in Chapter 4.

The important style properties for this class of effects are:

- **color** properties
- **clip** properties
- **filter** properties
- the **visibility** property
- **border** properties

These style properties can be set as described earlier. The following common tasks illustrate some useful ends for this functionality.

onMouseOver highlighting

Before Dynamic HTML, **onMouseOver** highlighting meant swapping images, which wasn't always that fast. Not anymore as the Internet Explorer 4.0 example shows:

```
<HTML><BODY>
Pick any item ... <BR>
<OL>
<LI ONMOUSEOVER="this.style.color='green'"
ONMOUSEOUT="this.style.color='black'">
Pick me!
<LI ONMOUSEOVER="this.style.color='green'"
ONMOUSEOUT="this.style.color='black'">
No, pick me!
<LI ONMOUSEOVER="this.style.color='green'"
ONMOUSEOUT="this.style.color='black'">
Don't listen to them! Pick me!
<LI ONMOUSEOVER="this.style.color='green'"
ONMOUSEOUT="this.style.color='black'">
Pick me, or else I'll cry.
</OL>
</BODY></HTML>
```

The background color, or in fact any combination of style information, can be just as easily set. However, the background color in particular is a little trickier. This is because the tag might not end on the screen where you think it ought to—try replacing **'color'** with **'backgroundColor'** in the above example. The solution is to use **<SPAN>** tags to give finer control to the script:

```
<HTML><BODY>
Pick any item ... <BR>
<OL>
<LI>
<SPAN ONMOUSEOVER="this.style.backgroundColor='yellow'"
       ONMOUSEOUT="this.style.backgroundColor='white'"
>
Don't pick me!
</SPAN>
<LI>
<SPAN ONMOUSEOVER="this.style.backgroundColor='yellow'"
       ONMOUSEOUT="this.style.backgroundColor='white'"
>
Don't pick me either!
</SPAN>
</OL></BODY></HTML>
```

There's always a catch. In this case, it's Netscape browsers. You can't set style properties in Navigator 4.0. However, there is an escape hatch: all Netscape Window objects can have their background color changed, and that includes layers. So this will work:

```
<HTML><BODY>
Before layer.
<BR>
<LAYER ONMOUSEOVER="this.bgColor='red'" ONMOUSEOUT="this.bgColor='white'">
MouseOver me!
</LAYER>
<BR>
After layer.
</BODY></HTML>
```

With Netscape, for changes more general than just the background color you must resort to more desperate tactics. See 'Making a fancy entrance' below for a solution.

Improved menus

Again, prior to Dynamic HTML, your choices for menus were restricted to the `<SELECT>` tag, and image swap tricks. The ability to clip HTML elements after the page is displayed opens up whole new possibilities. Again, here is an Internet Explorer 4.0-specific example:

```
<HTML><BODY>
<STYLE TYPE="text/css">
#menu1 { position: absolute; clip: rect(auto auto 32 auto) }
#item   { background-color: red }
</STYLE>

<SCRIPT>
   function   pick(obj) { obj.style.backgroundColor="yellow"; return true; }
   function unpick(obj) { obj.style.backgroundColor="red"; return true;}
</SCRIPT>

<STRONG><PRE>
<DIV id="menu1"
 ONMOUSEOVER="this.style.clip = 'rect(auto auto auto auto)'"
 ONMOUSEOUT ="this.style.clip = 'rect(auto auto 32 auto)'"
>
   <SPAN ID="item">File  </SPAN>
   <SPAN ID="item">        </SPAN>
   <SPAN ID="item" ONMOUSEOVER="pick(this)" ONMOUSEOUT="unpick(this)">Open   </
SPAN>
   <SPAN ID="item" ONMOUSEOVER="pick(this)" ONMOUSEOUT="unpick(this)">Edit   </
SPAN>
   <SPAN ID="item" ONMOUSEOVER="pick(this)" ONMOUSEOUT="unpick(this)">Export</
SPAN>
   <SPAN ID="item" ONMOUSEOVER="pick(this)" ONMOUSEOUT="unpick(this)">Import</
SPAN>
   <SPAN ID="item" ONMOUSEOVER="pick(this)" ONMOUSEOUT="unpick(this)">Save   </
SPAN>
   <SPAN ID="item">        </SPAN>
   <SPAN ID="item" ONMOUSEOVER="pick(this)" ONMOUSEOUT="unpick(this)">Exit   </
SPAN>
</DIV>
</PRE></STRONG>
</BODY></HTML>
```

The keys to this example are the two handlers in the first `<DIV>` tag. They expose and hide most of the content of that element in response to the mouse, leaving only the word 'file ' permanently visible. Without clipping, the menu of seven items and two blank lines would always appear. By the position of the bottom clip, the menu is exposed or removed as desired.

Note that this example is only an illustration. It needs quite a bit more handler work to be a fully working system: the **onMouseOver**/**onMouseOut** handlers for the **ID="menu1"** tag should be replaced with a fancier **onClick** handler; the `<SPAN>` tags require **onClick** handlers; the menu does not "roll up" in all cases because event bubbling is not fully managed (try exposing the menu and moving off the side, compared with off the top).

This kind of behavior is still possible in Netscape 4.0, but is not nearly as simple. The highlighting of singular menu items requires a significant amount of work, since each one must be a layer. Using layers can be as non-portable as sticking to Internet Explorer 4.0-only features.

Making a fancy entrance

Normally a document appears in the browser window as it downloads. The **visibility** style property can be used to alter this behavior. This Internet Explorer 4.0 example mimics the kind of behavior you might typically see from a Java applet:

```
<HTML><HEAD>
<STYLE TYPE="text/css">
  #loading { position: absolute }
  #content { position: absolute; visibility: hidden }
</STYLE>
<SCRIPT>
function display_it()
{
  document.all.content.style.visibility='visible';
  document.all.loading.style.visibility='hidden';
}
</SCRIPT>
</HEAD>
<BODY ONLOAD="setTimeout('display_it()', 4000)">
<DIV ID="loading" STYLE="color: orange">
  <H1>Loading, please wait ...</H1>
</DIV>
<DIV ID="content">
  Regrettably, anticipation exceeds the event in this case.
</DIV>
</BODY>
</HTML>
```

The **setTimeout()** call is only present to help simulate a slow-loading document—normally you would call **display_it()** immediately from the **onLoad** handler. To achieve the same effect in Netscape, just replace the **display_it()** function as follows:

```
function display_it()
{
  document.layers.content.visibility='visible';
  document.layers.loading.visibility='hidden';
}
```

This next example uses visibility to support fancy **onMouseOver** style changes for Netscape browsers:

```
<HTML><BODY>
<STYLE TYPE="text/css">
.alternate { visibility: hidden; color: red; background-color: yellow; }
</STYLE>
Before layer.
<BR>
<LAYER ONMOUSEOVER="
window.document.layers[1].visibility='visible';
this.visibility='hidden'
">
MouseOver me!
</LAYER>
<LAYER CLASS="alternate" ONMOUSEOUT="
window.document.layers[0].visibility='show';
this.visibility='hidden'
">
MouseOver me!
</LAYER>
<BR>
```

```
After layer.
</BODY></HTML>
```

In this example there are two layers, one exactly on top of the other, both with the same content. When the mouse moves over one, it disappears and the other appears. When the mouse moves out again, the reverse happens.

For Internet Explorer 4.0, filters are a further trick you can pull to control visibility of HTML elements. Filters are a Microsoft proprietary extension to style sheets that provide a grab-bag of special effects. The effects can be applied to **<DIV>** tags and images. If used without thought, the effects produced can look very amateurish. The **invert**, **chroma**, and **blendtrans** options are the safest in terms of style. Refer to Wrox's *Instant IE4 Dynamic HTML* for a detailed discussion of filters.

Border decorations and other nasties

Border style properties are yet another way of highlighting content in an HTML document. An extremely simple use for Internet Explorer 4.0:

```
<HTML><BODY><CENTER>
<H3 STYLE="color: green">Easy games of the Paeolithic Age #3: Trap the Rock</
H3>
<DIV ID="prey"> One Rock </DIV>
<FORM>
<INPUT TYPE="button"
   VALUE="Trap it now"
   ONCLICK="document.all.prey.style.border='medium solid'"
>
</FORM>
</CENTER></BODY></HTML>
```

Here are the before and after images:

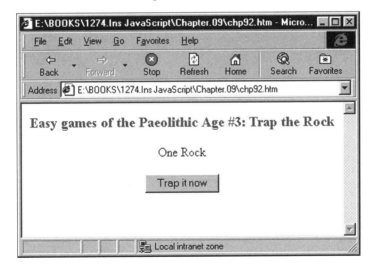

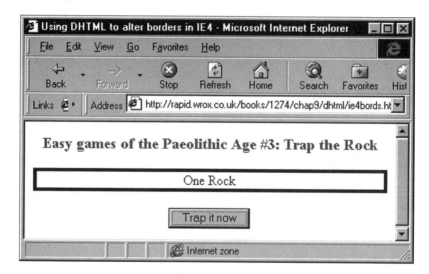

At first glance this example might not seem to reveal anything new, but look closely: when the button is pressed, the **<DIV>** tag is boxed, expanding slightly in the process, and the button moves slightly down the window to compensate (observe the after case has earned a scrollbar). Reload the document and press the button again to repeat the effect. The change in the **<DIV>** tag has resulted in the rest of the document being re-organized

This behavior is a powerful feature specific to Internet Explorer 4.0 called **reflowing** the document. In simple examples as above it is very handy, taking care of the layout changes for you much like a modern word processor. In fact, most of the style properties not touched on yet in this chapter are likely to cause reflow to occur. All the margin, font, padding, border, spacing and text attributes are implicated.

It's worth being aware of this effect. There are several cases where you might not want reflow to occur:

- In very large documents, reflow can take some time if the changed point is near the top.

- In carefully laid out documents, you might not want your exact pixel settings to be moved around.

- If the user has an unusual font size as their default for the browser, reflow might ruin a document that otherwise appears well laid out.

All the style properties illustrated earlier don't cause any reflow. 'Modifying content and structure' below explains how to deliberately exploit the reflow feature of Internet Explorer 4.0. Netscape browsers don't have this capability.

Moving HTML elements around

Beyond simple style enhancements to HTML documents lies re-organising how the existing document parts are laid in the browser window. Changing the layout of an HTML document comes down to manipulating the CSS-P style attributes of absolutely and relatively positioned elements.

The important style properties for this class of effect are:

- `position`
- `left`, `top`, `width and height`
- `clip and overflow`
- `z-index`

The **position** style property is absolutely critical. If it is not set to 'relative' or 'absolute', then the element that the style applies to will not be movable at all. Setting the position property 'frees' the element for movement, otherwise it is 'embedded' in the rest of the document.

The idea of 2.5-D animation pervades this kind of Dynamic HTML. For complex movement effects, the z-order must be carefully planned for all the movable elements in the page. However, for simple effects this is not usually necessary.

A further restriction on moving HTML around is that of coordinate systems: there must be some way to tell the difference between 'here' and 'there'. You need to decide at the start whether to fit in with the browser's layout of the document and use percentage measures, or whether to go straight to specific pixel-by-pixel measurements. If the user can resize the window displaying the document, or if the document must work for browsers running at many different screen resolutions, then choose percentage measures. If you want to do highly accurate movement, then you should create a non-resizable browser window using **window.open()** and perform all your movement within that window on a pixel-by-pixel basis.

Types of Movement

Movement of HTML elements can be expressed in several different ways. In the following examples, **balloon.gif** looks like this:

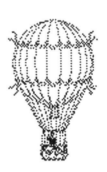

Of course, movement is not restricted to images—any kind of content can be used, from simple text to complex chunks of HTML markup.

Automated movement

User input isn't always required before HTML elements can move around. Via JavaScript, motion can be had automatically. This first example illustrates:

```
<HTML><HEAD>
<STYLE>
#zephyr { position: absolute; left: 0; top: 0; }
</STYLE>
<SCRIPT>
function drift()
{
  var z = document.all.zephyr.style;
  if ( z.pixelTop < 200 && z.pixelLeft == 0 ) z.pixelTop +=5;
  else if ( z.pixelLeft < 200 && z.pixelTop == 200 ) z.pixelLeft +=5;
  else if ( z.pixelTop <= 200 && z.pixelTop > 0 ) z.pixelTop -=5;
  else if ( z.pixelLeft <= 200 && z.pixelLeft > 0) z.pixelLeft -= 5;
}
</SCRIPT></HEAD>
<BODY ONLOAD="setInterval('drift()',1)">
<DIV ID="zephyr">
  <IMG SRC="balloon.gif"><BR>
  Out, out and about!
</DIV>
</BODY></HTML>
```

When viewed in Internet Explorer 4.0, this example displays the balloon moving in a square with diagonally opposite corners at pixel coordinates (0,0) and (200,200). There are several points to note here:

- Redrawing the absolutely positioned element takes time. The **setInterval()** delay is one millisecond; if the computer could perform at that pace, the balloon would travel around the square about 7 times a second, which it clearly does not.

- The script must finish ('let go') before the HTML element is redrawn - if you replace the **setInterval()** timing mechanism with a **while()** or **for** loop inside the **drift()** function, it won't work, because JavaScript will always be in charge.

- Note the use of style properties that report pixel values as integers, not strings. Recall that '**20px**' is a valid positional value, but that format is not as easy to work with as a plain number.

To make the example work in Netscape Navigator 4.0, replace the main function with this alternative:

```
function drift()
{
  var z = document.layers[0];
  if ( z.top < 200 && z.left == 0 ) z.top +=5;
  else if ( z.left < 200 && z.top == 200 ) z.left +=5;
  else if ( z.top <= 200 && z.top > 0 ) z.top -=5;
  else if ( z.left <= 200 && z.left > 0) z.left -= 5;
}
```

This example shows very typical differences between the two browsers. One of the detection techniques described in Chapter 2 could be used to make both browsers workable from the one HTML document.

This next very similar example shows how **z-order** can be used to plan overlapping animated areas:

```html
<HTML><HEAD>
<STYLE>
#zephyr { position: absolute; left: 0; top: 0; z-index: 1; background-color:
yellow;}
#sirocco { position: absolute; left: 150; top: 150; z-index: 2; }
</STYLE>
<SCRIPT>
function drift()
{
   var z = document.all.zephyr.style;

   if ( z.pixelLeft == 0 && z.pixelTop == 0 )
     z.zIndex = ( z.zIndex == 1 ) ? 3 : 1;

   if ( z.pixelTop < 200 && z.pixelLeft == 0 ) z.pixelTop +=5;
   else if ( z.pixelLeft < 200 && z.pixelTop == 200 ) z.pixelLeft +=5;
   else if ( z.pixelTop <= 200 && z.pixelTop > 0 ) z.pixelTop -=5;
   else if ( z.pixelLeft <= 200 && z.pixelLeft > 0) z.pixelLeft -= 5;

   z = document.all.sirocco.style;
   if ( z.pixelTop < 250 && z.pixelLeft == 150 ) z.pixelTop +=5;
   else if ( z.pixelLeft < 250 && z.pixelTop == 250 ) z.pixelLeft +=5;
   else if ( z.pixelTop <= 250 && z.pixelTop > 150 ) z.pixelTop -=5;
   else if ( z.pixelLeft <= 250 && z.pixelLeft > 150) z.pixelLeft -= 5;
}
</SCRIPT></HEAD>
<BODY ONLOAD="setInterval('drift()',1)">
<IMG ID="zephyr" SRC="balloon.gif"></IMG>
<DIV ID="sirocco"><IMG SRC="balloon.gif"><BR>In, in with a spin!</DIV>
</BODY></HTML>
```

Non-obvious in the first balloon example was the transparent nature of the balloon image. 'Black' and 'transparent' are the only colors in that example, not 'black' and 'white'. In this second example, the original image now has a z-order that switches with each pass around the square, and a solid background color. The result is that on odd-numbered passes around the square, the first image can be seen 'through' the second image, but on even-numbered occasions, the first image blocks out the second image due to its solid background color.

User Drag-Drop

Rather than rely on the browser, sometimes the users want to move an HTML element around on the page themselves. This is more likely to be the case if the Web page provides puzzles or games. There is an important distinction between dragging an item from *outside* the browser onto a browser window (such as a file icon), and just moving an element around *inside* the window it belongs to. Only the latter case is discussed here, since the former leads into the complexities of operating systems.

For the latter case, the script writer needs to provide the magic—there is no direct drag-and-drop support in the browser for moving positioned HTML elements. This can be a bit confusing to understand, so an analogy may help. Suppose the user is at a picnic, and sees a biscuit they want on the grass. Their hand reaches for the biscuit, but it moves. No matter how hard they try to grab the biscuit, it moves away. Eventually the picnickers organize to box the biscuit in, revealing thousands of bored ants underneath engaged in psychological warfare against the human race. The ants are moving the biscuit in response to the user's hand movements.

Back in the browser it works almost the same, except the script writer acts for the ants. When the user moves the mouse over the item to be dragged, the item moves in the mouse direction because JavaScript code underneath detected the mouse movement and moves the HTML item accordingly. The steps are:

- 'prime' the item for dragging with an appropriate handler
- catch all **onMouseMove** events and update the item's position
- 'defuse' the item for dragging with an appropriate handler

In other words, like this (for Internet Explorer 4.0):

```
<HTML><HEAD>
<STYLE> #zephyr { position: absolute; left: 0; top: 0;} </STYLE>
<SCRIPT>
var primed = false;
var new_x = 0;
var new_y = 0;

function set_drag() { window.primed = !window.primed; }

function handle_move()
{
  if ( window.primed == true)
  {
    window.new_x = window.event.x;
    window.new_y = window.event.y;
    setTimeout("drag_it()",1);
  }
}

function drag_it()
{
  with ( window.document.all.zephyr.style )
  {
    pixelLeft = window.new_x - pixelWidth/2;
    pixelTop  = window.new_y - pixelHeight/2;
  }
}

</SCRIPT></HEAD>
<BODY ONMOUSEMOVE="handle_move()">
<IMG ID="zephyr" ONCLICK="set_drag()" SRC="balloon.gif"></IMG>
</BODY></HTML>
```

This example lets you position the balloon anywhere you wish on the page, using the mouse. This is very specific to Internet Explorer 4.0.

There are three functions in this example. **set_drag()** is just a switch to turn dragging on and off; in this case the **onClick** handler is chosen, so the user must press and release the mouse button before dragging starts, and again on finishing. **handle_move()** picks up all move events from the window and updates the image. It uses a separate function **drag_it()** in a timer, not because of the limitation that JavaScript must 'let go' before the image's position changes, but because it gives the user time to move the mouse away from the dragged item. Try collapsing **drag_it()**'s statements into **handle_move()** and see how the dragged item 'sticks' to the mouse pointer in a frustrating way.

Modifying content and structure

As remarked earlier, even simple style changes in an HTML document can cause the current layout of a document to be disturbed. Thus most style changes aren't possible in Navigator 4.0, and in Internet Explorer 4.0 they cause the browser to automatically reflow as a result. For small changes, like expanding text by increasing its font size, this latter possibility is a useful but trivial feature. However, it can be exploited more thoroughly for good effect.

The most obvious example of this effect is collapsing menus, such as you might find in the Apple Macintosh's Finder, or in the Windows Explorer utility of Microsoft Windows. Using the **innerHTML** and **outerHTML** properties discussed earlier, this is fairly straightforward to achieve. This example is Internet Explorer 4.0 only:

```
<HTML><HEAD><SCRIPT>
var hairy_exposed = false;
var scaly_exposed = false;
var bugs_exposed = false;

function show_details(obj)
{
  if ( eval(obj.id+"_exposed" ) == false )   // show the exploded list
  {
    obj.innerHTML = document.all[obj.id+"_list"].innerHTML;
    eval(obj.id+"_exposed=true");
  }
  else                                       // collapse the list
  {
    obj.children[0].outerHTML='';
    eval(obj.id+"_exposed=false");
  }
}
</SCRIPT></HEAD><BODY>
<DIV ID="hairy_list" STYLE="display: none">
<UL> <LI> Mammals <LI> Marsupials <LI> Monotremes </UL>
</DIV>

<DIV ID="scaly_list" STYLE="display: none">
<UL> <LI> Fish <LI> Reptiles <LI> Birds .. sort of </UL>
</DIV>

<DIV ID="bugs_list" STYLE="display: none">
<UL> <LI> Creepy crawlies <LI> Stinging things
     <LI> Slugs and stuff <LI> Ugh - Germs </UL>
</DIV>

<H2> Amateur's guide to the animal kingdom</H2>
<UL>
<LI ID="hairy" ONCLICK="show_details(this)">Hairy things</LI>
<LI ID="scaly" ONCLICK="show_details(this)">Scaly things</LI>
<LI ID="bugs" ONCLICK="show_details(this)">Bugs</LI>
</UL></BODY></HTML>
```

In this example, the three <DIV> elements are just invisible storage areas for HTML used as replacement text later, hence the **'display:none'** style information. You could just as easily store the HTML in plain JavaScript strings, but that's very cumbersome to type in. Since the <DIV> tags appear as objects in the DOM hierarchy, access to their original HTML is as easy (or easier in this case) as literal strings. When the user clicks on the line items, they get an expanded, two level view for that item. Note the careful use of **innerHTML** and **outerHTML** to make this happen.

However, this example has a problem. When you replace one tag's contents with another, you lose the original contents. In this example, the main headings disappear forever, even though their bullet-points remain. The script could save the old values somewhere and replace them later, but there is a better way.

Each tag object supports an **insertAdjacentHTML()** method. This method allows new content to be slipped into the document before or after the tag of the current tag object. It takes two arguments: a special keyword indicating exactly where to insert ("**BeforeBegin**", "**AfterBegin**", "**BeforeEnd**", "**AfterEnd**"), and the HTML content to insert. As for the **innerHTML/ innerText** pair of properties, there is also an **insertAdjacentText()** method. To fix the behavior of the above example, replace the first branch of the **'if'** statement with these statements:

```
        obj.insertAdjacentHTML("BeforeEnd",
    document.all[obj.id+"_list"].innerHTML);
        eval(obj.id+"_exposed=true");
```

These features provide a flexible way to manipulate the document's source. They rely on some knowledge of the document's current structure in order to identify the bits that are of interest. Browser users, on the other hand, aren't encumbered with structured views of HTML. When a browser user selects part of a document in a browser window by dragging and highlighting with the mouse, any amount of content might be selected. The user doesn't care where tag boundaries might lie. To handle that behavior, Internet Explorer 4.0 supports a special **TextRange** object. **TextRange** objects require a bit of study before you can exploit them usefully, so their features are left to books more closely focussed on dynamic HTML.

Summary

Netscape and Microsoft 4.0 browsers expose a lot of new host objects to JavaScript's control. The ability to manipulate fragments of a single HTML document, known as Dynamic HTML puts a number of new techniques at the script writer's (and HTML author's) disposal. Using these techniques, a browser window graduates from a mostly static information display device, to a (possibly highly) animated and interactive communication media. This evolution allows browsers to take up some of the space normally reserved by other tools, such as in the area of presentation graphics.

Regrettably, both vendors continue to add incompatible features as they anticipate or innovate ahead of the standardization process. Fortunately, the Document Object Model is both standard-driven and central to these new features. Because of its more recent release, Internet Explorer 4.0 has far greater support for this standard than Netscape's 4.0 browser offering does.

Chapter

10

Further Topics

Some topics in JavaScript don't warrant a whole chapter. They are collected here.

Probably of greatest interest is the way HTML intrinsic events are enhanced in the Netscape and Microsoft version 4.0 browsers, allowing more sophisticated treatment of user input. Intrinsic events need not be seen as a "flat" list—they can be organized into hierarchical structures.

Second, the business of locating a named variable or property in JavaScript is more complex than it may first seem. A named variable can be searched for via two separate mechanisms: there is the matter of prototype-based inheritance and there is the matter of scope chains. The two are briefly discussed.

Third, Netscape has worked hard to exploit JavaScript in a number of unique ways. Their Netcaster Communicator 4.0 component uses JavaScript as a configuration mechanism. BeanConnect is a Netscape 4.0 enhancement to LiveConnect whose goal is to broaden the reach of LiveConnect. It has some implications for JavaScript too.

Finally, the success of HTML and JavaScript brings with it a new class of problems. One of those problems is support for large-scale development, where Web pages are complex, or many people are involved. The main problem with large-scale development is finding a mechanism for chopping the work up into pieces without creating chaos in the process. Chopping the work up is often called '**componentising**'.

There are two contending technologies for this mechanism. The **JavaScript Beans** specification fostered by Netscape is designed to parallel the **Java Beans** initiative from Sun Microsystems. **Scriptlets** from Microsoft, on the other hand, provide a system that requires special support in the browser. Both approaches solve the componentising problem and also make the development of highly productive drag-and-drop development tools both attractive and feasible.

Browser Event Models

Web browsers were originally designed to display plain HTML and that was all. The handling of user input via HTML intrinsic events is a more recent innovation. Client-side languages like JavaScript came after HTML, and for earlier browsers it shows. It is only with advent of the 4.0 browsers that event handling mechanisms are organized in a general and flexible way.

The bad old days

In the simplest model for events, an event occurs, a handler fires and then the event is over. This is generally how Netscape and Microsoft 3.0 browsers work. However, even for these older browsers, that simple model is not really sufficient. This table shows that for some events, more than one handler of the same type might fire:

Event	3.0 handlers that might fire	User action that fires multiple handlers
onBlur	frame, window, text and password fields	Click on a different frame or window.
onError[1]	frame, window, image	Load a document containing a bad image.
onFocus	frame, window, text and password fields	Click on a field in a different frame. Click on a field or frame in a different window.
onLoad	frame, window, image	Load a document or frameset
onReset[1]	reset button, form	Clear a form
onSubmit[1]	submit button, form	Submit a form

1. Netscape Navigator 3.0 only.

For these browsers there is little you can do to control this behavior, except avoid using specific combinations of handlers. It follows that if more events or more features are added to the browser, something has to happen to give more control to the scriptwriter.

Event innovations in 4.0 browsers

Because of the enhancements chosen by Microsoft and Netscape, the two main 4.0 browsers aren't that different in overall approach but they do differ in the specific details.

When all the details (and learning) regarding event features for a given vendor are lumped into a pile, that pile is big enough that committing to a single browser suddenly seems very attractive. Of course, this is a bad idea for public web pages, because it restricts you to less than half of the Internet users. If you are concerned about portability, you need to make a deliberate decision at the start to keep it simple, or else you will be locked into a particular browser in no time.

Additional events

The HTML 4.0 standard mandates a number of new intrinsic events and these are supported to a lesser or greater degree by both 4.0 browsers. In addition to the events already specified in the 3.0 browsers, there are 10 general user input events that apply to every tag in the HTML document. They are: **onKeyPress**, **onKeyup**, **onKeyDown**, **onClick**, **onDblClick**, **onMouseOver**, **onMouseOut**, **onMousecMove**, **onMouseDown** and **onMouseUp**.

For Microsoft Internet Explorer 4.0, these events are supported as described by the HTML 4.0 standard.

For Netscape Navigator 4.0, only windows, frames, layers and Link objects (the **<A HREF>** and **<AREA>** tags are Link objects) support all these events. The **onMouseMove** handler is supported only via JavaScript, not via HTML tag attributes.

Both browsers support events beyond the HTML 4.0 standard; Netscape supports 3: **onResize**, **onDragDrop** and **onMove**; Microsoft supports a multitude. Refer to the specific browser documentation—the detail is beyond this book's scope.

Netscape's lack of support for the 10 user input events can be partially worked around by exploiting the support that is present for links. This example illustrates:

```
<HTML><HEAD>
<STYLE TYPE="text/css">
A:link { text-decoration: none; color: none }
</STYLE>
</HEAD><BODY>
Normal text
<A HREF="http://localhost/" ONCLICK="return false;" ONDBLCLICK="return false;">
<STRONG>Interesting part <P> with tags<P><STRONG>
</A>
Normal text
</BODY></HTML>
```

If any mouse events are required for the **<STRONG>** tag, then use the event handlers of the surrounding **<A>** tag. Key press and click events can be captured by the window and passed to **<A>** tag handlers as well—see the discussion further on. Generally speaking, Internet Explorer 4.0 has a much more rich event model.

Additional structure

For Microsoft and Netscape 3.0 browsers, event handlers are organized in a "flat" list: when an event occurs, all the appropriate handlers in the list are fired. In the 4.0 browsers, they are stored in a hierarchy that dictates which handler is the first candidate for a given event. An event may pass through several handlers, but if so, there is a definite order. Since event handlers are properties of JavaScript host objects, the hierarchy follows the browser's object model.

265

The crucial difference between Netscape and Microsoft implementations is that for Netscape, events travel down the hierarchy, for Microsoft they travel up. The Microsoft approach is favored for adoption by the DOM (Document Object Model) standard. That standard is still in early draft at this time of writing. A diagram of a typical document illustrates the difference:

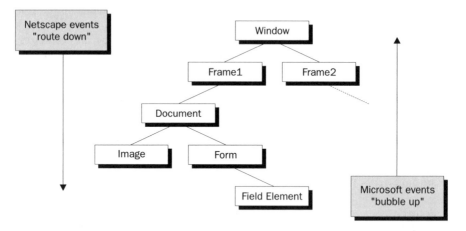

Not all events can flow through the hierarchy. Many of the Internet Explorer 4.0 event handlers, for example, are attached to specific objects. If the matching event occurs, either that object's handler or no handler at all will be called.

Not all objects in the hierarchy are exploited when an event flows through the structure. In the Navigator 4.0 case, typically only "large" objects like windows, layers and documents get a chance. This is because Navigator 4.0 only has partial support for the DOM. The object whose tag actually contains the handler will always be a candidate for the event, regardless of its size.

Additional objects

As well as new event handlers and better-organized event handlers, the 4.0 browsers also provide more event information. A new JavaScript object called the Event object (Netscape) or event (Microsoft) stores this data.

The event object is handled differently in the two browsers. In the Microsoft case, there is only one event object per browser window. All the event handlers must refer to this object. In the Netscape case, an event object is created for each event and is passed to the handler as an argument. This table gives an at-a-glance comparison of the two styles of event object:

Internet Explorer 4.0 window.event properties	Netscape Navigator 4.0 Event object properties
User input	
`type`	`type`
`altKey, ctrlKey, shiftKey, keyCode, button`	`which, modifiers`
Graphical position of event	
`screenX, screenY, clientX, clientY, offsetX, offsetY, x, y`	`screenX, screenY, layerX, layerY, pageX, pageY`
Items marked out by mouse movements	
`fromElement, toElement`	`data`
Progress and control information	
`reason, returnValue, cancelBubble`	(a separate routing mechanism is available)
Document element originating the event	
`srcElement, srcFilter`	`target`
Special constants	
	`MOUSEDOWN, MOUSEUP, CLICK, KEYDOWN, KEYUP, KEYPRESS`

You can make a JavaScript function, which inspects such an object and acts as a general event handler. This is a good way to illustrate how the browsers differ. For Internet Explorer 4.0 such a handler looks like this:

```
function handy_event_handler()
{
  if ( window.event.type == "click" )
  {
    // do click stuff ...
    return true;
  }
  // and so on for other possibilities...
  return false
}
```

For Netscape Navigator 4.0, such a handler looks like this:

```
function handy_event_handler(new_event)
{
  if ( new_event.type == "click" )
  {
    // do click stuff ...
    return true;
  }
```

```
   // and so on for other possibilities...
   return false
}
```

For both browsers, a portable handler that works for simple handler tasks only:

```
function handy_event_handler(netscape_event)
{
  var real_event;
  real_event = (netscape_event) ? netscape_event : window.event;

  if ( real_event.type == "click" )
  {
    // do click stuff ...
    return true;
  }
  // and so on for other possibilities...
  return false
}
```

Managing events in the handler hierarchy

If a given document has no event handlers, then the entire event flow and structure provided by the browser has no effect. So, leaving event handlers out is a good way to avoid complexity. This isn't very practical if you are designing a highly interactive page.

If you restrict yourself to handlers that are attached to the most-specific HTML tags only, you avoid event flow effects up or down the hierarchy and still get to receive events. In this case you are operating in a similar manner to the 3.0 browser event model, except more events are possible.

If you need to use events at several levels of the object model, the real differences between Netscape and Microsoft show up. A different approach must be adopted for each brand if you want to fully exploit the object hierarchy. The general strategy for each browser type can be described this way:

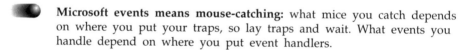 **Microsoft events means mouse-catching:** what mice you catch depends on where you put your traps, so lay traps and wait. What events you handle depend on where you put event handlers.

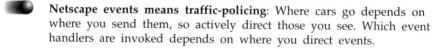 **Netscape events means traffic-policing**: Where cars go depends on where you send them, so actively direct those you see. Which event handlers are invoked depends on where you direct events.

Microsoft

Managing events for Microsoft's 4.0 browser proceeds in the familiar pattern of previous browsers, so there's nothing radical to learn. When events proceed through handlers in the new event hierarchy, they do so one at a time - only one handler is active at any time. Two of the new properties of the **window.event** object need to be particularly borne in mind:

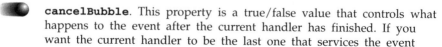 **cancelBubble**. This property is a true/false value that controls what happens to the event after the current handler has finished. If you want the current handler to be the last one that services the event

caught, set this property to **true**. Beware that Microsoft documentation says that a few events cannot be cancelled! This example illustrates canceling, it displays **'MIDDLE'** and **'INNER'** alert boxes only:

```
<HTML><BODY>
<DIV ONCLICK="alert('OUTER'); return true;">
<DIV ONCLICK="alert('MIDDLE'); window.event.cancelBubble=true; return true;">
<DIV ONCLICK="alert('INNER'); window.event.cancelBubble=false; return true;">
Click Me
</DIV>
</DIV>
</DIV>
</BODY></HTML>
```

returnValue. This property is a true/false value that controls whether the normal action of the event occurs (for example, submitting a form or navigating a link). Beware that a few events' actions cannot be stopped, such as the unloading of a document associated with an **onUnLoad** event. The action for an event occurs after the last handler has finished. It is the return value of that last handler that normally dictates whether the action will happen, as for 3.0 browsers. This presents a problem if an earlier handler wants to have a say in the event's ultimate impact. The **returnValue** property provides an override mechanism for those earlier handlers. If it is ever set to **true** or **false**, so that it is no longer undefined, its value is used regardless of the return value of the last handler. This example will not follow the link even though all handlers return **true**:

```
<HTML><BODY>
<A HREF="about:blank" ONCLICK="alert('A tag'); return true;">
<DIV ONCLICK="alert('DIV tag'); window.event.returnValue=false; return true;">
Click Me
</DIV>
</A>
</BODY></HTML>
```

The bubbling and event action mechanisms are separate and don't affect each other.

Netscape

For Netscape, ordinary event handlers proceed in the same pattern as for 3.0 browsers, but the advanced features require a whole new concept. This concept is that window, document and layer objects can be interposed between the user and the object that an event is normally associated with, such as a button. This interposed object may then handle the event first. A general term for this kind of behavior is **filtering**, but it's just as easy to think of it as events arriving at the top of the document object model first, as described above. To do this requires three steps:

Create handlers for the interposing object. It is better to create and assign these directly in JavaScript, because their meaning in the web page is not as trivial as typical event handlers. When one of these handlers is called and then finishes, that is the end of all event processing for that event. Therefore, the return value of that handler dictates whether the event's action is cancelled or not, as for earlier browser versions. If tag attributes are not used to define these handlers, the appropriate properties of the window, document or layer object must be assigned to.

● **Start collecting events.** An interposed object does not automatically use these new handlers. The special function **captureEvents()** must be used to determine which events an interposed object will collect. The sole argument is a bitwise-OR'ed list of constants. These constants are similar to other JavaScript constants such as **Math.PI**. They represent the 10 general user input events specified by HTML 4.0. **'Event.MOUSEUP | Event.MOUSEDOWN | Event.KEYPRESS'** is an example of three values bitwise-OR'ed together. The matching function **releaseEvents()** stops an interposed object from collecting events.

● **Decide routing policy.** Once the interposed object is collecting events, those events will never be forwarded to their original destination (such as a form element) unless extra efforts are made. These efforts takes the form of two methods: **routeEvent()** and **handleEvent()**. A call to **routeEvent()** from within an event handler tells the browser to suspend the current handler, call other handlers that are involved and then return back to the point of suspension. So **routeEvent()** provides the mechanism for events to "route down" the object hierarchy. This behavior means handlers are **nested**—one handler is invoked from inside another. The other function **handleEvent()** is more radical. It is a method of the Window and Document (not Layer) objects. If such an object's method is called from within another handler then the event is passed to that object directly, ignoring any other objects expecting the event, and ignoring the normal hierarchy entirely.

Here is an example of two frames that illustrate a simple case of **handleEvent()**. To see it happen, click in either frame. To illustrate **routeEvent()**, add a button to each frame with an onClick handler, and change **'top.first.handleEvent(e)'** to read **'routeEvent(e)'**.

```
<!-- frameset.htm -->
<HTML>
<FRAMESET ROWS="*,*">
<FRAME NAME="first" SRC="anyframe.htm">
<FRAME NAME="second" SRC="anyframe.htm">
</FRAMESET>
</HTML>
```

```
<!-- anyframe.htm -->
<HTML><BODY><SCRIPT>

document.write('This is the frame named "'+self.name+'"'); // visible content

function handle_it(e)                          // ordinary event handler,
e is the event
{
    alert("Caught by frame: " + window.name);
    if ( window.name == "first" )
        alert("Preventing infinite loop");
    else
        return top.first.handleEvent(e);
    return true;
}
```

```
window.onMouseDown = handle_it;        // assign handler
window.captureEvents(Event.MOUSEDOWN); // in this case, filter just one event

</SCRIPT></BODY></HTML>
```

There is one complication that is due to frames. A frame might display a URL from a Web site that is different to the web site of the frameset document. A security hobble prevents parent documents from capturing that frame's events ("Every window is free"—Chapter 6.). However, if the parent document and its scripts are signed or otherwise secure, the methods
window.enableExternalCapture() and
window.disableExternalCapture() can be used to free up or re-impose this restriction.

Prototype and Scope Chains

JavaScript is an interpreted language. If it were a compiled language, the compilation stage could be used to organize the identifiers that appear in the script. This would "ready" the identifiers for use. An interpreted language requires a more sophisticated approach, since it can be called on at any time to identify and manage a newly named variable.

The question is, how does JavaScript know to display 99.95 for the **new_price** variable in this (or any other) script:

```
<HTML><BODY><SCRIPT>
eval('var new_price = 99.95; ');    // no variables - just a string
document.write(new_price);
</SCRIPT></BODY></SCRIPT>
```

Details of JavaScript's solution are the topic of this section.

Simplifications revisited

JavaScript allows objects to be constructed as described in Chapter 1, using constructor functions and the **prototype** property. In that discussion, the implications of the **prototype** property were glossed over to a degree. In Chapter 7 'Disappearing Data', one of the common problems discussed was that of forgetting that the 'current object' or 'current scope' within a form element's event handler is different to the usual scope, which is the window object. In that discussion, just what a 'current scope' might be was glossed over to a degree as well.

Recall that methods, variables and objects are all just properties of some other object, even if that other object is merely the global object. When a name for a property (an **identifier**) appears in a JavaScript program, two questions need answering in order to find out what it stands for:

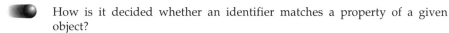 How is it decided whether an identifier matches a property of a given object?

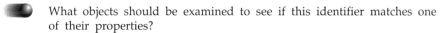 What objects should be examined to see if this identifier matches one of their properties?

271

The answers lie in the prototype mechanism in the first case, and in the scope chain mechanism in the second.

Prototype Inheritance Chains

Prototype inheritance chains allow the JavaScript interpreter to determine whether a property exists for an object or not. Here is a typical object created via a JavaScript constructor:

```
function Thingy(name)
{
  this.name = name;
}

Thingy.prototype.colour = 'blue';
Thingy.prototype.shape = 'round';

var thing = new Thingy('Jack');
```

Consider the composition of the **thing** object. JavaScript objects have properties, and each property can have only one value. If more than one value is required, the property must refer to another object.

Therefore the **prototype** property in this example must refer to another object, since it has two properties **colour** and **shape**. In fact, **typeof(Thingy.prototype)** reports "**object**". If the **prototype** property is an object, it must have its own prototype, assumedly called **Thingy.prototype.prototype**. What about that object's prototype? This type of behavior could go on forever.

Fortunately, in the normal case the ECMAScript standard says that a constructor function's **prototype** property is of type Object, and the actual prototype object's own **prototype** property is **null**, so there is only one step. Normally, the only places to look for a property with a given name are directly in the object, and directly in the object's prototype object.

The example could be re-written to explicitly define the object's prototype, rather than relying on the built-in Object prototype as above. Here is such a re-write:

```
function Thingy_common_bits()
{
  this.prototype = null;
  this.colour = 'blue';
  this.shape = 'round';
}

function Thingy(name)
{
  this.name = name;
}

Thingy.prototype = new Thingy_common_bits();
var thing = new Thingy('Jack');
```

The behavior for the **thing** object is the same as before. The only difference is that now the **prototype** property is explicitly set to a new object using an object constructor **Thingy_common_bits()**. This example could be further changed to show a more general case:

```
function Thingy_bit1()            // prototype's prototype constructor
{
  this.prototype = null;
  this.colour = 'blue';
}

function Thingy_bit2()            // prototype constructor
{
  this.shape = 'round';
}

function Thingy(name)            // object constructor
{
  this.name = name;
}

Thingy.prototype      = new Thingy_bit1();
Thingy_bit1.prototype = new Thingy_bit2();

var thing = new Thingy('Jack');    // object
```

The **thing** object still looks the same as the other examples, but this time it is contributed to by two prototype objects, one directly (its own prototype), and one indirectly (its prototype's prototype). This is a prototype chain. If the chain is exhausted without a given property name being found, the property is **undefined**.

A word on inheritance

Inheritance in software is a concept made widely popular by object-oriented modeling techniques. A specific interpretation of what inheritance really is acts as a cornerstone of that modeling technique. The prototype approach to inheritance used by JavaScript doesn't match that interpretation.

The main risk here is getting drawn into arguments with OO (object-oriented) pedants about what rubbish JavaScript is, and how it corrupts the very moral fiber of the OO temple. There are two approaches:

 Call JavaScript object-based, not object oriented to sooth these people. Object based systems don't have any inheritance. Use the prototyping features anyway.

 Construct a careful argument based on the theme that inheritance can be conceived a number of different ways. The artificial intelligence community has a different view of what inheritance might be to the OO community, and the ECMAScript standard has some words on the subject as well. Your parents probably have their own view of human inheritance as well. You might also point out that there is no fundamentally correct modeling technique, in the same way that there is no fundamentally correct solution to any problem involving subjective human beings. There's more than one way to skin a cat— JavaScript's approach to inheritance is just one more perspective on the subject.

273

Scope Chains

A scope chain is used by the JavaScript interpreter to determine which objects to examine for a given property name. Each object so determined will then have its prototype chain examined. There must always be at least one candidate object, even if it is just the global object.

A scope chain's details are not accessible to the script writer. It is part of the script's 'execution context', or 'thread of execution', or 'interpreter instance' or 'housekeeping data', whichever you prefer.

According to ECMAScript, the script writer can't directly interact with the scope chain. However, it is easy to change it, particularly using the **with** statement as this example shows:

```
<HTML><SCRIPT>
var plant = 'Geranium';            // == window.plant

var outside = new Object;          // == window.outside
outside.furniture = 'Banana Lounge'; // == window.outside.furniture
outside.plant = 'Willow';          // == window.outside.plant

outside.inside = new Object;       // == window.outside.inside
outside.inside.plant = 'Ficus';    // == window.outside.inside.plant

alert(plant);
with ( outside )
{
  alert(plant);
  with ( inside )
  {
    alert(plant);
    alert(furniture);
  }
}
</SCRIPT></HTML>
```

Not surprisingly, the example displays alerts for '**Geranium**', '**Willow**' and '**Ficus**' in that order. It may come as a surprise that '**Banana Lounge**' is displayed as well, even though the **inside** object has no **furniture** property.

The reason 'Banana Lounge' is displayed is that the **with** statement does not **replace** the object usually scrutinized when an identifier name is encountered, it **adds** an object to the scrutiny process.

The object added (the argument of the **with** statement) is the 'current object' or 'current scope', to use familiar terminology, but it is really just the first in a list of such objects. This list is called the **scope chain**. Objects in the scope chain are consulted in order until the identifier matches one of the object's properties.

In the above example, each **with** statement adds an object to the front of the scope chain when it starts, and removes that item when it ends. When the innermost statements are executed, the chain consists of three objects: **inside**, **outside**, and **window**. The object consulted first is **inside**.

The business of scope chains is a subtle source of bugs. Since it is possible to locate all the property names of all the objects in the scope chain, not just those of the object at the head of the chain, there are many more opportunities to accidentally clash with an existing name.

Finally, this extremely simple example shows that the interpreter may organize the scope chain before a piece of script even starts running:

```
<HTML><HEAD><SCRIPT>
function show_name(name)
{
   alert(name);
}
</SCRIPT></HEAD><BODY>
<FORM METHOD="POST" NAME="foofoo">
<INPUT TYPE="button" NAME="Test Name" ONCLICK="show_name(name)">
</FORM>
</BODY></HTML>
```

In this example, both the **show_name()** function and the **name** property are correctly identified inside the event handler. However, **show_name()** is only a property of the **window** object, while **name** is a property of the **window**, **form** and **form element (button)** objects. Since the button's name is passed to the alert box, both window and button objects must be in the scope chain, and the **button** object must be before the **window** object. Very convenient, as it saves using '**window.show_name()**' in the event handler code, but creates extra opportunities for name mixups, as in the non-handler case.

Particularly confusing can be use of identifiers such as **location** which exist in both the Window and Document objects—that is why it is still wise to prefix identifiers with '**window.**' everywhere that is practical.

Netscape Netcaster

Netscape's Communicator 4.0 product has a **window.components** property that is an array. Obviously the plan must be to populate this array with a suite of add-on components in the same way that the **window.plugins** array can be populated with a suite of third-party plugins. Netcaster is the first and only such offering to date. It is downloaded and installed separate to the main Communicatior installation process.

This is what Netcaster means to the script writer:

- Yet another place to configure Netscape's browsers via JavaScript.

- Two further host objects to interact with in the browser.

- Special constraints to take into account when developing client-side JavaScript.

- Functionality to do graphics and text *outside* of any browser window.

- A chance to taste the shape of Netscape things to come.

Push technology

Before plunging into the details, a few marketing dragons need slaying first. The implications of **push technology** on the Internet were a topic of much discussion in 1997. Push technology derives from comparisons between the Web and other media such as television, radio and print. In those other media, the user/consumer/audience is almost entirely passive, whereas the Web generally requires the user to direct matters with the mouse and keyboard. Push technology opens the opportunity for Web pages to "push" information (whether documents, applets or otherwise) into the user's browser (or wherever) without much user interaction, rather than the user actively "pulling" (downloading). Hysteria surrounding the advent of push technology stems from the possibility that a Web content provider can take a much larger role in the user's viewing choices: the user subscribes/tunes in/buys a content agreement, and the provider varies the content over time. This is the type of opportunity that television stations, newspaper publishers, stock exchanges and CNN represent— potentially big business. Furthermore, if the content is software rather than just data, it also represents a chance for software vendors to update user's computers remotely—more power to the vendors.

Unfortunately, it is not so easy. For TV, radio and print, it doesn't matter if a user switches off - TV and radio signals are broadcast without regard for individual users, and newspapers are disposed of if they are not sold. For the Internet and the Web, there needs to be an understanding that the user's computer is switched on before anything can be pushed to it. So Web content can't just be blindly pushed into the arms of a browser from the content provider end. Since security is an issue, the user's computer can't be rummaged through by the content provider to see what to update, either. Finally, with Internet bandwidth increasing oh-so-slowly, the content provider can't saturate the Internet with content updates on the assumption that someone might want them.

Enter Netscape and Microsoft's browsers and Marimba's Castanet technology. These tools are seen as central to the possibility of push. Netcaster is Netscape's offering aimed at this market. While these tools may look like push technology on the surface, underneath it is a different story; no content server takes the initiative, although one might respond to a "push" tool's request.

These tools also promote the idea of **channels** - a stream of content from one source - paralleling radio and TV. Netscape and Microsoft have gone to great lengths to sign up channel providers that will add value to the technology that they sell to users.

What Netcaster is really

At the core of Netcaster is the same old stuff as the rest of the Netscape browser: Web pages, URLs, HTML, Java, JavaScript and HTTP. The fancy "push" content is typically just Web pages. Separate to the core are four innovations:

 Fancy browser graphics. There is a new user control called the 'Channel Finder' which looks like a toolbar crossed with a bookmark list—that is roughly all it is.

- A new **webtop** window. This is a variant on the possibilities of the `window.open()` method. It allows the whole computer screen to be used as a single browser window, and can be located behind other screen elements such as icons, menus and applications. It wastes no space with window decorations.

- A configurable **web crawler**. A web crawler is just a piece of software that browses the web automatically as though it were a highly methodical user.

- Marimba software included. The Netscape browser can use this software to download content instead of its normal, direct approach via HTTP if the Netcaster user so chooses. Castanet is beyond the scope of this book.

Without the distractions of the graphical enhancements, what you have is a web browser that can browse on its own.

How it works

When the Netcaster component is installed and activated, the Channel Finder contains a little database of channels, just as the bookmark list is a database of bookmarks. When the browser is running, there are two people steering in parallel: the user who controls the normal Web, e-mail and news windows, and the Netcaster web crawler functionality that controls any "active" channels.

Each channel is defined by a URL, some timing information, some window positioning information and some trivia. The timing information controls how often the web crawler will examine the URL of the channel. The web crawler retrieves the URL's document, and recursively follows all the HTML-embedded links, retrieving subsidiary documents as well, up to a configured limit. These are stored in a document cache similar to the normal browser cache. If the channel is visible, the content is displayed as well. Once the web crawler has finished, it stops activity until the timing information tells it to try again. At that point it crawls again, fetching any updates that might have occurred in the meantime.

The Netcaster component is designed to be useable when the browser is offline —not connected to the Internet. In that case, attempts to view a channel just result in the channel's cached documents being displayed.

What it is good for

Netcaster gives the user several new ways to interact with the Web:

- A lazy way to find out what's new. By subscribing to a channel, the user makes the content provider do the work of searching out and assembling content.

- A cheaper way to surf the web. By efficiently crawling the Web, the user can download heaps of information at the fastest rate possible, then disconnect and view the information offline at a more relaxed pace.

277

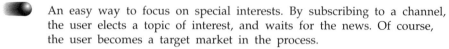 An easy way to focus on special interests. By subscribing to a channel, the user elects a topic of interest, and waits for the news. Of course, the user becomes a target market in the process.

A non-intrusive way to stay up-to-date. Since the Netcaster channels can appear on the screen's backdrop ('webtop'), the user can do other tasks without interruption, while the backdrop updates according to channel content changes.

Because Netcaster is partially an automated Web browsing system, it obeys the etiquette rules for **Web robots**. Web robots are automated web browsers ('web crawlers'), and etiquette rules are a system of checks that stop automated web browsers from dominating the Internet with their activities. Each Web site has a **robots.txt** file, which defines how much (if any), web crawling is allowed at that site. The Netcaster component of Communicator follows the etiquette rules by identifying itself as a robot. This has a downside: some sites might refuse to respond to Netcaster URL requests. Obviously, channel sites are unlikely to refuse.

Working with channels

Development of web pages viewed via a channel is much the same as any web page. It is the creation of new channels that is unique.

New host objects

There are two JavaScript host objects worth considering.

The **window.components["netcaster"]** is one of these objects. This is the 'top level' object for the Netcaster subsystem of Communicator. Its most interesting features are as follows:

active property. Contains a Boolean value indicating whether Netcaster is running or not.

activate() method. Start Netcaster.

getChannelObject() method. Ask for a new **Channel** object.

addChannel() method. Submit a channel object to Netcaster, creating a new channel.

The last two functions represent a change of tack for JavaScript objects. Up until now, it has usually been sufficient to use the JavaScript **new** operator to create new objects. The approach used by Netcaster is more formal—the script writer must request a new object from the Netcaster subsystem and submit it back after it has been worked on. Here is a simple example:

```
var nc_top = components["netcaster"];
nc_top.activate();          // make sure Netcaster is turned on
if (nc_top.active == true)
{
   import nc_top.getChannelObject;  // Extract usable functions from
   import nc_top.addChannel;        // Netcaster, which is otherwise secure.
```

```
        var channel = nc_top.getChannelObject();    // new Channel object.

        // work on the 'channel' object ...

        addChannel(channel);               // modified and 'submitted' to Netcaster.
    }
```

The **Channel** object itself is a configuration object. It contains no methods, only properties. The script writer's job is to assign values to the properties until the new channel is fully defined. To read about all the channel object properties, consult the Netscape Netcaster manual: **http://developer.netscape.com/library/documentation/netcast/devguide/index.html**. Here is an example that shows the critical properties required to get going quickly:

```
// add to the above example:

channel.url = ("http://www.wrox.com");    // channel URL
channel.name = ("WROX Books");            // name appearing in Channel Finder

channel.depth = 2;                        // how many links deep the webcrawler goes

channel.intervalTime = 3600;              // optional update frequency in minutes.
                                          // No updates occur if not specified

channel.maxCacheSize = 1000000;           // optional limit on disk space (bytes)

channel.mode = "webtop";                  // appearance (others: "full", "window")
channel.type = 1;                         // retrieval mechanism (2 = Castanet)
```

JavaScript inside channels

Web pages designed for channel viewing force two constraints onto the scriptwriter.

Firstly, channels can be viewed offline. The webcrawler inside Netcaster attempts to ensure that all files required for the channel are sniffed out when the channel is downloaded. However it only looks at URLs embedded in tags in HTML documents. This means that any URLs referred to from inside JavaScript, such as Image pre-loading or random links will not work unless the URLs are also visible from HTML. The script writer should therefore avoid these features.

Secondly, if the channel is displayed to the user in "webtop" or "full" mode, the script writer can't really open new windows or use multi-window tricks such as help. Scrollbars, toolbars and menus aren't available either. This puts all the responsibility on the scriptwriter to provide navigation mechanisms for the user. Apart from ordinary **<A HREF>** links, this means extensive use of Dynamic HTML.

Netscape BeanConnect

The Applets and Java chapter described how JavaScript and Java can communicate with each other via LiveConnect or ActiveX. With the release of Netscape 4.0 browser, the LiveConnect functionality has been enhanced, and dubbed BeanConnect in the process. This has some implications for JavaScript.

The major improvements made available by BeanConnect have nothing to do with JavaScript—they are Java specific. Even the improvements, which do relate to JavaScript require a good working knowledge of Java, so the possibilities are only briefly sketched out here.

Recall from the Applets and Java chapter that JavaScript can access locally stored Java classes even if no applet is present. JavaScript can also access Java classes via the main Java class of an HTML-embedded applet.

In summary, and avoiding the Java specific features, BeanConnect allows you to create new elements on the screen beyond those made available by the HTML **<INPUT>** tag. You can then handle user interaction to those elements directly from JavaScript, even though they are written in Java. No applet is required to do this.

This is an enhancement to LiveConnect because:

- No applet is required in the HTML page to draw the element.

- Previously, you couldn't access a Java class by itself if it required screen space to draw on.

This new tactic lays open Netscape's IFC ('Internet Foundation Class') Java components and all Java Beans to direct exploitation by JavaScript.

In order to pursue this further, the script writer needs to understand:

- Java Beans, and a Java class library such as IFC, JFC (Java Foundation Classes) or Swing.

- The Java event model, and how a target adaptor fits into it.

- Netscape's new javabean: URLs and **<OBJECT>** tags interact.

- The **netscape.javascript.JSTargetAdaptor** Java class.

Once all that is covered, it is possible in not too many lines of code to have a mini-applet in a HTML document. Just correctly embed a JavaScript function that will be invoked when the user interacts with a Java component or Bean displayed on the page. Look for BeanConnect references on Netscape's **http://developer.netscape.com** Web site for all the gory details. Java must still be enabled for this functionality to work.

JavaScript Beans

JavaScript Beans are useless to the script writer unless one of several things is happening:

- A visual "drag and drop" style development tool is being used for JavaScript development, such as Acadia's Infuse.

- The script writer is developing re-useable software aimed at developers who do use visual development tools for JavaScript.

The script writer is working in a project that emphasizes formal specifications. Very large projects might have this requirement.

What's a Bean?

Modern software, especially graphical or client software tends to be made up of other, smaller, software components. A bean is a type of component that is particularly easy to take advantage of when building software. The software meaning for "bean" was coined by Sun Microsystems, who also invented the bean specification for the Java language. The name emerged during the general wordplay about coffee that was used by marketeers to associate products with the Java language. Allegorically, a Java program is a coffee drink, and beans are used to make up the coffee.

A bean is a piece of software that conforms to a bean specification. All such a specification does is constrain software objects to present a well-behaved and predictable interface to the outside world. Predictable objects are easy to manage, and give development tools a chance to provide the developer with quite powerful features. These can be used to combine beans into larger programs. Part of the predictability is called **introspection**. Introspection allows a tool to examine a previously unknown bean and discover all its features. This removes the need for tools to build up a possibly unmanageable store of information about "known beans".

At the purely technical level, an object consists of method, property and event behavior. For Java objects, a class definition defines all of these things, and is an integral part of the language. The class definition plus rules of good behavior—the bean specification—is all that's required for Java Beans.

What's a JavaScript Bean?

For JavaScript objects, there is no class definition akin to Java, since JavaScript objects are loosely typed and interpreted to boot. The nearest you get in JavaScript is the constructor function that is used to create a custom object.

If such a definition method existed for JavaScript objects, they could be exploited in visual development tools in the same powerful way that Java Beans are. Netscape have developed such a definition method, hence JavaScript Beans.

Within JavaScript, JavaScript beans are all implemented as custom JavaScript objects, not host objects, and use the JavaScript constructor mechanism to name those custom objects for the **'new'** operator.

Since JavaScript is interpreted, the mechanism for introspection can occur at two levels: the bean specific information is available to bean-knowledgable development tools and language features like **typeof()** and **for... in...** allow examination of objects at run time.

JavaScript Bean Specification

A JavaScript bean is a piece of JavaScript code stored in a file along with some special information. This file has the suffix `.jsb`. Beans that rely on other files (such as a `.js` file containing a library of functions) can be collected together with those files into a JAR file.

Goals of the specification

For those readers generally nervous with JavaScript's loosely-typed nature relief is in sight. For those who couldn't get away from C++ fast enough, welcome back. The JavaScript Beans specification, which amounts to a file format and some conventions, is intended to nail down every last detail and type that a JavaScript object contains. Fundamentally, the language is still loosely-typed, but if the spirit of the specification is followed, the issues are more like those of a strongly-typed language.

Some of the things the specification tries to achieve are:

- **Similarity with Java Beans**. The features of the Java BeanInfo class are closely mimicked.

- **Familiarity to script writers**. The `.jsb` file format is reminiscent of HTML.

- **Integration with Java**. Since it's a Netscape show, and Netscape's LiveConnect allows close integration between JavaScript and Java, Java types can be used for JavaScript object properties.

- Sufficiently specific for development tools to exploit.

JSB file format

Eons ago in Internet terms, you may have learnt that HTML is a specific example of a markup language, and is defined by the SGML markup definition language. The file format of `.jsb` files follow a simple markup language of its own, analogous to HTML. Apart from the tags that make up the markup language, the content of the `.jsb` file is pure JavaScript (and possibly Liveconnect'ed Java). This example shows the list of tags, in the order that they commonly occur. Ellipses (three dots) indicates the previous line can appear more than once.

```
<JSB>
    <JSB_DESCRIPTOR CUSTOMISER ENV VISUAL DETAILS>
    <JSB_ICON ICONNAME>
    <JSB_INTERFACE NAME>
    <JSB_PROPERTY DEFAULTVALUE ENV ISBOUND ISDEFAULT PROPERTYEDITOR PROPTYPE
            READMETHOD TYPE WRITEMETHOD VALUESET DETAILS>
    ...
    <JSB_EVENT ADDLISTENERMETHOD EVENTMODEL ISDEFAULT LISTENERMETHOD
LISTENERTYPE
            REMOVELISTENERMETHOD DETAILS>
    ...
    <JSB_METHOD ENV TYPE DETAILS>
    ...
        <JSB_PARAMETER TYPE DETAILS>
        ...
```

```
    </JSB_METHOD>
    ...
    <JSB_CONSTRUCTOR> </JSB_CONSTRUCTOR>
</JSB>
<JSB_LISTENER NAME> </JSB_LISTENER>
...
```

Where a **DETAILS** tag attribute appears, read these attributes instead, which usually appear to the user when the bean is read by a visual development tool:

```
NAME DISPLAYNAME SHORTDESCRIPTION
```

Here is an example of a very simple JavaScript Bean, but of course, its unrunnable without using a tool like Netscape's Visual JavaScript to read it and construct a normal web page with it:

```
<JSB>
    <JSB_DESCRIPTOR NAME="PanicObject">
    <JSB_PROPERTY NAME="panic_message" TYPE="string">
    <JSB_PROPERTY NAME="panic_level" TYPE="string">
    <JSB_METHOD NAME="do_panic" TYPE="void"> </JSB_METHOD>
    <JSB_CONSTRUCTOR>
        function do_panic() {
            if ( this.panic_level == "low" )
            alert(panic_message);
        else
            top.location.href = "javascript:'<HTML><H1>"+panic_message+"</H1></HTML>'"
        }

        function PanicObject(params) {
            this.panic_message = params.panic_message;
            this.panic_level   = params.panic_level;
            this.do_panic      = do_panic;
        }
    </JSB_CONSTRUCTOR>
</JSB>
```

This object displays an alert with a message if the panic level is set to low, otherwise it erases the current document and writes the message as a replacement in the biggest size (destroying the JavaScript object in the process, since it's stored in the old document). It has two properties the user can read and alter, and one method the user can call.

Applying JavaScript Beans

Using visual development tools for JavaScript development is another book, but a few remarks are salient:

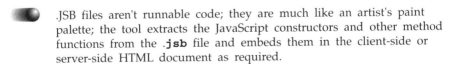

- .JSB files aren't runnable code; they are much like an artist's paint palette; the tool extracts the JavaScript constructors and other method functions from the **.jsb** file and embeds them in the client-side or server-side HTML document as required.

- Nothing stops the developer from hacking up the JavaScript produced by a development tool—it's still an interpreted environment. Such hacks are fairly pointless though, and might be difficult to keep up to date.

Although custom JavaScript objects are central to the JavaScript Beans concept, there's no reason why such an object can't interact with other objects in a HTML page, such as form elements, Java applets and plugins, and CORBA objects. There is some support for these other object via tag attribute values.

Scriptlets

The JavaScript Bean specification doesn't in theory require a specific browser. Microsoft's Scriptlet technology requires Internet Explorer 4.0. At the cost of portability, the script writer gains back a component system that is simpler than the JavaScript Bean approach.

Scriptlet technology helps to control web development complexity in the following ways:

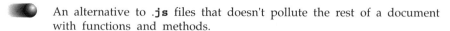 An alternative to .**js** files that doesn't pollute the rest of a document with functions and methods.

Another way of dividing up the window space in a document as styles, frames and layers do.

A way of producing part of an HTML document separate to the rest of it.

Unlike JavaScript Beans, Scriptlets have nothing to do with Java. At this time of writing there are no visual development tools for Scriptlets. Scriptlets apply to all Microsoft's scripting languages, such as VBScript, not just JavaScript. Finally, Scriptlets encompass HTML as well as pure JavaScript.

What's a Scriptlet?

There are three ways of looking at Scriptlets:

A new kind of browser plugin

A way to componentize JavaScript and HTML

A faster development tool than ActiveX

In all cases, Scriptlets are a JavaScript and HTML-friendly technology. The name 'Scriptlet' is either a Microsoft invention or is derived from discussions in the JavaScript Internet newsgroups. In either case, a JavaScript Scriptlet is meant to be similar in style and focus to a Java applet.

Scriptlets as Web plugins

A web browser displaying an HTML document can have areas of that document reserved for the display of plugin data. Provided the correct plugin is present, visual information in a format foreign to HTML can be displayed in that area. All that is required is the use of the **<EMBED>** or **<OBJECT>** tag.

One format for visual information is HTML itself. Internet Explorer 4.0 allows HTML documents to be displayed in a plugin-style area. The 'plugin' that displays these documents is built into the browser. Just like other plugins, the **<OBJECT>** tag is used. Here is an example:

```
<!-- top.htm -->
<HTML><BODY>
I am above the scriptlet<BR>
<OBJECT WIDTH=100 HEIGHT=100 TYPE="text/x-scriptlet" DATA="scriptlet.htm"></
OBJECT>
<BR>I am below the scriptlet
</BODY></HTML>
```

```
<!-- scriptlet.htm -->
<HTML><BODY STYLE="background-color: yellow">
I <STRONG>AM</STRONG> the scriptlet!
</BODY></HTML>
```

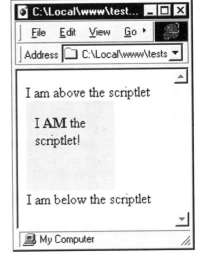

This document appears like this in Internet Explorer 4.0:

Any HTML document could be put in the place of **scriptlet.htm**—the Scriptlet's area can display scrollbars if the document is too big for the area. Since HTML documents can contain JavaScript, this document could be used instead of **scriptlet.htm** for the same effect:

```
<!-- scriptlet2.htm -->
<HTML><BODY STYLE="background-color: yellow">
<SCRIPT>
document.write( "I " + "AM".strong() + " the scriptlet!");
</SCRIPT>
</BODY></HTML>
```

By itself, this is not a very interesting use of Scriptlets, since you already have **<IFRAME>**. The next section expands on the possibilities. One noteworthy feature is that the **<OBJECT>** tag for the Scriptlet has no **CLSID** attribute— therefore Scriptlets have the potential to be quite portable.

Scriptlets as JavaScript components

Since a Scriptlet can contain JavaScript, it's not hard for the scriptwriter to organize matters so that inter-related JavaScript code is collected together into a Scriptlet. By itself, this does nothing except appeal to the orderly and organized. However, the collected JavaScript inside the Scriptlet can be accessed from the containing document. This allows the Scriptlet to be treated as a component. Here is the example of the last section again, slightly modified:

```
<!-- top.htm -->
<HTML><BODY ONLOAD='setTimeout("test.show_message()",5000);'>
I am above the scriptlet<BR>
<OBJECT ID="test" WIDTH=100 HEIGHT=100 TYPE="text/x-scriptlet"
DATA="scriptlet.htm">
</OBJECT>
<BR>I am below the scriptlet
</BODY></HTML>
```

```
<!-- scriptlet.htm -->
<HTML><BODY STYLE="background-color: yellow">
I <STRONG>AM</STRONG> the scriptlet!
<SCRIPT>
function public_show_message()
{
  alert("And I'm proud of it.");
}
</SCRIPT>
</BODY></HTML>
```

In this example, the Scriptlet pops up an alert five seconds after loading in response to a function called by the main document. The main document calls the function without its **public_** prefix—more on that later. The Scriptlet needn't take up any visible space on the screen. It may just perform computation. To achieve this, merely use **STYLE="display: none"** in the object tag that contains the Scriptlet.

The method **show_message** is said to be **exposed**, or **published**, meaning that it is available outside of the Scriptlet itself. Both methods and properties can be exposed. In addition, the document containing the Scriptlet's **<OBJECT>** tag can specify an **onScriptletEvent** event handler that will catch any events the Scriptlet might create.

Scriptlets as ActiveX development tools

A third way of describing Scriptlets is to consider them as ActiveX controls. Most ActiveX controls are written in compiled languages such as C++, but it needn't be the case. Scriptlets embedded in another HTML document were previously compared with plugins, but it is more accurate to say that they are contained within an ActiveX COM object. That COM object is the same one used for normal browser windows, and supports the HTML and JavaScript languages.

For other ActiveX controls, the control is developed and compiled, and when needed it is downloaded to the browser where it executes directly on the PC's CPU with the assistance of the ActiveX infrastructure and Windows runtime libraries. For the Scriptlet model, the control is developed in a scripting language, so no compile is required. When it is downloaded, it is executed by being interpreted by the Internet Explorer COM object.

Describing exposed Scriptlet features

Without any special steps being taken, none of the JavaScript inside a Scriptlet is accessible from the document containing the Scriptlet's **<OBJECT>** tag. This is the principal of information hiding, designed to force good manners onto the user of the Scriptlet.

In order to make something available to the containing document, the Scriptlet must use special naming conventions that the browser is aware of. These conventions revolve around the prefix **public_**. There are not one, but two approaches.

Using the public_description object

An HTML document might be displayed by a whole browser window, or just inside a Scriptlet area. In the latter case a special object can be created which can be used to expose properties and methods of the Scriptlet. This is the **public_description** object.

If this object exists in the Scriptlet code, then it will be the authority the browser uses to decide which methods and functions are exposed to the parent document. Every method or property in the Scriptlet that matches a property name of the **public_description** object will be accessible from outside the Scriptlet. The **public_description** object is itself quite ordinary. Here is a simple example:

```
<HTML><HEAD><SCRIPT>

function do_this() { alert('do_this() called'); }
function do_that() { alert('do_that() called'); }

var this_data;
var that_data;

var public_description = new Object;
public_description.do_that = do_this;
public_description.that_data = that_data;

</SCRIPT></HEAD></HTML>
```

In this example, the **do_that()** method can be called from outside the Scriptlet, and the **that_data** property can be read and set from outside the Scriptlet. The two '**this**' items cannot. It doesn't really matter what values the properties of this special object have—it is the existence of those properties that is important.

For Scriptlet properties, flexibility beyond that of Scriptlet methods is possible. These two examples are equivalent:

```
public_description.that_data = that_data;
```

and

```
public_description.get_that_data = that_data;
public_description.set_that_data = that_data;
```

The special use of the **get_** and **set_** prefixes allows the Scriptlet creator to specify whether the property should externally be just readable (**'get_'**), just writeable (**'set_'**), or readable and writeable (**'get_'** and **'set_'**).

Using property name prefixes

If the **public_description** object is not used, then the actual methods and properties can be named so that they are automatically exposed outside the Scriptlet. All that is required is that they be prefixed with the string **'public_'**. Here is the example of the last section repeated using this alternate notation:

```
<HTML><HEAD><SCRIPT>

function do_this()       { alert('do_this() called'); }
function public_do_that() { alert('do_that() called'); }

var         this_data;
var public_that_data;

</SCRIPT></HEAD></HTML>
```

When used externally, the prefix **'public_'** is not required, so this example looks identical to the last. You still have the more detailed approach to exposing properties. Again, these two examples are equivalent:

```
public_that_data = that_data;
```

and

```
public_get_that_data = that_data;
public_set_that_data = that_data;
```

Summary

JavaScript's apparent simplicity might be an attractive solution for "quick and dirty" programming designed to freshen up plain HTML pages, but it has some industrial-strength features as well. The common theme for all these features is flexibility.

At the 4.0 browser level, HTML intrinsic event handling is a highly organized, yet complex and partially incompatible matter. Without these events much of Dynamic HTML wouldn't be possible.

Resolution of JavaScript identifiers in the core language proceeds in a highly predictable way and allows ordered lists of objects to be automatically consulted when a variables origin is in debate.

Netscape continues to enhance the utility of JavaScript. For the end user of a browser, Netcaster provides a step up from the hide-and-seek game that tracking down one's favorite subjects has become on the Web. Netcaster is configured by JavaScript. For the developer, BeanConnect creates even more opportunity for JavaScript to interact with Java.

For the developer, formal specifications in the form of JavaScript Beans and Scriptlet technology allows the developer to control complexity and quickly built web components, sometimes with easy-to-use development tools.

ECMAScript Core Language

The ECMAScript standard describes the central features of the JavaScript language. A vendor's particular implementation conforms to the standard if it implements all the features described in the standard. An implementation may add further features, particularly host objects, and still conform.

 Host objects are described in later Reference Sections.

 Non-host object enhancements are described in Section B.

 The features listed in this section are discussed in more detail in Chapter 1.

Comparison tables at the end of each section only show a value if there is a non-conformance to the standard.

Script Formatting and Comments

 Unicode 2.0 characters may be used to write a script. Only ASCII characters can appear outside string literals and comment text.

 Whitespace separates language elements not otherwise separated by punctuation characters, improves readability and consists of one or more of these characters:

Character name	Unicode value	ASCII decimal code
Tab	\u0009	9
Vertical Tab	\u000B	11
Form Feed	\u000C	13
Space	\u0020	32

 Line terminators also separate language elements, but cannot appear directly inside a string literal:

Character name	Unicode value	ASCII decimal code
Line Feed	\u000A	10
Carriage Return	\u000D	14

Comments are non-functional text. Single line comments can appear inside multi-line comments but no other combination is possible.

```
// single line comment
```

```
/* multi-line
   comment */
```

Identifiers consist of one or more alphabetic letters, decimal digits, underscores ('_') or dollar signs ('$'), and are case-sensitive. The first character may not be a decimal digit.

Automatic semicolon insertion. Statements normally end with a semicolon(';'). If left out, the interpreter will assume one, except within the parentheses of a **for** loop. If a **return** statement with an argument, or an expression with a post-increment('++') or post-decrement ('--') operator is split over two lines, an unexpected semicolon may be inserted.

Literals

Literals are data values embedded directly in a script.

void is an operator, not a literal.

There is no literal representation of the Undefined type's sole value.

null is the Null type's sole literal value.

true and **false** are the Boolean type's literal values.

Numeric literals for the Number type may be represented in several ways:

Signed integer: an optional **+** or **-** leads at least one character instance from the set **0123456789**, but the first may not be **0** (zero) if there is more than one character instance.

Signed decimal: either a signed integer, **+** , **-** or nothing, then a **.** (full stop) followed by at least one character instance from the set **0123456789**.

Signed scientific: a signed decimal followed by one of **eE** followed by a signed integer.

Octal: a **0** (zero) followed by at least one character instance from the set **01234567**.

- **Hexadecimal:** a **0x** (zero-x) or **0X** (zero-X) followed by at least one character instance from the set **0123456789abcdefABCDEF**. Therefore, hexadecimal numbers are case-insensitive.

- **NaN and Infinity:** There are no literal representations—see the **global** object for properties with these values.

Numeric literals may not exactly match any computer-representable number. In that case, rounding will occur when interpreted—see Data Types.

String literals for the String type may be represented as follows:

- A harmless item is any Unicode character except line terminators, \ (backslash), ' (single quote) and " (double quote).

- A String literal is a " followed by at least zero items from the set of harmless items plus ', and then a further ".

- A String literal is a ' followed by at least zero items from the set of harmless items plus ", and then a further '.

A String literal may also contain escape sequences. An escape sequence is a \ followed by special characters which together identify a single Unicode character. If a non-special character follows the \, the \ is ignored. The list of escape sequences is:

Escape Sequence	Name	Unicode value
\b	backspace	\u0008
\t	horizontal tab	\u0009
\n	line feed (new line)	\u000A
\f	form feed	\u000C
\r	carriage return	\u000D
\"	double quote: "	\u0022
\'	single quote: '	\u0027
\\	backslash: \	\u005C
\0DDD (see below)	octal sequence	\u0000 to \u00FF
\xDD (see below)	hexadecimal sequence	\u0000 to \u00FF
\uDDDD (see below)	Unicode sequence	\u0000 to \uFFFF

- An **octal escape sequence** is a backslash followed by **0** (zero), followed by an optional character from the set **0123**, followed by one or two characters from the set **01234567**. This is an octal value in the range 0 to 255 (decimal).

- A **hexadecimal escape sequence** is a backslash followed by one of **xX**, followed by two character instances from the set 0123456789abcdefABCDEF. This is a case-insensitive hexadecimal number in the range 0 to 255 (decimal).

293

A **Unicode escape sequence** is a backslash followed by a **u**, followed by four character instances from the set **0123456789abcdefABCDEF**. This is a case-insensitive hexadecimal number in the range 0 to 65535 (decimal).

Data Types

Every data item in a script has a type. Variables can contain any type of data. The standard draws a distinction between the names of types and allowable values for those types - names of types start with an uppercase letter. The standard doesn't say how the values of various types should be output to the user, except for rounding of numbers. See also the Native Objects heading.

Undefined. The type of a variable that hasn't been assigned a value: e.g. **'var x;'**. This type has one value: undefined, with no literal representation.

Null. The type for empty values. This type has one value: null, written **null** literally.

Boolean. The type for truth values. This type has two unique values: true and false, written **true** and **false** literally.

Number. The type for integral and floating point numbers. The Number type is a double precision 64-bit IEEE 754 value, with special values NaN (Not a Number) and positive and negative infinity. Numbers as big as 1×10^{300}, and as small as 1×10^{-300} are possible, as well as their negatives. Roughly 18 significant digits are possible.

Because computers are finite, real numbers such as π cannot always be exactly represented.

> **Special care must be taken to convert those numbers to a human readable format so that they appear as expected—this is a rounding problem.**

Mathematics introduces tiny errors when numbers with many digits are operated on. This usually only interests mathematicians and statisticians, and is a general problem with computers. Small integer operations, such as **234 * 12**, are usually unaffected.

> **Some numbers can be represented in more than one way. There are positive and negative zeros, and many different values of NaN. This is invisible to the scriptwriter.**

String. The type for sequences of Unicode characters. The minimum length is 0; the standard mandates no maximum length. Current implementations allow for strings of at least a Megabyte in size. According to the standard, the String type uses a Unicode 2.0 encoding which covers the whole world of characters.

294

Browsers at version 4.0 or less only support smaller character sets such as ISO 8859-1 (Latin1) which is English ASCII plus Western European characters. So, no Chinese symbols are available without changing the browser's language. The subject of character sets versus character set encodings is a complex one. For more information read the Unicode standard, or investigate on the Web.

Object. The underlying type of all ECMAScript/Javascript objects. It has no innate values exposed to the script writer's control. Instead it supplies behavior that the script writer can use (see Chapter 1) and that other object types can inherit:

- properties may be attached to it.
- The **prototype** property may be exploited to support inheritance.
- The **typeof()** method returns **"Object"** for Object type values.

In addition there are Reference, List and Completion type, but these are invisible to the script writer. The Reference type is of some conceptual use to script writers in that it is used to track values of the Object type - see Chapter 1. **void** is not a type, it is an operator.

Read the standard for all the gory details regarding types.

The **typeof()** strings are:

Type operated on	Resulting string
Undefined	"undefined"
Null	"object"
Boolean	"boolean"
Number	"number"
String	"string"
Object (native object that isn't a function)	"object"
Object (native object that is a function)	"function"
host object	No standard. Depends on the specific object.

Type conversion

The full type conversion story is very complex. See Chapter 1 for an easy way out, or read the standard very carefully. Two specific unusual cases are bit operators and array indices.

- Bit operators temporarily convert their left argument to a 32-bit value, and their right argument to an unsigned 5-bit value.
- Any number value (not string) used as an array element index will be converted to an unsigned 32-bit value.

295

Operators and Expressions

The ECMAScript operators are:

Operator	Name	Operator	Name
Unary operators			
`delete`	deletes an object	+	unary plus
`void`	force the undefined value to be returned	-	unary minus
`typeof`	report a value's type	~	bitwise **NOT**
`++`	pre- and post-increment	!	logical **NOT**
`--`	pre- and post-decrement		
Binary operators			
`*`	multiplication	`<<`	left shift
`/`	division	`>>`	right shift
`%`	modulus or remainder	`>>>`	unsigned right shift
`+`	addition or concatenation		
`-`	subtraction	`&`	bitwise **AND**
		`|`	bitwise **OR**
`<`	less than	`^`	bitwise **XOR**
`>`	greater than		
`<=`	less than or equal	`&&`	logical **AND**
`>=`	greater than or equal	`||`	logical **OR**
`==`	equal		
`!=`	not equal		
Special operators			
`this`	refers to the current scope's object	?:	ternary conditional operator; allows 'if' inside an expression
`new`	construct an object of given type	,	'comma': separates function arguments or sequences of expressions
`=`	assigns result of right hand expression to left hand variable	( )	delimits function arguments and groups operators in expressions

Operator	Name	Operator	Name
op=, *=, /=, %=, +=, -=, <<=, >>=, >>>=, &=, ^= or |=	assignment with binary operator applied to old value and new value before final assignment:	[]	Associates a property name with an object in an array-like manner.
.	Associates a property name with an object		

Operator Precedence

Does 1 + 2 * 3 = 1 + (2 * 3) = 7 or does it equal (1 + 2) * 3 = 6?

The ECMAScript standard doesn't yet clearly document operator precedence. However, JavaScript closely follows Java, and Java closely follows C. The table shows precedence with highest at the top, and like operators grouped together. The third column explains whether to read 1+2+3+4 as ((1+2)+3)+4 or 1+(2+(3+(4))).

Operator type	Operators	Evaluation order for like elements
postfix operators	[] () . expr++ expr--	left to right
unary operators	++expr --expr +expr -expr ~ !	right to left
object management or cast	new delete void	right to left
multiplicative	* / %	left to right
additive	+ -	left to right
shift	<< >> >>>	left to right
relational	< > <= >= typeof(expr)	left to right
equality	== !=	left to right
bitwise AND	&	left to right
bitwise exclusive OR	^	left to right
bitwise inclusive OR	|	left to right
logical AND	&&	left to right
logical OR	||	left to right
conditional	? :	right to left
assignment	= += -= *= /= %= &= ^= |= <<= >>= >>>=	right to left

Statements and Control Flow

Statements are the basic unit of work in the language. Statements are terminated with a semi-colon which can be left out if the line ends after the statement. A block is a collected sequence of statements. Blocks and statements are generally interchangeable.

```
statement-body;    // a statement
```

```
{
    statement;        // one or more statements plus braces equal a block
}
```

If ... else ...

```
if ( condition )
    statement or block
```

or

```
if ( condition )
    statement or block
else
    statement or block
```

While ...

```
while ( condition )
    statement or block
```

If a block is used it may contain instances of

```
break;
```

or

```
continue;
```

For ...

```
for ( setup-expression; continue-condition; change-expression )
    statement or block
```

or

```
for ( variable in object-variable )
    statement or block
```

Only properties without the **DontEnum** special ECMAScript property attribute are revealed by the second form.

If a block is used it may contain instances of

```
break;
```

or

```
continue;
```

With ...

```
with ( object )
   statement or block
```

Scope, functions and methods

There is always a current object, accessible via the special variable/operator **this**.

Functions are sections of executable script associated with a property name, also called a function name. The name follows the rules for property/variable names. Functions are first declared, then invoked.

Declarations can occur as follows:

```
function example1()
{
// zero or more statements
}
```

or

```
function example2(arg1, arg2)      // as many named variables as needed
{
// zero or more statements possibly using arg1, arg2
}
```

or

```
new Function("a", "b", "c", "return a+b+c");      // a,b,c are arguments
```

or

```
new Function("a, b, c", "return a+b+c");      // a,b,c are arguments
```

or

```
new Function("a,b", "c", "return a+b+c");      // a,b,c are arguments
```

or

```
new Function("return arguments[0]+arguments[1]+arguments[2]"); // no arguments
```

Functions may contain one or more instances of

```
return;
```

or

```
return expression;
```

Invocation of functions occurs as follows:

```
example1(var1, var2)                              // zero or more arguments
```

or

```
object_variable.method_property_name(var1, var2)    // zero or more arguments
```

- Any number of arguments can be passed to a function, regardless of its declaration.

- All function arguments are passed by value, if they are primitive types, otherwise by reference.

- Functions can be called recursively, therefore care needs to be taken to avoid infinite loops.

- The standard does not require that functions be declarable inside other functions.

If a function's body (main statement block) uses the **this** operator, it is said to be a method and must be invoked as a property of an object. Also see the Function object below.

Native Objects

Native objects are part of the JavaScript interpreter and the standard. The only built in object is Math. The standard explains the gory details of 'prototype inheritance', which allows one object to take on properties of another.

Objects and their properties commonly form a tree data structure, with the global object at the root of the tree. Because properties and variables can track any object, more general structures than trees are possible. The most general structure possible where objects are tracked with no apparent plan is called a **cyclic directed graph**.

There is a full listing of all the ECMAScript host objects below. Note that because all objects inherit their prototype's properties, objects can call methods and properties of their own using the syntax

```
obj.property()
```

rather than using the full prototype syntax:

```
obj.prototype.property()
```

To aid reference, therefore, only the root name is given here. Where the argument of the property is the current object itself, then we have used the keyword **this** to indicate it.

All the objects of ECMAScript have **toString()** and **valueOf()** methods. However, these return different results depending on the object from which they are called, and are so detailed for each object.

Internal Properties

These are the internal properties of all ECMAScript objects. Note that instantiations of particular objects can have these properties read using the **Get** property, but they are internal properties and not accessible to the language. However, see Reference Section B for details of JScript mechanisms for doing so.

Property	Parameters	Description
[[Prototype]]	none	The prototype of this object.
[[Class]]	none	The kind of this object.
[[Value]]	none	Internal state information associated with this object.
[[Get]]	(PropertyName)	Returns the value of the property.
[[Put]]	(PropertyName, Value)	Sets the specified property to Value.
[[CanPut]]	(PropertyName)	Returns a boolean value indicating whether a [[Put]] operation with the specified PropertyName will succeed.
[[HasProperty]]	(PropertyName)	Returns a boolean value indicating whether the object already has a member with the given name.
[[Delete]]	(PropertyName)	Removes the specified property from the object.
[[DefaultValue]]	(Hint)	Returns a default value for the object, which should be a primitive value (not an object or reference).
[[Construct]]	a list of argument values provided by the caller	Constructs an object. Invoked via the **new** operator. Objects that implement this internal method are called *constructors*.
[[Call]]	a list of argument values provided by the caller	Executes code associated with the object. Invoked via a function call expression. Objects that implement this internal method are called *functions*.

Global Object

In every case, a **length** property of a built-in function object described in this section has the attributes **ReadOnly**, **DontDelete**, **DontEnum**, and no others. Note that all objects inherit the methods from the **Global** object:

Property Name	Read/write?	Enumerable?	Description
NaN	Yes	No	Initial value is NaN
Infinity	Yes	No	Initial value is $+\infty$

Method Name	Arguments	Return	Description
eval()	x	string object	Returns either **x** if not a string object, the result of **x** as a program, a runtime error if **x** does not execute as a program or the **undefined** value.
parseInt()	string, radix	integer value	The **parseInt** function produces an integer value by interpreting the contents of the *string* argument according to the specified *radix*. Default radix is 10.
parseFloat()	string	NaN or number value	Interprets the string value as a decimal literal to give a number.
escape()	string	string	Replaces characters in string with special URL meanings with their corresponding hexadecimal escape sequence.
unescape()	string	string	Translates hexadecimal escape sequences in a string back into characters.
isNaN()	number	True|False	Returns True if the argument is **NaN**, otherwise False
isFinite()	number	True|False	False if the argument is **NaN**, +∞, or −∞, otherwise True.
Object(...)	Value or empty	Object object	If value, must be **null** or **undefined**. Creates a new Object object.
Function(...)	as required	Function object	Creates a new Function object, with the arguments providing formal parameters. The last argument is executable code.
Array(...)	Array items or length or empty	Array object	Instantiates an Array object with the arguments as members. Length creates an array of length equal to length, empty creates an empty array.
String(...)	value or empty	string value; empty string	Value returns a string value computed by **ToString(value)**; empty returns " "
Boolean(...)	value or empty	boolean value; false	Calculates a boolean value using **ToBoolean(value)**; or simply returns false.

Method Name	Arguments	Return	Description
Number(...)	value or empty	Number value; +0	Calculates a number value according to ToNumber(value), or returns 0.
Date(...)	see description	string value	Returns a string value representing the current time in UTC (GMT)
Math	No	No	It is not possible to call the Math object as a method.

Object

There are no special properties for the Object object, other than those which it inherits from the special built-in prototype object; it does not have an initial **value**:

Property Name	Read/write?	Enumerable?	Description
constructor	Yes	No	Holds the built-in Object constructor

Method Name	Arguments	Return	Description
toString()	this	String value	Returns a string for the object of the form "[object ", class, and "]"
valueOf()	this	Object	Returns the object.

Function

The **function** object can be called instead of a function value.

Property Name	Read/write?	Enumerable?	Description
length	No	No	Establishes expected number of arguments as an integer.
arguments	No	No	Value depends on

Method Name	Arguments	Return	Description
toString()	this	String value	Returns an string value representation of the function. Precise whitespacing, formatting etc are left to the implementation.

Array

The **array** object is used to store collections of information in an easily accessible fashion.

Property Name	Read/write?	Enumerable?	Description
Length	Yes	No	This is always numerically greater than the names of all members of the array.

Method	Arguments	Returns	Description
join (separator)	see description	string	The array elements are converted to strings, then concatenated with the separator. Default separator is **comma**.
reverse()	this	Array	Returns a new array object with the elements reversed.
sort (comparefn)	Function	Array	Sorts the array according to function of a form that establishes (**x>y** as –ve; **x=y** as 0; **x<y** as +ve)

String

The String object can be thought of as a wrapper for a simple string value. The string value passed to the object when it is created becomes in essence an unnamed, implicit, property of the object itself.

Property Name	Read/write?	Enumerable?	Description
fromCharCode (char0, char1…)	yes	no	Returns a string value containing as many characters as the resulting string.
length	No	No	An integer equal to the number of characters in the string; once created, it is unchanging.

Method Name	Arguments	Return	Description
toString()	this	string value	Returns this String value. Note that the **toString** method is not generic.
charAt(pos)	number	string value	Returns character number pos in the string as a string value.

Method Name	Arguments	Return	Description
charCodeAt (pos)	number	Number	Returns a non negative number that represents, according to Unicode, the character at position **pos**, else **NaN**.
indexOf (searchString , position)	string, number	Index of rightmost character; -1	Searches string for the next substring, **searchstring**, to the right of position **pos**. Returns index position, or −1 if string is not found. Default position is 0.
lastIndexOf (searchString , position)	string, number	Index of leftmost character; -1	Searches string for the nearest substring, **searchstring**, to the left of position **pos**. Returns index position, or −1 if string is not found. Default position is 0.
split (separator)	string	**Array** object containing substrings.	Splits a string, left to right, by each instance of the **separator**, which are not included in the resulting array. If separator = **'empty string'**, then returns array containing one character per array element, and of a **length** equal to the **length** of the string.
substring (start)	number	string value	Returns a string value beginning at character **start** and running to end of string. If start is NaN or negative, then begins at pos 0.
substring (start, end)	number, number	string value	Returns a string value of the characters between start and end positions. Will be reversed if **start>end**; treated as 0 if negative or NaN; as string length if larger than string.
toLowerCase()	this	string value	Converts entire string to lowercase string value
toUpperCase()	this	string value	Converts entire string to uppercase string value.
valueOf()	this	string value	Returns the string, else runtime error if not a String object.

Boolean

The Boolean object can be seen as a 'wrapper' for a simple Boolean value. When created, the value of the boolean becomes essentially an implicit, unnamed, property of the object

Property Name	Read/write?	Enumerable?	Description
Boolean (value)	Yes	No	returns a boolean value computed by toBoolean(value)

Method Name	Arguments	Return	Description
toString()	this	"true" or "false"	Returns a string "true" if true, "false" if false.
valueOf()	this	true or false	Returns value of object; generates a runtime error if not a boolean object

Number

Like the String and Boolean objects, the Number object is primarily a wrapper, although it has a number of in built properties that represent significant values for ECMAScript

Property Name	Read/write?	Enumerable?	Description
MAX_VALUE	No	No	The largest possible value, approx $1.7976931348623157e^{308}$
MIN_VALUE	No	No	The smallest positive non-zero value, approx $5e^{-324}$
NaN	No	No	Value is NaN
NEGATIVE_ INFINITY	No	No	Value is $-\infty$
POSITIVE_ INFINITY	No	No	Value is $+\infty$

Method Name	Arguments	Returns	Description
toString()	radix	See description	If radix is 10 or not supplied, then a toString opration is carried out; if another integer from 2 to 36, the result is an implementation dependent string.
valueOf()	this	Number object	Gives error if not a number.

Math

The Math object is unusual in that essentially it provides a number of useful mathematical operations that are accessible through the Math object.

Property Name	Read/write?	Enumerable?	Description
E	No	No	The number value for e, base of the natural logarithms. Approx **2.7182818284590452354**
LN10	No	No	Number value of the natural log of 10, approx **2.302585092994046**.
LN2	No	No	Number value of the natural log of 2, approx **0.6931471805599453**
LOG2E	No	No	Number value of the base-2 logarithm of 2, which is approx **1.4426950408889634**
LOG10E	No	No	Number value of the base-10 logarithm, which is approx **0.4342944819032518**
PI	No	No	The number value for π (ratio of a circle's circumference to its diameter) approx **3.14159265358979323846**
SQRT1_2	No	No	The value for the square root of ½, which is approx **0.7071067811865476**
SQRT2	No	No	The number value of the square root of 2, which is approx **1.4142135623730951**

Note that every method of the math object first carries out a **toNumber()** operation on each of the arguments, then performs a computation on the resulting value(s). For familiar expressions (e.g. acos, asin etc.) the implementor will use available mathematical libraries, such as those available to C programmers. ECMAScript recommends the use of the freely downloadable Maths library **fdlibm**.

Method Name	Arguments	Returns	Description
abs()	x	absolute number	Returns the absolute value of x; in general, has the same magnitude as the value but a positive sign
acos()	x	Number in radians	Approximates the inverse cosine of the argument; expressed in radians.
asin()	x	Number in radians	Approximates the inverse sine of the argument; expressed in radians
atan()	x	Number in radians	Approximates the inverse tan of the argument; expressed in radians
atan2()	y, x	Number in radians	Returns the inverse tan of the quotient y/x where the argument signs determine the quadrant of the result.
ceil()	x	Integer number	Returns the smallest mathematical integer larger than x. If x is already an integer, then equal to x.
cos()	x	Number in radians	Gives an implementation-dependent approximation of the cosine of the argument.
exp()	x	Number value	Returns an approximation of e to the power x.
floor()	x	Number value	Returns the greatest mathematical integer smaller than x. If x is already an integer, then return is equal to x.
log()	x	Number value	Approximates the natural logarithm of x.
max()	x,y	x or y	Returns the larger of the two arguments.
min()	x,y	x or y	Returns the smaller of the two arguments.
pow()	x,y	x^y	Returns x to the power y
random()	None	Number value	Returns a randomly generated number greater than or equal to 0, less than 1.
round()	x	Integer	Returns the closest integer to the argument; rounds up if two are equally close. If x is an integer, then return = x

Method Name	Arguments	Returns	Description
sin()	x	Number in radians	Gives an implementation-dependent approximation of the sine of the argument.
sqrt()	x	Number value	Returns an approximation of the square root of the argument.
tan()	x	Number value	Gives an implementation-dependent approximation of the tan of the argument.

Date

The **date** object contains a number that represents a given time in milliseconds, relative to Midnight, January 1st, 1970. Readers are referred to the ECMAScript standard for full details of the operations carried out to convert this number to specific dates and times under implementations of ECMAScript. Note that Months are represented by an integer from 0 to 11, inclusive, with 0 being January and 11 being December. Days of the week are integers from 0 to 6, with 0 being Sunday and 6 being Saturday. Note that UTC is Universal Coordinated Time, or GMT.

Property Name	Read/write?	Enumerable?	Description
length	No	No	Initial value is 7

Method Name	Arguments	Returns	Description
parse(string)			
UTC(year, [month, [date, [hours, [minutes, [seconds, ms]]]]])		Number	Creates a date value in UTC, rather than a local time date. Note that arguments can not be 'skipped', and that if date or larger unit is omitted (e.g. month, year) then result is implementation dependent.
toString()		String	Implementation dependent, but intended to return a human readable time value. Not generic.
getTime()	**Value** stored in date object.	time value	Returns the time value of the object
getYear()	**Value** stored in date object.	19xx	Specified only for backward compatibilty; returns two digit year.

Method Name	Arguments	Returns	Description
getFullYear()	**Value** stored in date object.	xxxx	Returns four digit year in human readable form. Based on local time
getUTCFull_Year()	**Value** stored in date object.	xxxx	As above; based on UTC.
getMonth()	**Value** stored in date object.	0-11	Calculates month, based on local time
getUTCMonth()	**Value** stored in date object.	0-11	Calculates month, based on UTC.
getDate()	**Value** stored in date object.	1-31	Calculates date, based on local time.
getUTCDate()	**Value** stored in date object.	1-31	Calculates date, based on UTC.
getDay()	**Value** stored in date object.	0-6	Calculates day, based on local time.
getUTCDay()	**Value** stored in date object.	0-6	Calculates day, based on UTC.
getHours()	**Value** stored in date object.	0-23	Calculates hour, based on local time
getUTCHours()	**Value** stored in date object.	0-23	Calculates hour, based on UTC time
getMinutes()	**Value** stored in date object.	0-59	Returns number of minutes past the hour according to local time.
getUTC_Minutes()	**Value** stored in date object.	0-59	Returns number of minutes past the hour according to UTC time.
getSeconds()	**Value** stored in date object.	0-59	Returns number of seconds past the minute according to local time.
getUTC_Seconds()	**Value** stored in date object.	0-59	Returns number of seconds past the minute according to UTC time.
getMilli_seconds()	**Value** stored in date object.	0-999	Returns number of milliseconds past the minute according to local time.
getUTCMilli_seconds()	**Value** stored in date object.	0-999	Returns number of milliseconds past the minute according to UTC time.
getTimezone_Offset()		Integer	Returns difference between UTC time and local time in minutes.

Method Name	Arguments	Returns	Description
setTime(*time*)	time	time	sets date object's value to specified time.
setMilli_ seconds(*ms*)	integer	**date** value (integer)	Sets date object's value to specified milliseconds, local time.
setUTCMilli_ seconds(*ms*)	integer	**date** value (integer)	Sets date object's value to specified milliseconds, UTC.
setSeconds_ (sec [, *ms*])	integer,	**date** value (integer)	Sets date object's value to specified seconds and milliseconds, local time.
setUTC_ Seconds_ (*sec* [, *ms*])	integer	**date** value (integer)	Sets date object's value to specified seconds, UTC.
setMinutes_ (*min* [, *sec* [, _]])	integer	**date** value (integer)	Sets date object's value to specified minutes, local *ms* time.
setUTC_ Minutes(*min* _ [, *sec* [, *ms*]])	integer	**date** value (integer)	Sets date object's value to specified minutes, UTC.
setHours_ (*hour* [, *min* _ [, *sec* [, *ms*]]])	integer	**date** value (integer)	Sets date object's value to specified minutes, local time.
setUTCHours_ (*hour* [, *min* _ [, *sec* [, *ms*]]])	integer	**date** value (integer)	Sets date object's value to specified minutes, UTC.
setDate(*date*)	integer	**date** value (integer)	Sets date object's value to specified date, local time.
setUTCDate_ (*date*)	integer	**date** value (integer)	Sets date object's value to specified date, UTC.
setMonth_ (*mon* [, *date*])	integer	**date** value (integer)	Sets date object's value to specified month, local time.
setUTCMonth_ (*mon* [, *date*])	integer	**date** value (integer)	Sets date object's value to specified month, UTC.
setFullYear_ (*year* [, *mon* [, *date*]])	integer	**date** value (integer)	Sets date object's value to specified full year, local time.
setUTCFull_ Year(*year* [, _ *mon* [, *date*]])	integer	**date** value (integer)	Sets date object's value to specified full year, UTC.
setYear(*year*)	integer	**date** value (integer)	Sets date object's value to specified year, local time, two digits. Deprecated.

Method Name	Arguments	Returns	Description
toLocale_ String()	**value** of date object	**string**	Returns a human readable string based on local time & representation. Implementation dependent.
toUTCString()	**value** of date object	**string**	Returns a human readable string based on UTC.
toGMTString()	**value** of date object	**string**	Returns a human readable string based on GMT (Included for backward compatability).

Note that for **set...** methods, where optional arguments (such as [s]) are omitted, they are retrieved using the appropriate **get** method.

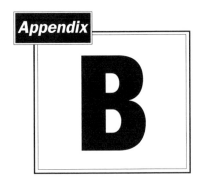

Core Language Enhancements

The headings in this section match those of Section A. JavaScript vendors can't leave the language alone; they have to add features. This section describes those features. Host objects are covered in later sections.

Script Formatting and Comments

Microsoft supports a special formatting comment, @cc, or conditional compilation. This allows JScript browsers to use new JavaScript features without affecting non-JScript browsers.

Keywords	Description
@cc_on	Activates conditional compilation support.
@if, @elif, @end	Conditionally executes a group of statements
@set	Allows creation of variables used in conditional compilation statements.

The following predefined variables are available for conditional compilation. If a variable is not true, it is not defined and behaves as **NaN** when accessed.

Variable	Behavior
@_win32	**true** if running on a win32 system
@_win16	**true** if running on a win16 system
@_mac	**true** if running on an Apple Macintosh system
@_alpha	**true** if running on a Dec Alpha processor
@_x86	**true** if running on an Intel processor
@_mc680x0	**true** if running on a Motorola 680x0 processor
@_PowerPC	**true** if running on a PowerPC
@_jscript	Always **true**

Variable	Behavior
`@_jscript_build`	Contains the build number of the JScript scripting engine.
`@_jscript_version`	Contains the JScript version number in major.minor format.

Literals

Using Object Initializers in Netscape 4.0x

Previously, objects could only be created by using either a constructor function or a function supplied for the creation of a certain object. In Navigator 4.0, however, you can also create objects using an 'object initializer'. This method should be used when only one instance of an object is needed and the ability to create multiple instances of the object is not required.

The syntax for an object using an object initializer is:

```
objectName = {property1:value1, property2:value2,..., property N:value N}
```

where **objectName** is the name of the new object, each **property n** is an identifier (either a name, a number, or a string literal), and each **value n** is an expression whose value is assigned to the property **n**. The **objectName** and assignment are defined by the script writer.

If you do not need to refer to this object elsewhere, you do not need to assign it to a variable.

If an object is created with an object initializer in a top-level script, JavaScript interprets the object each time it evaluates the expression containing the object literal. In addition, an initializer used in a function is created each time the function is called.

A slightly different syntax is needed to create an array with object initializers:

```
arrayName = [element0, element1, ..., element N]
```

where **arrayName** is the name of the new array and each **element n** is a value for one of the array's elements.

When you create an array using an initializer, it is initialized with the specified values as its elements, and its length is set to the number of arguments. As with other objects, assigning the array to a variable name is optional. You do not have to specify all elements in the new array. If you put two commas in a row, the array is created with spaces for the unspecified elements.

Data Types

JavaScript Data Tainting in Navigator 3.0

JavaScript for Navigator 3.0 had a feature called *data tainting*. When data tainting was enabled, the JavaScript used in one window could see the properties of another window, no matter what server the other window's document was loaded from. However, the author of the other window *tainted* (marked) property values or other data that should have been secure or private, and JavaScript would not pass these tainted values on to any server without the user's permission.

Data Tainting has been omitted from Javascript 1.2 / Navigator 4.0

Operators and Expressions

JScript Identity Operators

In addition to the ECMAScript compliant comparison operators, JScript also adds the following comparators

Operator type	Operators	Evaluation order for like elements
identity operators	===, !==	left to right

These operators behave identically to the equality operators except that no type conversion is done, and the types must be the same to be considered equal.

Support for Regular Expressions

Both JScript and JavaScript provide support for string searches by regarding both regular expressions and strings as objects, providing them with properties and methods as with other objects.

The JScript RegularExpression Object

Regular Expression objects store patterns used when searching strings for character combinations. After the Regular Expression object is created, it is either passed to a string method, or a string is passed to one of the regular expression methods. Information about the most recent search performed is stored in the RegExp object.

Unlike other objects, this can be created in two ways with the following pieces of syntax

```
var regularexpression = /pattern/
var regularexpression = /pattern/switch
```

or

```
var regularexpression = new RegExp("pattern")
var regularexpression = new RegExp("pattern","switch")
```

317

"Pattern" denotes the expression string you want to search for, and is obligatory. **Switch** is optional and denotes the type of search you wish to conduct. Available switches are:

- **i** (ignore case)
- **g** (global search for all occurrences of pattern)
- **gi** (global search, ignore case)

The **RegularExpression** Object has four properties and three methods, as follows:

Property	Description
global	Boolean value denoting whether the global switch (g) has been used.
ignorecase	Boolean value denoting whether the ignore case (i) switch has been used.
lastIndex	Specifies the index point form which to begin the next match.
source	Contains the text of the regular expression pattern.

Method	Description	Return Values	Required Arguments
compile	Compiles a string expression containing a regular expression pattern into an internal format.	(internal conversion)	**pattern**
exec	Searches for a match in the specified string.	**null** or **array**	**string**
test	Tests whether a pattern exists in a string.	**boolean**	**string**

The JScript RegExp Object

The **RegExp** object stores information on regular expression pattern searches. It cannot be created directly—only as a side effect of using the **RegularExpression** object—but is always available for use. Its properties have undefined as their value until a successful regular expression search has been completed.

The **RegExp** object has nine properties and no methods:

Property	Description
`index`	Returns the beginning position of the first successful match in a searched string.
`input`	Contains the string against which a search was performed. Read-only Also written as `$_` instead of `input`
`lastindex`	Returns where the last successful match begins in a string that was searched.
`lastmatch`	Returns the last matched characters. Read only. Also written as `$&` instead of `lastmatch`
`lastParen`	Returns the last substring match within parentheses, if any. Read-only. Also written as `$+` instead of `lastParen`
`leftContext`	Returns the input string up to the most recent match. Read-only Also written as `` $` `` instead of `leftContext`
`multiline`	Boolean value specifying whether searching continued across line breaks. Read-only. Also written as `$*` instead of `multiline`
`rightContext`	Returns the input string past the most recent match. Read-only. Also written as `$'` instead of `rightContext`
`$1, $2, ..., $9`	Returns the nine most-recently memorized strings found during pattern matching. Read-only

The JavaScript RegExp Object

While JavaScript expresses the concept of JavaScript as a single object called `RegExp`, JScript uses two objects, `RegExp` and `RegularExpression` to implement the idea. The JavaScript `RegExp` object however, uses all the methods and properties that apply to both the JScript objects, and the syntax is also the same.

Regular Expression Syntax

Special characters and sequences are used in writing patterns for regular expressions. The table that follows details them and includes short examples showing how the characters are used.

Character	Description
\	Marks the next character as special. `/n/` matches the character "n". The sequence `/\n/` matches a linefeed or newline character.
^	Matches the beginning of the input or line.
$	Matches the end of the input or line.
*	Matches the preceding character zero or more times. `/zo*/` matches "z" and "zoo."

319

Character	Description
+	Matches the preceding characters one or more times. **/zo+/** matches "zoo" but not "z."
?	Matches the preceding character zero or one time. **/a?ve?/** matches the "ve" in "never."
.	Matches any single character except a newline character.
pattern	Matches pattern and remembers the match. The matched substring can be retrieved from the resulting Array object elements **[1]**...**[n]** or the **RegExp object's** **$1**...**$9** properties. To match parentheses characters, (), use "\(" or "\)".
x|y	Matches either x or y. /z|food?/ matches "zoo" or "food."
{n}	n is a nonnegative integer. Matches exactly n times. **/o{2}/** does not match the "o" in "Bob," but matches the first two o's in "foooood."
{n,}	n is a nonnegative integer. Matches at least n times. **/o{2,}/** does not match the "o" in "Bob" and matches all the o's in "foooood." **/o{1,}/** is equivalent to /o+/.
{n,m}	m and n are nonnegative integers. Matches at least n and at most m times. **/o{1,3}/** matches the first three o's in "fooooood."
[xyz]	A character set. Matches any one of the enclosed characters. **/[abc]/** matches the "a" in "plain."
[^xyz]	A negative character set. Matches any character not enclosed. **/[^abc]/** matches the "p" in "plain."
[\b]	Matches a backspace (Javascript only)
\b	Matches a word boundary, such as a space. **/ea*r\b/** matches the "er" in "never early."
\B	Matches a nonword boundary. **/ea*r\B/** matches the "ear" in "never early."
\cX	Where X is a control character. Matches a control character in a string. For example, **/\cM/** matches control-M in a string. (Javascript only)
\d	Matches a digit character. Equivalent to **[0-9]**.
\D	Matches a nondigit character. Equivalent to **[^0-9]**.
\f	Matches a form-feed character.
\n	Matches a linefeed character.
\r	Matches a carriage return character.
\s	Matches any white space including space, tab, form-feed, and so forth. Equivalent to **[\f\n\r\t\v]**
\S	Matches any nonwhite space character. Equivalent to **[^ \f\n\r\t\v]**
\t	Matches a tab character.
\v	Matches a vertical tab character.

Character	Description
\w	Matches any word character including underscore. Equivalent to **[A-Za-z0-9_]**.
\W	Matches any nonword character. Equivalent to c.
\num	Matches num, where num is a positive integer. A reference back to remembered matches. \1 matches what is stored in **RegExp.$1**.
/n/	Matches n, where n is an octal, hexadecimal, or decimal escape value. Allows embedding of ASCII codes into regular expressions. (Jscript only)
\o octal \x hex	Where \o octal is an octal escape value or \x hex is a hexadecimal escape value. Allows you to embed ASCII codes into regular expressions.

Statements and Control Flow

This is a short guide to the non-standard statements used in browser implementations of JavaScript. Except where stated, JavaScript commands are valid for Navigator 2.0 onwards and the most recent implementations of JScript.

Break (JavaScript,JScript)

The **break** statement is available in both JavaScript and JScript. It terminates the current **while** or **for** loop and transfers program control to the statement following the terminated loop. If a label is used in conjunction with the **break**, it will terminate the associated label. The syntax for both Jscript and JavaScript is:

```
break [label]
```

The optional label argument specifies the label of the statement you are breaking from.

As an example, this simple function breaks out of the loop when the loop count reaches 3, and returns **x** times 3:

```
function testBreak(x) {
var i = 0
while (i < 6) {
        if (i == 3)
                break
        i++
    }
return i*x
```

continue (JavaScript, JScript)

Statement that terminates execution of the block of statements in a **while** or **for** loop, but, unlike **break**, continues execution of the loop with the next iteration. The syntax for both JScript and JavaScript is:

```
continue [label]
```

As with **break, label** is an optional argument that transfers the effect of the **continue** statement to the appropriate labeled statement.

do...while (JavaScript, JScript)

Carries out the statement until the test condition evaluates to **false**. The statement is always carried out at least once. Syntax is:

```
do
  statement
while(condition)
```

export (JavaScript)

Allows a signed script to provide properties, functions, and objects to all other signed or unsigned scripts—used for establishing security. The receiving script uses the equivalent, **import**.

```
export name1, name2, ..., nameN
export *
```

The **nameN** parameters supply the names of properties, functions, objects etc to be exported; * makes all the script's properties, functions and objects available.

for...in (JavaScript, JScript)

Statement that iterates a specified variable over all the properties of an object (or array, in JScript). For each distinct property, JavaScript executes the specified statements. Note that you cannot control the order in which the statement runs through the properties.

```
for (variable in object | array)
  statement
```

variable is the number to be assigned to each element of the object, **object|array** is the object or array to be affected and **statement** (which may be a compound statement)

import (JavaScript)

Allows a script to import properties, functions, and objects from a signed script which has exported the information. Syntax and parameters are similar, but not identical, to those of export:

```
import object.name1, object.name2,… object.nameN
import object.*
```

object is the object that will hold the names; * will import all the elements of the object.

@if Statement (JScript)

Enables conditional execution of one of a group of statements, depending on the truth value of an expression.

322

Syntax is

```
@if (expression1)
 statement1
@elif (expression2)
 statement2
...
else
 statementn
@end
```

expression1 and **expression2** are expressions that can give a Boolean result. The statements are evaluated in series, with **statement1** being passed if **expression1** is true, **statement2** only if **expression2** is **true** <u>and</u> **expression1** is **false** and so on. An **@if** statement can be written on a single line. It is also possible to use multiple **@elif** clauses, although they must come before an **@else** clause.

According to the Jscript documentation, the **@if** statement is best used to determine which text among several options should be used for text output, using the **@(platform)** syntax detailed under Conditional Compilation.

labeled (JavaScript, Jscript)

Provides an identifier that can be referred to by **break** or **continue** to indicate whether or not the program should continue execution. Syntax is:

```
label :
 statement
```

statement can be a block of statements.

@set Statement (JScript)

@set Statement is specific to JScript, and is used to create variables for conditional compilation statements. The syntax is:

```
@set @variablename = term
```

variablename establishes the variable name and must be preceded by the **@** symbol. **term** establishes the variable, and can be composed of a constant, a conditional compilation, or a parenthesized expressions. Note that only Numeric and Boolean variables are supported; strings can't be set. Variables created using **@set** are generally used in conditional compilation statements, but need not be.

Switch (JavaScript, JScript)

Allows a program to evaluate an expression and attempt to match the expression's value to one of several case labels. Syntax is:

```
switch (expression){
 case label :
      statement;
              break;
 case label :
          statement;
              break;
```

323

```
              ...
    default : statement;
    }
```

expression is the statement to be evaluated; **label** is the possible result the expression is to be evaluated against. If (and only if) **label** exactly matches the expression result (without a type conversion) then **statement** (which may be a series of statements) will be carried out. **break** is optional, but can be used to jump straight out of the case cycle. **default** is also optional; if it is present, it will be applied if the expression is not matched, but otherwise the program will simply move onto the statements following the **switch.**

while (JavaScript, JScript)

The **while** statement creates a loop that evaluates a boolean expression, and if it is **true**, executes a block of statements. Syntax is:

```
    while (expression) {
    statements
    }
```

expression is the boolean function to be examined; **statements** are the statements to be carried out until **expression** is false.

Scope, functions and methods

caller (JScript)

The **caller** property of a function contains a reference to the function that invoked the current function. It is described as **functionname.caller**. It is only defined for a function while that function is executing. If the function is called from the top level of a JScript program, caller contains **null**

Native Objects

JScript Extra Date Methods

Method	Description	Required Arguments
getVarDate	Returns the VT_DATE value stored in the Date object.	date.getVarDate( )

JScript Array Handling

In addition to the normal array handling methods, there are two additional methods which apply to all arrays. They are as follows:-

Method	Description	Required Arguments
concat	Combines two arrays to create a new array.	`array1.concat(array2)`
slice	Returns a section of an array	`array1.slice(start)` `array1.slice(start,end)`

The VBArray Object (JScript)

JScript also provides support for a new kind of object. A **VBArray** provides access to Visual Basic safe arrays. They are read-only, and cannot be created directly. The safeArray argument must have obtained a VBArray value before being passed to the VBArray constructor. This can only be done by retrieving the value from an existing ActiveX or other object. VBArrays can have multiple dimensions. The indices of each dimension can be different. This object has five methods associated with it.

Method	Description	Required Arguments
dimensions	Returns the number of dimensions in a VBArray	`array.dimensions()`
getItem	Retrieves the item at the specified location	`Array.getItem` `(dimension1,..., dimn)`
lbound	Returns the lowest index value used in the specified dimension of a VBArray.	`Array.lbound()` `Array.lbound(dimension)`
toArray	Converts a VBArray to a standard JScript array.	`safeArray.toArray( )`
ubound	Returns the highest index value used in the specified dimension of the VBArray.	`Array.ubound()` `Array.ubound(dimension)`

JScript and Javascript String Handling

In addition to the ECMA-compliant string object methods in both the major implementations of Javascript, there are a number of extra methods existing in both JScript and JavaScript which can be divided into the following categories:-

String Addition and Subtraction

Identical in name to the array methods, concat and slice also apply to strings

Method	Description	Required Arguments
concat	Combines two strings to create a new string.	`string1.concat(string2)`
slice	Returns a section of a string.	`string1.slice(start)` `string1.slice(start, end)`

325

String Searches and Regular Expressions

Three methods—**match**, **replace** and **search**—can be used to formulate searches for regular expressions within strings

Method	Description	Required Arguments
match	Executes a search on a string object using the supplied Regular Expression object.	`stringObj.match(RegExp)`
replace	Replaces the text found matching a regular expression within a string with some other text	`stringObj.match(RegExp, newText)`
search	Searches a string for matches to a regular expression	`stringObj.search (RegExp)`

HTML Creation

The following methods take a text string and then surround it with certain HTML tags

Method	Description	Required Arguments
anchor	Puts a named HTML anchor around the string text. Returns strVar as `<A NAME="aname">`strVar`</A>`	`Text = Text.anchor(aname)`
big	Puts HTML `<big>` tags around text in the string Returns Text as `<big>`Text`</big>`	`Text=Text.big( )`
blink	Puts HTML `<blink>` tags around the string text Returns Text as `<blink>`Text`</blink>`	`Text=Text.blink( )`
bold	Puts HTML `<b>` tags around the string text Returns Text as `<b>`Text`</b>`	`Text=Text.bold( )`
fixed	Puts HTML `<tt>` tags around the string text Returns Text as `<tt>`Text`</tt>`	`Text=Text.fixed( )`
fontcolor	Puts colored font tags around the string text Returns `<font color="fcolor">`Text`</font>`	`Text = Text.fontcolor ("fcolor")`
fontsize	Puts 'sized' font tag around the string text Returns `<font size='fsize'>`Text`</font>`	`Text.fontsize(fsize)`

Method	Description	Required Arguments
`italics`	Puts HTML `<i>` tags around the string text Returns Text as `<i>`Text`</i>`	`Text = Text.italics( )`
`link`	Puts a set of site link tags around the string text Returns Text as `<A HREF= "linkedsite">`Text`</A>`	`Text = Text.link("linkedsite")`
`small`	Puts HTML `<SMALL>` tags around the string text Returns Text as `<SMALL>`Text`</SMALL>`	`Text=Text.small( )`
`strike`	Puts HTML `<STRIKE>` tags around the string text Returns Text as `<STRIKE>`Text`</STRIKE>`	`Text=Text.strike( )`
`sub`	Puts HTML `<SUB>` tags around the string text Returns Text as `<SUB>`Text`</SUB>`	`Text=Text.sub( )`
`sup`	Puts HTML `<SUP>` tags around the string text Returns Text as `<SUP>`Text`</SUP>`	`Text=Text.sup( )`

None of the above methods check to see if the tag has already been applied to the string.

The Enumerator Object (JScript)

Collection members are not immediately accessible. Rather than using array indices, you can only select first or next element of a collection. The JScript Enumerator object provides a way to access any member of a collection. It has the following four methods:

Method	Description
`atEnd()`	Returns a Boolean value indicating if the enumerator is at the end of the collection.
`item()`	Returns the current item in the collection.
`moveFirst()`	Resets the current item in the collection to the first item.
`moveNext()`	Moves the current item to the next item in the collection.

JScript ScriptEngine Functions

As a refinement/replacement of the 'language' property which JavaScript uses to return whether a piece of script or applet is written in JavaScript or JScript, Microsoft's scripting language contains four functions which can access a little more detail:

327

Function	Description	Returns
ScriptEngine	Returns a string representing the scripting language in use.	**JScript, VBA** or **VBScript**
ScriptEngine_ BuildVersion	Returns the build version number of the scripting engine in use	The return value corresponds directly to the version information contained in the DLL for the scripting language in use.
ScriptEngine_ MajorVersion	Returns the major version number of the scripting engine in use	*See above*
ScriptEngine_ MinorVersion	Returns the minor version number of the scripting engine in use	*See above*

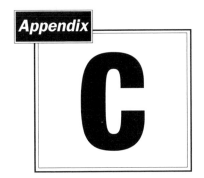

C-The Browser Object Model

The Browser Object Model offers a very useful resource for accessing the properties of the client browser with JavaScript. The diagram below is, strictly, for IE4. However, it shares its basic structure with the Navigator browser object model.

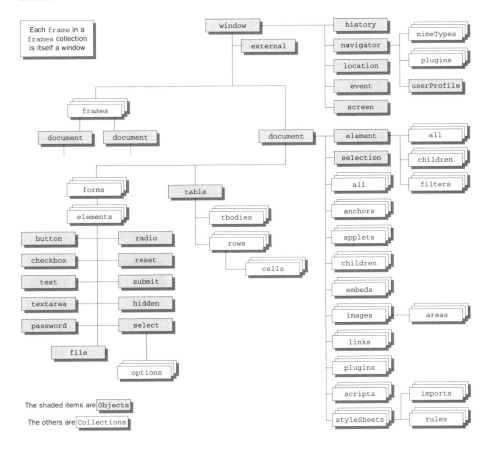

Browser Object Table

This is by no means a complete listing; full details of browsers' Object Models can usually be found in their SDKs. Note that in particular, because of its DOM compliance, IE4 can treat almost all HTML tags as individual objects, and the script writer can access these.

Objects	Browser?	Description
anchor	NC	An object that represents an anchor created with `<A NAME="..">` in the document.
A	IE4	IE equivalent of anchor
area		An area created within a `<MAP>` element by an `<AREA>` tag.
button	NC	An object that represents a control created with an `<INPUT>` tag where TYPE=BUTTON.
button	IE4	
checkbox	NC	An object that represents a control created with an `<INPUT>` tag where TYPE=CHECKBOX.
document		Exposes the contents of the HTML document through a number of arrays and properties.
element	NC4	An object that represents a control in the array of all the controls on a `<FORM>`.
event		The global event object exposed for accessing an event's parameters.
fileUpload	NC	An object that represents a control created with an `<INPUT>` tag where TYPE=FILE.
form		An object that represents the section of a page contained within a `<FORM>` tag.
frame		An object that represents a `<FRAME>` within a `<FRAMESET>`.
hidden	NC	An object that represents a control created with an `<INPUT>` tag where TYPE=HIDDEN.
history		Contains information on the URLs that the client has visited.
image		An object that represents an element created with an `<IMG>` tag.
layer		An object that represents a `<LAYER>` or `<ILAYER>` in a document.
link		An object that represents a link created in the page with an `<A HREF="..">` tag.
location		Contains information about the current URL being displayed.
mimeType		Contains information about the MIME types supported by the browser.

Objects	Browser?	Description
navigator		An object representing the browser itself, and its properties.
option		An individual **<OPTION>** item in a list created by a **<SELECT>** tag.
password	NC4	An object that represents a control created with an **<INPUT>** tag where **TYPE=PASSWORD**.
plugin	NC4	An object that represents the features of an installed plugin component.
radio	NC4	An object that represents a control created with an **<INPUT>** tag where **TYPE=RADIO**.
reset	NC4	An object that represents a control created with an **<INPUT>** tag where **TYPE=RESET**.
screen		Contains information about the client's screen and rendering abilities.
select	NC4	An object that represents a list control created with a **<SELECT>** tag.
StyleSheet	IE4	Exposes all the styles within a single style sheet in the styleSheets collection.
submit	NC4	An object that represents a control created with an **<INPUT>** tag where **TYPE=SUBMIT**.
text	NC4	An object that represents a control created with an **<INPUT>** tag where **TYPE=TEXT**.
textarea		An object that represents a text area control created with a **<TEXTAREA>** tag.
TextRange	IE4	Represents sections of the text stream making up the HTML document.
window		An object that provides information about the current browser window.

Note that these tables are by no means complete; full details of browser's Object Models can usually be found in their SDKs

JavaScript Universal Properties and Methods

These properties and methods apply to all objects within the model, as they all apply to the primitive OBJECT object.

Property	Description
name	Specifies the name to use to refer to the anchor.

Methods	Description	Required Arguments
eval	Evaluates a string of JavaScript code in the context of the specified object.	eval(string)
toString	Returns a string representing the specified object	toString() toString(i) where 2<=i<=16
valueOf	Returns the primitive value of the specified object	valueOf()
watch	Watches for a property to be assigned a value and runs a function when that occurs.	watch(property)
unwatch	Removes a watchpoint from a property of the object	unwatch(property)

Notes : **eval** was removed as a method of objects in Navigator 4, but retained as a global function, as specified in ECMAScript

The ActiveXObject Object (IE)

Enables and returns a reference to an automation object

No properties or methods

The Anchor Object (Navigator 2+)

A place in a document that is the target of a hypertext link.

No properties or methods

The Applet Object (Navigator 3+,IE)

Includes a Java applet in a web page.

Has all the properties and methods of a Java applet

The Area Object (Navigator 3+,IE)

Defines an area of an image as an image map. When the user clicks the area, the area's hypertext reference is loaded into its target window. Area   objects are a type of Link   object.

Properties	Description
hash	The string following the # symbol, the anchor name, in the URL
host	The **hostname:port** part of the location or URL.
hostname	The **hostname** part of the location or URL.

Properties	Description
`href`	The destination URL or anchor point.
`pathname`	The file or object path name following the third slash in a URL.
`port`	The `port` number in a URL.
`protocol`	Specifies the beginning of the URL, including the colon..
`search`	Any query string or form data following the ? in the complete URL.
`target`	Specifies the window or frame where the new page will be loaded.
`text`	A string containing the content of the corresponding A tag

Methods	Description	Required Arguments
`handleEvent`	Invokes the appropriate event handling code of the object for this event.	`handleEvent(eventName)`

The Button Object (Navigator 2+)

Represents a control created with an `<INPUT>` tag where `TYPE=CHECKBOX`

Properties	Description
`form`	Specifies the form that contains the button.
`name`	Specifies the name to use to refer to the button.
`type`	Must be `"BUTTON"` for a Button element.
`value`	The caption of the button.

Methods	Description	Required Arguments
`blur`	Causes the element to lose the focus, and fires its `onBlur` event.	`blur()`
`click`	Simulates a click on the element, but does not fire its `onClick` event.	`click()`
`focus`	Causes the element to receive the focus, and fire its `onFocus` event.	`focus()`
`handleEvent`	Invokes the appropriate event handling code of object for this event.	`handleEvent(eventName)`

335

The Checkbox Object (Navigator 2+, IE)

Represents a control created with an **<INPUT>** tag where **TYPE=CHECKBOX**

Properties	Description
checked	Indicates that the checkbox is selected (i.e. 'on' or ticked).
defaultChecked	Denotes if the checkbox is checked by default.
form	Reference to the form object that contains the element.
name	Specifies the name to use to refer to the checkbox.
type	Must be "CHECKBOX" for a Checkbox element.
value	The value of the control when checked.

Methods	Description	Required Arguments
blur	Causes the control to lose the focus, and fire its **onBlur** event.	blur()
click	Simulates a click on the control, and fires its **onClick** event.	click()
focus	Causes the control to receive the focus, and fire its **onFocus** event.	focus()
handleEvent	Invokes the appropriate event handling code of the object for this event.	handleEvent(eventname)

The Document Object

Contains information about the current document, and provides methods for displaying HTML output to the user.

Properties	Description
activeElement	Identifies the element that has the focus
alinkColor	The color for active links in the page - i.e. while the mouse button is held down
anchors	An array containing an entry for each anchor in the document
applets	An array containing an entry for each applet in the document
bgColor	Specifies the background color to be used for an element.

Properties	Description
`body`	Read-only reference to the document's implicit body object, as defined by the `<BODY>` tag
`cookie`	The string value of a cookie stored by the browser.
`domain`	Sets or returns the domain of the document that served the document for use in cookies and security
`embeds`	An array containing an entry for each embedded object in the document
`fgColor`	Sets the color of the document foreground text
`formName`(NC4)	A separate property for each named form in the document
`forms`	An array containing an entry for each form in the document
`images`	An array containing an entry for each image in the document
`lastModified`	The date that the source file for the page was last modified, as a string, where available
`layers`	An array containing an entry for each layer in the document
`linkColor`	The color for unvisited links in the page
`links`	An array containing an entry for each link in the document
`location`	The full URL of the document
`parentWindow`	Returns the parent window that contains the document.
`plugins`(NC4 only)	An array containing an entry for each plugin in the document
`readyState`	Specifies the current state of an object being downloaded
`referrer`	The URL of the page that referenced (loaded) the current page
`selection` (NC4 only)	Read-only reference to the document's selection object.
`title`	Provides advisory information about the element, such as when loading or as a tooltip, contained in the `<TITLE>` tag.
`url`	Uniform Resource Locator (address) for the current document or in a <META> tag
`vlinkColor`	The color for visited links in the page

337

Methods	Description	Required Arguments
`captureEvents`	Instructs the document to capture events of a particular type	`captureEvents_` `(eventType)`
`clear` (IE4)	Clears the contents of a selection or document object	
`close`	Closes a document forcing written data to be displayed, or closes the browser window	`close()`
`createElement` (IE4)	Creates an instance of an image or option element object	
`createStyle_` `sheet`(IE4 only)	Creates a Stylesheet	
`elementFrom_` `Point`(IE4)	Returns the element at the specified x and y coordinates with respect to the window.	
`execCommand` (IE4)	Executes a command over the document selection or range	
`getSelection`	Returns a string currently containing the text selected in the document	`getSelection( )`
`handleEvent`	Invokes the handler for the specified event	`handleEvent(eventName)`
`open`(IE4)	Opens a stream to collect output of **write** or **writeln** methods	`open( )` `open(mime-type)` `open(text/html,` `replace)`
`queryCommand_` `Enabled`(IE4)	Denotes if the specified command is available for a document or TextRange	
`queryCommand_` `Indeterm`(IE4)	Denotes if the specified command is in the indeterminate state	
`queryCommand_` `State`(IE4)	Returns the current state of the command for a document or TextRange object.	
`queryCommand_` `Supported`(IE4)	Denotes if the specified command is supported for a document or TextRange object	
`queryCommand_` `Value`(IE4)	Returns the value of the command specified for a document or TextRange object	
`releaseEvents`	Releases an event that has been captured back up through the normal event hierarchy	`releaseEvents_` `(eventType)`

Methods	Description	Required Arguments
`routeEvent` (NC4 only)	Passes an event that has been captured back up through the normal event hierarchy	
`write` (IE4)	Writes text and HTML to a document in the specified window	`write(expr1, ..., expr N)`
`writeln` (IE4)	Writes text and HTML to a document in the specified window, followed by a carriage return	`writeln(expr1, ..., expr N)`

The Element Object (NC4)

Represents a control in the array of all the controls on a `<FORM>`

Properties	Description
`checked`	Indicates that a checkbox or radio element is selected (i.e. 'on' or ticked).
`defaultChecked`	Denotes if a checkbox or radio element is checked by default.
`defaultValue`	The text displayed as the initial contents of a text-based control.
`form`	Reference to the form object that contains the element.
`length`	Returns the number of elements in an element sub-array.
`name`	Specifies the name to use to refer to the element.
`selectedIndex`	An integer specifying the index of the selected option in a `<SELECT>` element.
`type`	The type of the element, such as **TEXT**, **BUTTON** or **RADIO**.
`value`	The default value of text/numeric controls, or the value when the control is 'on' for Boolean controls.

Methods	Description	Required Arguments
`blur`	Causes the element to lose the focus, and fire its **onBlur** event.	`blur( )`
`click`	Simulates a click on the element, and fires its **onClick** event.	`click( )`

Methods	Description	Required Arguments
`focus`	Causes the element to receive the focus, and fire its **onFocus** event.	`focus( )`
`handleEvent`	Invokes the appropriate event handling code of object for this event.	`handleEvent(eventName)`
`select`	Highlights the input area of a text-based element.	`select( )`

The Event Object (Navigator 4)

The global object provided to allow the scripting language to access an event's parameters.

Properties	Description
`altKey` (IE4)	Returns the state of the *Alt* key when an event occurs
`button` (IE only)	The mouse button, if any, that was pressed to fire the event
`cancelBubble` (IE only)	Set to prevent the current event from bubbling up the hierarchy
`clientX` (IE only)	Returns the *x* coordinate of the element, excluding borders, margins, padding, scrollbars, etc
`clientY` (IE only)	Returns the *y* coordinate of the element, excluding borders, margins, padding, scrollbars, etc
`ctrlKey` (IE only)	Returns the state of the *Ctrl* key when an event occurs
`data`	The URLs of the objects dropped onto the Navigator window, as an array of strings
`fromElement` (IE only)	Returns the element being moved from for an **onmouseover** or **onmouseout** event
`height`	Represents the height of the window or frame
`keyCode` (IE only)	ASCII code of the key being pressed. Changing it sends a different character to the object.
`layerX` (NC)	Horizontal position of the mouse pointer in pixels in relation to the containing layer. layerX is synonymous with x
`layerY` (NC)	Vertical position of the mouse pointer in pixels in relation to the containing layer. layerY is synonymous with y
`modifiers` (NC)	String containing the names of the keys held down for a key-press event. Modifier key values are: **ALT_MASK, CONTROL_MASK, SHIFT_MASK,** and **META_MASK.**

Properties	Description
offsetX (IE only)	Returns the *x* coordinate of the mouse pointer when an event occurs, relative to the containing element.
offsetY (IE only)	Returns the *y* coordinate position of the mouse pointer when an event occurs, relative to the containing element
pageX (NC)	Horizontal position in pixels of the mouse pointer or a layer in relation to the page
pageY (NC)	Vertical position in pixels of the mouse pointer or a layer in relation to the page
reason (IE)	Indicates whether data transfer to an element was successful, or why it failed
returnValue (IE)	Allows a return value to be specified for the event or a dialog window
screenX (NC)	Returns the *x* coordinate of the mouse pointer when an event occurs, in relation to the screen
screenY (NC)	Returns the *y* coordinate of the mouse pointer when an event occurs, in relation to the screen
shiftKey (IE)	Returns the state of the *Shift* key when an event occurs
srcElement (IE)	Returns the element deepest in the object hierarchy that a specified event occurred over.
srcFilter (IE)	Returns the filter that caused the element to produce an **onfilterchange** event.
target	The name of the object where the event was originally sent
toElement (IE)	Returns the element being moved to for an **onmouseover** or **onmouseout** event.
type (NC)	Returns the name of the event as a string, without the 'on' prefix, such as 'click' instead of 'onclick'.
which (IE)	ASCII value of a key that was pressed, or indicates which mouse button was clicked
width (IE)	Represents the width of the window or frame
x (IE)	Returns the *x* coordinate of the mouse pointer relative to a positioned parent, or otherwise to the window
y (IE)	Returns the *y* coordinate of the mouse pointer relative to a positioned parent, or otherwise to the window

The FileUpload object (Navigator 2+)

Represents a control created with an <INPUT> tag where TYPE=FILE

Properties	Description
form	Reference to the form object that contains the element.
name	Specifies the name to use to refer to the element.
type	Must be "FILE" for a FileUpload element.
value	The text value of the control. ie The name of the file to upload

Methods	Description	Required Arguments
blur	Causes the element to lose the focus, and fire its onBlur event.	blur( )
focus	Causes the element to receive the focus, and fire its onFocus event.	focus( )
handleEvent	Invokes the appropriate event handling code of object for this event.	handleEvent(eventName)
select	Selects the input area of the file upload field	select( )

The Form object (Navigator 2+)

Represents the section of a page contained within a <FORM> tag.

Properties	Description
action	The URL where the form is to be sent.
elements	An array reflecting all the elements in a form
encoding	Defines the type of mime-encoding to be used when submitting the form.
length	Returns the number of elements in the form.
method	How the form data should be sent to the server; either GET or POST.
name	Specifies the name to use to refer to the form.
target	Specifies the window or frame where the return page will be loaded.

Methods	Description	Required Arguments
handleEvent	Invokes the appropriate event handling code of object for this event.	handleEvent(eventName)
reset	Simulates a mouse click on a RESET button in the form.	reset( )
submit	Submits the form, as when the SUBMIT button is clicked.	submit( )

The Frame object (Navigator 2+)

Represents a **<FRAME>** within a **<FRAMESET>**. Every frame object is also the same as a window object and has the same properties and methods. See 'Window Object' for this list.

The Hidden object (Navigator 2+)

Represents a control created with an **<INPUT>** tag where **TYPE=HIDDEN**

Properties	Description
`form`	Specifies the form containing the hidden object
`name`	Specifies the name to use to refer to the element.
`type`	Must be "**HIDDEN**" for a Hidden element.
`value`	Reflects the current value of the hidden object

The History Object   (Navigator 2+)

Contains information about the URLs that the client has visited, as stored in the browser's History list, and allows the script to move through the list.

Properties	Description
`current`	The current item in the browser's history list
`length`	Returns the number of elements in the history list
`next`	Refers to the next item in the browser's history list
`previous`	Refers to the previous item in the browser's history list

Methods	Description	Required Arguments
`back`	Loads the previous URL in the browser's History list.	`back( )`
`forward`	Loads the next URL in the browser's History list	`forward( )`
`go`	Loads a specified URL from the browser's History list	`go(part of url in history list)` `go(number in history list)`

The Image Object (Navigator 3+)

Represents an element created with an **<IMG>** tag

Properties	Description
border	Specifies the border to be drawn around the image.
complete	Indicates if the image has completed loading.
height	Sets the height for the image in pixels.
hspace	The horizontal spacing between the image and its neighbors.
lowsrc	Specifies the URL of a lower resolution image to display.
name	Specifies the name to use to refer to the image.
prototype	Allows the addition of properties to an image object
src	An external file that contains the source data for the image.
vspace	The vertical spacing between the image and its neighbors.
width	Sets the width for the image in pixels.

Methods	Description	Required Arguments
handleEvent	Invokes the appropriate event handling code of object for this event.	handleEvent(eventName)

The Layer Object (Navigator 4)

Corresponds to a layer in an HTML document created by a **<LAYER>** or an **<ILAYER>** tag.

Properties	Description
above	Indicates that the layer should be above another element in the z-order of the page, or returns the element above it.
background	URL of an image to display behind the elements in the layer.
below	Indicates that the layer should be below another element in the z-order of the page, or returns the element below it.
bgColor	Specifies the background color to be used for the layer.
clip.bottom	Y co-ordinate of the bottom of the clipping rectangle for the layer.
clip.height	Height of the clipping rectangle for the layer.
clip.left	X co-ordinate of the left of the clipping rectangle for the layer.
clip.right	X co-ordinate of the right of the clipping rectangle for the layer.
clip.top	Y co-ordinate of the top of the clipping rectangle for the layer.
clip.width	Width of the clipping for the layer.
document	The layer's associated document

Properties	Description
`left`	Position in pixels of the left-hand side of the layer in relation to its containing layer or the document.
`name`	Specifies the name to use to refer to the layer.
`pageX`	Horizontal position of the mouse pointer in pixels with respect to the layer.
`pageY`	Vertical position of the mouse pointer in pixels with respect to the layer.
`parentLayer`	Reference to the layer that contains the current layer.
`siblingAbove`	Reference to the layer above the current layer if they share the same parent layer.
`siblingBelow`	Reference to the layer below the current layer if they share the same parent layer.
`src`	An external file that contains the source data for the layer.
`top`	Position of the top of the layer.
`visibility`	Defines whether the layer should be displayed on the page.
`zIndex`	Position in the z-order or stacking order of the page, i.e. the z co-ordinate.

Methods	Description	Required Arguments
`captureEvents`	Instructs the layer to capture all events of a particular type.	`captureEvents_ (eventType)`
`handleEvent`	Invokes the appropriate event handling code of the object for this event.	`handleEvent(eventName)`
`load`	Loads a file into a layer, and can change the width of the layer it loads the file into.	`load(filename, layerWidth)`
`moveAbove`	Changes the z-order so that the layer is rendered above (overlaps) the specified layer.	`moveAbove(aLayer)`
`moveBelow`	Changes the z-order so that the layer is rendered below (covered by) the specified layer.	`moveBelow(aLayer)`
`moveBy`	Moves the layer horizontally and vertically by a specified number of pixels.	`moveBy(horiz, vert)`
`moveTo`	Moves the layer so that the top left is at a position x, y (in pixels) within its container layer.	`moveTo(x,y)`

Methods	Description	Required Arguments
moveToAbsolute	Moves the layer to a position specified in x and y with respect to the page and not the container.	moveToAbsolute(x,y)
releaseEvents	Instructs the layer to stop capturing events of a particular type.	releaseEvents_ (eventType)
resizeBy	Resizes the layer horizontally and vertically by a specified number of pixels.	resizeBy(width, height)
resizeTo	Resizes the layer to a size specified in x and y (in pixels).	resizeTo(width, height)
routeEvent	Passes an event that has been captured back up through the normal event hierarchy.	routeEvent(eventName)

The Link Object (Navigator 2+)

Represents a link created in the page with an **<A HREF='...'>** tag.
NB In general, a URL has this form - protocol://host:port/
pathname#hash?search

Properties	Description
hash	The string following the # symbol, the anchor name, in the HREF value.
host	Specifies the host and domain name, or IP address, of a network host.
hostname	Specifies the host:port portion of the URL.
href	The destination URL or anchor point.
pathname	The file or object path name following the third slash in a URL.
port	The port number in a URL.
protocol	The initial sub-string indicating the URL's access method.
search	Any query string or form data following the ? in the complete URL.
target	Specifies the window or frame where the new page will be loaded.
text	A string containing the content of the corresponding A tag.

Methods	Description	Required Arguments
`handleEvent`	Invokes the appropriate event handling code of object for this event.	`handleEvent(eventName)`

The Location Object (Navigator 2+)

Contains information on the current URL. It also provides methods that will reload a page
NB In general, a URL has this form -
protocol://host:port/pathname#hash?search

Properties	Descriptions
`hash`	The string following the # symbol in the URL
`host`	Specifies the host and domain name, or IP address, of a network host.
`hostname`	Specifies the host:port portion of the URL.
`href`	The entire URL as a string
`pathname`	The file or object path name following the third slash in a URL
`port`	The port number in a URL
`protocol`	The initial substring up to and including the first colon, indicating the URL's access method
`search`	The contents of the query string or form data following the ? (question mark) in the complete URL

Methods	Description	Required Arguments
`assign` (IE only)	Loads another page. Equivalent to changing the **window.location.href** property	
`reload`	(Forces a) reload of the current page in the window	`reload( )` `reload(ForceGet)`
`replace`	Loads the specified URL over the current element in the browser's history list	`replace('URL')`

The Mime-Type Object (Navigator 3+, IE4)

The object representing a Mime-Type supported by the browser

Properties	Description
description	Returns a description of the **MimeType**
enabledPlugin	Returns the plug-in that can handle the specified **MimeType**
suffixes	A list of filename extensions used with the specified **MimeType**
type (NC4)	The name of the mime-type. e.g. video/mpeg.

The Navigator Object (Navigator 2+, IE)

The object representing the browser itself

Properties	Description
appCodeName	The code name of the browser
appName	The product name of the browser
appVersion	The version of the browser
cookieEnabled (IE4 only)	Indicates if client-side cookies are enabled in the browser
language	Returns the language the browser was compiled for
mimeTypes (NC4)	An array of all the mime types supported by the client
platform (NC4)	Returns the name of the operating system the browser was compiled for
plugins (NC4)	An array of all the plugins loaded in by the client.
userAgent (NC4)	The user-agent (browser name) header sent in the HTTP protocol from the client to the server

Method	Description	Return Values	Required arguments
javaEnabled	Returns True or False, depending on whether a Java VM is installed and enabled	true false	javaEnabled( )
preference (NC4)	Allows a signed script to get and set certain Navigator preferences.		preference (prefName) preference(prefName, setValue)
taintEnabled	Specifies whether data tainting is enabled (Navigator 3 only, IE)	true false	taintEnabled( )

The Option Object (Navigator 2+)

An individual **<OPTION>** item in a list created by a **<SELECT>** tag.

Properties	Description
defaultSelected	Specifies the initial selection state of the option
index (IE only)	Returns the ordinal position of the option in a list.
length (IE only)	Returns the number of elements in an element sub-array.
selected	Specifies the current selection state of the option
selectedIndex (IE only)	An integer specifying the index of the selected option in a list.
text	The text displayed for the option
value	The value returned when the option is selected and the form is submitted.

The Password Object (Navigator 2+)

Represents a control created with an **<INPUT>** tag where **TYPE=PASSWORD**

Properties	Description
defaultValue	The text displayed as the initial contents of the control.
form	Reference to the form object that contains the control.
name	Specifies the name to use to refer to the control.
type	Must be "PASSWORD" for a Password control.
value	The text value of the control.

Methods	Description	Required Arguments
blur	Causes the control to lose the focus, and fire its **onBlur** event.	**blur( )**
focus	Causes the control to receive the focus, and fire its **onFocus** event.	**focus( )**
handleEvent	Invokes the appropriate event handling code of object for this event.	**handleEvent(eventName)**
select	Highlights the input area of the control.	**select( )**

The Plugin Object (Navigator 3+)

Represents the features of an installed plugin component

Properties	Description
description	A description of the plugin
filename	Name of the plugin file on disk
length	Returns the number of mime types the plugin supports
name	Specifies the name to use to refer to the plugin.

Methods	Description	Required Arguments
refresh	Makes newly installed plug-ins available and optionally reloads open documents that contain plug-ins.	refresh()

The Radio Object (NC4 only)

Represents a control created with an **<INPUT>** tag where TYPE=RADIO

Properties	Description
checked	Lets you set an individual radio object to 'ON'
default_ Checked	Denotes if the individual radio button is checked.
form	Reference to the form object that contains the element.
name	Specifies the name to use to refer to the group of radio buttons.
type	Must be "RADIO" for a Radio element.
value	The 'value' attribute given to the radio button when declared

Methods	Description	Required Arguments
blur	Causes the control to lose the focus, and fire its **onBlur** event.	blur( )
click	Simulates a click on the control, and fires its **onClick** event.	click( )
focus	Causes the control to receive the focus, and fire its **onFocus** event.	focus( )
handleEvent	Invokes the appropriate event handling code of the object for this event.	handleEvent(eventName)

The Reset Object (Navigator 2+)

Represents a reset button on an HTML form

Properties	Description
`form`	Reference to the form object that contains the element.
`name`	Specifies the name to use to refer to the element.
`type`	Must be "RESET" for a Reset element.
`value`	The text used for the reset button's caption.

Methods	Description	Required Arguments
`blur`	Causes the control to lose the focus, and fire its onBlur event.	`blur( )`
`click`	Simulates a click on the control, and fires its onClick event.	`click( )`
`focus`	Causes the control to receive the focus, and fire its onFocus event.	`focus( )`
`handleEvent`	Invokes the appropriate event handling code of the object for this event.	`handleEvent(eventName)`

The Screen Object (Navigator 4, IE4)

Contains properties describing the display screen and colors.

Properties	Description
`availHeight` (NC4)	Height of the available screen space in pixels (excluding screen furniture)
`availWidth` (NC4)	Width of the available screen space in pixels (excluding screen furniture)
`bufferDepth` (IE4 only)	Specifies if and how an off-screen bitmap buffer should be used
`colorDepth`	Returns the number of bits per pixel of the user's display device or screen buffer
`height`	Returns the height of the user's display screen in pixels
`pixelDepth` (NC4)	Returns the number of bits used per pixel by the system display hardware
`updateInterval` (IE4 only)	Sets or returns the interval between screen updates on the client
`width`	Returns the width of the user's display screen in pixels

The Select Object (Navigator 2+)

Contains properties describing a selection list in an HTML form

Properties	Description
form	Reference to the form object that contains the list element.
length	Number of items in the selection list.
name	Specifies the name to use to refer to the list element.
options	Reflects the text associated with the items
selectedIndex	The numeric position within the list of the (first) selected item.
type	Indicates the type of list, i.e. SELECT-ONE, SELECT-MULTI.
text (NC4 only)	The text of the currently selected item.

Methods	Description	Required Arguments
blur	Causes the control to lose the focus, and fire its onBlur event.	blur( )
focus	Causes the control to receive the focus, and fire its onFocus event.	focus( )
handleEvent	Invokes the appropriate event handling code of the object for this event.	handleEvent(eventName)

The Selection Object (IE4 only)

Returns the active selection on the screen, allowing access to all the selected elements including the plain text in the page.

Properties	Description
type	The type of the selection, i.e. a control, text, a table, or none

Methods	Description
clear	Clears the contents of the selection
createRange	Returns a copy of the currently selected range
empty	Deselects the current selection and sets selection type to none

The Style Object (IE4 only) (In Netscape as JavaScript Style Properties)

This provides access to the individual style properties for an element. These could have been previously set by a style sheet, or by an inline style tag within the page.

Property Name	Description
background	Specifies a background picture that is tiled behind text and graphics.
background_Attachment	Defines if a background image should be fixed on the page or scroll with the content.
backgroundColor	Specifies the background color of the page or element.
backgroundImage	Specifies a URL for the background image for the page or element.
backgroundPosition	The initial position of a background image on the page.
background_PositionX	The x coordinate of the background image in relation to the containing window.
background_PositionY	The y coordinate of the background image in relation to the containing window.
BackgroundRepeat	Defines if and how a background image is repeated on the page.
border	Specifies the border to be drawn around the element.
borderBottom	Used to specify several attributes of the bottom border of an element.
borderBottomColor	The color of the bottom border for an element.
borderBottomStyle	The style of the bottom border for an element.
borderBottomWidth	The width of the bottom border for an element.
borderColor	The color of all or some of the borders for an element.
borderLeft	Used to specify several attributes of the left border of an element.
borderLeftColor	The color of the left border for an element.
borderLeftStyle	The style of the left border for an element.
borderLeftWidth	The width of the left border for an element.
borderRight	Used to specify several attributes of the right border of an element.
BorderRightColor	The color of the right border for an element.
BorderRightStyle	The style of the right border for an element.
BorderRightWidth	The width of the right border for an element.
borderStyle	Used to specify the style of one or more borders of an element.

Property Name	Description
borderTop	Used to specify several attributes of the top border of an element.
borderTopColor	The color of the top border for an element.
borderTopStyle	The style of the top border for an element.
borderTopWidth	The width of the top border for an element.
borderWidth	Used to specify the width of one or more borders of an element.
clear	Causes the next element or text to be displayed below left-aligned or right-aligned images.
clip	Specifies how an element's contents should be displayed if larger that the available client area.
color	The text or foreground color of an element.
cssText	The text value of the element's entire **STYLE** attribute.
cursor	Specifies the type of cursor to display when the mouse pointer is over the element.
display	Specifies if the element will be visible (displayed) in the page.
filter	Sets or returns an array of all the filters specified in the element's style property.
font	Defines various attributes of the font for an element, or imports a font.
fontFamily	Specifies the name of the typeface, or 'font family'.
fontSize	Specifies the font size.
fontStyle	Specifies the style of the font, i.e. normal or italic.
fontVariant	Specifies the use of small capitals for the text.
fontWeight	Specifies the weight (boldness) of the text.
height	Specifies the height at which the element is to be drawn, and sets the **posHeight** property.
left	Specifies the position of the left of the element, and sets the **posLeft** property.
letterSpacing	Indicates the additional space to be placed between characters in the text.
lineHeight	The distance between the baselines of two adjacent lines of text.
listStyle	Allows several style properties of a list element to be set in one operation.
listStyleImage	Defines the image used as a background for a list element.
listStylePosition	Defines the position of the bullets used in a list element.

Property Name	Description
listStyleType	Defines the design of the bullets used in a list element.
margin	Allows all four margins to be specified with a single attribute.
marginBottom	Specifies the bottom margin for the page or text block.
marginLeft	Specifies the left margin for the page or text block.
marginRight	Specifies the right margin for the page or text block.
marginTop	Specifies the top margin for the page or text block.
overflow	Defines how text that overflows the element is handled.
paddingBottom	Sets the amount of space between the bottom border and content of an element.
paddingLeft	Sets the amount of space between the left border and content of an element.
paddingRight	Sets the amount of space between the right border and content of an element.
paddingTop	Sets the amount of space between the top border and content of an element.
pageBreakAfter	Specifies if a page break should occur after the element.
pageBreakBefore	Specifies if a page break should occur after the element.
pixelHeight	Sets or returns the height style property of the element in pixels, as a pure number, rather than a string.
pixelLeft	Sets or returns the left style property of the element in pixels, as a pure number, rather than a string.
pixelTop	Sets or returns the top style property of the element in pixels, as a pure number, rather than a string.
pixelWidth	Sets or returns the width style property of the element in pixels, as a pure number, rather than a string.
posHeight	Returns the value of the height style property in its last specified units, as a pure number rather than a string.
position	Returns the value of the position style property, defining whether the element can be positioned.
posLeft	Returns the value of the left style property in its last specified units, as a pure number rather than a string.
posTop	Returns the value of the top style property in its last specified units, as a pure number rather than a string.
posWidth	Returns the value of the width style property in its last specified units, as a pure number rather than a string.
styleFloat	Specifies if the element will float above the other elements in the page, or cause them to flow round it.

Property Name	Description
textAlign	Indicates how text should be aligned within the element.
textDecoration	Specifies several font decorations (underline, overline, strikethrough) added to the text of an element.
textDecoration_ Blink	Specifies if the font should blink or flash. Has no effect in IE4.
textDecoration_ LineThrough	Specifies if the text is displayed as strikethrough, i.e. with a horizontal line through it.
textDecorationNone	Specifies if the text is displayed with no additional decoration.
textDecoration Overline	Denotes if the text is displayed as overline, i.e. with a horizontal line above it.
textDecoration Underline	Denotes if the text is displayed as underline, i.e. with a horizontal line below it.
textIndent	Specifies the indent for the first line of text in an element, and may be negative.
textTransform	Specifies how the text for the element should be capitalized.
top	Position of the top of the element, sets the **posTop** property. Also returns topmost window object.
verticalAlign	Sets or returns the vertical alignment style property for an element.
visibility	Indicates if the element or contents are visible on the page.
width	Specifies the width at which the element is to be drawn, and sets the **posWidth** property.
zIndex	Sets or returns the z-index for the element, indicating whether it appears above or below other elements.

MethodName	Description	Required Attributes
getAttribute	Returns the value of an attribute defined in an HTML tag.	
removeAttribute	Causes the specified attribute to be removed from the HTML element and the current page.	
setAttribute	Adds and/or sets the value of an attribute in a HTML tag.	

356

The Stylesheet Object (IE only)

Exposes all the styles within a single style sheet in the styleSheets collection

Property Name	Description
`disabled`	Sets or returns whether an element is disabled.
`href`	The entire URL as a string.
`id`	Identifier or name for an element in a page or style sheet, or as the target for hypertext links.
`owningElement`	Returns the style sheet that imported or referenced the current style sheet, usually through a `<LINK>` tag.
`parentStyleSheet`	Returns the style sheet that imported the current style sheet, or null for a non-imported style sheet.
`readOnly`	Indicates that an element's contents are read only, or that a rule in a style sheet cannot be changed.
`type`	Specifies the type of list style, link, selection, control, button, MIME-type, rel, or the CSS language.

Methods	Description
`addImport`	Adds a style sheet to the imports collection for the given style sheet.
`addRule`	Creates a new style rule for the styleSheet object and returns the index into the Rules collection.

The Submit Object (Navigator 2+)

Represents a Submit button in an HTML form.

Properties	Description
`form`	Reference to the form object that contains the element.
`name`	Specifies the name to use to refer to the element.
`type`	Must be "SUBMIT" for a Submit element.
`value`	The text used for the submit button's caption.

Methods	Description	Required Arguments
`blur`	Causes the control to lose the focus, and fire its **onBlur** event.	`blur ()`
`click`	Simulates a click on the control, and fires its **onClick** event.	`click ()`
`focus`	Causes the control to receive the focus, and fire its **onFocus** event.	`focus()`
`handleEvent`	Invokes the appropriate event handling code of the object for this event.	`handleEvent(eventName)`

The Text Object (Navigator 2+)

Represents a single line text input area in an html form

Properties	Description
`defaultValue`	The text displayed as the initial contents of the control.
`form`	Reference to the form object that contains the element.
`name`	Specifies the name to use to refer to the element.
`type`	Must be `"TEXT"` (or omitted) for a text element.
`value`	The text currently within the text box.

Methods	Description	Required Arguments
`blur`	Causes the control to lose the focus, and fire its **onBlur** event.	`blur( )`
`focus`	Causes the control to receive the focus, and fire its **onFocus** event.	`focus( )`
`handleEvent`	Invokes the appropriate event handling code of the object for this event.	`handleEvent(eventName)`
`select`	Highlights the input area of the object.	`select( )`

The Textarea Object (Navigator 4)

Represents a multi line text input area in an html form.

Properties	Description
defaultValue	The text displayed as the initial contents of the control.
form	Reference to the form object that contains the element.
name	Specifies the name to use to refer to the element.
type	Information about the type of the control.
value	The text currently within the text box.

Methods	Description	Required Arguments
blur	Causes the control to lose the focus, and fire its onBlur event.	blur( )
focus	Causes the control to receive the focus, and fire its **onFocus** event.	focus( )
handleEvent	Invokes the appropriate event handling code of the object for this event.	handleEvent(eventName)
select	Highlights the input area of a form element.	select( )

The TextRange Object (IE only)

This object represents the text stream of the HTML document. It can be used to set and retrieve the text within the page.

Property Name	Description
htmlText	Returns the contents of a **TextRange** as text and HTML source.
text	The plain text contained within a block element, a **TextRange** or an **<OPTION>** tag.

Method Name	Description
collapse	Shrinks a TextRange to either the start or end of the current range.
compareEnd_ Points	Compares two text ranges and returns a value indicating the result.
duplicate	Returns a duplicate of a TextRange object.
execCommand	Executes a command over the document selection or range.
expand	Expands the range by a character, word, sentence or story so that partial units are completely contained.

Method Name	Description
findText	Sets the range start and end points to cover the text if found within the current document.
getBookmark	Sets String to a unique bookmark value to identify that position in the document.
inRange	Denotes if the specified range is within or equal to the current range.
isEqual	Denotes if the specified range is equal to the current range.
move	Changes the start and end points of a TextRange to cover different text.
moveEnd	Causes the range to grow or shrink from the end of the range.
moveStart	Causes the range to grow or shrink from the beginning of the range.
moveTo_Bookmark	Moves range to encompass the range with a bookmark value previously defined in String.
moveTo_ElementText	Moves range to encompass the text in the element specified.
moveToPoint	Moves and collapses range to the point specified in x and y relative to the document.
parent_Element	Returns the parent element that completely encloses the current range.
pasteHTML	Pastes HTML and/or plain text into the current range.
query_Command_Enabled	Denotes if the specified command is available for a document or TextRange.
query_Command_Indeterm	Denotes if the specified command is in the indeterminate state.
query CommandState	Returns the current state of the command for a document or TextRange object.
query_Command_Supported	Denotes if the specified command is supported for a document or TextRange object.
query_CommandText	Returns the string associated with a command for a document or TextRange object
query_CommandValue	Returns the value of the command specified for a document or TextRange object.
scrollInto_View	Scrolls the element or TextRange into view in the browser, optionally at the top of the window.
select	Makes the active selection equal to the current object, or highlights the input area of a form element.
setEndPoint	Sets the end point of the range based on the end point of another range.

The Window Object (Navigator 2+, IE)

The window object refers to a window or frame on display by the browser.

Property Name	Description
client (IE only)	Returns the navigator object for the browser
client_ **Information** (IE only)	A reference that returns the navigator object for the browser.
closed	Indicates if a window is closed.
defaultStatus	The default message displayed in the status bar at the bottom of the window
dialogArguments (IE only)	Returns the arguments that were passed into a dialog window, as an array.
dialogHeight (IE only)	Sets or returns the height of a dialog window.
dialogLeft (IE only)	Sets or returns the x coordinate of a dialog window.
dialogTop (IE only)	Sets or returns the y coordinate of a dialog window.
dialogWidth (IE only)	Sets or returns the width of a dialog window.
document	Read-only reference to the window's document object.
frames	An array of objects corresponding to child frames (created with the **FRAME** tag) in source order.
history	Read-only reference to the window's history object.
innerHeight (NC4)	Height of the window excluding the window borders
innerWidth (NC4)	Width of the window excluding the window borders
length	Returns the number of child frames in a window
location (NC4)	The current URL in the window
locationbar (NC4)	Defines whether the address bar will be displayed in the browser window
menubar	Represents the browser window's menu bar
name	A string specifying the window's name
offScreen_ **Buffering** (IE4 only)	Specifies whether to use off-screen buffering for the document
opener	Returns a reference to the window that created the current window

Property Name	Description
outerHeight (NC4)	Height of the window including the window borders
outerWidth (NC4)	Width of the window including the window borders
pageXOffset (NC4)	Horizontal offset of the top left of the visible part of the page within the windows in pixels
pageYOffset (NC4)	Vertical offset of the top left of the visible part of the page within the windows in pixels
parent	Returns the parent window or frame in the window/frame hierarchy
personalbar (NC4)	Represents the browser window's user's personal bar
returnValue (IE only)	Allows a return value to be specified for the event or a dialog window
scrollbars (NC4)	Defines whether the window will provide scrollbars if all the content cannot be displayed
self	Provides a reference to the current window.
status	Text displayed in the window's status bar, or an alias for the value of an option button.
statusbar (NC4)	Defines whether the status bar will be displayed in the browser window
toolbar (NC4)	Defines whether the toolbar will be displayed in the browser window
top	The topmost window object.
window	Read-only reference to the current window object, same as _self

Methods	Description	Required Arguments
Alert	Displays an Alert dialog box with a message and an OK button	**alert('message')**
back	Loads the previous URL in the browser's history list	**back( )**
blur	Causes a control to lose focus and fire its **onblur** event	**blur( )**
capture_Events (NC4)	Instructs the window to capture events of a particular type	**captureEvents_(eventType)**
clearInterval	Cancels an interval timer that was set with the **setInterval** method.	**clearInterval_(intervalID)**

Methods	Description	Required Arguments
clearTimeout	Cancels a timeout that was set with the **setTimeout** method.	clearTimeout_ (timeoutID)
close	Closes a document forcing written data to be displayed, or closes the browser window.	close( )
confirm	Displays a Confirm dialog box with a message and OK and Cancel buttons.	confirm('message')
disable_ External_ Capture (NC4)	Prevents a window that includes frames from capturing events in documents loaded from different locations	disable_ ExternalCapture( )
enable_ External_ Capture (NC4)	Allows a window that includes frames to capture events in documents loaded from different locations	enable_ ExternalCapture( )
execScript (IE only)	Executes a script. The **alert** default language is JScript	
find (NC4)	Returns true if a specified string is found in the text in the current window	find(string) find(string, casesensitive) find(string, casesensitive, backward)
focus	Causes a control to receive the focus and fires its **onfocus** event	focus( )
forward (NC4)	Loads the next URL in the browser's history list	forward( )
handleEvent (NC4)	Invokes the appropriate event handling code of the object for this event	handleEvent(eventName)
home (NC4)	Loads the user's home page into the browser window	home( )
moveBy (NC4)	Moves the window horizontally and vertically	moveBy(horiz, vert)
moveTo (NC4)	Moves the window so that the top left is at a position (x,y)	moveTo (x,y)
open	Opens the document as a stream to collect output of **write** or **writeln** methods	open(URL, windowName) open(URL, windowName, windowFeatures)
print (NC4)	Prints the contents of the window, equivalent to pressing the Print button.	print( )

Methods	Description	Required Arguments
prompt (NC4)	Displays a Prompt dialog box with a message and an input field	`prompt(message)` `prompt(message, inputDefault)`
release_ Events (NC4)	Instructs the window to stop capturing events of a particular type.	`releaseEvents_ (eventType)`
resizeBy (NC4)	Resizes the window horizontally and vertically	`resizeBy(horiz,vert)`
resizeTo (NC4)	Resizes the window to a size x, y specified in pixels	`resizeTo(x,y)`
routeEvent (NC4)	Passes an event that has been captured up through the normal event hierarchy	`routeEvent(event)`
scroll (Nav 3 only)	Scrolls the window to the specified x and y offset relative to the entire document	`scroll(x,y)`
scrollBy (NC4)	Scrolls the window horizontally and vertically within the window by a number of pixels	`scrollBy(horiz, vert)`
scrollTo (NC4)	Scrolls the document within the window so that the point x,y is at the top left corner	`scrollTo(x,y)`
setInterval	Denotes a code routine to execute repeatedly every specified number of milliseconds	`setInterval(exp, msec)` `setInterval(function, msec, arg1, ..., argN)`
setTimeout	Denotes a code routine to execute a specified number of milliseconds after loading the page	`setTimeout(exp, msec)` `setTimeout(function, msec, arg1, ..., arg N)`
showHelp (IE only)	Opens a window to display a Help file	
showModal_ Dialog (IE only)	Displays an HTML dialog window, and returns the **returnValue** property of its document when closed	
stop (NC4)	Stops the current download, equivalent to pressing the Stop button	`stop( )`

364

Special JScript Objects

The following objects are unique to JScript, and extend the functionality of the browser within the host system.

Drive Object

Gives the script access to the properties of the drive tree; allows various aspects of the drive system to be manipulated using JScript. The **Drive** object has no available methods.

Property Name	Description
AvailableSpace	Returns the amount of space available on the drive to the user.
DriveLetter	Returns drive letter.
DriveType	Returns drive type as an integer. **0** is unknown, **1** is removable, **2** is fixed, **3** is Network, **4** is CD-ROM, **5** is RAM disk
FileSystem	Returns file system type, such **FAT**, **NTFS** or **CDF**S
FreeSpace	Read-only value giving amount of freespace available to the user
IsReady	Returns **True** if drive is ready, otherwise **False**
Path	Returns the path for the specified drive
RootFolder	Returns a **Folder** object representing the root drive; read only
SerialNumber	Returns a unique decimal serial number for the specified drive
ShareName	Returns the shared network name for a network drive
TotalSize	Returns the total bytes available on the specified disk
VolumeName	Sets or returns the name of the drive volume; name is a string, in syntax: **VolumeName=string**

File Object

Allows the browser to treat a file as if it were an object.

Property Name	Description
Attributes	Sets or returns the attributes of the folder. Can read/write as well read only; syntax is **file.Attributes [= newattributes]**. Values are 0 (normal), 1(ReadOnly), 2(Hidden), 4(System), 8(Disk drive volume label) 16 (folder/directory), 32(changed file), 64 (link or shortcut), 128 (compressed file).

365

Property Name	Description
DateCreated	Read only property that returns the date that the specified file was created.
DateLastAccessed	Read only property that returns date and time of last access
DateLastModified	Read only property that returns date file was last modified.
Drive	Returns the drive letter of the file's home drive.
Name	Read/write value that sets or returns file/folders name.
ParentFolder	Returns a folder object containing the parent object for the specified file
Path	Returns directory path for specified object.
ShortName	Returns a DOS 8.3 naming convention.
ShortPath	Returns a path using the DOS 8.3 naming convention
Size	Returns size of the object in bytes. For folders, this is the total of all files and subfolders.
type	Returns a description of the folders type, based on the three letter extension.

Methods	Description	Required Arguments
Copy	Copies a file from one location to another; overwrite is an optional Boolean with a default of **true**.	object.Copy(destination[, overwrite]);
Delete	Deletes the specified file or folder object. **force** is an optional Boolean with default of **false** that will not allow deletion of read-only files.	object.Delete(force);
Move	Moves specified file or folder to the destination drive.	object.Move(destination);
OpenAsText_ Stream	Opens file and returns a **textstream** object that can be read, written too or appended. **iomode** (optional) is one of three constants: **ForReading, ForWriting**, or **ForAppending**. Default **format** is ACSII	object._ OpenAsTextStream_ ([iomode, [format]])

FileSystemObject

Allows the browser to access the host computer's file system as if it were an object.

Property Name	Description
`drives`	Returns a collection of all the drives available on the machine.

Methods	Description	Required Arguments
`BuildPath`	Appends a name to the end of a path. Will insert a separator.	`BuildPath(path, name)`
`CopyFile`	Copies a file from one location to another; overwrite is an optional Boolean with a default of **true**.	`CopyFile (source, destination[, overwrite] )`
`CopyFolder`	Copies a folder from one location to another; overwrite is an optional Boolean with a default of **true**.	`CopyFolder ( source, destination[, overwrite] )`
`CreateFolder`	Creates a folder; gives an error if **foldername** is already in use.	`CreateFolder_ (foldername)`
`CreateText_ File`	Creates a file with name filename, and returns a **TextStream** object that can be used to read/write the file.	`CreateTextFile_ (filename[, overwrite[, unicode]])`
`DeleteFile`	Deletes the specified file object. **force** is an optional Boolean with default of **false** that will not allow deletion of read-only files.	`DeleteFile ( filespec[, force] )`
`DeleteFolder`	Deletes the specified folder object. **force** is an optional Boolean with default of **false** that will not allow deletion of read-only files.	`DeleteFolder ( folderspec[, force]);`
`DriveExists`	Boolean return value; **True** if it exists, otherwise **false**.	`DriveExists(drivespec)`
`FileExists`	Boolean return value; **True** if it exists, otherwise **false**.	`FileExists(filespec)`
`FolderExists`	Boolean return value; **True** if it exists, otherwise **false**.	`FolderExists_ (folderspec)`
`GetAbsolute_ PathName`	Returns an explicit path.	`GetAbsolutePath_ Name(pathspec)`

Methods	Description	Required Arguments
GetBaseName	Returns a **string** value of the last item in the specified path, minus any file extension details.	GetBaseName(path)
GetDrive	Returns a **Drive** object for the specified drive; drive spec can be a letter, letter with colon or network share spec.	GetDrive(drivespec);
GetDriveName	Returns **Drive** name as a **string** for the specified path.	GetDriveName(path)
Get_Extension_Name	Returns the file type extension for last item in path as a **string**	GetExtensionName(path)
GetFile	Returns a **file** object corresponding to the last file in the path.	GetFile(filespec)
GetFileName	Returns the last item in the **pathspec string** as a **string**. It will return empty string if the path only has drives. Note that it does NOT check path existence; simply parses string.	GetFileName(pathspec)
GetFolder	Returns a **folder** object corresponding to the last folder in the path.	GetFolder(folderspec)
GetParent_FolderName	Returns the parent folder of the last item in the **pathspec string** as a **string**. It will return empty string if the path has no folders. Note that it does NOT check path existence; simply parses string.	GetParent_FolderName(path)
GetSpecial_Folder	Returns the special folder specified as an object. folderspec can be one of **0** (Windows folder), **1**(System Folder), **2**(Temporary folder)	GetSpecial_Folder(folderspec)
GetTempName	Provides a temporary file name, not an actual folder. Used for operations requiring a temporary file/folder.	GetTempName();
MoveFile	Moves one or more **file** objects from one location to another. **source** is the path to the files, and may include wildcards; **destination** may not.	MoveFile (source, destination)

Methods	Description	Required Arguments
MoveFolder	Moves **folders** from one location to another. **source** is the path to the folder, and may include wildcards; **destination** may not.	MoveFolder (source, destination);
OpenTextFile	Opens specified file and returns a **TextStream** object that can be read/written. **iomode** (optional) is one of three constants: **ForReading**, **ForWriting**, or **ForAppending**. Default **format** is ACSII.	OpenTextFile(filename[, iomode[, create[, format]]])

Folder Object

Allows JScript to manipulate the files on the browser's computer under suitably secure situations.

Property Name	Description
Attributes	Sets or returns the attributes of the folder. Can read/write as well read only; syntax is **folder.Attributes [= newattributes]**. Values are 0 (normal), 1(ReadOnly), 2(Hidden), 4(System), 8(Disk drive volume label) 16 (folder/directory), 32(changed file), 64 (link or shortcut), 128 (compressed file).
DateCreated	Read only property that returns the date that the specified file or folder was created.
DateLastAccessed	Read only property that returns date and time of last access
DateLastModified	Read only property that returns date file was last modified.
Drive	Returns the drive letter of the file's home drive.
IsRootFolder	Returns Boolean value indicating whether specified folder is a root directory or not.
Name	Read/write value that sets or returns folder's name.
ParentFolder	Returns a folder object containing the parent object for the specified file
Path	Returns directory path for specified object.
ShortName	Returns a DOS 8.3 naming convention.
ShortPath	Returns a path using the DOS 8.3 naming convention
Size	Returns size of the object in bytes. For folders, this is the total of all files and subfolders.

Property Name	Description
SubFolders	Returns a **folders** collection consisting of all sub folders in a folder, including hidden or system folders.
type	Returns a description of the folders type, based on the three letter extension.

Methods	Description	Required Arguments
Copy	Copies a folder from one location to another; overwrite is an optional Boolean with a default of **true**.	**object.Copy(destination[, overwrite]);**
Delete	Deletes the specified folder object. **force** is an optional Boolean with default of **false** that will not allow deletion of read-only files.	**object.Delete(force);**
Move	Moves specified folder to the destination drive.	**object.Move(destination);**
OpenAsText_ Stream	Opens file and returns a **textstream** object that can be read, written too or appended. **iomode** (optional) is one of three constants: **ForReading**, **ForWriting**, or **ForAppending**. Default **format** is ACSII	**object.OpenAsText_ Stream([iomode, [format]])**

TextStream

Properties	Description
AtEndOfLine	Returns a boolean value; **true** if at the end of as line; **false** otherwise.
AtEndOfStream	Returns a boolean value; **true** if at the end of the **TextStream**, **false** if otherwise.
Column	Returns the column **number** of the current character in the **TextStream**
Line	Read-only **number** value for the current line number in the **TextStream**

Methods	Description	Required Arguments
Close	Closes the **TextStream** object.	object.Close( );
Read	Reads the specified number of characters and returns the result as a **string** value.	object.Read(integer)
ReadAll	Returns the entire **TextStream** as a **string**	object.ReadAll( );
ReadLine	Reads a single line form a **TextStream**; from line start up to (but not including) a new line character.	object.ReadLine( )
Skip	Skips the specified number of characters when reading a **TextStream** object.	object.Skip(integer)
SkipLine	Skips the next line while reading the **TextStream**	object.SkipLine( )
Write	Writes the specified string to the **TextStream** object.	object.Write(string)
WriteBlank_ Lines	Inserts an **integer** number of newline characters, i.e. blank lines.	object.WriteBlank_ Lines(integer)
WriteLine	Writes the specified string followed by a newline character to the **TextStream**	object.WriteLine_ ([string])

HTML Tags & Colors

This section is intended to provide a quick reference to some of the more useful HTML tags and the attributes they support, together with a listing of color values and names sorted by type. A full listing of all the HTML tags is available from the Wrox web site, in the Wrox Ultimate HTML Reference Database. The URL is: **http://rapid.wrox.co.uk/html4db/**.

The HTML tags we have provided here are those directly relevant to JavaScript. Browser compatibility information is also provided

A

Defines a hypertext link. The **HREF** or the **NAME** attribute must be specified. **ALL**.

Attributes	2.0	3.2	4.0	N2	N3	N4	IE2	IE3	IE4
`<event_name>=script_code`	✗	✗	✓	✗	✗	✓	✗	✓	✓
`ACCESSKEY=key_character`	✗	✗	✓	✗	✗	✗	✗	✗	✓
`CHARSET=`*string*	✗	✗	✓	✗	✗	✗	✗	✗	✗
`CLASS=`*classname*	✗	✗	✗	✗	✗	✓	✗	✓	✓
`COORDS=`*string*	✗	✗	✓	✗	✗	✓	✗	✗	✗
`DATAFLD=column_name`	✗	✗	✗	✗	✗	✗	✗	✗	✓
`DATASRC=id`	✗	✗	✗	✗	✗	✗	✗	✗	✓
`DIR=LTR`|`RTL`	✗	✗	✓	✗	✗	✗	✗	✗	✗
`HREF=url`	✓	✓	✓	✓	✓	✓	✓	✓	✓
`HREFLANG=langcode`	✗	✗	✓	✗	✗	✗	✗	✗	✗
`ID=`*string*	✗	✗	✓	✗	✗	✓	✗	✓	✓
`LANG=language_type`	✗	✗	✓	✗	✗	✗	✗	✗	✓
`LANGUAGE=JAVASCRIPT`|`JSCRIPT`|`VBSCRIPT`|`VBS`	✗	✗	✗	✗	✗	✗	✗	✗	✓
`METHODS=`*string*	✓	✗	✗	✗	✗	✗	✗	✗	✓

Attributes	2.0	3.2	4.0	N2	N3	N4	IE2	IE3	IE4
NAME=*string*	✓	✓	✓	✓	✓	✓	✓	✓	✓
REL=**SAME** | **NEXT** | **PARENT** | **PREVIOUS** | *string*	✓	✓	✓	✗	✗	✗	✗	✓	✓
REV=*string*	✓	✓	✓	✗	✗	✗	✗	✓	✓
SHAPE=**CIRC** | **CIRCLE** | **POLY** | **POLYGON** | **RECT** | **RECTANGLE**	✗	✗	✓	✗	✗	✗	✗	✗	✗
STYLE=*string*	✗	✗	✓	✗	✗	✓	✗	✓	✓
TABINDEX=*number*	✗	✗	✓	✗	✗	✗	✗	✗	✓
TARGET=**<window_name>** | **_parent** | **_blank** | **_top** | **_self**	✗	✗	✓	✓	✓	✓	✗	✓	✓
TITLE=*string*	✓	✓	✓	✗	✗	✗	✗	✓	✓
TYPE=**BUTTON** | **RESET** | **SUBMIT**	✗	✗	✓	✗	✗	✗	✗	✗	✓
URN=*string*	✓	✗	✗	✗	✗	✗	✗	✗	✓

ADDRESS

Specifies information such as address, signature and authorship. **ALL**.

Attributes	2.0	3.2	4.0	N2	N3	N4	IE2	IE3	IE4
<event_name>=**script_code**	✗	✗	✓	✗	✗	✗	✗	✗	✓
CLASS=**classname**	✗	✗	✓	✗	✗	✓	✗	✗	✓
DIR=**LTR** | **RTL**	✗	✗	✓	✗	✗	✗	✗	✗	✗
ID=*string*	✗	✗	✓	✗	✗	✓	✗	✗	✓
LANG=**language_type**	✗	✗	✓	✗	✗	✗	✗	✗	✓
LANGUAGE=**JAVASCRIPT** | **JSCRIPT** | **VBSCRIPT** | **VBS**	✗	✗	✗	✗	✗	✗	✗	✗	✓
STYLE=**STRING**	✗	✗	✓	✗	✗	✓	✗	✗	✓
TITLE=**STRING**	✗	✗	✓	✗	✗	✗	✗	✗	✓

APPLET

Places a Java Applet or other executable content in the page. **HTML 3.2, N2, N3, N4, IE3, IE4, deprecated in HTML 4.0**.

Attributes	2.0	3.2	4.0	N2	N3	N4	IE2	IE3	IE4
<event_name>=**script_code**	✗	✗	D	✗	✗	✗	✗	✗	✗
ALIGN=**TOP** | **MIDDLE** | **BOTTOM** | **LEFT** | **RIGHT** | **ABSMIDDLE** | **BASELINE** | **ABSBOTTOM** | **TEXTTOP**	✗	✓	D	✓	✓	✓	✗	✓	✓
ALT=**text**	✗	✓	D	✓	✓	✓	✗	✓	✓
ARCHIVE=**url**	✗	✗	D	✗	✓	✓	✗	✗	✗
BORDER=**number**	✗	✗	D	✗	✗	✗	✗	✗	✗
CLASS=**classname**	✗	✗	D	✗	✗	✓	✗	✗	✓

Attributes	2.0	3.2	4.0	N2	N3	N4	IE2	IE3	IE4
CODE=filename	x	✓	D	✓	✓	✓	x	✓	✓
CODEBASE=Path|url	x	✓	D	✓	✓	✓	x	✓	✓
DATAFLD=column_name	x	x	x	x	x	x	x	x	✓
DATASRC=id	x	x	x	x	x	x	x	x	✓
DOWNLOAD=number	x	x	x	x	x	x	x	✓	x
HEIGHT=number	x	✓	D	✓	✓	✓	x	✓	x
HSPACE=number	x	✓	D	x	x	✓	x	✓	✓
ID=*string*	x	x	D	x	x	✓	x	x	✓
MAYSCRIPT=YES|NO	x	x	x	x	x	✓	x	x	x
NAME=*string*	x	✓	D	x	x	x	x	✓	✓
OBJECT=*string*	x	x	D	x	x	x	x	x	x
SRC=url	x	x	x	x	x	x	x	x	✓
STYLE=*string*	x	x	D	x	x	✓	x	x	✓
TITLE=*string*	x	x	D	x	x	x	x	✓	✓
VSPACE=number	x	✓	D	x	x	✓	x	✓	✓
WIDTH=number	x	✓	D	✓	✓	✓	x	✓	✓

BODY

Defines the beginning and end of the body section of the page. **ALL**.

Attributes	2.0	3.2	4.0	N2	N3	N4	IE2	IE3	IE4
<event_name>=script_code	x	x	✓	x	x	✓	x	x	✓
ALINK=color	x	✓	D	✓	✓	✓	x	✓	✓
BACKGROUND=*string*	x	✓	D	✓	✓	✓	✓	✓	✓
BGCOLOR=color	x	✓	D	✓	✓	✓	✓	✓	✓
BGPROPERTIES=FIXED	x	x	x	x	x	x	✓	✓	✓
BOTTOMMARGIN=number	x	x	x	x	x	x	x	x	✓
CLASS=classname	x	x	✓	x	x	✓	x	✓	✓
DIR=LTR|RTL	x	x	✓	x	x	x	x	x	x
ID=*string*	x	x	✓	x	x	✓	x	✓	✓
LANG=language_type	x	x	✓	x	x	x	x	x	✓
LANGUAGE=JAVASCRIPT|JSCRIPT| VBSCRIPT|VBS	x	x	x	x	x	x	x	x	✓
LEFTMARGIN=number	x	x	x	x	x	x	✓	✓	✓
LINK=color	x	✓	D	✓	✓	✓	✓	✓	✓
RIGHTMARGIN=number	x	x	x	x	x	x	x	x	✓
SCROLL=YES|NO	x	x	x	x	x	x	x	x	✓
STYLE=*string*	x	x	✓	x	x	✓	x	✓	✓
TEXT=color	x	✓	D	✓	✓	✓	✓	✓	✓

Attributes	2.0	3.2	4.0	N2	N3	N4	IE2	IE3	IE4
TITLE=*string*	✗	✗	✓	✗	✗	✗	✗	✗	✓
TOPMARGIN=number	✗	✗	✗	✗	✗	✗	✓	✓	✓
VLINK=color	✗	✓	D	✓	✓	✓	✓	✓	✓

BUTTON

Renders an HTML button, the enclosed text used as the button's caption. **HTML 4.0, IE4**.

Attributes	2.0	3.2	4.0	N2	N3	N4	IE2	IE3	IE4
<event_name>=script_code	✗	✗	✓	✗	✗	✗	✗	✗	✓
ACCESSKEY=ley_character	✗	✗	✓	✗	✗	✗	✗	✗	✓
CLASS=classname	✗	✗	✓	✗	✗	✗	✗	✗	✓
DATAFLD=column_name	✗	✗	✗	✗	✗	✗	✗	✗	✓
DATAFORMATAS=HTML | TEXT	✗	✗	✗	✗	✗	✗	✗	✗	✓
DATASRC=id	✗	✗	✗	✗	✗	✗	✗	✗	✓
DIR=LTR | RTL	✗	✗	✓	✗	✗	✗	✗	✗	✗
DISABLED	✗	✗	✓	✗	✗	✗	✗	✗	✓
ID=*string*	✗	✗	✓	✗	✗	✗	✗	✗	✓
LANG=language_type	✗	✗	✓	✗	✗	✗	✗	✗	✓
LANGUAGE=JAVASCRIPT | JSCRIPT | VBSCRIPT | VBS	✗	✗	✗	✗	✗	✗	✗	✗	✓
NAME=*string*	✗	✗	✓	✗	✗	✗	✗	✗	✗
STYLE=*string*	✗	✗	✓	✗	✗	✗	✗	✗	✓
TABINDEX=number	✗	✗	✓	✗	✗	✗	✗	✗	✗
TITLE=*string*	✗	✗	✓	✗	✗	✗	✗	✗	✓
TYPE=BUTTON | RESET | SUBMIT	✗	✗	✓	✗	✗	✗	✗	✗	✓
VALUE=*string*	✗	✗							

EMBED

Embeds documents of any type in the page, to be viewed in another suitable application. **N2, N3, N4, IE3, IE4**.

Attributes	2.0	3.2	4.0	N2	N3	N4	IE2	IE3	IE4
ALIGN=ABSBOTTOM | ABSMIDDLE | BASELINE | BOTTOM | LEFT | MIDDLE | RIGHT | TEXTTOP | TOP	✗	✗	✗	✗	✗	✓	✗	✗	✓
ALT=text	✗	✗	✗	✗	✗	✗	✗	✗	✓
BORDER=number	✗	✗	D	✗	✗	✓	✗	✗	✗
CLASS=classname	✗	✗	✗	✗	✗	✓	✗	✗	✓
CODE=filename	✗	✗	✗	✗	✗	✗	✗	✗	✓

Attributes	2.0	3.2	4.0	N2	N3	N4	IE2	IE3	IE4
CODEBASE=url	✗	✗	✗	✗	✗	✗	✗	✗	✓
HEIGHT=number	✗	✗	✗	✓	✓	✓	✗	✓	✓
HIDDEN=string	✗	✗	✗	✗	✗	✓	✗	✗	✗
HSPACE=number	✗	✗	✗	✗	✗	✓	✗	✗	✓
ID=string	✗	✗	✗	✗	✗	✓	✗	✗	✓
NAME=string	✗	✗	✗	✓	✓	✓	✗	✓	✓
PALETTE=FOREGROUND|BACKGROUND	✗	✗	✗	✗	✗	✓	✗	✓	✗
PLUGINSPAGE=string	✗	✗	✗	✗	✗	✓	✗	✗	✗
SRC=url	✗	✗	✗	✓	✓	✓	✗	✓	✓
STYLE=string	✗	✗	✗	✗	✗	✓	✗	✗	✓
TITLE=string	✗	✗	✗	✗	✗	✗	✗	✗	✓
TYPE=mime-type	✗	✗	✗	✗	✗	✓	✗	✗	✗
UNITS=EN|EMS|PIXELS	✗	✗	✗	✗	✗	✓	✗	✓	✓
VSPACE=number	✗	✗	✗	✗	✗	✓	✗	✗	✓
WIDTH=number	✗	✗	✗	✓	✓	✓	✗	✓	✓

FORM

Denotes a form containing controls and elements, whose values are sent to a server. ALL.

Attributes	2.0	3.2	4.0	N2	N3	N4	IE2	IE3	IE4
<event_name>=script_code	✗	✗	✓	✗	✗	✓	✗	✓	✓
ACCEPT-CHARSET=string	✗	✗	✓	✗	✗	✗	✗	✗	✗
ACTION=string	✓	✓	✓	✓	✓	✓	✓	✓	✓
CLASS=classname	✗	✗	✓	✗	✗	✓	✗	✗	✓
DIR=LTR|RTL	✗	✗	✓	✗	✗	✗	✗	✗	✗
ENCTYPE=string	✓	✓	✓	✓	✓	✓	✗	✗	✓
ID=string	✗	✗	✓	✗	✗	✓	✗	✗	✓
LANG=language_type	✗	✗	✓	✗	✗	✗	✗	✗	✓
LANGUAGE=JAVASCRIPT|JSCRIPT| VBSCRIPT|VBS	✗	✗	✗	✗	✗	✗	✗	✗	✓
METHOD=GET|POST	✓	✓	✓	✓	✓	✓	✓	✓	✓
NAME=string	✗	✗	✗	✗	✗	✓	✗	✗	✓
STYLE=string	✗	✗	✓	✗	✗	✓	✗	✗	✓
TARGET=<window_name>|_parent| _blank|_top|_self	✗	✗	✓	✓	✓	✓	✗	✓	✓
TITLE=string	✗	✗	✓	✗	✗	✗	✗	✗	✓

FRAME

Specifies an individual frame within a frameset. **HTML 4.0, N2, N3, N4, IE3, IE4.**

Attributes	2.0	3.2	4.0	N2	N3	N4	IE2	IE3	IE4
`<event_name>=script_code`	✗	✗	✗	✗	✗	✓	✗	✗	✓
`ALIGN=CENTER│LEFT│RIGHT`	✗	✗	✗	✗	✗	✓	✗	✓	✗
`BORDERCOLOR=color`	✗	✗	✗	✗	✓	✓	✗	✗	✓
`CLASS=classname`	✗	✗	✓	✗	✗	✓	✗	✗	✓
`DATAFLD=column_name`	✗	✗	✗	✗	✗	✗	✗	✗	✓
`DATASRC=id`	✗	✗	✗	✗	✗	✗	✗	✗	✓
`FRAMEBORDER=NO│YES│0│1`	✗	✗	✓	✗	✓	✓	✗	✓	✓
`ID=string`	✗	✗	✓	✗	✗	✓	✗	✗	✓
`LANG=language_type`	✗	✗	✗	✗	✗	✗	✗	✗	✓
`LANGUAGE=JAVASCRIPT│JSCRIPT│` `VBSCRIPT│VBS`	✗	✗	✗	✗	✗	✗	✗	✗	✓
`LONGDESC=url`	✗	✗	✓	✗	✗	✗	✗	✗	✗
`MARGINHEIGHT=number`	✗	✗	✓	✓	✓	✓	✗	✓	✓
`MARGINWIDTH=number`	✗	✗	✓	✓	✓	✓	✗	✓	✓
`NAME=string`	✗	✗	✓	✓	✓	✓	✗	✓	✓
`NORESIZE=NORESIZE│RESIZE`	✗	✗	✓	✓	✓	✓	✗	✓	✓
`SCROLLING=AUTO│YES│NO`	✗	✗	✓	✓	✓	✓	✗	✓	✓
`SRC=url`	✗	✗	✓	✓	✓	✓	✗	✓	✓
`STYLE=string`	✗	✗	✓	✗	✗	✗	✗	✗	✓
`TITLE=string`	✗	✗	✓	✗	✗	✓	✗	✗	✓

FRAMESET

Specifies a frameset containing multiple frames and other nested framesets. **HTML 4.0, N2, N3, N4, IE3, IE4**

Attributes	2.0	3.2	4.0	N2	N3	N4	IE2	IE3	IE4
`<event_name>=script_code`	✗	✗	✓	✗	✗	✗	✗	✗	✗
`BORDER=number`	✗	✗	D	✗	✓	✓	✗	✗	✓
`BORDERCOLOR=color`	✗	✗	✗	✗	✓	✓	✗	✗	✓
`CLASS=classname`	✗	✗	✓	✗	✗	✓	✗	✗	✓
`COLS=number`	✗	✗	✓	✓	✓	✓	✗	✓	✓
`FRAMEBORDER=NO│YES│0│1`	✗	✗	✗	✗	✓	✓	✗	✓	✓
`FRAMESPACING=number`	✗	✗	✗	✗	✗	✗	✗	✓	✓
`ID=string`	✗	✗	✓	✗	✗	✓	✗	✗	✓
`LANG=language_type`	✗	✗	✗	✗	✗	✗	✗	✗	✓

Attributes	2.0	3.2	4.0	N2	N3	N4	IE2	IE3	IE4
LANGUAGE=JAVASCRIPT|JSCRIPT|VBSCRIPT|VBS	x	x	x	x	x	x	x	x	✓
ROWS=number	x	x	✓	✓	✓	✓	x	✓	✓
STYLE=string	x	x	✓	x	x	x	x	x	✓
TITLE=string	x	x	✓	x	x	x	x	x	✓

HEAD

Contains tags holding unviewed information about the document. **ALL**.

Attributes	2.0	3.2	4.0	N2	N3	N4	IE2	IE3	IE4
CLASS=classname	x	x	x	x	x	✓	x	x	✓
DIR=LTR|RTL	x	x	✓	x	x	x	x	x	x
ID=string	x	x	x	x	x	✓	x	x	✓
LANG=language_type	x	x	✓	x	x	x	x	x	x
PROFILE=url	x	x	✓	x	x	x	x	x	x
TITLE=string	x	x	x	x	x	x	x	x	✓

HTML

The outer tag for the page, which identifies the document as containing HTML elements. **ALL**.

Attributes	2.0	3.2	4.0	N2	N3	N4	IE2	IE3	IE4
DIR=LTR|RTL	x	x	✓	x	x	x	x	x	x
LANG=language_type	x	x	✓	x	x	x	x	x	x
TITLE=string	x	x	x	x	x	x	x	x	✓
VERSION=url	x	x	✓	x	x	x	x	x	x

IFRAME

Used to create in-line floating frames within the page. **HTML 4.0, IE3, IE4**

Attributes	2.0	3.2	4.0	N2	N3	N4	IE2	IE3	IE4
ALIGN=ABSBOTTOM|ABSMIDDLE|BASELINE|BOTTOM|LEFT|MIDDLE|RIGHT|TEXTTOP|TOP	x	x	D	x	x	x	x	x	✓
BORDER=number	x	x	D	x	x	x	x	x	✓
BORDERCOLOR=color	x	x	x	x	x	x	x	x	✓
CLASS=classname	x	x	✓	x	x	x	x	x	✓
DATAFLD=column_name	x	x	x	x	x	x	x	x	✓
DATASRC=id	x	x	x	x	x	x	x	x	✓

Attributes	2.0	3.2	4.0	N2	N3	N4	IE2	IE3	IE4
FRAMEBORDER=NO|YES|0|1	✗	✗	✓	✗	✗	✗	✗	✗	✓
FRAMESPACING=number	✗	✗	✗	✗	✗	✗	✗	✗	✓
HEIGHT=number	✗	✗	✓	✗	✗	✗	✗	✗	✓
HSPACE=number	✗	✗	✗	✗	✗	✗	✗	✗	✓
ID=*string*	✗	✗	✓	✗	✗	✗	✗	✗	✓
LANG=language_type	✗	✗	✗	✗	✗	✗	✗	✗	✓
LANGUAGE=JAVASCRIPT|JSCRIPT|VBSCRIPT|VBS	✗	✗	✗	✗	✗	✗	✗	✗	✓
LONGDESC=url	✗	✗	✓	✗	✗	✗	✗	✗	✗
MARGINHEIGHT=number	✗	✗	✓	✗	✗	✗	✗	✗	✓
MARGINWIDTH=number	✗	✗	✓	✗	✗	✗	✗	✗	✓
NAME=*string*	✗	✗	✓	✗	✗	✗	✗	✗	✓
NORESIZE=NORESIZE|RESIZE	✗	✗	✗	✗	✗	✗	✗	✗	✓
SCROLLING=AUTO|YES|NO	✗	✗	✓	✗	✗	✗	✗	✗	✓
SRC=url	✗	✗	✓	✗	✗	✗	✗	✗	✓
STYLE=*string*	✗	✗	✓	✗	✗	✗	✗	✗	✓
TITLE=*string*	✗	✗	✓	✗	✗	✗	✗	✗	✓
VSPACE=number	✗	✗	✗	✗	✗	✗	✗	✗	✓
WIDTH=number	✗	✗	✓	✗	✗	✗	✗	✗	✓

ILAYER

Defines a separate area of the page as an inline layer that can hold a different page. **N4 only**.

Attributes	2.0	3.2	4.0	N2	N3	N4	IE2	IE3	IE4
<event_name>=script_code	✗	✗	✗	✗	✗	✓	✗	✗	✗
ABOVE=object_id	✗	✗	✗	✗	✗	✓	✗	✗	✗
BACKGROUND=*string*	✗	✗	✗	✗	✗	✓	✗	✗	✗
BELOW=object_id	✗	✗	✗	✗	✗	✓	✗	✗	✗
BGCOLOR=color	✗	✗	D	✗	✗	✓	✗	✗	✗
CLASS=classname	✗	✗	✗	✗	✗	✓	✗	✗	✗
CLIP=number[,number,number,number]	✗	✗	✓	✗	✗	✓	✗	✗	✗
ID=*string*	✗	✗	✗	✗	✗	✓	✗	✗	✗
LEFT=number	✗	✗	✗	✗	✗	✓	✗	✗	✗
NAME=*string*	✗	✗	✗	✗	✗	✓	✗	✗	✗
PAGEX=number	✗	✗	✗	✗	✗	✓	✗	✗	✗
PAGEY=number	✗	✗	✗	✗	✗	✓	✗	✗	✗
SRC=url	✗	✗	✗	✗	✗	✓	✗	✗	✗
STYLE=*string*	✗	✗	✗	✗	✗	✓	✗	✗	✗

Attributes	2.0	3.2	4.0	N2	N3	N4	IE2	IE3	IE4
TOP=number	x	x	x	x	x	✓	x	x	x
VISIBILITY=SHOW|HIDE|INHERIT	x	x	x	x	x	✓	x	x	x
WIDTH=number	x	x	x	x	x	✓	x	x	x
Z-INDEX=number	x	x	x	x	x	✓	x	x	x

IMG

Embeds an image or a video clip in the document. **Supported by ALL**.

Attributes	2.0	3.2	4.0	N2	N3	N4	IE2	IE3	IE4
<event_name>=script_code	x	x	✓	x	x	✓	x	x	✓
ALIGN=BASBOTTOM|ABSMIDDLE|BASELINE| BOTTOM|LEFT|MIDDLE|RIGHT|TEXTTOP|TOP	✓	✓	D	✓	✓	✓	✓	✓	✓
ALT=text	✓	✓	✓	✓	✓	✓	✓	✓	✓
BORDER=number	x	✓	D	✓	✓	✓	✓	✓	✓
CLASS=classname	x	x	✓	x	x	✓	x	✓	✓
CONTROLS	x	x	x	x	x	x	✓	✓	x
DATAFLD=column_name	x	x	x	x	x	x	x	x	✓
DATASRC=id	x	x	x	x	x	x	x	x	✓
DIR=LTR|RTL	x	x	✓	x	x	x	x	x	x
DYNSRC=string	x	x	x	x	x	x	✓	✓	✓
HEIGHT=number	x	✓	✓	✓	✓	✓	✓	✓	✓
HSPACE=number	x	✓	✓	✓	✓	✓	✓	✓	✓
ID=string	x	x	✓	x	x	✓	x	✓	✓
ISMAP	✓	✓	✓	✓	✓	✓	✓	✓	✓
LANG=language_type	x	x	✓	x	x	x	x	x	✓
LANGUAGE=JAVASCRIPT|JSCRIPT| VBSCRIPT|VBS	x	x	x	x	x	x	x	x	✓
LONGDESC=url	x	x	✓	x	x	x	x	x	x
LOOP=number	x	x	x	x	x	x	✓	✓	✓
LOWSRC=url	x	x	x	✓	✓	✓	x	x	✓
NAME=string	x	x	x	x	x	✓	x	x	✓
SRC=url	✓	✓	✓	✓	✓	✓	✓	✓	✓
START=number | string	x	x	x	x	x	x	✓	✓	x
STYLE=string	x	x	✓	x	x	✓	x	✓	✓
TITLE=string	x	x	✓	x	x	x	x	✓	✓
USEMAP=url	x	✓	✓	✓	✓	✓	✓	✓	✓
VSPACE=number	x	✓	✓	✓	✓	✓	✓	✓	✓
WIDTH=number	x	✓	✓	✓	✓	✓	✓	✓	✓

INPUT

Specifies a form input control, such as a button, text or check box. **Supported by ALL**.

Attributes	2.0	3.2	4.0	N2	N3	N4	IE2	IE3	IE4
`<event_name>=script_code`	✗	✗	✓	✗	✗	✓	✗	✓	✓
`ACCEPT=`*string*	✗	✗	✓	✗	✗	✗	✗	✗	✗
`ACCESSKEY=key_character`	✗	✗	✓	✗	✗	✗	✗	✗	✓
`ALIGN=CENTER|LEFT|RIGHT`	✓	✓	D	✓	✓	✓	✓	✓	✓
`ALT=text`	✗	✗	✓	✗	✗	✗	✗	✗	✗
`CHECKED=FALSE|TRUE`	✓	✓	✓	✓	✓	✓	✓	✓	✓
`CLASS=classname`	✗	✗	✓	✗	✗	✓	✗	✓	✓
`DATAFLD=column_name`	✗	✗	✗	✗	✗	✗	✗	✗	✓
`DATAFORMATAS=HTML|TEXT`	✗	✗	✗	✗	✗	✗	✗	✗	✓
`DATASRC=id`	✗	✗	✗	✗	✗	✗	✗	✗	✓
`DIR=LTR|RTL`	✗	✗	✓	✗	✗	✗	✗	✗	✗
`DISABLED`	✗	✗	✓	✗	✗	✗	✗	✗	✓
`ID=`*string*	✗	✗	✓	✗	✗	✓	✗	✓	✓
`LANG=language_type`	✗	✗	✓	✗	✗	✗	✗	✗	✓
`LANGUAGE=JAVASCRIPT|JSCRIPT|` `VBSCRIPT|VBS`	✗	✗	✗	✗	✗	✗	✗	✗	✓
`MAXLENGTH=number`	✓	✓	✓	✓	✓	✓	✓	✓	✓
`NAME=`*string*	✓	✓	✓	✓	✓	✓	✓	✓	✓
`NOTAB`	✗	✗	✗	✗	✗	✗	✗	✓	✗
`READONLY`	✗	✗	✓	✗	✗	✗	✗	✗	✓
`SIZE=number`	✓	✓	✓	✓	✓	✓	✓	✓	✓
`SRC=url`	✓	✓	✓	✓	✓	✗	✓	✓	✓
`STYLE=`*string*	✗	✗	✓	✗	✗	✓	✗	✓	✓
`TABINDEX=number`	✗	✗	✓	✗	✗	✗	✗	✓	✓
`TITLE=`*string*	✗	✗	✓	✗	✗	✗	✗	✓	✓
`TYPE=BUTTON|CHECKBOX|FILE|HIDDEN|` `IMAGE|PASSWORD|RADIO|RESET|SUBMIT|TEXT`	✓	✓	✓	✓	✓	✓	✓	✓	✓
`USEMAP=url`	✗	✗	✓	✗	✗	✗	✗	✗	✗
`VALUE=`*string*	✓	✓	✓	✓	✓	✓	✓	✓	✓

LABEL

Defines the text of a label for a control-like element. **HTML 4.0, IE4**.

Attributes	2.0	3.2	4.0	N2	N3	N4	IE2	IE3	IE4
`<event_name>=script_code`	x	x	✓	x	x	x	x	x	✓
`ACCESSKEY=key_character`	x	x	✓	x	x	x	x	x	✓
`CLASS=classname`	x	x	✓	x	x	x	x	x	✓
`DATAFLD=column_name`	x	x	x	x	x	x	x	x	✓
`DATAFORMATAS=HTML│TEXT`	x	x	x	x	x	x	x	x	✓
`DATASRC=id`	x	x	x	x	x	x	x	x	✓
`DIR=LTR│RTL`	x	x	✓	x	x	x	x	x	x
`FOR=element_name`	x	x	✓	x	x	x	x	x	✓
`ID=string`	x	x	✓	x	x	x	x	x	✓
`LANG=language_type`	x	x	✓	x	x	x	x	x	✓
`LANGUAGE=JAVASCRIPT│JSCRIPT│` `VBSCRIPT│VBS`	x	x	x	x	x	x	x	x	✓
`STYLE=`*string*	x	x	✓	x	x	x	x	x	✓

LAYER

Defines a separate area of the page as a layer that can hold a different page.
N4 only.

Attributes	2.0	3.2	4.0	N2	N3	N4	IE2	IE3	IE4
`<event_name>=script_code`	x	x	x	x	x	✓	x	x	x
`ABOVE=object_id`	x	x	x	x	x	✓	x	x	x
`BACKGROUND=`*string*	x	x	x	x	x	✓	x	x	x
`BELOW=object_id`	x	x	x	x	x	✓	x	x	x
`BGCOLOR=color`	x	x	D	x	x	✓	x	x	x
`CLASS=classname`	x	x	x	x	x	✓	x	x	x
`CLIP=number[,number,number,number]`	x	x	x	x	x	✓	x	x	x
`ID=`*string*	x	x	x	x	x	✓	x	x	x
`LEFT=number`	x	x	x	x	x	✓	x	x	x
`NAME=string`	x	x	x	x	x	✓	x	x	x
`PAGEX=number`	x	x	x	x	x	✓	x	x	x
`PAGEY=number`	x	x	x	x	x	✓	x	x	x
`SRC=url`	x	x	x	x	x	✓	x	x	x
`STYLE=`*string*	x	x	x	x	x	✓	x	x	x
`TOP=number`	x	x	x	x	x	✓	x	x	x
`VISIBILITY=SHOW│HIDE│INHERIT`	x	x	x	x	x	✓	x	x	x
`WIDTH=number`	x	x	x	x	x	✓	x	x	x
`Z-INDEX=number`	x	x	x	x	x	✓	x	x	x

LINK

Defines a hyperlink between the document and some other resource. **HTML 2.0, 3.2 & 4.0, IE3, IE4**.

Attributes	2.0	3.2	4.0	N2	N3	N4	IE2	IE3	IE4
`<event_name>=script_code`	x	x	✓	x	x	x	x	x	x
`CHARSET=charset`	x	x	✓	x	x	x	x	x	x
`CLASS=classname`	x	x	✓	x	x	x	x	x	x
`DIR=LTR|RTL`	x	x	✓	x	x	x	x	x	x
`DISABLED`	x	x	x	x	x	x	x	x	✓
`HREF=url`	✓	✓	✓	✓	✓	✓	x	✓	✓
`HREFLANG=langcode`	x	x	✓	x	x	x	x	x	x
`ID=`*string*	x	x	✓	x	x	✓	x	x	✓
`LANG=language_type`	x	x	✓	x	x	x	x	x	✓
`MEDIA=SCREEN|PRINT|PROJECTION|` `BRAILLE|SPEECH|ALL`	x	x	✓	x	x	x	x	x	✓
`METHODS=`*string*	✓	x	x	x	x	x	x	x	x
`REL=relationship`	✓	✓	✓	✓	✓	✓	x	✓	✓
`REV=relationship`	✓	✓	✓	✓	✓	✓	x	✓	x
`STYLE=`*string*	x	x	✓	x	x	✓	x	x	x
`TARGET=<window_name>|_parent|` `_blank|_tope|_self`	x	x	✓	x	x	x	x	x	x
`TITLE=`*string*	✓	✓	✓	✓	✓	✓	x	✓	✓
`TYPE=MIME-type`	x	x	✓	x	x	✓	x	✓	✓
`URN=`*string*	✓	x	x	x	x	x	x	x	x

OBJECT

Inserts an object or other non-intrinsic HTML control into the page. **HTML 4.0, IE3, IE4**.

Attributes	2.0	3.2	4.0	N2	N3	N4	IE2	IE3	IE4
`<event_name>=script_code`	x	x	✓	x	x	x	x	x	✓
`ACCESSKEY=key_character`	x	x	x	x	x	x	x	x	✓
`ALIGN=ABSBOTTOM|ABSMIDDLE|BASELINE|` `BOTTOM|LEFT|MIDDLE|RIGHT|TEXTTOP|TOP`	✓	✓	D	x	x	x	x	✓	✓
`ARCHIVE=urllist`	x	x	✓	x	x	x	x	x	x
`BORDER=number`	x	x	D	x	x	x	x	✓	x
`CLASS=classname`	x	x	✓	x	x	x	x	x	✓
`CLASSID=`*string*	x	x	✓	x	x	x	x	✓	✓
`CODE=filename`	x	x	x	x	x	x	x	x	✓

Attributes	2.0	3.2	4.0	N2	N3	N4	IE2	IE3	IE4
CODEBASE=url	x	x	✓	x	x	x	x	✓	✓
CODETYPE=url	x	x	✓	x	x	x	x	✓	✓
DATA=*string*	x	x	✓	x	x	x	x	✓	✓
DATAFLD=column_name	x	x	x	x	x	x	x	x	✓
DATASRC=id	x	x	x	x	x	x	x	x	✓
DECLARE	x	x	✓	x	x	x	x	✓	x
DIR=LTR|RTL	x	x	✓	x	x	x	x	x	x
EXPORT	x	x	✓	x	x	x	x	x	x
HEIGHT=number	x	x	✓	x	x	x	x	✓	✓
HSPACE=number	x	x	✓	x	x	x	x	✓	x
ID=*string*	x	x	✓	x	x	x	x	x	✓
LANG=language_type	x	x	✓	x	x	x	x	x	✓
LANGUAGE=JAVASCRIPT|JSCRIPT|VBSCRIPT|VBS	x	x	x	x	x	x	x	x	x
NAME=*string*	x	x	✓	x	x	x	x	✓	✓
NOTAB	x	x	x	x	x	x	x	✓	x
SHAPES	x	x	✓	x	x	x	x	✓	x
STANDBY=*string*	x	x	✓	x	x	x	x	✓	x
STYLE=*string*	x	x	✓	x	x	x	x	x	✓
TABINDEX=number	x	x	✓	x	x	x	x	✓	✓
TITLE=*string*	x	x	✓	x	x	x	x	✓	✓
TYPE=MIME-type	x	x	✓	x	x	x	x	x	x
USEMAP=url	x	x	✓	x	x	x	x	✓	x
VSPACE=number	x	x	✓	x	x	x	x	✓	x
WIDTH=number	x	x	✓	x	x	x	x	✓	✓

OPTION

Denotes one choice in a **SELECT** drop-down or list element. **ALL**.

Attributes	2.0	3.2	4.0	N2	N3	N4	IE2	IE3	IE4
<event_name>=script_code	x	x	✓	x	x	x	x	x	✓
CLASS=classname	x	x	✓	x	x	✓	x	x	✓
DIR=LTR|RTL	x	x	✓	x	x	x	x	x	x
DISABLED	x	x	✓	✓	✓	x	x	x	x
ID=*string*	x	x	✓	x	x	✓	x	x	✓
LABEL=*string*	x	x	✓	x	x	x	x	x	x
LANG=language_type	x	x	✓	x	x	x	x	x	x
LANGUAGE=JAVASCRIPT|JSCRIPT|VBSCRIPT|VBS	x	x	x	x	x	x	x	x	✓

385

Attributes	2.0	3.2	4.0	N2	N3	N4	IE2	IE3	IE4
PLAIN	✗	✗	✗	✓	✓	✓	✗	✗	✗
SELECTED	✓	✓	✓	✓	✓	✓	✓	✓	✓
STYLE=*string*	✗	✗	✓	✗	✗	✓	✗	✗	✗
TITLE=*string*	✗	✗	✓	✗	✗	✗	✗	✗	✗
VALUE=*string*	✓	✓	✓	✓	✓	✓	✓	✓	✓

PARAM

Used in an **OBJECT** or **APPLET** tag to set the object's properties. **ALL except HTML 2.0.**

Attributes	2.0	3.2	4.0	N2	N3	N4	IE2	IE3	IE4
DATAFLD=column_name	✗	✗	✗	✗	✗	✗	✗	✗	✓
DATAFORMATAS=HTML｜TEXT	✗	✗	✗	✗	✗	✗	✗	✗	✓
DATASRC=id	✗	✗	✗	✗	✗	✗	✗	✗	✓
ID	✗	✗	✓	✗	✗	✗	✗	✗	✗
NAME=*string*	✗	✓	✓	✓	✓	✓	✗	✓	✓
TYPE=*string*	✗	✗	✓	✗	✗	✗	✗	✓	✗
VALUE=*string*	✗	✓	✓	✓	✓	✓	✗	✓	✓
VALUETYPE=DATA｜REF｜OBJECT	✗	✗	✓	✗	✗	✗	✗	✓	✗

SCRIPT

Specifies a script for the page that will be interpreted by a script engine. **HTML 3.2, 4.0, N2, N3, N4, IE3, IE4.**

Attributes	2.0	3.2	4.0	N2	N3	N4	IE2	IE3	IE4
ARCHIVE=url	✗	✗	✗	✗	✗	✓	✗	✗	✗
CHARSET=charset	✗	✗	✓	✗	✗	✗	✗	✗	✗
CLASS=classname	✗	✗	✗	✗	✗	✓	✗	✗	✓
DEFER	✗	✗	✓	✗	✗	✗	✗	✗	✗
EVENT=<event_name>	✗	✗	✗	✗	✗	✗	✗	✗	✓
FOR=element_name	✗	✗	✗	✗	✗	✗	✗	✗	✓
ID=*string*	✗	✗	✗	✗	✗	✓	✗	✗	✓
LANGUAGE=JAVASCRIPT｜JSCRIPT｜VBSCRIPT｜VBS	✗	✗	D	✓	✓	✓	✗	✓	✓
SRC=url	✗	✗	✓	✗	✓	✓	✗	✓	✓
STYLE=*string*	✗	✗	✗	✗	✗	✓	✗	✗	✓
TITLE=*string*	✗	✗	✗	✗	✗	✗	✗	✗	✓
TYPE=*string*	✗	✗	✓	✗	✗	✗	✗	✓	✓

SELECT

Defines a list box or drop-down list. **ALL**.

Attributes	2.0	3.2	4.0	N2	N3	N4	IE2	IE3	IE4
`<event_name>=script_code`	x	x	✓	x	x	✓	x	x	✓
`ACCESSKEY=key_character`	x	x	x	x	x	x	x	x	✓
`ALIGN=ABSBOTTOM|ABSMIDDLE|BASELINE|` `BOTTOM|LEFT|MIDDLE|RIGHT|TEXTTOP|TOP`	x	x	x	x	x	x	x	x	✓
`CLASS=classname`	x	x	✓	x	x	✓	x	x	✓
`DATAFLD=column_name`	x	x	x	x	x	x	x	x	✓
`DATASRC=id`	x	x	x	x	x	x	x	x	✓
`DIR=LTR|RTL`	x	x	✓	x	x	x	x	x	x
`DISABLED`	x	x	✓	x	x	x	x	x	✓
`ID=string`	x	x	✓	x	x	✓	x	x	✓
`LANG=language_type`	x	x	✓	x	x	x	x	x	✓
`LANGUAGE=JAVASCRIPT|JSCRIPT|` `VBSCRIPT|VBS`	x	x	x	x	x	x	x	x	✓
`MULTIPLE`	✓	✓	✓	✓	✓	✓	✓	✓	✓
`NAME=string`	✓	✓	✓	✓	✓	✓	✓	✓	✓
`SIZE=number`	✓	✓	✓	✓	✓	✓	✓	✓	✓
`STYLE=string`	x	x	✓	x	x	✓	x	x	✓
`TABINDEX=number`	x	x	✓	x	x	x	x	x	✓
`TITLE=string`	x	x	✓	x	x	x	x	x	✓

STYLE

Specifies the style properties (i.e. the style sheet) for the page. **HTML 3.2, 4.0, N4, IE3, IE4**.

Attributes	2.0	3.2	4.0	N2	N3	N4	IE2	IE3	IE4
`DIR=LTR|RTL`	x	x	✓	x	x	x	x	x	x
`DISABLED`	x	x	x	x	x	x	x	x	✓
`ID=string`	x	x	x	x	x	✓	x	x	x
`LANG=language_type`	x	x	✓	x	x	x	x	x	x
`MEDIA=SCREEN|PRINT|PROJECTION|` `BRAILLE|SPEECH|ALL`	x	x	✓	x	x	x	x	x	✓
`SRC=url`	x	x	x	x	x	✓	x	x	x
`TITLE=string`	x	x	✓	x	x	x	x	✓	✓
`TYPE=string`	x	x	✓	x	x	✓	x	✓	✓

TITLE

Denotes the title of the document and used in the browser's window title bar. **ALL**.

Attributes	2.0	3.2	4.0	N2	N3	N4	IE2	IE3	IE4
DIR=LTR|RTL	x	x	✓	x	x	x	x	x	x
ID=*string*	x	x	x	x	x	✓	x	x	✓
LANG=language.type	x	x	✓	x	x	x	x	x	x
TITLE=*string*	x	x	x	x	x	x	x	x	✓

Colors Sorted by Group

Color Name	Value	IE4 Color Constant
Blues		
azure	F0FFFF	htmlAzure
aliceblue	F0F8FF	htmlAliceBlue
lavender	E6E6FA	htmlLavender
lightcyan	E0FFFF	htmlLightCyan
powderblue	B0E0E6	htmlPowderBlue
lightsteelblue	B0C4DE	htmlLightSteelBlue
paleturquoise	AFEEEE	htmlPaleTurquoise
lightblue	ADD8E6	htmlLightBlue
blueviolet	8A2BE2	htmlBlueViolet
lightskyblue	87CEFA	htmlLightSkyBlue
skyblue	87CEEB	htmlSkyBlue
mediumslateblue	7B68EE	htmlMediumSlateBlue
slateblue	6A5ACD	htmlSlateBlue
cornflowerblue	6495ED	htmlCornflowerBlue
cadetblue	5F9EA0	htmlCadetBlue
indigo	4B0082	htmlIndigo
mediumturquoise	48D1CC	htmlMediumTurquoise
darkslateblue	483D8B	htmlDarkSlateBlue
steelblue	4682B4	htmlSteelBlue
royalblue	4169E1	htmlRoyalBlue
turquoise	40E0D0	htmlTurquoise
dodgerblue	1E90FF	htmlDodgerBlue
midnightblue	191970	htmlMidnightBlue

Color Name	Value	IE4 Color Constant
aqua	00FFFF	htmlAqua
cyan	00FFFF	htmlCyan
darkturquoise	00CED1	htmlDarkTurquoise
deepskyblue	00BFFF	htmlDeepSkyBlue
darkcyan	008B8B	htmlDarkCyan
blue	0000FF	htmlBlue
mediumblue	0000CD	htmlMediumBlue
darkblue	00008B	htmlDarkBlue
navy	000080	htmlNavy

Greens

Color Name	Value	IE4 Color Constant
mintcream	F5FFFA	htmlMintCream
honeydew	F0FFF0	htmlHoneydew
greenyellow	ADFF2F	htmlGreenYellow
yellowgreen	9ACD32	htmlYellowGreen
palegreen	98FB98	htmlPaleGreen
lightgreen	90EE90	htmlLightGreen
darkseagreen	8FBC8F	htmlDarkSeaGreen
olive	808000	htmlOlive
aquamarine	7FFFD4	htmlAquamarine
chartreuse	7FFF00	htmlChartreuse
lawngreen	7CFC00	htmlLawnGreen
olivedrab	6B8E23	htmlOliveDrab
mediumaquamarine	66CDAA	htmlMediumAquamarine
darkolivegreen	556B2F	htmlDarkOliveGreen
mediumseagreen	3CB371	htmlMediumSeaGreen
limegreen	32CD32	htmlLimeGreen
seagreen	2E8B57	htmlSeaGreen
forestgreen	228B22	htmlForestGreen
lightseagreen	20B2AA	htmlLightSeaGreen
springgreen	00FF7F	htmlSpringGreen
lime	00FF00	htmlLime
mediumspringgreen	00FA9A	htmlMediumSpringGreen
teal	008080	htmlTeal
green	008000	htmlGreen
darkgreen	006400	htmlDarkGreen

389

Color Name	Value	IE4 Color Constant
Pinks and Reds		
lavenderblush	FFF0F5	htmlLavenderBlush
mistyrose	FFE4E1	htmlMistyRose
pink	FFC0CB	htmlPink
lightpink	FFB6C1	htmlLightPink
orange	FFA500	htmlOrange
lightsalmon	FFA07A	htmlLightSalmon
darkorange	FF8C00	htmlDarkOrange
coral	FF7F50	htmlCoral
hotpink	FF69B4	htmlHotPink
tomato	FF6347	htmlTomato
orangered	FF4500	htmlOrangeRed
deeppink	FF1493	htmlDeepPink
fuchsia	FF00FF	htmlFuchsia
magenta	FF00FF	htmlMagenta
red	FF0000	htmlRed
salmon	FA8072	htmlSalmon
lightcoral	F08080	htmlLightCoral
violet	EE82EE	htmlViolet
darksalmon	E9967A	htmlDarkSalmon
plum	DDA0DD	htmlPlum
crimson	DC143C	htmlCrimson
palevioletred	DB7093	htmlPaleVioletRed
orchid	DA70D6	htmlOrchid
thistle	D8BFD8	htmlThistle
indianred	CD5C5C	htmlIndianRed
mediumvioletred	C71585	htmlMediumVioletRed
mediumorchid	BA55D3	htmlMediumOrchid
firebrick	B22222	htmlFirebrick
darkorchid	9932CC	htmlDarkOrchid
darkviolet	9400D3	htmlDarkViolet
mediumpurple	9370DB	htmlMediumPurple
darkmagenta	8B008B	htmlDarkMagenta
darkred	8B0000	htmlDarkRed
purple	800080	htmlPurple
maroon	800000	htmlMaroon

Color Name	Value	IE4 Color Constant
Yellows		
ivory	FFFFF0	htmlIvory
lightyellow	FFFFE0	htmlLightYellow
yellow	FFFF00	htmlYellow
floralwhite	FFFAF0	htmlFloralWhite
lemonchiffon	FFFACD	htmlLemonChiffon
cornsilk	FFF8DC	htmlCornsilk
gold	FFD700	htmlGold
khaki	F0E68C	htmlKhaki
darkkhaki	BDB76B	htmlDarkKhaki
Beiges and Browns		
snow	FFFAFA	htmlSnow
seashell	FFF5EE	htmlSeashell
papayawhite	FFEFD5	htmlPapayaWhite
blanchedalmond	FFEBCD	htmlBlanchedAlmond
bisque	FFE4C4	htmlBisque
moccasin	FFE4B5	htmlMoccasin
navajowhite	FFDEAD	htmlNavajoWhite
peachpuff	FFDAB9	htmlPeachPuff
oldlace	FDF5E6	htmlOldLace
linen	FAF0E6	htmlLinen
antiquewhite	FAEBD7	htmlAntiqueWhite
beige	F5F5DC	htmlBeige
wheat	F5DEB3	htmlWheat
sandybrown	F4A460	htmlSandyBrown
palegoldenrod	EEE8AA	htmlPaleGoldenRod
burlywood	DEB887	htmlBurlywood
goldenrod	DAA520	htmlGoldenRod
tan	D2B48C	htmlTan
chocolate	D2691E	htmlChocolate
peru	CD853F	htmlPeru
rosybrown	BC8F8F	htmlRosyBrown
darkgoldenrod	B8860B	htmlDarkGoldenRod
brown	A52A2A	htmlBrown

Color Name	Value	IE4 Color Constant
sienna	A0522D	htmlSienna
saddlebrown	8B4513	htmlSaddleBrown
Whites and Grays		
white	FFFFFF	htmlWhite
ghostwhite	F8F8FF	htmlGhostWhite
whitesmoke	F5F5F5	htmlWhiteSmoke
gainsboro	DCDCDC	htmlGainsboro
lightgray	D3D3D3	htmlLightGray
silver	C0C0C0	htmlSilver
darkgray	A9A9A9	htmlDarkGray
gray	808080	htmlGray
lightslategray	778899	htmlLightSlateGray
slategray	708090	htmlSlateGray
dimgray	696969	htmlDimGray
darkslategray	2F4F4F	htmlDarkSlateGray
black	000000	htmlBlack

JavaScript Reserved Words

There is an extensive range of words that, for a number of reasons, are reserved in JavaScript, and can not or should not be used as identifiers. Some of these are common across all implementations of JavaScript; others are reserved in only some implementations. Others still – particularly in ECMAscript- cover proposed extensions to the language which have not yet been implemented. Furthermore, because JavaScript can be combined with a number of other languages, as well as aspects of HTML and CSS, it is advisable to also avoid reserved words for these languages as well.

JavaScript-specific Keywords

These are organized by implementation; if you've decided to specialize in a single browser implementation, then you may choose not to worry about reserved keywords for other browsers, though we advise against this. Ticks mean the word is reserved, crosses that it is free for use.

	Netscape	JScript	ECMAScript
abstract	✓	✗	✗
boolean	✓	✗	✗
break	✓	✓	✓
byte	✓	✗	✗
case	✓	✓	✓
catch	✓	✓	✓
char	✓	✗	✗
class	✓	✓	✓
const	✓	✓	✓
continue	✓	✓	✓
debugger	✗	✓	✓
default	✓	✓	✓
delete	✗	✓	✓
do	✓	✓	✓

	Netscape	JScript	ECMAScript
double	✓	✗	✗
else	✓	✓	✓
enum	✗	✓	✓
export	✗	✓	✓
extends	✓	✓	✓
false	✓	✓	✗
final	✓	✗	✗
finally	✓	✓	✓
float	✓	✗	✗
for	✓	✓	✓
function	✓	✓	✓
goto	✓	✗	✗
if	✓	✓	✓
implements	✓	✗	✗
import	✓	✓	✓
in	✓	✓	✓
instanceof	✓	✗	✗
int	✓	✗	✗
interface	✓	✗	✗
long	✓	✗	✗
native	✓	✗	✗
new	✓	✓	✓
null	✓	✓	✗
package	✓	✗	✗
private	✓	✗	✗
protected	✓	✗	✗
public	✓	✗	✗
return	✓	✓	✓
short	✓	✗	✗
static	✓	✗	✗
super	✓	✓	✓
switch	✓	✓	✓
synchronized	✓	✗	✗
this	✓	✓	✓
throw	✓	✓	✓
throws	✓	✗	✗
transient	✓	✗	✗

	Netscape	JScript	ECMAScript
true	✓	✓	✗
try	✓	✓	✓
typeof	✗	✓	✓
var	✓	✓	✓
void	✓	✓	✓
while	✓	✓	✓
with	✓	✓	✓

Keywords in Java

The following keywords are reserved in Java so you should avoid using them as names in your programs, regardless of implementation:

abstract	finally	public
boolean	float	return
break	for	short
byte	goto	static
case	if	super
catch	implements	switch
char	import	synchronized
class	instanceof	this
const	int	throw
continue	inerface	throws
default	long	transient
do	native	try
double	new	void
else	package	volatile
extends	private	while
final	protected	

You should also not attempt to use the boolean values **true** and **false**, or **null** as names in your programs.

Reserved Words in C

The words in the following list are **keywords** in C, so you should avoid using them as names in your programs, regardless of implementation:

auto	extern	sizeof
break	float	static
case	for	struct
char	goto	switch
const	if	typedef
continue	int	union
default	long	unsigned
do	register	void
double	return	volatile
else	short	while
enum	signed	

StyleSheet/JSS property names

This is a list of property names used in StyleSheets (as defined in CSS1) and the alternative Netscape technology, JavaScript StyleSheet. As with reserved words, they should be avoided in JavaScript programming.

CSS1	JSS
font	fontFamily
font-family	fontSize
font-size	fontStyle
font-style	fontWeight
font-variant	color
font-weight	backgroundColor
color	backgroundImage
background	lineHeight
background-attachment	listStyleType
background-color	textAlign
background-image	textDecoration
background-position	textIndent
background-repeat	textTransform
letter-spacing	verticalAlign
line-height	borderColor

CSS1	JSS
list-style	borderStyle
list-style-image	borderTopWidth
list-style-position	border-left
list-style-type	border-bottom
text-align	border-right
text-decoration	borderRightWidth, borderBottomWidth, borderLeftWidth
text-indent	borderWidths()
text-transform	clear
vertical-align	display
word-spacing	align
border-color	height
border-style	marginTop
border-top	marginRight
border	marginBottom
border-right-width	marginLeft()
border-bottom-width	margins
border-left-width	paddingTop
border-width	paddingRight
border-top-width	paddingBottom
clear	paddingLeft
display	paddings()
float	whiteSpace
height	width
left	
margin-top	
margin-right	
margin-bottom	
margin-left	
margin	
overflow	
padding-top	
padding-right	
padding-bottom	
padding-left	
padding	

CSS1	JSS
position	
top	
visibility	
white-space	
width	
z-index	

HTML Tags

You should, of course avoid using any of the HTML tags, properties or attributes as anything except themselves in JavaScript programming. Although they are far too numerous to list here, you can find a complete listing of them in the Wrox Press book:

Instant HTML Programmer's Reference (ISBN 1-861001-56-8)

To quickly check the availability of any names, use the Wrox Press Ultimate HTML database, available online at **http://rapid.wrox.co.uk/html4db**.

Appendix

F

Standards

This table provides a guide to the location of all the standards mentioned in the book. Except where indicated, all of these are free for download, and provide an invaluable selection of resources for the JavaScript programmer determined to get the most out of JavaScript and its related technologies.

Standards	Location
HTML 4.0	`http://www.w3.org/TR/PR-html40/`
HTML 3.2	`http://www.w3.org/TR/REC-html32/`
ECMAScript	`http://www.ecma.ch/stand/ecma-262.htm`
Javascript 1.0, 1.1, 1.2	`http://developer.netscape.com/library/documentation/index.html`
JSRef Jscript 1.0 2.0 3.0	`http://www.microsoft.com/JScript/us/Jslang/Jstoc.htm`
CSS1, CSS1-positioning.	`http://www.w3.org/TR/REC-CSS1`
DOM	`http://www.w3.org/DOM/`
URL encoding RFC 1738	`http://globecom.net/(nobg)/ietf/rfc/rfc1738.shtml`
Unicode 2.0	`http://www.unicode.org/unicode/uni2book/uc20toc.html`
Perl regexps.	`http://www.perl.org/com`
CGI standards	`http://www.ast.cam.ac.uk/%7Edrtr/cgi-spec.html`
XMP	`http://luna.bearnet.com/w3org/HTML_2.0/dtd/xmp.html`
POSIX	`http://www.pasc.org/abstracts/1003p1.htm`
C - ANSI X3.159-1989	`ftp://ftp.uu.net/doc/standards/ansi/X3.159-1989`
floating point ANSI/IEEE 1754-1985	available to buy from IEEE

Appendix

Support and Errata

One of the most irritating things about any programming book can be when you find that a bit of code you've just spent an hour typing simply doesn't work. You check it a hundred times to see if you've set it up correctly and then you notice the spelling mistake in the variable name on the book page. Grrrr! Of course, you can blame the authors for not taking enough care and testing the code, the editors for not doing their job properly, or the proofreaders for not being eagle-eyed enough, but this doesn't get around the fact that mistakes do happen.

We try hard to ensure no mistakes sneak out into the real world, but we can't promise you that this book is 100% error free. What we can do is offer the next best thing by providing you with immediate support and feedback from experts who have worked on the book and try to ensure that future editions eliminate these gremlins. The following section will take you step by step through how to post errata to our web site to get that help:

- Finding a list of existing errata on the web site
- Adding your own errata to the existing list
- What happens to your errata once you've posted it (why doesn't it appear immediately?)

and how to mail a question for technical support:

- What your e-mail should include
- What happens to your e-mail once it has been received by us

Finding an Errata on the Web Site

Before you send in a query, you might be able to save time by finding the answer to your problem on our web site, **http:\\www.wrox.com**. Each book we publish has its own page and its own errata sheet. You can get to any book's page by using the drop down list box on our web site's welcome screen.

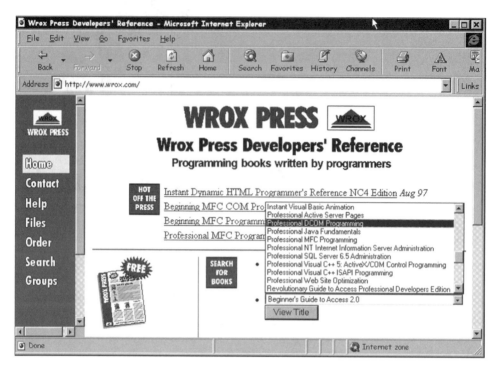

From this you can locate any book's home page on our site. Select your book and click View Title to get the individual title page:

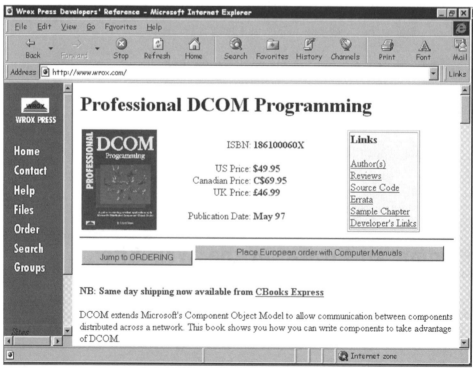

Each book has a set of links. If you click on the Errata link, you'll immediately be transported to the errata sheet for that book:

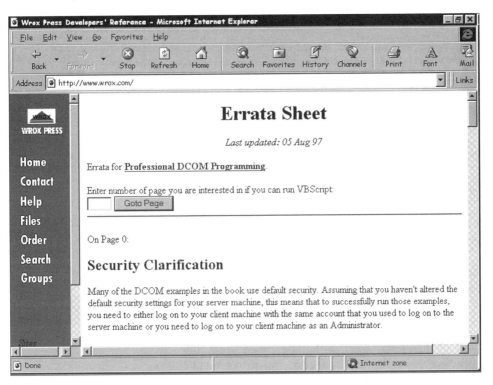

If you're using Internet Explorer 3.0 or later, you can jump to errors more quickly using the text box provided. The errata lists are updated daily, ensuring that you always have the most up-to-date information on bugs and errors.

Adding an Errata to the Sheet Yourself

It's always possible that you may not find your error listed, in which case you can enter details of the fault yourself. It might be anything from a spelling mistake to a faulty piece of code in a book. Sometimes you'll find useful hints that aren't really errors on the listing. By entering errata you may save another reader some hours of frustration and, of course, you will be helping us to produce even higher quality information. We're very grateful for this sort of guidance and feedback. Here's how to do it:

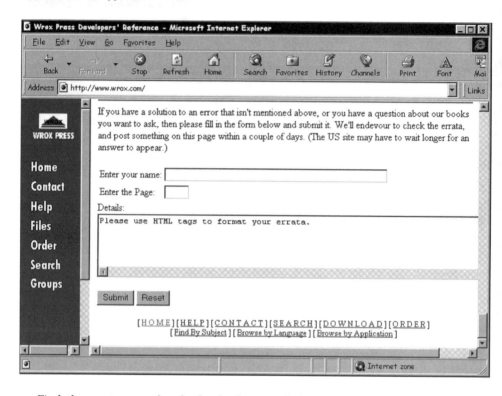

Find the errata page for the book, then scroll down to the bottom of the page, where you will see a space for you to enter your name (and e-mail address for preference), the page the errata occurs on and details of the errata itself. The errata should be formatted using HTML tags - the reminder for this can be deleted as you type in your error.

Once you've typed in your message, click on the Submit button and the message is forwarded to our editors. They'll then test your submission and check that the error exists, and that any suggestions you make are valid. Then your submission, together with a solution, is posted on the site for public consumption. Obviously this stage of the process can take a day or two, but we will endeavor to get a fix up sooner than that.

E-mail Support

If you wish to directly query a problem in the book with an expert who knows the book in detail then e-mail **support@wrox.com**, with the title of the book and the last four numbers of the ISBN in the Subject field of the e-mail. A typical e-mail should include the following things:

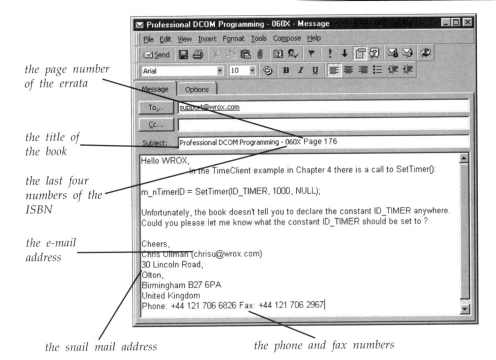

the page number of the errata

the title of the book

the last four numbers of the ISBN

the e-mail address

the snail mail address

the phone and fax numbers

We won't send you junk mail. We need details to help save your time and ours. If we need to replace a disk or CD we'll be able to get it to you straight away. When you send an e-mail it will go through the following chain of support;

Customer Support

Your message is delivered to one of our customer support staff who are the first people to read it. They have files on the most frequently asked questions and will answer anything immediately. They answer general questions about the books and web site.

Editorial

Deeper queries are forwarded on the same day to the technical editor responsible for that book. They have experience with the programming language or particular product and are able to answer detailed technical questions on the subject. Once an issue has been resolved, the editor can post the errata to the web site.

The Author(s)

Finally, in the unlikely event that the editor can't answer your problem, he/she will forward the request to the author. We try to protect the author from any distractions from writing. However, we are quite happy to forward specific requests to them. All Wrox authors help with the support on their books. They'll mail the customer and editor with their response, and again, all readers should benefit.

What we can't answer

Obviously with an ever growing range of books and an ever-changing technology base, there is an increasing volume of data requiring support. While we endeavor to answer all questions about a book, we can't answer bugs in your own programs that you've adapted from our code. So, while you might have loved the help desk system examples in our Active Server Pages book, don't expect too much sympathy if you cripple your company with a live application you customized from chapter 12. But do tell us if you're especially pleased with a successful routine you developed with our help.

How to tell us exactly what you think!

We understand that errors can destroy the enjoyment of a book and can cause many wasted and frustrated hours, so we seek to minimize the distress that they can cause.

You might just wish to tell us how much you liked or loathed the book in question. Or you might have ideas about how this whole process could be improved. In which case you should e-mail **feedback@wrox.com**. You'll always find a sympathetic ear, no matter what the problem is. Above all you should remember that we do care about what you have to say and we will do our utmost to act upon it.

Symbols

423

I

427

O

Q

U

V

Z

X

ASP Today

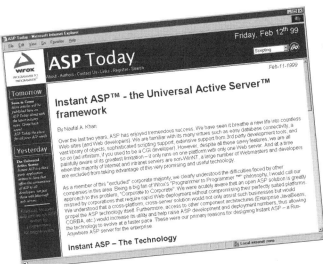

It's not easy keeping up to date with what's hot and what's not in the ever-changing world of internet development. Even if you stick to one narrow topic like ASP, trawling through the mailing lists each day and finding new and better code is still a twenty-four-seven job. Which is where we come in.

You already know Wrox Press from its series of titles on ASP and its associated technologies. We realise that we can't bring out a book everyday to keep you all up to date, so from March 1, we're starting a brand new website at www.asptoday.com which will do all the hard work for you. Every week you'll find new tips, tricks and techniques for you to try out and test in your development, covering ASP components, ADO, RDS, ADSI, CDO, Security, Site Design, BackOffice, XML and more. Look out also for bug alerts when they're found and fixes when they're available.

We hope that you won't be shy in telling us what you think of the site and the content we put on it either. If you like what you'll see, we'll carry on as we are, but if you think we're missing something, then we'll address it accordingly. If you've got something to write, then do so and we'll include it. We're hoping our site will become a global effort by and for the entire ASP community.

In anticipation,
Dan Maharry, ASPToday.com